Revenue Statistics 1965-2016

SPECIAL FEATURE:
COMPLEMENTARY INDICATORS
OF TAX REVENUES

OECD
BETTER POLICIES FOR BETTER LIVES

This work is published on the responsibility of the Secretary-General of the OECD. The opinions expressed and arguments employed herein do not necessarily reflect the official views of the Organisation or of the governments of its member countries.

This document, as well as any data and map included herein, are without prejudice to the status of or sovereignty over any territory, to the delimitation of international frontiers and boundaries and to the name of any territory, city or area.

Please cite this publication as:
OECD (2017), *Revenue Statistics 1965-2016*, OECD Publishing, Paris.
http://dx.doi.org/10.1787/10.1787/9789264283183-en

ISBN 978-92-64-28317-6 (print)
ISBN 978-92-64-28318-3 (PDF)
ISBN 978-92-64-28440-1 (ePub)

Annual: Revenue Statistics
ISSN 2522-7696 (print)
ISSN 2522-770X (online)

The statistical data for Israel are supplied by and under the responsibility of the relevant Israeli authorities. The use of such data by the OECD is without prejudice to the status of the Golan Heights, East Jerusalem and Israeli settlements in the West Bank under the terms of international law.

Corrigenda to OECD publications may be found on line at: *www.oecd.org/publishing/corrigenda*.

Foreword

This annual publication provides information on tax levels and tax structures in OECD countries. It was prepared under the auspices of the Working Party on Tax Policy Analysis and Tax Statistics of the Committee on Fiscal Affairs and is published under the responsibility of the Secretary-General of the OECD.

Table of contents

Tables

Figures

Executive summary

The OECD average tax-to-GDP ratio increased again in 2016 to a new high of 34.3%, continuing the steady increases in tax levels since 2009, their low-point following the financial crisis. Since then, personal taxes continue to play an increasingly important role in OECD tax revenues, while revenues from social security contributions and value-added taxes are slowly decreasing from post-crisis peaks, and corporate income tax revenues have still not recovered.

Taxes are defined as compulsory, unrequited payments to general government. They are unrequited in that the benefits provided by governments to taxpayers are not normally allocated in proportion to their payments. Taxes are classified by their base: income, profits and capital gains; payroll; property; goods and services; and other taxes. Compulsory social security contributions (SSCs) paid to general government are also treated as taxes. Revenues are analysed by level of government: federal or central; state; local; and social security funds. Detailed information on the classifications is set out in the Interpretative Guide in Annex A.

Tax levels in 2016

Between 2015 and 2016, the OECD average tax-to-GDP ratio increased from 34.0% to 34.3%. This is the seventh consecutive annual increase, and means that the OECD average tax-to-GDP level is, again, the highest in the fifty-year period covered by *Revenue Statistics*. OECD average tax levels have remained above pre-crisis levels since 2014.

An increase in tax-to-GDP ratios from 2015 to 2016 is also observed in 20 of the 33 countries for which preliminary 2016 data is available. In all of these countries, the increase was due to tax revenues increasing more than GDP. The increase in the tax-to-GDP ratio was largest in Greece, due to higher revenues from taxes on income and taxes on goods and services, with increases above one percentage point experienced in four other countries (Korea, Latvia, the Netherlands and Poland). Thirteen countries experienced a decrease in tax-to-GDP ratios in 2016, relative to 2015. The falls were smaller, with no decreases exceeding one percentage point. The largest decreases were experienced by Austria and New Zealand, due to a decrease in taxes on income and profits and also a decrease in taxes on goods and services for New Zealand. Decreases were also seen in Belgium, Canada, Chile, Iceland, Ireland, Israel, Italy, Norway, Portugal, Spain and the United States. In all countries but Norway, the falls were due to tax revenues increasing less than GDP, whereas in Norway, both tax revenues and GDP fell.

Across OECD countries, tax-to-GDP ratios in 2016 ranged from 17.2% in Mexico to 45.9% in Denmark, with 18 countries within five percentage points of the OECD average of 34.3%. Eighteen OECD countries reported tax-to-GDP ratios in 2016 that were higher than those in 2007, with the greatest increases being in Greece and Mexico. Among the remaining 15 countries, tax levels in 2016 remained more than three percentage points lower in Ireland and Norway.

Tax structure in 2015

In 2015, the share of personal income tax revenues in total tax revenues, on average, increased from 24.1% to 24.4%. At the same time, the share of SSCs and taxes on goods and services, including VAT, fell slightly, while corporate income tax revenues and property taxes remained relatively stable.

These annual changes are a continuation of the trends that have emerged in the average OECD tax structure since the financial crisis of 2008. Since the crisis, the share of revenues from personal income taxes initially fell (from 23.7% in 2007 to 23.2% of total revenues in 2010) before increasing steadily to 24.4% in 2015. Property taxes followed a similar trend, decreasing from 5.6% in 2007 to 5.5% in 2010 and increasing to 5.8% in 2015. By contrast, the share of SSCs and taxes on goods and services, including value-added taxes, increased initially (from 24.6% and 31.9% in 2007, respectively to peaks of 26.6% in 2009 for SSCs and 33.0% in 2010 for taxes on goods and services), before falling steadily to 25.8% and 32.4% in 2015, respectively. Corporate income tax revenues fell sharply as a share of revenues during the financial crisis, from 11.2% to 8.8% in 2010, and have remained at this lower level since, accounting for 8.9% of total revenues in 2015.

Changes by level of government

Tax revenues at different levels of government remained stable in 2015 relative to 2014, both on an OECD average basis and in individual countries. The federal share of revenues in 2015 remained at 54.0% of general government revenue in federal countries and at 63.5% in unitary countries. In federal countries, 24.7% of revenues were received at subnational level on average (ranging from 4.5% in Austria to 49.9% in Canada), with roughly two-thirds of revenues being received by state governments and one-third by local governments. In unitary countries, the share of local government revenues was 11.8% on average, ranging from less than 2% in the Czech Republic, Estonia and Mexico, to 36.0% in Sweden.

Share of total government revenues in 2015

A special feature in this report compares total tax revenues in each country against additional macroeconomic and fiscal indicators, including gross national income, tax per capita, total government revenues (including non-tax revenues), and total government expenditure.

In 2015, tax revenues accounted for 82.0% of total government revenues, on average, in the OECD. Among OECD countries, the contribution of taxation to total government revenue ranges from 68.6% and 69.9% of total revenues in Mexico and Norway, respectively, to 91.4% in Italy. In 23 OECD countries, the contribution of tax to total government revenue was between 80 and 90%.

Although the OECD average tax-to-GDP ratio has increased to exceed pre-crisis levels since 2014, the share of taxes to total revenues is still lower in 2015 than in the years prior to the crisis, although it has partially recovered from its fall from 82.6% in 2007 to 80.4% in 2009. Since 2009, the share of taxes in total revenues has increased in 28 OECD countries (excluding the Czech Republic, Greece, Hungary, Norway, the Slovak Republic, Slovenia and Switzerland) although remains lower than 2007 levels in 18 countries.

Introduction

The purpose of this annual publication is to provide internationally comparative data on tax levels and tax structures in member countries of the OECD. The taxes imposed in each country are presented in a standardised framework based upon the OECD classification of taxes and its Interpretative Guide as contained in Annex A to this Report.

Starting in 2004, the data for recent years in this publication are mainly reported on an accrual basis, rather than the cash basis that was used in previous editions. The reasons for this change were discussed in Special Feature S.2 of the 2003 edition. Details of the practical implementation of this change were given in Special Feature S.1 of the 2004 edition.

The data for the Report has, for the most part, been provided by Delegates to Working Party No. 2 on Tax Policy Analysis and Tax Statistics of the Committee on Fiscal Affairs. The OECD acknowledges the co-operation of the International Monetary Fund, whose classification of tax revenues – although in a number of respects less detailed – is in many respects similar to that of the OECD.[1] The most important of the other classifications currently in use is the System of National Accounts (henceforth referred to as SNA) and the European System of Integrated Economic Accounts of EU member states (henceforth referred to as ESA), which is primarily an elaboration of SNA, though differing from it in certain respects. Subject to a few exceptions, SNA/ESA figures can be reconciled with the figures in the present Report, since SNA criteria and definitions have been adopted unless the contrary is specifically indicated.

The material is organised in six chapters. Chapter 1 summarises tax trends of the past 50 years focusing in turn on tax-to-GDP ratios (section 1.1), tax structures (section 1.2) and taxes by level of government (section 1.3). Section 1.4 discusses the impact of alternate treatments of non-wastable tax credits. This year's issue also carries in Chapter 2 a special feature on "Complementary indicators of tax revenues". Chapter 3 contains a set of comparative statistical tables for years 1965-2016. Chapter 4 provides country tables with tax revenue and tax-to-GDP ratios broken down by selected tax categories and by level of government for years between 1990 and 2015 (section 4.1).[2] Two memorandum tables show how countries finance their social benefits, and report taxes and social security contributions paid by general government (section 4.2). Chapter 5, which is available on line only, provides statistical tables with a detailed breakdown of tax revenues by country for years between 1965 and 2015 (section 5.1).[2] Two memorandum tables show how countries finance their social benefits, and report taxes and social security contributions paid by general government (section 5.2). Chapter 6, which is also only available on line, attributes tax revenues to general government by the following sub-sectors: central, state; local and social security funds. It contains a set of comparative statistical tables for years 1975-2015 (section 6.1) and a second series of tables with a detailed breakdown of tax revenues by country for years between 1975 and 2015 (section 6.2).

Notes

1. See IMF, *Government Finance Statistics Manual 2014* (Washington, DC: International Monetary Fund, 2014).
2. Because of space limitations data are shown for selected years between 1965 and 2015. Data for years not shown are available on line.

Chapter 1

Tax revenue trends 1965-2016

Revenue Statistics 2017 presents detailed internationally comparable data on tax revenues of OECD countries for all levels of government. The latest edition provides final data on tax revenues in 1965-2015. In addition, provisional estimates of tax revenues in 2016 are included for almost all OECD countries.[1]

Box 1. **Revenue Statistics in OECD Countries – definitions and classifications**

In *Revenue Statistics 2017*, taxes are defined as compulsory, unrequited payments to general government. Taxes are unrequited in the sense that benefits provided by government are not normally in proportion to their payments.

In the OECD classification, taxes are classified by the base of the tax:

- Income and profits (heading 1000)
- Compulsory social security contributions paid to general government, which are treated as taxes (heading 2000)
- Payroll and workforce (heading 3000)
- Property (heading 4000)
- Goods and services (heading 5000)
- Other (heading 6000)

Much greater detail on the tax concept, the classification of taxes and the accrual basis of reporting is set out in the OECD Interpretative Guide at Annex A of this report.

All of the averages presented in this summary are unweighted.

1.1. Tax-to-GDP ratios

a. Tax ratios for 2016 (provisional data)

New OECD data in the annual *Revenue Statistics* publication show that tax revenues as a percentage of GDP (i.e. the tax-to-GDP ratio) continue to increase since the low-point experienced in almost all countries in 2008 and 2009 as a result of the financial and economic crisis. The average tax-to-GDP ratio in OECD countries was 34.3%[2] in 2016 compared with 34.0% in 2015 and 33.9% in 2014. The 2016 figure is the highest recorded OECD average tax-to-GDP ratio since records began in 1965 (Figure 1.1).

Country tax-to-GDP ratios in 2016 varied considerably (Table 1.1), both across countries and since 2015. Key observations include:

- Denmark had the highest tax-to-GDP ratio in 2016 (45.9%) and Mexico the lowest (17.2%).
- Of the 33 countries for which data for 2016 are available the ratio of tax revenues to GDP compared to 2015 rose in 20 and fell in 13.
- Between 2015 and 2016, the largest tax ratio increases were in Greece (2.2 percentage points explained by an increase in taxes on income and profits and in taxes on goods and services) and in the Netherlands (1.5 percentage points due to an increase in social

Figure 1.1. **Trends in tax-to-GDP ratios, 1965-2016p (as % of GDP)**

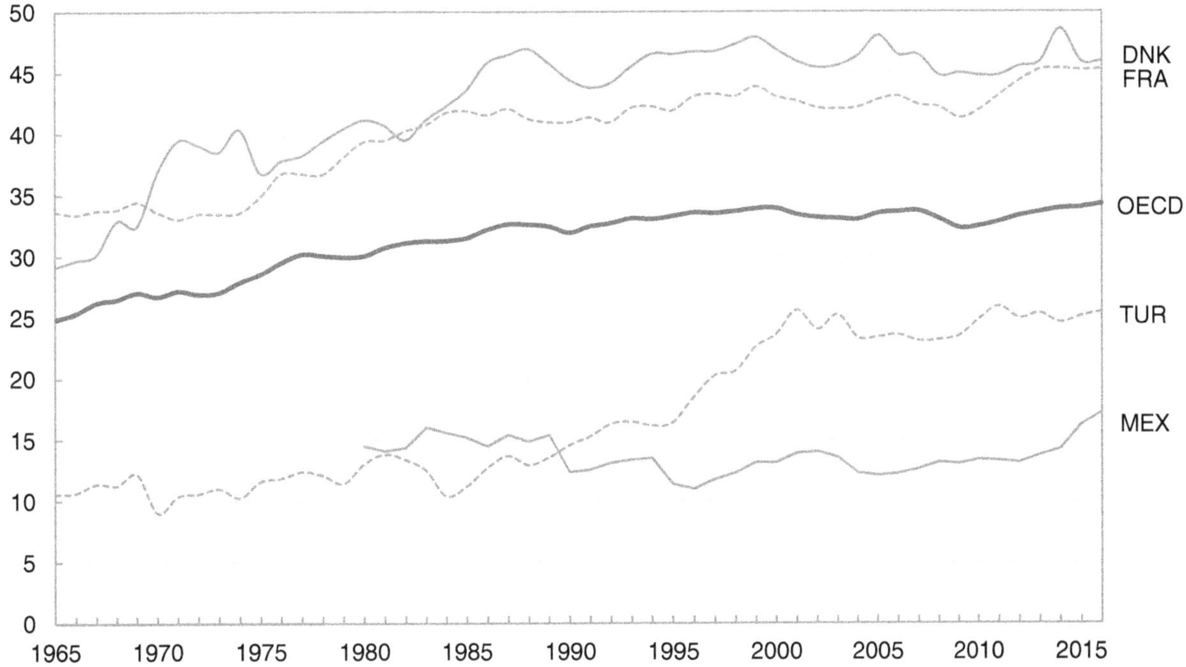

Note: Data for 2016 is preliminary. The OECD average in 2016 is calculated by applying the unweighted average percentage change for 2016 in the 33 countries providing data for that year to the overall average tax-to-GDP ratio in 2015.
Source: Table 3.1.

StatLink http://dx.doi.org/10.1787/888933611392

security contributions and in taxes on goods and services). Other countries with increases in their tax-to-GDP ratio between 2015 and 2016 of more than one percentage point were Korea, Latvia and Poland (Figure 1.2).

- The largest falls in the tax-to-GDP ratio between 2015 and 2016 were in Austria and New Zealand (just under one percentage point) due to a decrease in taxes on income and profits and also a decrease in taxes on goods and services for New Zealand.

Although the OECD average tax-to-GDP ratio was higher in 2016 than in 2007 (pre-crisis), this was not the case in nearly half of OECD countries: 15 OECD countries had lower tax-to-GDP ratios in 2016 than in 2007. In particular, the ratio in 2016 remains at least 3 percentage points lower in two countries; Ireland and Norway. The biggest fall has been in Ireland, from 30.4% in 2007 to 23.0% of GDP in 2016, largely due to the exceptional increase in GDP in 2015. Excluding Ireland, the largest fall has been in Norway, from 42.1% of GDP in 2007 to 38.0% in 2016 (Figure 2). In contrast, the strongest increase over this period was in Greece (7.4 percentage points, from 31.2% to 38.6%between 2007 and 2016. Three other countries, Estonia, Mexico and the Slovak Republic experienced increases of 3 percentage points or more over the same period.

Changes in the tax-to-GDP ratio are driven by the relative changes in nominal tax revenues and in nominal GDP. From one year to the next, if tax revenues rise more than GDP (or fall less than GDP) the tax-to-GDP ratio will increase. Conversely, if tax revenues rise less than GDP, or fall further, the tax-to-GDP ratio will go down. Therefore, the tax-to-GDP ratio does not necessarily mean that the amount of tax revenues have increased in nominal, or even real, terms.

Table 1.1. **Summary of key tax revenue ratios in the OECD**

	Tax revenue as % of GDP				Tax revenue as % of total tax revenue in 2015						
	2016p	2015	2014	2000	1100 Taxes on income, individuals (PIT)	1200 Taxes on income, corporates (CIT)	2000 Social security contributions (SSC)	4000 Taxes on property	5111 Value added taxes	Other consumption taxes[6]	All other taxes[7]
OECD - Average[1]	**34.3**	**34.0**	**33.9**	**33.9**	**24.4**	**8.9**	**25.8**	**5.8**	**20.0**	**12.4**	**2.7**
Australia	..	28.2	27.6	30.4	41.5	15.3	0.0	10.7	13.0	14.5	5.0
Austria	42.7	43.7	43.1	42.4	24.1	5.2	33.6	1.3	17.7	9.6	8.4
Belgium	44.2	44.8	45.0	43.5	28.3	7.4	31.9	7.8	15.0	8.8	0.8
Canada	31.7	32.0	31.2	34.8	36.9	9.9	15.1	11.8	13.2	9.9	3.2
Chile	20.4	20.5	19.6	18.8	9.8	21.0	6.9	4.4	40.8	13.3	3.8
Czech Republic	34.0	33.3	33.1	32.4	10.7	10.8	43.1	1.4	21.7	11.7	0.5
Denmark[2]	45.9	45.9	48.6	46.9	55.2	5.6	0.1	4.1	20.0	11.6	3.4
Estonia	34.7	33.9	32.8	31.1	17.2	6.2	33.4	0.8	27.3	14.5	0.5
Finland	44.1	43.9	43.8	45.8	30.2	4.9	28.9	3.3	20.6	11.8	0.3
France[2]	45.3	45.2	45.3	43.1	18.9	4.6	37.1	9.0	15.3	9.1	6.1
Germany[3]	37.6	37.1	36.8	36.2	26.5	4.7	37.6	2.9	18.8	9.0	0.5
Greece[2]	38.6	36.4	35.9	33.4	15.0	5.9	29.4	8.5	20.1	19.2	1.8
Hungary	39.4	39.0	38.2	38.6	13.7	4.6	32.4	3.3	24.9	18.8	2.2
Iceland	36.4	36.7	38.6	36.2	36.7	6.5	9.8	5.4	22.6	9.7	9.3
Ireland	23.0	23.1	28.5	30.8	31.6	11.3	16.8	6.4	19.7	12.9	1.2
Israel[4]	31.2	31.3	31.1	34.9	19.4	9.5	16.4	10.6	24.9	13.0	6.1
Italy	42.9	43.3	43.5	40.6	26.0	4.7	30.1	6.5	14.2	13.1	5.4
Japan	..	30.7	30.3	25.8	18.9	12.3	39.4	8.2	13.7	7.3	0.3
Korea	26.3	25.2	24.6	21.5	17.2	13.1	26.6	12.4	15.3	12.7	2.7
Latvia	30.2	29.0	28.8	29.1	20.4	5.5	28.7	3.4	26.5	14.8	0.6
Luxembourg	37.1	36.8	37.4	36.9	24.5	11.9	29.0	8.9	17.6	7.9	0.3
Mexico[5]	17.2	16.2	14.2	13.1	20.6	20.1	13.9	2.0	23.9	14.7	4.9
Netherlands	38.8	37.4	37.5	37.2	20.5	7.2	37.8	3.8	17.6	12.0	1.1
New Zealand	32.1	33.0	32.4	32.5	38.1	13.8	0.0	6.1	29.7	8.7	3.6
Norway	38.0	38.3	38.9	41.9	27.9	11.5	27.3	2.9	21.4	9.0	0.0
Poland	33.6	32.4	32.0	32.9	14.4	5.7	38.5	4.2	21.6	14.4	1.3
Portugal	34.4	34.6	34.3	31.1	21.2	9.0	26.1	3.7	24.8	13.6	1.6
Slovak Republic	32.7	32.3	31.2	33.6	9.7	11.5	42.7	1.3	21.3	12.4	1.1
Slovenia	37.0	36.6	36.5	36.6	14.0	4.0	39.7	1.7	22.9	17.1	0.5
Spain[2]	33.5	33.8	33.7	33.2	21.3	7.0	33.8	7.7	19.0	10.7	0.5
Sweden	44.1	43.3	42.6	49.0	29.1	6.9	22.4	2.4	20.9	7.2	11.1
Switzerland	27.8	27.7	27.0	27.4	31.1	10.8	24.6	6.7	12.4	9.3	5.0
Turkey	25.5	25.1	24.6	23.6	14.6	5.7	29.0	4.9	20.6	23.7	1.5
United Kingdom	33.2	32.5	32.2	33.2	27.7	7.5	18.7	12.6	21.2	11.7	0.5
United States	26.0	26.2	25.9	28.2	40.5	8.5	23.7	10.3	0.0	17.0	0.0

1. 2016 provisional average calculated by applying the unweighted average percentage change for 2016 in the 33 countries providing data for that year to the overall average tax to GDP ratio in 2015.
2. The total tax revenue has been reduced by the amount of any capital transfer that represents uncollected taxes.
3. From 1991 the figures relate to the united Germany.
4. The data for Israel are supplied by and under the responsability of the relevant Israeli authorities. The use of such data by the OECD is without prejudice to the status of the Golan Heights, East Jerusalem and Israeli settlements in the West Bank under the terms of international law.
5. 2016 provisional: Secretariat estimate, including expected revenues collected by state and local governments.
6. Calculated as 5000 Taxes on goods and services less 5111 Value added taxes.
7. Includes 1300 Unallocable between personal and corporate income tax, 3000 Taxes on payroll and workforce and 6000 Other taxes.

StatLink http://dx.doi.org/10.1787/888933611658

In 2016, 20 OECD countries had an increase in their tax-to-GDP ratio relative to 2015. In all of these countries, GDP growth was positive, although to a lesser degree than tax revenue growth. Of the thirteen OECD countries that experienced a decline in their tax-to-GDP ratio in 2016, twelve had higher levels of tax revenues, although to a lesser degree than nominal GDP levels; no countries had positive nominal GDP growth and negative tax growth; and one country (Norway) experienced declines in both nominal tax revenues and

Figure 1.2. **Changes in tax-to-GDP ratios, p.p., 2015-16p and 2007-16p**

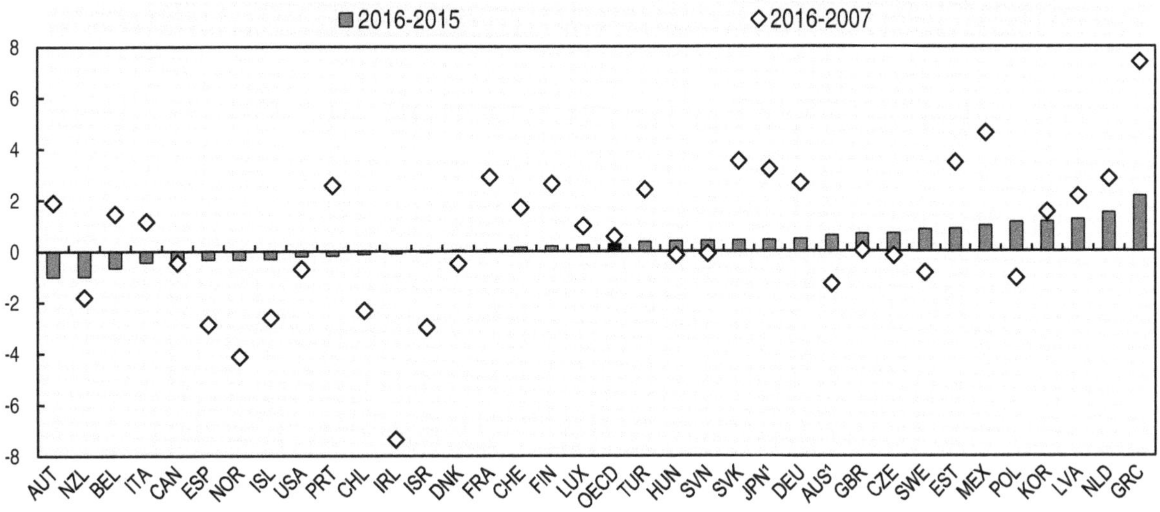

1. Preliminary data for 2016 was not available for Australia and Japan. For these countries the comparison shown is 2015-14 and 2015-17 data.

Source: Secretariat calculations based on Table 3.1.

StatLink http://dx.doi.org/10.1787/888933611411

Box 2. **Methodology: the tax-to-GDP ratio**

The tax-to-GDP ratios shown in *Revenue Statistics 2017* express aggregate tax revenues as a percentage of GDP. The value of this ratio depends on its denominator (GDP) as well as its numerator (tax revenue), and that the denominator – GDP – is subject to historical revision.

The numerator (tax revenue)

- For the numerator, the OECD Secretariat uses revenue figures that are submitted annually by correspondents from national Ministries of Finance, Tax Administrations or National Statistics Offices. Although provisional figures for most countries become available with a lag of about six months, finalised data become available with a lag of around one and a half years. Final revenue data for 2015 were received during the period May-August 2017.
- In thirty-two OECD countries the reporting year coincides with the calendar year. Three countries – Australia, Japan and New Zealand – have different reporting years. Reporting year 2014 includes Q2/2014-Q1/2015 (Japan) and Q3/2014-Q2/2015 (Australia, New Zealand) respectively (Q = quarter).

The denominator (GDP)

- For the denominator, the GDP figures used for *Revenue Statistics 2017* are the most recently available on 1 September 2017. By that time, the 2015 and 2016 GDP figures were available for all OECD countries.
- Using these GDP figures ensures a maximum of consistency and international comparability for the reported tax-to-GDP ratios.
- The GDP figures are based on the OECD Annual National Accounts (ANA – SNA) for the OECD countries where the reporting year is the actual calendar year.
- Where the reporting year differs from the calendar year, the annual GDP estimates are obtained by aggregating quarterly GDP estimates provided by the OECD Statistics Directorate for those quarters corresponding to each country's fiscal (tax) year. For example, in the case of Japan Q2/2015-Q1/2016.

GDP (Figure 1.3). In addition, changes between 2014 and 2015 are shown for Australia and Japan, where the tax-to-GDP ratio is not available in 2016. In both countries, nominal tax revenues grew faster than GDP, leading to increases in the tax-to-GDP ratio.

Figure 1.3. **Relative changes in nominal tax revenues and nominal GDP, %, 2015-16p**

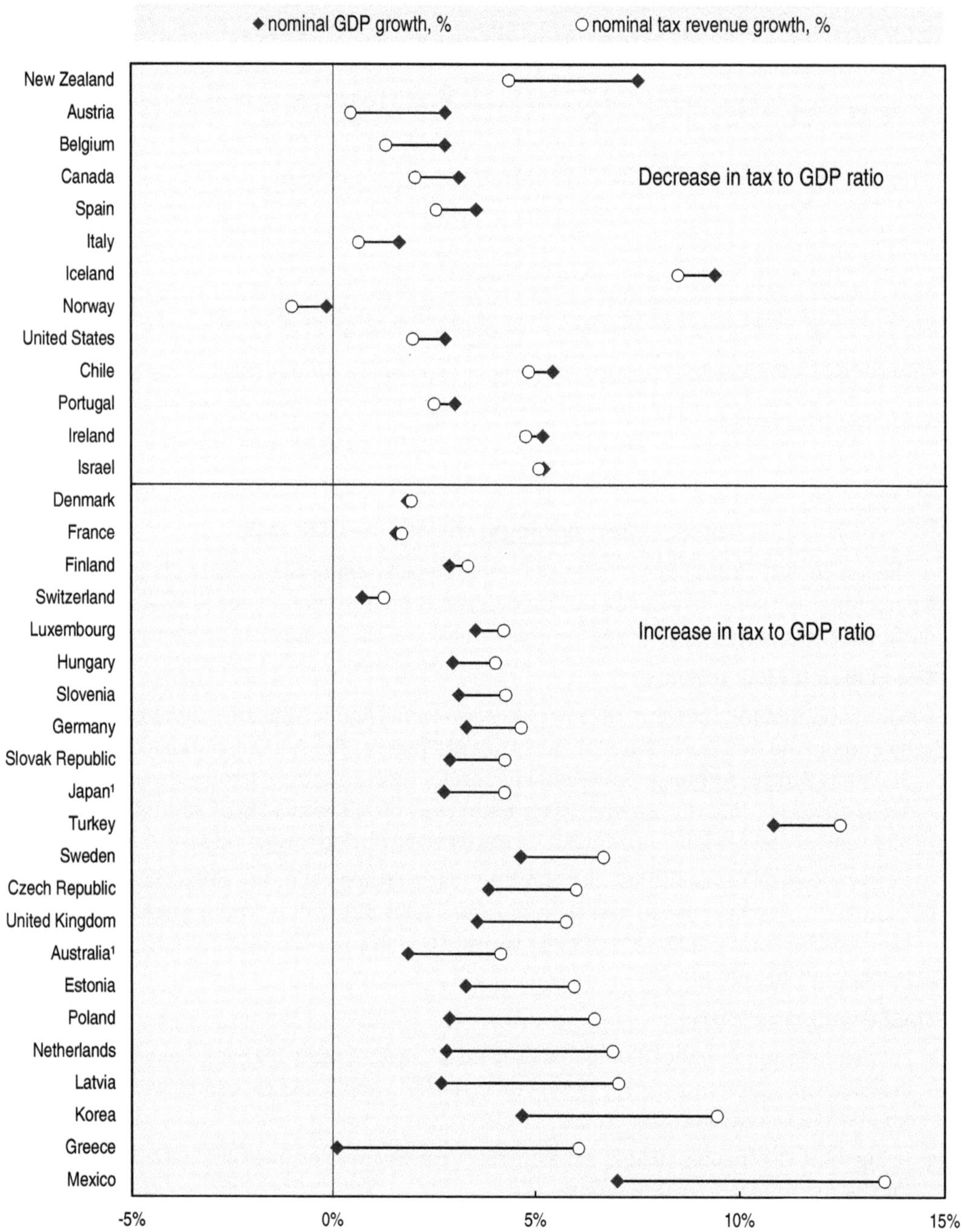

1. Data for Australia and Japan shows the change between 2014 and 2015, as preliminary data for 2016 was not available.

Source: Secretariat calculations based on chapter 4 (tax revenues) and table 3.19 (GDP).

StatLink http://dx.doi.org/10.1787/888933611430

Figure 1.4. **Tax-to-GDP ratios in 2015 and 2016p (as % of GDP)**

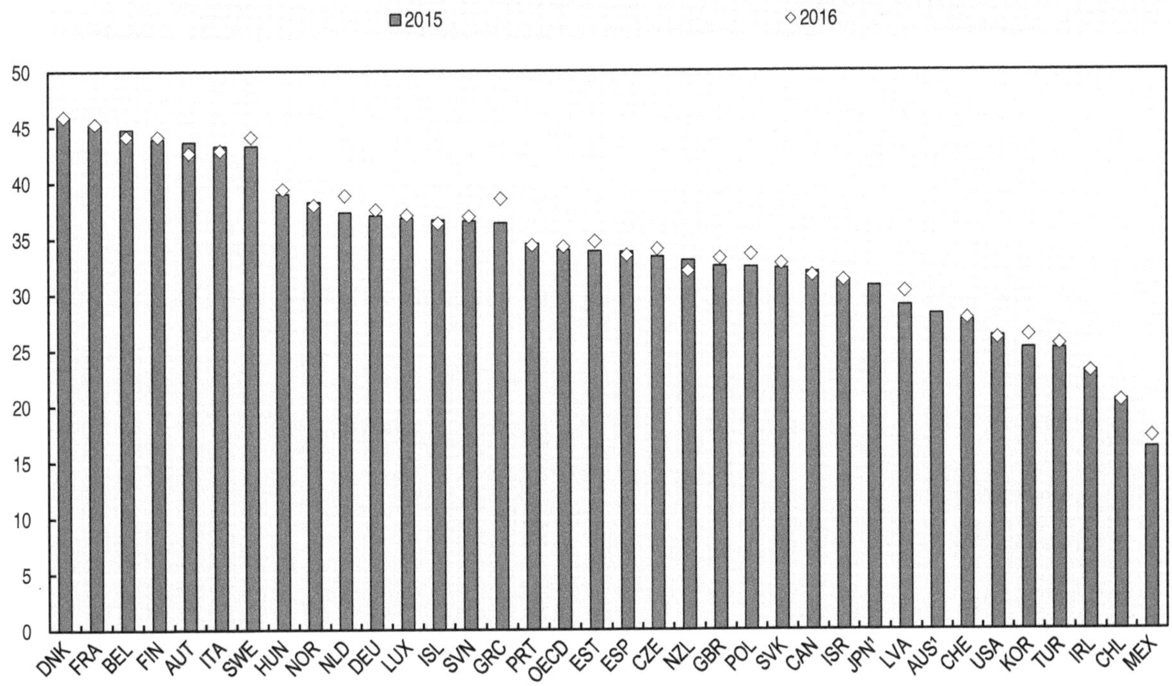

1. Preliminary data for 2016 was not available for Australia and Japan.
Source: Secretariat calculations based on Table 3.1.

StatLink http://dx.doi.org/10.1787/888933611449

b. Tax-to-GDP ratios for 2015 (final data)

The latest year for which tax-to-GDP ratios are based on final revenue data and available for all OECD countries is 2015 (Figure 1.4). These data show that tax ratios vary considerably across countries:

- In 2015, Denmark had the highest tax-to-GDP ratio (45.9%), followed by France (45.2%), Belgium (44.8%) and Finland (43.9) and Sweden (43.3%) and Mexico had the lowest ratio at 16.2% followed by Chile at 20.5%.
- Seven countries – Austria, Belgium, Denmark, Finland, France, Italy and Sweden – had tax-to-GDP ratios of above 40%.
- In contrast, nine countries – Australia, Chile, Ireland, Korea, Latvia, Mexico, Switzerland, Turkey and the United States – had tax-to-GDP ratios of below 30%.
- The tax-to-GDP ratio in the OECD area as a whole (un-weighted average) was 34.0% in 2015 and rose by 0.1 percentage points from 2014.
- Relative to 2014, overall tax ratios rose in 26 OECD member countries and fell in 9.
- The largest increases in the tax-to-GDP ratio were in Mexico (2.0 percentage points), Estonia (1.1), the Slovak Republic (1.1) and Chile (0.9).
- The largest reductions were in Ireland (5.4 percentage points, due to the extraordinary increase in GDP in 2015), Denmark (2.7 percentage points) and Iceland (1.9 percentage points).

Between 2014 and 2015, the key changes in the tax-to-GDP ratio were largely driven by increases in revenues from goods and services taxes. Revenues from taxes on income (personal and corporate income taxes together) as a percentage of GDP were unchanged at 11.5% on average (Table 1.2). The largest increase was in Mexico (1.1 percentage points) and Chile (1.0 percentage points). Denmark and Ireland reported the largest falls in this ratio (by 2.7 and 1.5 percentage points of GDP respectively).

On average, revenues from personal income taxes were unchanged at 8.4% in 2015, while revenues from corporate income tax were unchanged at 2.8% over the same period (Table 1.2). Revenues from goods and services taxes increased from 10.8% in 2014 to 10.9% in 2015. The other ratios were largely unchanged between 2014 and 2015.

Table 1.2. **Tax structures in the OECD area, selected years (unweighted average as % of GDP)**

Per cent

	1965	1990	2000	2007	2010	2012	2013	2014	2015
Total tax revenue	24.8	31.9	33.9	33.7	32.5	33.3	33.6	33.9	34.0
1000 Taxes on income, profits and capital gains	8.7	12.2	12.0	12.2	10.8	11.2	11.3	11.5	11.5
of which:									
1100 Taxes on income, profits and capital gains of individuals	6.8	9.7	8.7	8.2	7.7	8.1	8.2	8.4	8.4
1200 Taxes on income, profits and capital gains of corporates	2.1	2.5	3.2	3.6	2.7	2.8	2.8	2.8	2.8
2000 Social security contributions (SSC)	4.5	7.4	8.6	8.4	8.8	8.9	9.0	9.0	9.0
3000 Taxes on payroll and workforce	0.3	0.3	0.4	0.4	0.3	0.4	0.4	0.4	0.4
4000 Taxes on property	1.9	1.8	1.8	1.8	1.7	1.8	1.9	1.9	1.9
5000 Taxes on goods and services	9.4	10.0	10.9	10.6	10.6	10.7	10.8	10.8	10.9
of which:									
5111 Value added taxes	0.7	5.2	6.4	6.5	6.4	6.6	6.6	6.7	6.7
5121 Excises	3.5	2.6	2.9	2.6	2.7	2.7	2.6	2.6	2.6
6000 Other Taxes	0.1	0.3	0.2	0.2	0.2	0.2	0.2	0.2	0.2

Note: Percentage share of major tax categories in GDP. Data are included from 1965 onwards for Australia, Austria, Belgium, Canada, Denmark, Finland, France, Germany, Greece, Iceland, Ireland, Italy, Japan, Luxembourg, the Netherlands, New Zealand, Norway, Portugal, Spain, Sweden, Switzerland, Turkey, United Kingdom and United States; from 1972 for Korea; from 1980 for Mexico; from 1990 for Chile; from 1991 for Hungary and Poland; from 1993 for the Czech Republic and from 1995 for Estonia, Israel, Latvia, the Slovak Republic and Slovenia.

Source: OECD (2017), "Revenue Statistics: Comparative tables", *OECD Tax Statistics (database)*, *DOI:* http://dx.doi.org/10.1787/data-00262-en.

StatLink http://dx.doi.org/10.1787/888933611677

c. *Tax ratio changes between 1965 and 2015*

Between 1965 and 2015, the average tax-to-GDP ratio in the OECD area increased from 24.8% to 34.0% (an increase of 9.2 percentage points) between 1965 and 2015 (Figure 1.1). Despite the increase in the average across the OECD countries, total tax revenues as a percentage of GDP have fallen in Ireland.

Before the first oil shock (1973 to 1974), strong, almost uninterrupted income growth enabled tax levels to rise in all OECD countries. In part, tax levels rose automatically through the effect of fiscal drag on personal income tax schedules. From 1975 to 1985, the tax burden in the OECD area increased by 2.9 percentage points. After the mid-1970s, the combination of slower real income growth and higher levels of unemployment apparently limited the revenue raising capacity of governments. But during and after the deep recession following the second oil shock (1980), countries in Europe saw tax levels rise further, to finance higher spending on social security and rein in budget deficits.

After the mid-1980s, most OECD countries substantially reduced the statutory rates of their personal and corporate income tax, but the negative revenue impact of widespread tax reforms was often offset by reducing or abolishing tax reliefs. By 2000, the average

OECD tax-to-GDP ratio had risen to 34.0%, its highest recorded level at that time. It fell back slightly between 2001 and 2004, but then rose again between 2005 and 2007 before falling back following the crisis. Taking these changes together the average tax level in the OECD area increased by 0.7 percentage points between 1995 and 2015 (Figure 1.1).

The OECD average conceals the great variety in national tax-to-GDP ratios. In 1965, tax-to-GDP ratios in OECD countries ranged from 10.6% in Turkey to 33.6% in France. By 2015 the corresponding range was from 16.2% in Mexico to 45.9% in Denmark. The trend towards higher tax levels over this period reflects the need to finance a significant increase of public sector outlays in almost all OECD countries.

1.2. Tax structures

Tax structures are measured by the share of major taxes in total tax revenue. In 2015, the tax structures of OECD countries varied. Seventeen countries raised the largest part of their revenues from income taxes (both corporate and personal), nine countries raised the largest part of their revenues from SSCs, and nine countries raised the largest part of their revenues from consumption taxes (including VAT). Taxes on property and payroll taxes played a smaller role in the revenue systems of OECD countries in 2015, both on average and within most countries (Figure 1.5).

Figure 1.5. **Tax structures in 2015 (as % of total tax revenue)**

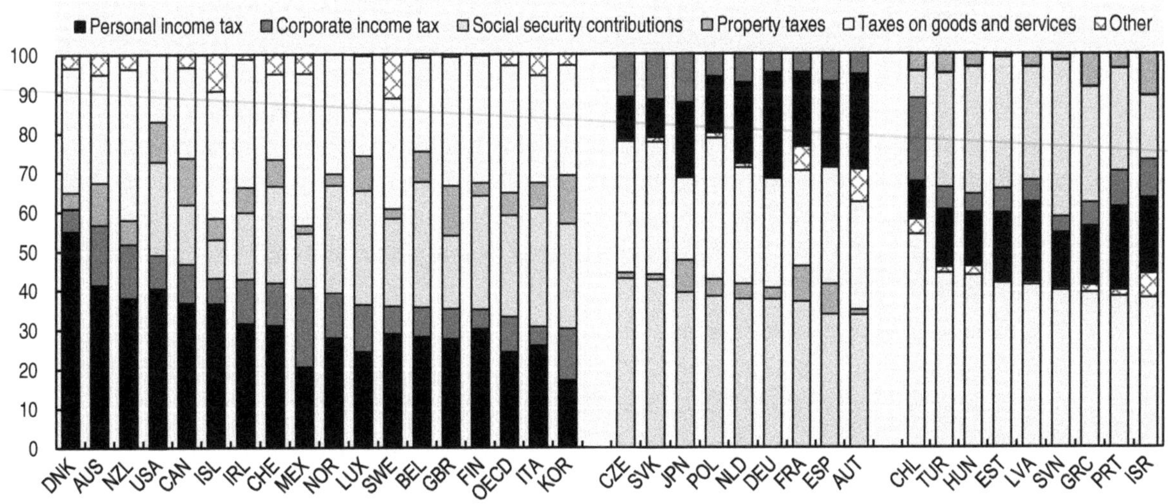

Note: Countries are grouped and ranked by those where income tax revenues (personal and corporate) form the highest share of total tax revenues, followed by those where social security contributions, or taxes on goods and services, form the highest share.
Source: Secretariat calculations based on data in chapter 4.

StatLink http://dx.doi.org/10.1787/888933611468

While, on average, tax levels have generally been rising, the tax structure or tax "mix" has been remarkably stable over time. Nevertheless, several trends have emerged up to 2015 – the latest year for which data is available for all 35 OECD countries.

a. Taxes on income and profits

On average, in 2015, OECD countries collected 34.1% of their tax revenues through taxes on income and profits (personal and corporate income taxes taken together). Taxes on personal and corporate incomes remain the most important source of revenues used to finance public spending in 17 OECD countries, and in nine of them – Australia, Canada,

Figure 1.6. **Trends in tax structures (1965-2015, as % of total tax revenue)**

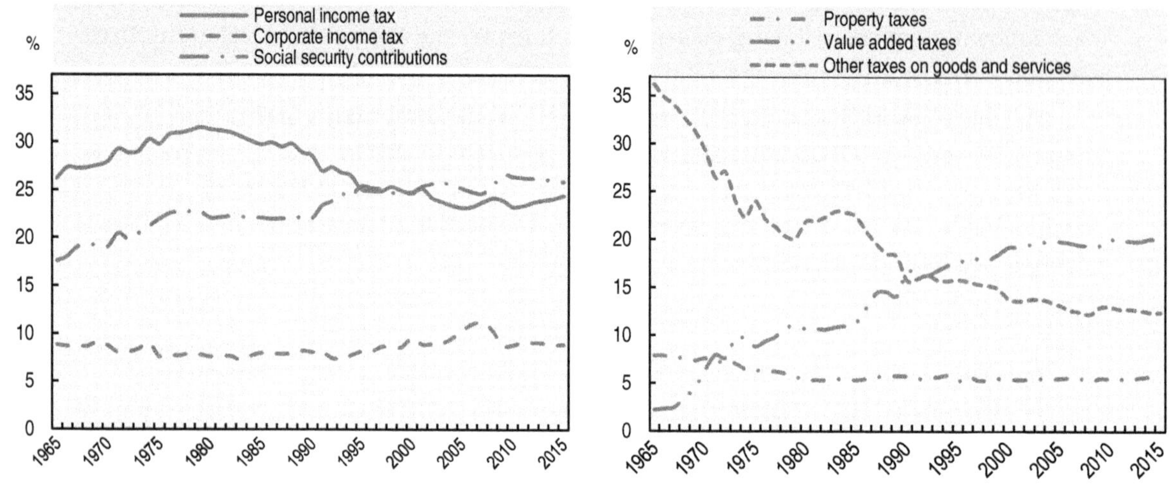

Source: Secretariat calculations based on tables 3.8 to 3.14.

StatLink http://dx.doi.org/10.1787/888933611487

Denmark, Iceland, Ireland, Mexico, New Zealand, Switzerland and the United States – the share of income taxes in the tax mix exceeds 40%.

Within taxes on income and profits, the shares of personal and corporate income taxes vary:

- Revenues from personal income taxes are 24.4% of total taxes on average in 2015 compared with around 30% in the 1980s. About two percentage points of this reduction can be attributed to the impact on the average of a number of relatively new entrants to the OECD from Eastern Europe for which tax revenue data is only available from the 1990s onwards. These countries tend to have relatively low personal income tax revenues and high revenues from social security contributions, but this impact is observed on the post 1990 data only.
- The variation in the share of the personal income tax between countries is considerable. In 2015, it ranged from a low of 9.7% and 9.8% in the Slovak Republic and Chile respectively to 41.5% in Australia and 55.2% in Denmark (Figure 1.5).
- The sharp fall in the share of revenues from corporate income taxes in total taxation in 2008 and 2009 did not continue into 2011 and 2012, but the share of these taxes in total revenues remains, at 8.9% of total tax revenues in 2015, below its 11.2% share in 2007.
- The share of the corporate income tax in total tax revenues varies considerably across countries from less than 5% (Finland, France, Germany, Hungary, Italy and Slovenia) to 20.1% (Mexico) and 21.0% (Chile). Apart from the spread in statutory rates of the corporate income tax, these differences are at least partly explained by institutional and country specific factors, for example:
  - the degree to which firms in a country are incorporated,
  - the breadth of the corporate income tax base, for example some narrowing may occur as a consequence of generous depreciation schemes and of tax incentives,
  - the degree of cyclicality of the corporate tax system, for which one of the important elements are loss offset provisions,

- the extent of reliance upon tax revenues from the exploitation of oil and/or mineral deposits, and
- other instruments to postpone the taxation of earned profits.

b. Social security contributions

Social security contributions as a share of total tax revenues on average across the OECD accounted for 25.8% in 2015. They were highest in the Czech Republic and the Slovak Republic (43.1% and 42.7%, respectively). In contrast, Australia and New Zealand do not levy social security contributions.

There is also wide variation across OECD countries in the relative proportions of social security contributions paid by employees and employers (Figure 1.7):

- Eight countries (Chile, Denmark, Greece, Israel, Luxembourg, the Netherlands, Slovenia and Switzerland) raise more revenues from employee SSCs, whereas the remainder raise more from employer SSCs.
- The highest share of employee SSC revenues are found in Slovenia, at 20.6% of total revenues. Germany, Greece, Japan, the Netherlands and Poland also have employee SSC revenues of over 15% of total tax revenues. Denmark had the lowest share, at 0.1% of total revenues. Only Estonia also had revenues from employee SSCs of less than 5% of total revenues.
- The highest share of employer social security contribution revenues are found in Estonia, at 31.7% of total revenues. The Czech Republic also had employer SSC revenues of over 25% of total tax revenues. Denmark and Chile had the lowest shares, at 0.1% and 0.2% of total revenues respectively.
- The highest share of self-employed or non-employed social security contribution revenues are found in the Czech Republic and the Slovak Republic, at 7.1% and 8.5% of total revenues respectively.

Figure 1.7. **Composition of social security contributions, as % of total social security contributions, 2015**

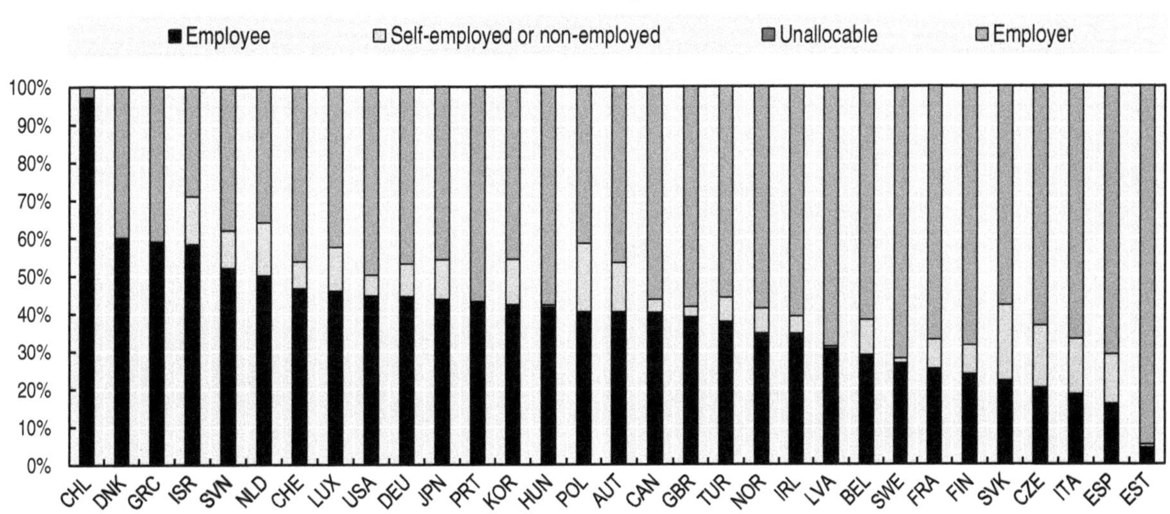

Note: Australia, Iceland, Mexico and New Zealand are not included within Figure 1.7. Although Iceland and Mexico collect social security contributions, disaggregated data is not available. New Zealand and Australia do not levy social security contributions.
Source: Secretariat calculations based on data in chapter 4.

StatLink http://dx.doi.org/10.1787/888933611506

c. Property taxes

Between 1965 and 2015, the share of taxes on property fell from 7.9% to 5.8% of total tax revenues on average across the OECD (Figure 1.6). Within OECD countries, they accounted for between 12.6% of total revenues in the United Kingdom, to less than 1% in Estonia:

- In relative terms, property taxes account for more than 10% of total tax revenue in six countries (Australia, Canada, Israel, Korea, the United Kingdom and the United States).
- Property taxes account for less than 2% of total revenue in five countries (Austria, Czech Republic, Estonia, Slovenia and the Slovak Republic).

d. Consumption taxes

- The share of taxes on goods and services fell from fell from 38.4% to 32.4% between 1965 and 2015 (Figure 1.6).
- During this period, the composition of taxes on goods and services has fundamentally changed. A fast-growing revenue source has been general consumption taxes, especially the value-added tax (VAT) which is now imposed in thirty-four of the thirty-five OECD countries.[3]
- General consumption taxes presently account for 20.6% of total tax revenue, compared with only 11.9% in the mid-1960s. In 2015, the vast majority of this was from VAT (20.0% of total tax revenues) (Figure 1.6).
- The substantially increased importance of the value-added tax has served to counteract the diminishing share of specific consumption taxes, such as excises and custom duties.
  - Between 1975 and 2015 the share of specific taxes on consumption (mostly on tobacco, alcoholic drinks and fuels, as well as some environment-related taxes) have almost halved from 17.7% to 9.7% of total revenues. In 2015, excises were the largest single category of total revenues, accounting for 7.7% of total revenues (Figure 1.8).
  - Rates of taxes on imported goods were considerably reduced across all OECD countries, reflecting a global trend to remove trade barriers.

Figure 1.8. **Share of consumption tax revenues as % of total revenues, 1975-2015**

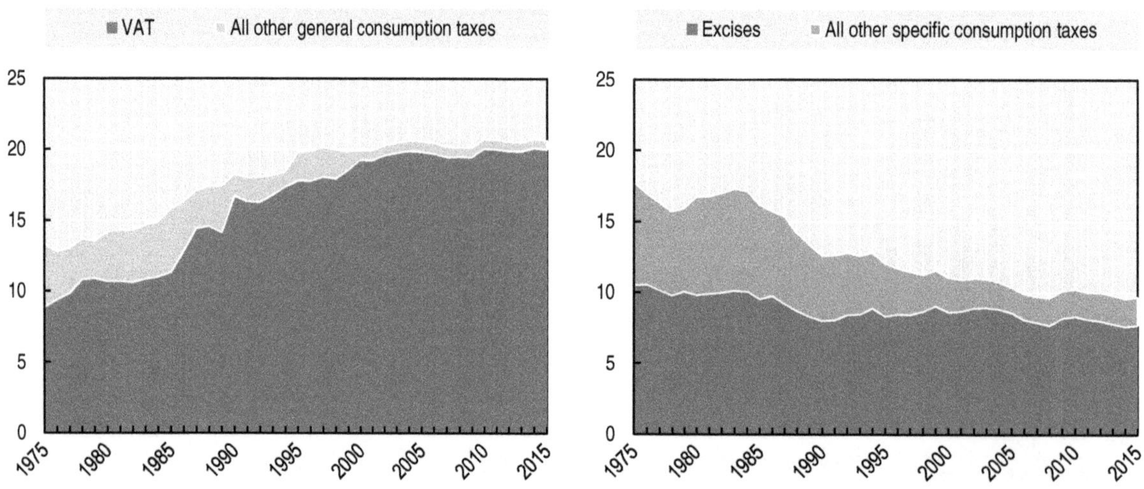

Note: The unweighted average for each year includes all countries which report revenue in the categories shown in that year.
Source: Secretariat calculations based on chapter 4

StatLink http://dx.doi.org/10.1787/888933611525

- Nevertheless, countries such as Mexico, Slovenia (around 14%) and Turkey (around 22%) still collect a relatively large proportion of their tax revenues through taxes on specific goods and services.

1.3. Taxes by level of government

This section discusses the relative share of tax revenues attributed to the various sub-sectors of general government in 2015. The different sub-sectors are:

- Central government
- State government (federal and regional countries only)
- Local government
- Social security funds
- Supranational (EU countries only)

The guidelines for attributing these revenue shares to the different levels of government are based on the final version of the 2008 System of National Accounts. These guidelines are discussed in the special feature S.1 in the 2011 edition of OECD Revenue Statistics.

a. Revenues of sub-national governments

Eight OECD countries have a federal structure. Among these countries, central governments received 54.0% of total revenues in 2015 on average. The second-highest share of revenues on average was received by social security funds, which are a sub-sector of general government, at 21.1% of total revenues, followed by 17.1% at the local level and 7.5% at the state level (Table 1.3). However, within countries there was considerable variation around these means:

- In 2015, the share of central government receipts in the eight federal OECD countries varied from 30.6% in Germany to 80.4% in Australia.
- In 2015, the share of the states varied from 1.5% in Austria, 4.2% in Mexico and 7.7% in Belgium to 39.5% in Canada. The share of local government varied from 1.6% in Mexico to 15.2% in Switzerland.
- Between 1975 and 2015 the share of federal government revenues declined by about eleven percentage points in Belgium and to a lesser extent in Canada, Germany and the United States.
- The share of federal government revenues increased in Austria and Switzerland by around 15 and five percentage points respectively. There was little change in Australia and Mexico.
- Of the seven federal countries with social security funds the share increased in five, the exceptions being Canada, where it slightly declined, and Mexico, where it declined by around 8 percentage points between 1995 and 2015.

Spain is classified as a regional rather than a unitary country because of its highly decentralised political structure. In 2015 the share of central government receipts was 42.5% compared with 14.0% for the regional government. Between 1975 and 2015, the share of local government receipts increased from around 4% to 10% and the share of social security funds declined from 48% to 33%.

The remaining twenty-six OECD countries have a unitary structure. In these countries, an average of 63.5% of revenues were derived at the central level, with 24.4% accounted for

Table 1.3. **Tax revenues of sub-sectors of general government as % of total tax revenue, federal countries**

	Supranational			Central government			State or Regional government			Local government			Social Security Funds		
	1975	1995	2015	1975	1995	2015	1975	1995	2015	1975	1995	2015	1975	1995	2015
Federal countries															
Australia	..	..	..	80.1	77.5	79.3	15.7	19.0	17.1	4.2	3.4	3.6	0.0	0.0	0.0
Austria	..	0.0	0.4	51.7	65.1	67.0	10.6	1.8	1.5	12.4	4.1	3.0	25.3	29.0	28.0
Belgium	1.4	1.0	0.9	65.3	60.1	54.3	..	1.8	7.7	4.4	4.8	4.9	28.8	32.2	32.2
Canada	..	..	..	47.6	39.1	40.9	32.5	37.1	39.5	9.9	9.8	10.3	10.0	14.0	9.2
Germany	1.2	0.6	0.5	33.5	31.4	30.6	22.3	21.6	23.0	9.0	7.4	8.3	34.0	39.0	37.6
Mexico	..	..	..	..	73.9	80.4	..	2.8	4.2	..	1.5	1.6	..	21.8	13.9
Switzerland	..	..	..	30.7	31.6	35.8	27.0	23.8	24.5	20.3	17.6	15.2	22.0	27.0	24.6
United States	..	..	..	45.4	41.4	43.3	19.5	20.0	19.4	14.7	13.3	13.6	20.5	25.2	23.7
Unweighted average	1.3	0.6	0.6	50.6	52.5	54.0	21.3	16.0	17.1	10.7	7.7	7.5	20.1	23.5	21.1
Regional country															
Spain[1,2]	..	0.5	0.5	48.2	51.3	42.5	..	4.8	14.0	4.3	8.8	9.9	47.5	34.6	33.1

1. Spain is constitutionally a non-federal country but has a highly decentralised political structure.
2. The total tax revenue has been reduced by the amount of any capital transfer that represents uncollected taxes.

StatLink http://dx.doi.org/10.1787/888933611696

Table 1.4. **Tax revenues of sub-sectors of general government as % of total tax revenue, unitary countries**

	Supranational			Central government			State or Regional government			Local government			Social Security Funds		
	1975	1995	2015	1975	1995	2015	1975	1995	2015	1975	1995	2015	1975	1995	2015
Unitary countries															
Chile	..	..	..	..	89.9	86.9	..	..	..	..	6.5	7.6	..	3.6	5.6
Czech Republic	..	..	0.5	..	57.7	55.3	..	..	..	..	0.9	1.2	..	41.4	43.1
Denmark[1]	1.1	0.5	0.4	68.9	68.2	72.8	..	..	..	30.0	31.3	26.8	0.1	0.0	0.1
Estonia	..	..	0.5	..	84.3	82.3	..	..	..	..	0.8	1.0	..	14.9	16.2
Finland	..	0.4	0.3	56.0	46.6	47.1	..	..	..	23.5	22.3	23.7	20.4	30.8	28.9
France[1]	0.7	0.4	0.2	51.2	42.3	33.3	..	..	..	7.6	11.0	13.2	40.6	46.3	53.3
Greece[1]	..	0.6	0.3	67.1	66.8	68.6	..	..	..	3.4	0.9	2.4	29.5	31.7	28.7
Hungary	..	..	0.3	..	63.8	60.8	..	..	..	..	2.5	5.8	..	33.6	33.1
Iceland	..	..	..	81.3	79.2	74.4	..	..	..	18.7	20.8	25.6	0.0	0.0	0.0
Ireland	2.3	1.5	0.5	77.4	83.1	83.0	..	..	..	7.3	2.7	2.4	13.1	12.7	14.0
Israel	..	..	..	..	79.6	75.5	..	..	..	..	6.4	8.1	..	14.0	16.4
Italy	..	0.4	0.3	53.2	62.7	53.1	..	..	..	0.9	5.4	16.5	45.9	31.5	30.1
Japan	..	..	..	45.5	41.2	36.7	..	..	..	25.6	25.2	23.9	29.0	33.6	39.4
Korea	..	..	..	89.0	69.2	55.4	..	..	..	10.1	18.7	18.0	0.9	12.1	26.6
Latvia	..	..	0.6	..	43.5	51.3	..	..	..	..	19.5	19.4	..	36.9	28.7
Luxembourg	0.8	0.4	0.1	63.6	66.5	68.3	..	..	..	6.7	6.5	3.5	29.0	26.6	28.1
Netherlands	1.5	1.3	1.0	58.9	56.0	57.4	..	..	..	1.2	3.1	3.8	38.4	39.5	37.8
New Zealand	..	..	..	92.3	94.7	93.2	..	..	..	7.7	5.3	6.8	0.0	0.0	0.0
Norway	..	..	..	50.6	58.4	84.7	..	..	..	22.4	19.6	15.3	27.0	22.0	0.0
Poland	..	..	0.5	..	61.9	48.1	..	..	..	..	8.3	12.9	..	29.8	38.5
Portugal	..	0.8	0.3	65.4	72.3	67.8	..	..	..	0.0	5.4	7.2	34.6	21.5	24.7
Slovak Republic	..	..	0.5	..	62.5	55.8	..	..	..	..	1.3	2.0	..	36.2	41.7
Slovenia	..	..	0.4	..	51.8	50.7	..	..	..	..	6.3	9.6	..	41.9	39.3
Sweden	..	0.4	0.3	51.3	46.9	51.3	..	..	..	29.2	30.9	36.0	19.5	21.8	12.4
Turkey	..	..	..	..	75.1	61.3	..	..	..	..	12.8	9.6	..	12.1	29.0
United Kingdom	1.0	1.0	0.5	70.5	77.5	75.9	..	..	..	11.1	3.7	4.9	17.5	17.8	18.7
Unweighted average	1.2	0.7	0.4	65.1	65.5	63.5	..	..	..	12.8	10.7	11.8	21.6	23.5	24.4

1. The total tax revenue has been reduced by the amount of any capital transfer that represents uncollected taxes.

StatLink http://dx.doi.org/10.1787/888933611715

by social security funds. A further 11.8% were raised by local governments. Among unitary OECD countries:

- The share of central government receipts in 2015 varied from 33.3% in France and 36.7% in Japan to 93.2% in New Zealand.
- The local government share varied from 1.0% in Estonia to 36.0% in Sweden.
- Between 1975 and 2015 there have been shifts to local government of 5 percentage points or more in six countries – France, Iceland, Italy, Korea, Portugal and Sweden and a smaller increase in the Netherlands. Shifts of 5 percentage points or more in the other direction occurred in two countries – Norway and the United Kingdom.
- Between 1975 and 2015, there were increases in the share of social security funds of 7 or more percentage points in four countries – Finland, France, Japan and Korea – and corresponding decreases in four other countries – Italy, Norway, Portugal and Sweden.

The "supranational" column of Tables 1.3 and 1.4 report taxes collected on behalf of the European Union (EU) by the twenty-two EU member states that are members of the OECD. For years prior to 1998, customs duties collected on behalf of the EU by national tax administrations of the EU member states are included under heading 5123.[4] From 1998 onwards they are shown as a memorandum item since they represent a tax imposed by the EU and collected by national administrations.

Table 1.5. **Customs duties collected on behalf of the European Union**

Millions of national currency

	2000	2005	2007	2009	2011	2012	2013	2014	2015	2016p
Austria[1]	356	325	397	320	378	344	328	369	415	446
Belgium[1]	960	1 208	1 388	1 147	1 285	1 247	1 185	1 250	1 363	1 557
Czech Republic	..	5 586	6 443	5 548	6 961	6 172	5 544	6 968	7 859	8 033
Denmark	2 325	2 833	3 282	2 647	3 177	2 962	2 824	3 001	3 285	3 069
Estonia[1]	..	22	35	20	29	29	29	30	34	34
Finland[1]	129	148	199	152	189	184	166	170	165	163
France[1]	1 513	1 583	1 657	1 461	1 866	1 883	1 842	1 827	1 931	1 818
Germany[1]	3 394	3 433	3 972	3 778	4 556	4 417	4 251	4 608	5 195	5 089
Greece[1]	210	262	307	252	186	162	148	163	181	199
Hungary	..	26 572	27 981	25 657	27 462	27 206	26 337	31 947	38 960	41 620
Ireland[1]	208	226	273	208	240	242	247	275	327	311
Italy[1]	1 536	1 785	2 261	2 008	2 319	2 077	1 890	2 022	2 246	2 270
Latvia[1]	..	26	37	21	31	32	28	36	40	47
Luxembourg[1]	27	21	23	13	17	15	15	24	24	26
Netherlands[1]	1 310	1 265	1 679	1 518	1 889	1 780	1 756	2 046	2 266	2 340
Poland	..	1 464	1 711	1 743	1 859	2 018	1 977	2 316	2 823	3 359
Portugal[1]	204	145	185	154	168	155	144	149	158	174
Slovak Republic[1]	..	75	136	111	157	129	115	127	119	124
Slovenia[1]	..	34	85	57	62	54	52	52	52	53
Spain[1]	971	1 436	1 722	1 328	1 553	1 436	1 315	1 512	1 754	1 885
Sweden	3 450	4 327	5 099	4 764	5 399	4 995	4 976	5 737	6 243	6 044
United Kingdom	1 800	1 908	2 074	2 435	2 925	2 885	2 914	2 949	3 077	3 318

Note: p: provisional
1. For euro area countries, the figures are in euros for all years.

StatLink http://dx.doi.org/10.1787/888933611734

b. Composition of central and sub central revenues

Figure 1.9 shows the revenues from each major category of tax revenue for central and sub central governments. For federal and regional countries, the sub central level includes revenues received by both state and local governments. Figure 1.9 demonstrates that:

- Central government revenues in almost all OECD countries are predominantly derived from income and goods and services taxes, with a negligible share from property taxes.
- At the subnational level, revenue from property taxes provides a much larger share of revenues than at the central level, and accounts for over 90% of revenues in four countries (Greece, Ireland, Israel and United Kingdom).
- By contrast, the share of income taxes and goods and services taxes is lower at the sub central level, the exceptions being Sweden, Finland and Luxembourg, where over 90% of sub central revenues are derived from income taxes.

Figure 1.9. **Composition of revenues of sub-sectors of general government, 2015**

(a) Federal or central government (b) Sub-national governments

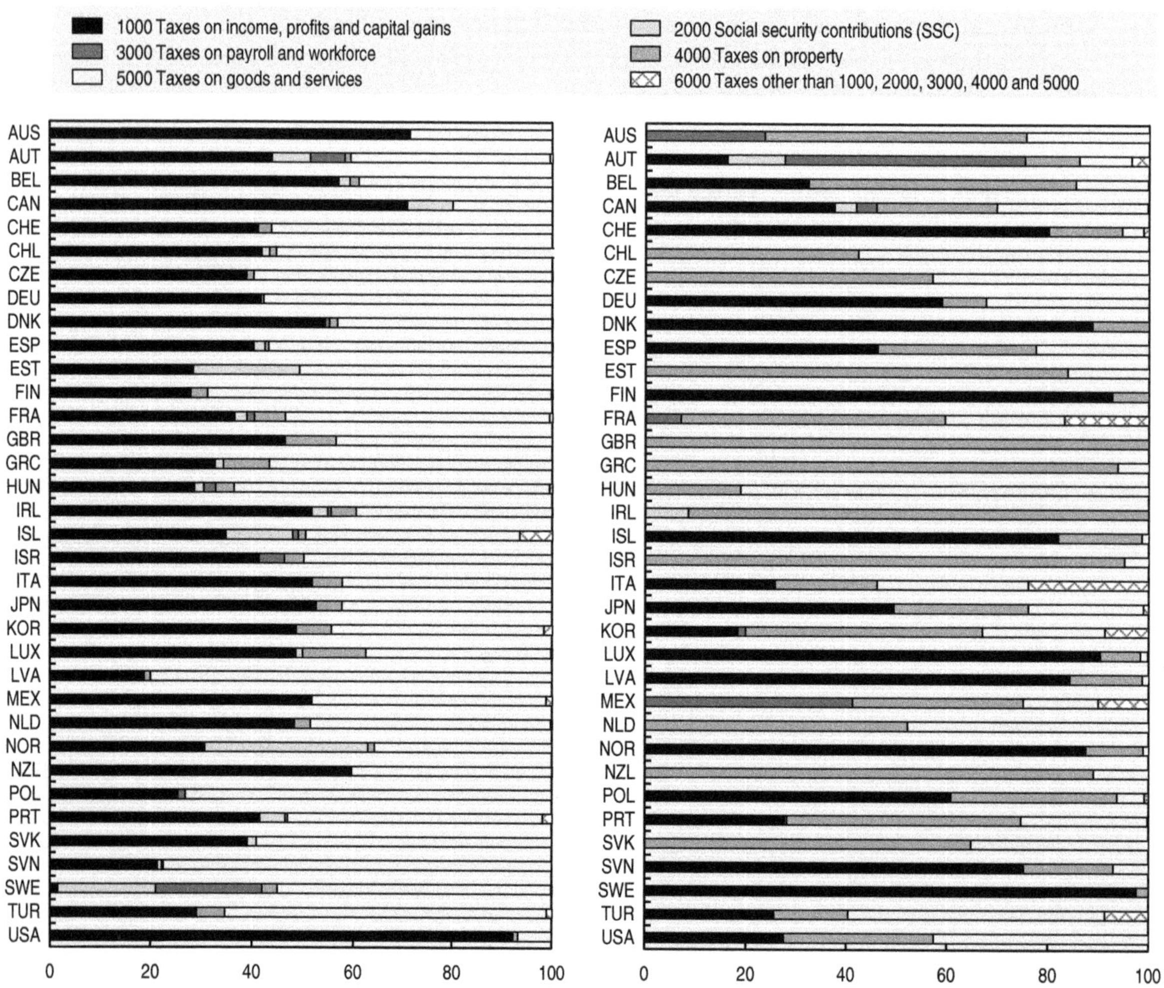

Note: The left-hand panel (a) refers to only those taxes which are classified as central government taxes. Social security contributions paid to social security funds are excluded. The right-hand panel (b) refers only to those taxes which are classified as sub-central taxes (local and (where relevant) state taxes). Social security contributions paid to social security funds are excluded.

Source: Secretariat calculations based on tables 3.16 to 3.18.

StatLink http://dx.doi.org/10.1787/888933611544

1.4. Non-wastable tax credits

There are two kinds of tax credits that apply to income taxes (both personal and corporate):

- Non-payable or wastable tax credits are those that can only ever be used to reduce or eliminate a tax liability. They cannot be paid out to either taxpayers or non-tax payers as a benefit. They are, therefore, the same as a tax allowance or relief.
- In contrast, payable or non-wastable tax credits can be partitioned into two parts. One part is used to reduce or eliminate a tax liability in the same way as a wastable tax credit. The other part can be paid directly to recipients as a benefit payment, when the benefit exceeds the tax liability.

The OECD methodology for classifying non-wastable tax credits is set out in paragraphs 19 and 20 of the *Interpretative Guide*. This states that only the part of a non-wastable tax credit that is used to reduce or eliminate a taxpayer's tax liability should be subtracted in the reporting of tax revenues. This is referred to as the "tax expenditure component" of the credit. In contrast, the part of the tax credit that exceeds the taxpayer's tax liability and is paid to that taxpayer is treated as an expenditure item and not subtracted in the reporting of tax revenues. This part is referred to as the "transfer component".

Table 1.6 provides information on the non-wastable tax credits in 2015 for those countries reporting them in the *Revenue Statistics 2017* (though it may be that some countries with non-wastable tax credits do not appear in the table). It shows the amounts of the non-wastable tax credits and their two components together with the results of using the figures to calculate tax revenue values and the associated tax-to-GDP ratios.

Table 1.6 also shows two alternative treatments:

- The "net basis" which treats non-wastable tax credits entirely as tax provisions, so that the full value of the tax credit reduces reported tax revenues, as shown in columns 4 and 7.
- The "gross basis" is the exact opposite, treating non-wastable tax credits entirely as expenditure provisions, with neither the transfer component nor the tax expenditure component being deducted from tax revenue, as shown in columns 6 and 9. This is the approach followed by the GFSM and the SNA.

Table 1.6 shows that, with some exceptions, the choice of method for reporting non-wastable tax credits has only a small impact on the ratio of total tax revenue to GDP. For the countries with available data, the differences between the ratios on a net basis and on a gross basis are one percentage point or more in only France, Germany, New Zealand and the United Kingdom, and between half a percentage point and one percentage point in Australia, Canada, Czech Republic, Italy and the United States.

Table 1.6. **Effect of alternative treatments of non-wastable tax credits, 2015**

	Non-wastable tax credits in billlions of national currency			Total tax revenue in milllions of national currency			Total tax revenue as a percentage of GDP		
	Total value	Transfer component	Tax expenditure component	Net basis	Split basis (per current guidance)	Gross basis	Net basis	Split basis (per current guidance)	Gross basis
Australia	9.3	6.8	2.5	456.3	463.1	465.6	27.8	28.2	28.4
Austria[1]	0.5	0.2	0.3	148.2	148.4	148.7	43.6	43.7	43.8
Belgium	0.7	0.3	0.4	183.6	183.8	184.3	44.7	44.8	44.9
Canada[2]	11.1	10.1	1.0	627.8	637.9	638.9	31.5	32.0	32.1
Chile[3]	175.5	129.7	45.8	32 532.4	32 662.0	32 707.8	20.5	20.6	20.6
Czech Republic	32.1	8.9	23.2	1 523.6	1 532.5	1 555.7	33.2	33.3	33.9
Denmark[4]	4.2	0.2	4.0	930.3	930.6	934.5	45.9	45.9	46.1
France[4]	25.8	10.4	15.4	981.7	992.1	1 007.5	44.7	45.2	45.9
Germany	42.2	15.7	26.4	1 112.6	1 128.4	1 154.8	36.6	37.1	37.9
Iceland	1.2	1.0	0.2	811.0	812.0	812.2	36.6	36.7	36.7
Ireland	0.5	..	0.5	..	60.6	61.1	..	23.1	23.3
Israel[5]	1.4	1.3	0.1	362.7	364.1	364.1	31.2	31.3	31.3
Italy	14.7	6.0	8.6	706.2	712.3	720.9	42.9	43.3	43.8
Luxembourg[6]	0.2	..	..	..	..	19.3	..	..	36.8
Mexico	43.8	1.0	42.8	2 952.2	2 953.2	2 996.0	16.2	16.2	16.5
New Zealand	2.4	1.6	0.8	81.3	82.8	83.6	32.4	33.0	33.4
Norway	1.7	1.3	0.4	1 192.9	1 194.2	1 194.5	38.3	38.3	38.3
Slovak Republic[6]	0.3	..	..	..	..	25.4	..	..	32.3
Spain[4]	1.0	0.2	0.8	363.4	363.7	364.5	33.8	33.8	33.9
United Kingdom	30.8	27.4	3.4	581.8	609.2	612.6	31.1	32.5	32.7
United States	157.2	113.9	43.4	4 638.5	4 752.4	4 795.8	25.6	26.2	26.5

Note: In *Revenue Statistics*, the tax revenue data are reported on a split basis, unless indicated otherwise.
1. The children's tax credit is not regarded as a tax credit in the *OECD Revenue Statistics* and is treated entirely as an expenditure provision.
2. Some non-wastable tax credits cannot be split into the transfer and tax expenditure components. Their total values have been added to the transfer component.
3. In *Revenue Statistics*, the tax revenue data for Chile are reported on a net basis.
4. The total tax revenue has been reduced by the amount of any capital transfer that represents uncollected taxes.
5. The data for Israel are supplied by and under the responsibility of the relevant Israeli authorities. The use of such data by the OECD is without prejudice to the status of the Golan Heights, East Jerusalem and Israeli settlements in the West Bank under the terms of international law.
6. In *Revenue Statistics*, the tax revenue data for Luxembourg and Slovak Republic are reported on a gross basis.

StatLink http://dx.doi.org/10.1787/888933611753

Notes

1. Provisional 2016 figures are not available for Australia and provisional figures on social security contributions in Japan are also not available as at the time *Revenue Statistics 2017* was published.
2. Calculated by applying the unweighted average percentage change for 2016 in the 33 countries providing data for that year to the overall average tax-to-GDP ratio in 2015.
3. The terms "value added tax" and "VAT" are used to refer to any national tax that embodies the basic features of a value added tax by whatever name or acronym it is known e.g. "Goods and Services Tax" ("GST").
4. From 1998 onwards, these custom duties are shown as a "memorandum" item since they represent a tax imposed by the EU and collected by national administrations. However, they continue to be part of the aggregate revenue figures that represent all taxes imposed within the territory of EU member states. This approach ensures consistency of the time series, and ensures that the tax-to-GDP ratio measures are immune to changes in the relative share of customs duties in (1) the composition of EU financing resources and (2) national tax mixes of EU member states.

Chapter 2

Special feature: Complementary indicators of tax revenues

Revenue Statistics presents taxes in national currency, in USD, and as a proportion of Gross Domestic Product (GDP). In addition, tax structure information is provided by expressing specific tax revenues as a percentage of total tax revenue. The primary indicator used in *Revenue Statistics* is the tax-to-GDP ratio, where tax revenues are expressed as a percentage of the GDP of a country.

Taxes as a percentage of GDP are an internationally-recognised and commonly-used indicator of tax levels within an economy, and will continue to be the primary indicator of *Revenue Statistics*. Expressing taxes as a percentage of GDP offers two main advantages: firstly, it permits comparisons of tax revenue data both across time and across countries, something that is not possible in national currency or USD due to inflation and fluctuating exchange rates. Secondly, the tax-to-GDP ratio provides an indication of the scale of tax revenues in the context of the economy from which they are generated.

This Special Feature estimates provides complementary indicators of the tax revenue data collected by *Revenue Statistics*. It considers two additional types of indicator: "macro" indicators, which use other summary measures of the economy or country to understand the tax revenues raised from that economy; and "fiscal" indicators to illustrate the contribution of tax revenues to the government's wider fiscal position. Specifically, this Special Feature presents total tax revenues as a proportion of Gross National Income (GNI), and on a purchasing power parity (PPP)-adjusted per capita basis (the macro indicators); and as a proportion of total government revenues and of total government expenditures (the fiscal indicators).

In this Special Feature, data on tax revenues are taken from *Revenue Statistics* (OECD, 2017), and data on GNI, population, total revenues, and total government expenditures are taken from *National Accounts of OECD Countries* (OECD, 2017, Issue 1). Where tax revenues have been adjusted for PPP, the conversion data are taken from the *Main Economic Indicators* (OECD, 2017, Issue 8).

2.1. Macro indicators

a. Tax as a percentage of national income: the tax-to-GNI ratio

Tax as a percentage of GDP calculates the tax burden against the production of the economy. A complementary indicator of tax revenues is to compare revenues against national income, measured as GNI in the System of National Accounts.

GNI is the sum of all income received from goods and services produced within a country in a year, as well as net primary income flows. This means adding all income that a country's residents receive from overseas and subtracting all income that is sent abroad to foreign residents. Therefore, GNI calculates the income from goods and services received by a country's residents, regardless of where that income was generated. This contrasts with GDP, which measures all production within an economy, regardless of whether it was subsequently exported, and not including any imports.

Equation 1 illustrates the difference between GNI and GDP.

Equation 1. Measuring Gross National Income

$$GNI = GDP + Primary\,income\,receivable\,from\,abroad - Primary\,income\,payable\,abroad$$

Source: System of National Accounts, 2008.

The tax-to-GNI ratio for all OECD countries is set out in Table 2.1 for a selection of years between 2000 and 2015. In 2015, the tax-to-GNI ratios varied considerably across OECD countries (Figure 2.2, left-hand panel). Luxembourg had the highest tax-to-GNI ratio, at 57.8%. Eight other European countries had ratios above 40% (Austria, Belgium, Denmark, Finland, France, Hungary, Italy and Sweden). A further seven European countries also had tax-to-GNI ratios above the OECD unweighted average of 34.9% (Czech Republic, Germany, Greece, Netherlands, Norway, Portugal and Slovenia). Mexico had the lowest tax-to-GNI ratio in 2015 at 16.7%, followed by Chile, Korea, and Turkey. Ratios in Australia, Canada, the United Kingdom and the United States were between 25% and 35% in 2015.

On an unweighted average basis, the OECD tax-to-GNI and tax-to-GDP ratios followed the same broad trends between 2000 and 2015 (Figure 2.1). In all years, the tax-to-GNI ratio was higher than the tax-to-GDP ratio, indicating that on an unweighted average basis, OECD countries have a net outflow of income, with an average of 1.0 percentage point (p.p.) difference across the period.[1] Key observations of the two unweighted averages include:

Figure 2.1. **OECD average tax-to-GNI and tax-to-GDP ratios, 2000-15**

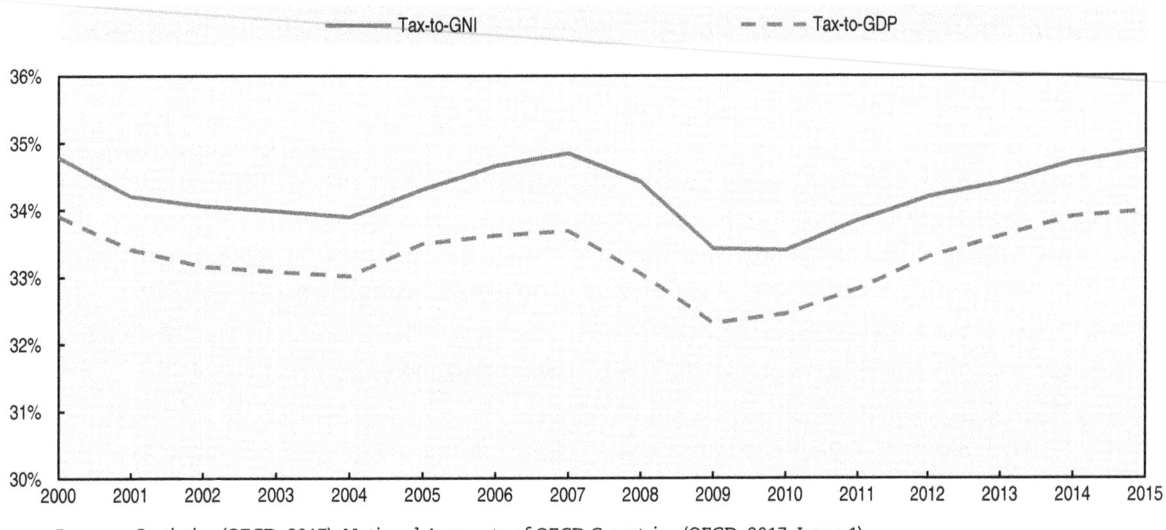

Source: Revenue Statistics (OECD, 2017), National Accounts of OECD Countries (OECD, 2017, Issue 1).

StatLink *http://dx.doi.org/10.1787/888933611563*

- The average OECD tax-to-GNI ratio varied slightly less than the tax-to-GDP ratio over this period. The difference between the highest and lowest tax-to-GNI ratios was 1.5 p.p., while this was 1.7 p.p. for the average OECD tax-to-GDP ratio;
- From 2006 to 2011, the difference between the tax-to-GNI ratio and the tax-to-GDP ratio was at its greatest. This was due to tax-to-GDP rising more slowly and decreasing more quickly than tax-to-GNI;

- The average tax-to-GNI and tax-to-GDP ratios experienced the same three peaks: in 2000 (at 34.8% and 33.9% respectively), in 2007 (at 34.8% and 33.7% respectively) and in 2015 (at 34.9% and 34.0% respectively);
- Following the crisis, the OECD average tax-to-GNI ratio reached its lowest point in 2010 at 33.4%, while tax-to-GDP reached its lowest point in 2009 at 32.3%. Following these low years, both measures increased steadily to overtake pre-crisis peaks and both reached their highest levels in 2015.

While the OECD average tax-to-GNI ratio experienced three peaks and two troughs during the years 2000 to 2015, country tax-to-GNI ratios differed in a variety of ways:

- In several countries, including Belgium, Germany, and Slovenia, there was little change in the level of tax-to-GNI ratios between 2000 and 2015. As these countries experienced GNI growth over the period, the steady tax-to-GNI ratio indicates that tax revenues increased with GNI.
- Spain and Hungary had similar tax-to-GNI levels in 2000 and 2015, but had fluctuations around the time of the crisis. In addition, Australia, Denmark, Estonia, Latvia, and the Netherlands had similar tax-to-GNI levels in 2000 and 2015, with fluctuations throughout.
- Canada, Finland, Israel, New Zealand, and Slovak Republic experienced an overall decrease in their tax-to-GNI ratios, though there were periods of stable tax-to-GNI ratios or growth in some years.
- Italy, Iceland, Japan, Korea, and Poland experienced overall increases in their tax-to-GNI ratio over the period, while Luxembourg experienced a large increase. In countries with minor increases, the growth of the tax-to-GNI ratio was steadier, while large increases were consistent with more volatility. The latter may be attributable to swings in GNI growth, rather than large changes in tax revenues.

The financial crisis in 2008 and the subsequent years were a period of some volatility for tax revenues. The OECD average tax-to-GNI ratio dropped from a pre-crisis peak in 2007 to its lowest point in 2010 and then increased to a new high in 2015. Among OECD countries, the U-shaped trend of the tax-to-GNI ratio was mirrored by some, but not all, countries, with four main types of country trend observed during the crisis:

- Chile, Greece, Israel, Japan, Latvia, Poland, Portugal, Spain, and the United States decreased to a post-crisis low in 2009 and subsequently increased.
- The Czech Republic, Germany, Denmark, Finland, France, Ireland, Italy, Korea, Mexico, Norway, Slovenia, Sweden, and the United Kingdom had relatively unchanged tax-to-GNI ratios during the crisis, with increases or decreases of less than one percentage point and minor troughs in either 2009 or 2010.
- A third group of countries experienced an increase in their tax-to-GNI ratio during the crisis, with an inverse U-shaped trend. This was most often due to GNI decreasing faster than tax revenues, as in Estonia, the Netherlands, and Slovak Republic. In Austria, both tax revenues and GNI increased, while in Luxembourg tax revenues increased while GNI decreased.
- Australia and Hungary experienced a steady decline in their tax-to-GNI ratios during the crisis.

Figure 2.2. **Tax-to-GNI ratios (left panel) and tax revenue per capita (PPP-adjusted current USD, right panel), 2015**

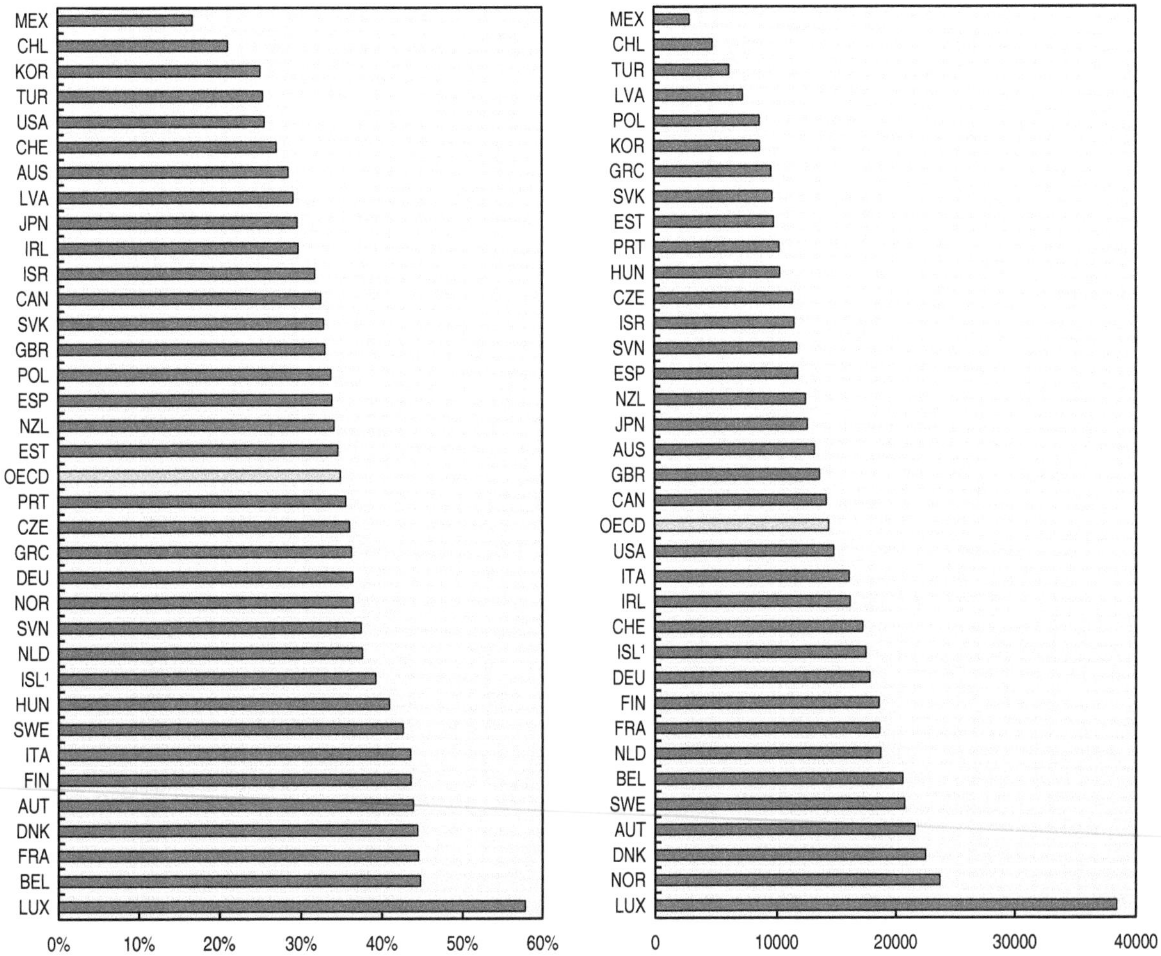

Note: Adjustments have been made for countries which have fiscal years that differ between Revenue Statistics and the National Accounts.

1. Tax-to-GNI data for Iceland are from 2014 as GNI data for 2015 were not available at the time of publication.

Source: Revenue Statistics (OECD, 2017), National Accounts of OECD Countries (OECD, 2017, Issue 1).

StatLink http://dx.doi.org/10.1787/888933611582

b. Tax per capita

Tax per capita measures tax revenues against the number of people resident in a country. Tax per capita is an indicator of the revenue that has been collected and is available to governments per resident in order to provide services and infrastructure for its residents. It is calculated by dividing total tax revenue by the country's population, which includes all individuals resident in the territory, regardless of legal status or citizenship.[2]

Tax per capita uses a base that typically experiences smaller year-on-year changes than other macroeconomic indicators. Tax per capita differs from tax-to-GNI and tax-to-GDP, as the latter are measures of a country's income or production, against which taxes are levied. By contrast, the tax per capita ratio expresses tax revenues as a function of a country's residents who both contribute to tax revenues and who receive government services.

Table 2.1. **Tax-to-GNI ratios and tax revenue per capita (PPP-adjusted current USD), 2000-15**

	Tax-to-GNI ratio[1] (%)					Tax per capita (PPP adjusted USD)				
	2000	2007	2009	2014	2015	2000	2007	2009	2014	2015
Australia	31.3	30.8	26.7	28.1	28.5	8 471	11 337	10 329	12 866	13 172
Austria	42.8	40.9	41.3	43.0	43.9	12 417	15 974	16 787	20 916	21 579
Belgium	42.5	42.2	42.3	44.8	44.8	12 178	15 755	16 132	20 254	20 548
Canada	35.7	32.6	32.7	31.7	32.5	10 348	12 813	12 525	14 022	14 157
Chile	19.5	25.6	18.6	20.3	21.1	1 794	3 807	2 805	4 465	4 757
Czech Republic	33.1	36.6	34.8	35.5	36.0	5 253	8 900	8 893	10 681	11 356
Denmark	47.9	46.2	44.5	46.9	44.4	13 424	18 097	18 161	23 224	22 496
Estonia	32.3	33.6	36.0	33.7	34.6	2 919	6 855	7 167	9 335	9 817
Finland	46.1	41.4	40.4	43.4	43.6	12 246	15 645	15 508	18 191	18 584
France	42.3	41.5	40.6	44.7	44.5	11 283	14 486	14 377	18 247	18 624
Germany	36.5	34.4	35.3	36.1	36.4	9 975	12 919	13 616	17 365	17 846
Greece	33.1	32.0	31.3	35.8	36.3	6 508	9 135	9 305	9 485	9 595
Hungary	40.5	42.4	41.0	39.8	40.9	4 577	7 506	8 022	9 715	10 289
Iceland[1]	37.3	41.0	38.9	39.2	..	10 677	15 812	13 030	17 137	17 533
Ireland	35.3	35.1	32.8	33.7	29.7	9 273	14 200	11 373	14 730	16 213
Israel	37.2	34.3	30.6	31.5	31.7	8 682	9 358	8 213	10 873	11 437
Italy	40.8	41.7	42.1	43.5	43.5	10 962	14 095	14 424	15 775	16 133
Japan	25.4	26.7	25.3	29.2	29.6	6 982	9 582	8 733	12 073	12 539
Korea	21.6	24.9	23.8	24.5	25.1	3 881	6 898	6 727	8 267	8 658
Latvia	29.2	29.0	26.0	28.9	29.1	2 334	5 089	4 707	6 882	7 223
Luxembourg	41.6	41.6	56.2	56.6	57.8	20 397	30 237	31 432	37 976	38 384
Mexico	13.4	12.9	13.2	14.6	16.7	1 309	1 780	1 875	2 561	2 905
Netherlands	36.6	35.7	35.3	37.6	37.6	11 759	15 669	15 596	18 396	18 711
New Zealand	34.5	36.8	31.6	33.2	34.1	7 070	10 081	9 281	11 941	12 397
Norway	42.4	42.2	41.0	37.5	36.5	15 471	23 507	22 871	25 523	23 765
Poland	33.1	35.8	32.2	33.2	33.7	3 514	5 799	6 003	8 121	8 624
Portugal	31.7	32.9	31.1	34.9	35.6	5 856	8 172	7 921	9 862	10 255
Slovak Republic	33.8	30.1	29.1	31.7	32.8	3 806	6 149	6 624	9 048	9 667
Slovenia	36.6	37.8	36.7	36.5	37.4	6 604	10 228	9 945	11 305	11 685
Spain	33.4	37.3	30.3	33.8	33.8	7 156	11 851	9 629	11 359	11 749
Sweden	49.0	43.6	43.0	41.7	42.6	14 332	18 251	17 498	19 759	20 702
Switzerland	25.7	25.9	26.5	26.7	27.1	9 704	12 898	13 893	16 563	17 258
Turkey	..	..	23.8	24.8	25.4	2 222	3 394	3 603	5 704	6 110
United Kingdom	33.0	32.8	31.5	32.6	33.0	8 637	11 670	10 878	13 099	13 599
United States	27.8	26.5	22.9	25.3	25.6	10 271	12 819	10 802	14 169	14 797
OECD average	**34.8**	**34.8**	**33.4**	**34.7**	**34.9**	**8 351**	**11 736**	**11 391**	**13 997**	**14 376**

Note: Adjustments have been made for countries with fiscal years that differ between Revenue Statistics and the National Accounts.
1. Tax-to-GNI data for Iceland are not included in 2015 as GNI data for 2015 were not available at the time of publication.
Source: Revenue Statistics (OECD, 2017), National Accounts of OECD Countries (OECD, 2017, Issue 1).

StatLink http://dx.doi.org/10.1787/888933611772

To calculate tax revenue per capita, tax revenues have been converted to current PPP-adjusted USD to equalise the purchasing power of the different currencies by adjusting for the price levels across countries in each year. This enables the measure to be more comparable across countries with different currencies and to better account for differences in prices across the OECD in a given year.

In 2015, PPP-adjusted tax per capita varied considerably across OECD countries (Figure 2.2, right-hand panel). Luxembourg had the highest tax per capita ratio, at USD 38 384, which was substantially higher than the next highest levels observed in Norway (USD 23 765) and Denmark (USD 22 496).[3] Twenty countries had tax per capita ratios between USD 10 000 and USD 20 000, and the OECD average level of PPP-adjusted tax per capita was USD 14 376.

Mexico had the lowest tax per capita in 2015 (USD 2 095), followed by Chile (USD 4 757), Turkey (USD 6 110), and Latvia (USD 7 223).

The amount of tax per capita paid may vary for different reasons and is influenced by both the level of tax as a proportion of GDP and the average per capita income (GDP) of the country. Figure 2.3 separates these two factors to better understand the levels of tax per capita shown. Figure 2.3 shows countries' tax-to-GDP ratios on the vertical axis and their level of GDP-per-capita on the horizontal axis.[4] The size of the area to the left and below a country's position therefore shows the tax paid per capita. The same level of tax per capita can result from a number of different combinations of tax-to-GDP and GDP per capita, with the curved lines showing different combinations for different levels of tax per capita. For example, France and the Netherlands both have a tax per capita level of around USD 18 500, but this is driven by higher GDP-per-capita in the Netherlands, and higher taxes as a proportion of GDP in France.

Figure 2.3. **Tax per capita (USD), 2015, decomposed by tax-to-GDP ratios and GDP per capita**

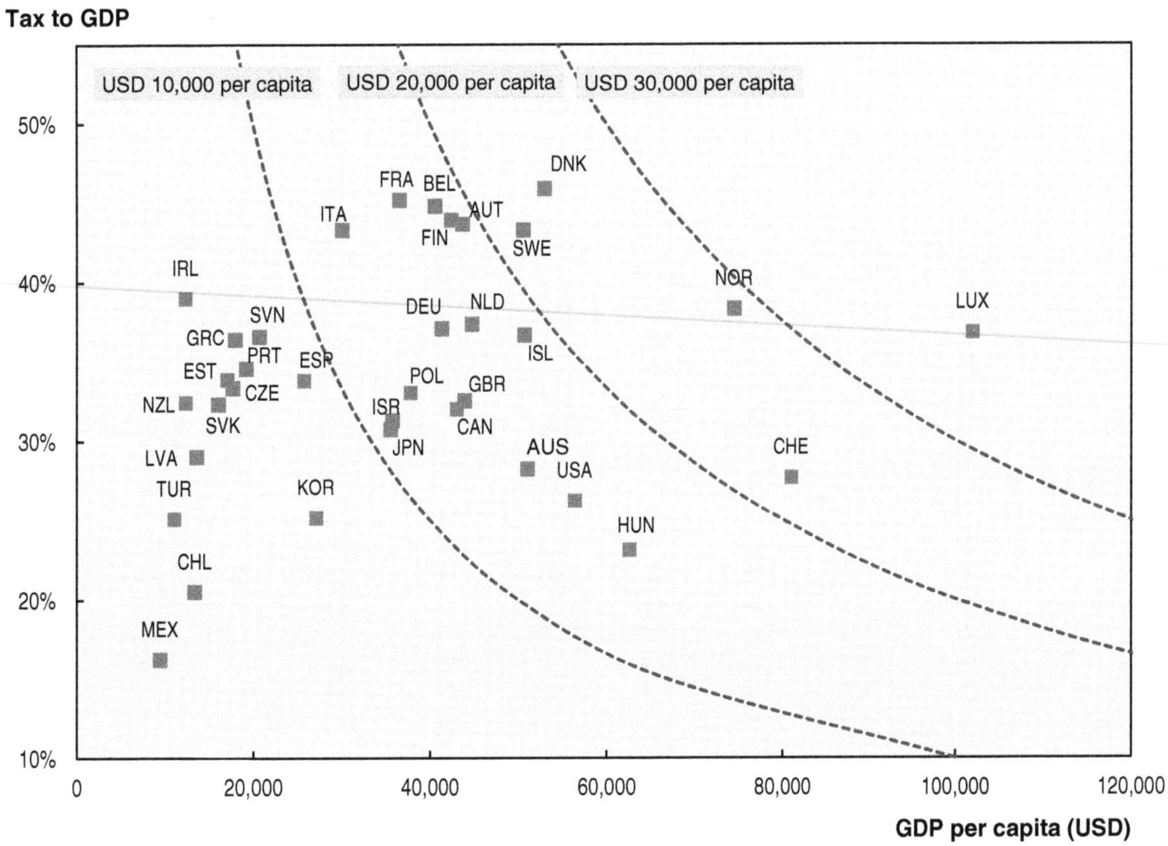

Source: Revenue Statistics (OECD, 2017), National Accounts of OECD Countries (OECD, 2017, Issue 1).

StatLink http://dx.doi.org/10.1787/888933611601

2.2. Fiscal indicators

a. Tax as a percentage of total government revenue

Tax as a percentage of total government revenue measures the proportion of government revenues derived from the tax base, with the remainder derived from non-tax sources. Non-tax sources of revenue may include dividends and interest from government assets, royalty and other resource revenues, or fines and penalties. Non-tax revenues, and the share of the different types of non-tax revenues, vary in importance across OECD countries.

Table 2.2 presents the ratio of tax to total government revenue for all OECD countries, from 2000 to 2015. In 2015, the unweighted OECD average of tax as a percentage of total

Table 2.2. **Tax revenue as a percentage of total government revenue (left-hand panel) and expenditure (right-hand panel), 2000-15**

	Tax revenue as a % of total revenue					Tax revenue as a % of government expenditure				
	2000	2007	2009	2014	2015	2000	2007	2009	2014	2015
Australia	86.7	84.6	79.4	81.2	82.1	84.1	86.3	67.7	75.5	75.7
Austria	87.2	84.7	84.1	86.0	86.1	83.6	82.4	75.8	81.6	84.3
Belgium	88.1	87.6	86.3	86.2	86.7	87.9	87.7	77.7	81.4	82.6
Canada	80.5	78.8	79.7	79.8	80.5	84.6	81.6	72.3	78.4	77.6
Czech Republic	88.2	86.9	84.5	81.7	80.8	80.6	85.4	73.8	78.0	79.6
Denmark	85.5	84.6	83.3	86.4	86.6	88.6	93.2	79.2	88.0	83.8
Estonia	85.6	84.4	79.3	83.3	83.3	85.4	91.1	75.5	84.8	83.5
Finland	83.3	79.7	78.2	79.7	80.8	95.2	88.5	74.6	75.3	76.9
France	86.2	85.1	83.1	85.1	85.0	84.0	81.0	72.6	79.2	79.6
Germany	79.1	81.9	82.1	82.6	83.3	80.6	82.3	76.5	83.1	84.6
Greece	78.4	76.9	78.4	76.2	75.2	71.5	66.0	56.4	70.7	67.0
Hungary	87.4	87.5	84.8	81.1	80.2	81.8	78.7	77.1	77.6	77.7
Iceland	85.2	84.9	82.2	85.4	87.2	87.8	95.1	65.8	85.3	85.5
Ireland	85.5	84.9	83.8	84.7	86.2	99.0	85.5	59.2	76.4	80.5
Israel	78.0	81.6	81.5	83.1	83.2	72.8	80.4	70.7	76.5	78.9
Italy	91.6	91.8	91.4	91.2	91.4	89.0	88.8	82.0	85.7	86.6
Japan	..	85.9	84.2	86.3	86.0	..	78.4	64.2	75.7	78.3
Korea	73.8	73.1	70.8	74.0	74.9	86.8	83.5	68.1	76.9	77.9
Latvia	84.4	83.8	80.1	79.8	80.6	78.2	82.3	63.4	76.4	77.9
Luxembourg	84.2	85.9	85.8	86.6	86.2	97.3	95.3	84.5	89.5	89.2
Mexico	..	60.6	56.9	59.2	68.6	..	61.0	55.4	57.7	66.2
Netherlands	84.5	83.7	82.0	84.6	86.3	88.3	84.1	72.8	80.5	82.4
New Zealand[1]	..	..	79.8	90.0	90.5	..	..	78.1	87.3	89.6
Norway	73.3	71.9	73.1	71.2	69.9	99.6	101.6	89.5	84.8	78.5
Poland	84.5	83.6	82.5	82.1	82.8	78.5	80.0	69.2	75.4	77.7
Portugal	78.3	76.4	73.8	76.6	78.4	72.4	71.3	59.4	66.0	71.3
Slovak Republic	84.1	84.3	79.1	78.9	75.1	64.6	79.8	65.1	73.8	70.6
Slovenia	86.2	87.5	85.2	81.3	80.6	79.4	87.3	74.8	72.6	75.7
Spain	86.9	88.6	85.2	86.4	87.3	84.6	92.9	64.8	74.9	77.1
Sweden	85.9	84.5	83.8	84.9	85.5	91.1	90.1	82.7	82.4	85.9
Switzerland	81.3	81.9	79.8	80.5	79.2	80.3	84.4	81.7	79.8	81.7
Turkey	..	..	67.7	72.4	72.9	..	..	57.5	72.9	75.8
United Kingdom	89.0	86.5	84.3	84.6	84.5	92.6	80.9	66.6	73.7	75.9
United States	81.7	80.0	76.0	78.1	78.6	83.6	72.3	53.6	68.2	69.8
OECD average	**83.8**	**82.6**	**80.4**	**81.5**	**82.0**	**84.5**	**83.7**	**70.8**	**77.8**	**79.0**

Note: Chile is not included as consolidated data on government revenue and expenditure are not available from the National Accounts. Total government revenue in the National Accounts includes tax revenues, imputed, voluntary, and compulsory social security contributions, and other non-tax revenues. Adjustments have been made for the different treatment of non-wastable tax credits between Revenue Statistics and the National Accounts (see section 1.4 of chapter 1 for more information); the supranational revenues which are included in total tax revenues of EU countries in Revenue Statistics; and for countries with fiscal years that differ between Revenue Statistics and the National Accounts.

1. Revenue and expenditure data for New Zealand are provided by Statistics New Zealand as consolidated data are not available from the National Accounts.

Source: Revenue Statistics (OECD, 2017), National Accounts of OECD Countries (OECD, 2017, Issue 1).

StatLink http://dx.doi.org/10.1787/888933611791

revenues was 82.0% (Figure 2.4, left-hand panel). There was also not much variation across OECD countries: 23 OECD countries sourced between 80 and 90% of government revenue from taxes and thirty OECD countries sourced between 70 and 90% of government revenue from taxes, with only Mexico and Norway having a ratio lower than 70%, at 68.6% and 69.9% respectively, partially due to non-tax resource revenues. Among OECD countries, Italy derived the highest proportion of revenues from taxes in 2015, at 91.4% tax to total revenue, followed by New Zealand at 90.5%, Spain at 87.3%, and Iceland at 87.2%. Among countries where tax accounted for less than 75% of total revenues, there was more variation: Mexico had the lowest ratio of tax to total revenue, at 68.6%, followed by Norway at 69.9%, Turkey at 72.9%, and Korea at 74.9%.

Figure 2.4. **Tax revenue as a percentage of total government revenue (left-hand panel) and expenditure (right-hand panel), 2015**

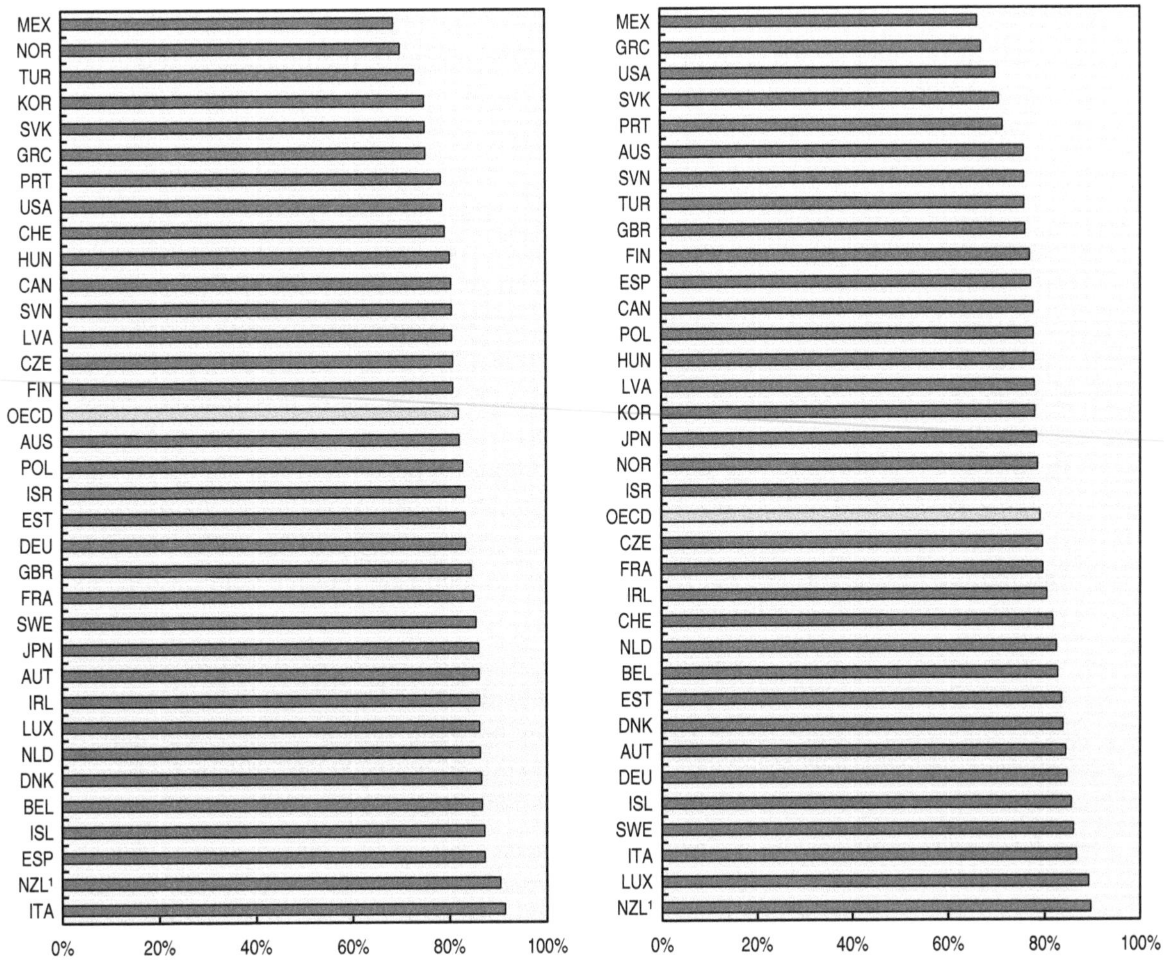

Note: Data for Chile are not included as consolidated data on government revenue and expenditure are not available from the National Accounts.

Total government revenue in the National Accounts includes tax revenues, imputed, voluntary, and compulsory social security contributions, and other non-tax revenues. Adjustments have been made for the different treatment of non-wastable tax credits between Revenue Statistics and the National Accounts (see section 1.4 of chapter 1 for more information); the supranational revenues which are included in total tax revenues of EU countries in Revenue Statistics; and for countries with fiscal years that differ between Revenue Statistics and the National Accounts.

1. Revenue and expenditure data for New Zealand are provided by Statistics New Zealand as consolidated data are not available in the National Accounts.

Source: Revenue Statistics (OECD, 2017), National Accounts of OECD Countries (OECD, 2017, Issue 1).

StatLink http://dx.doi.org/10.1787/888933611620

From 2000 to 2015, the average level of tax as a percentage of total revenue across OECD countries (on an unweighted basis for the countries in which data was available) fluctuated. From 2000 to 2006, there was a small and steady decline in the ratio of tax to total revenue, from 83.8% in 2000 to 82.2% in 2006, prior to a small increase to 82.6% in 2007. During the financial crisis, the share of tax revenues in total government revenues fell to a low point of 80.4% in 2009. Since 2009, the share of tax revenues in OECD countries has remained relatively flat, increasing very slightly to 82.0% in 2015. However, the share of tax revenues to total revenues still remains well below the level of 83.8% in 2000, despite the overall levels of tax revenue (measured as a percentage of GDP, on an unweighted average basis) being higher in 2015 than in 2000.

The behaviour of the OECD average tax to total revenue ratio depends on the levels of both tax and non-tax revenues across this period. During the financial crisis (observed in the fall in the tax to total revenue ratio from 2007 to 2009) the unweighted OECD average tax-to-GDP ratio also fell, from 33.7% in 2007, to 32.3% in 2009. At the same time, non-tax revenues increased by 2.9 p.p. of GDP between 2007 and 2009, then remained relatively steady until 2013. Since 2010, tax-to-GDP ratios have increased, to a new high of 34.0% in 2015, while the share of tax to total revenues has increased only slightly, indicating that since 2010, non-tax revenues have risen at a similar rate on average as tax revenues.

The OECD average trend since the financial crisis was not mirrored in all OECD countries. While most countries had a relatively stable tax to total revenue ratio following a low-point in 2009, some OECD countries have seen an increasing share of total revenues derived from taxation since 2012 or 2013. Key observations on country trends include:

- Austria, Estonia, the Netherlands, Switzerland, Spain, Sweden and the United States followed the OECD trend relatively closely through the period of the financial crisis, although Switzerland experienced its lowest tax to total revenue ratio in 2008, and Spain, Estonia and the Netherlands saw a slightly larger increase than the OECD average between 2013 and 2015. Australia, Estonia and Slovak Republic experienced a larger drop in their tax to total revenue ratios over the crisis period, of 5.3 p.p. in Australia, 5.1 p.p. in Estonia, and 5.2 p.p. in Slovak Republic. Mexico also saw relative volatility in tax revenues to total revenues across the period.
- In seven countries, the decrease in taxes as a percentage of total revenues occurred over a longer time period. The tax to total revenue ratio decreased by 2.0 p.p. in Belgium from 2007 to 2012; by 6.5 p.p. in the Czech Republic between 2008 and 2015; by 2.6p.p in Denmark between 2005 and 2011; by 5.3 p.p. in Finland from 2000 to 2010; by 5.4 p.p. in Hungary from 2008 to 2011; and by 5.6 p.p. in Norway from 2004 to 2008.
- A further six countries did not experience a decrease over this period; Greece saw an increase of 2.5 p.p. from 2008 to 2009, with volatility across the period; Italy saw an increase of 1.5 p.p. from 2004 to 2008 before falling back by 1 p.p. by 2014; and Germany saw an increase across the period as a whole, by 1.4.
- A number of countries had greater increases than the OECD average after the impact of the crisis in 2009. These include France, Iceland, Ireland, Japan, Korea, Portugal, and the United Kingdom.

b. Tax as a percentage of total expenditure

Measuring tax revenues as a proportion of total government expenditure indicates the level of expenditure supported by the tax system, rather than through non-tax revenues or debt. It is a measure of the sufficiency of taxation to fund government expenditure, although that is not to imply that tax should necessarily fund all expenditure. It is a useful complement in understanding the level of tax-to-GDP or tax-to-GNI, as it provides some indication of the scale of revenue required to fund government services.

Table 2.2 (right-hand panel) shows the ratio of tax revenues to total government expenditure from 2000 to 2015 for OECD countries. In 2015, the unweighted average OECD tax to expenditure ratio was 79.0% nearly three percentage points lower than the average OECD tax to total revenue ratio of 82.0%.

Across OECD countries, there was comparatively little variation around the unweighted average (Figure 2.5), although to a greater extent than for the tax to total revenue ratio. In 2015, the highest tax to expenditure ratio was seen in New Zealand at 89.6%, Luxembourg at 89.2%, with Italy at 86.6%, and Sweden at 85.9%. Twenty-four OECD countries had a tax to expenditure ratio of between 75 and 85%. The lowest ratio in 2015 was seen in Mexico at 66.2%. Other ratios below 70% are seen in Greece (67.0%), and the United States (69.8%).

Figure 2.5. **Tax revenues as a percentage of total government revenue and expenditure (left panel); Tax revenue, total government revenue and total government expenditure as a percentage of GDP (right panel), unweighted OECD average, 2000-15**

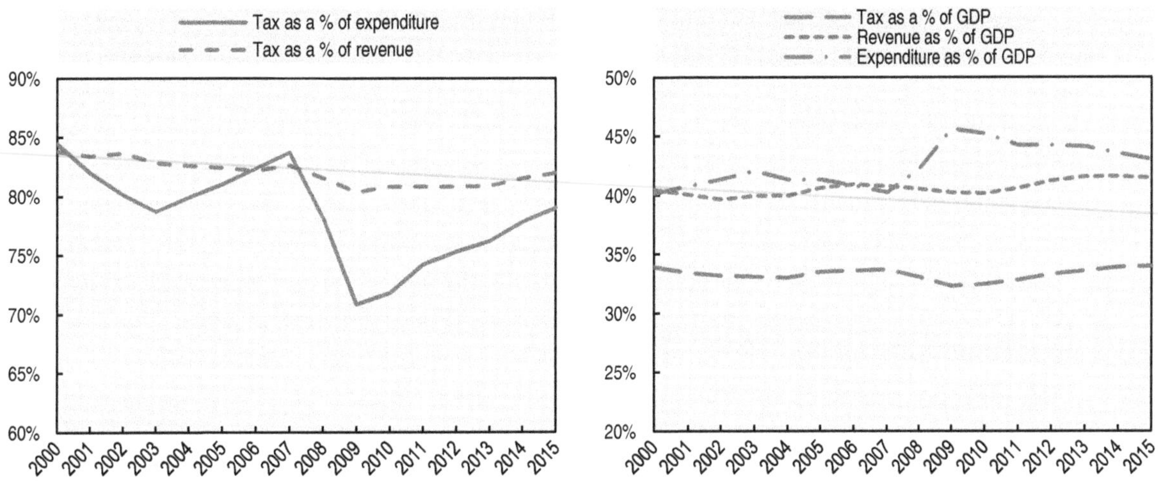

Note: Chile is not included as consolidated data on government revenue and expenditure are not available from the National Accounts. Revenue and expenditure data for New Zealand are provided by Statistics New Zealand as consolidated data are not available from the National Accounts.

Total government revenue in the National Accounts includes tax revenues, imputed, voluntary, and compulsory social security contributions, and other non-tax revenues. Adjustments have been made for the different treatment of non-wastable tax credits between Revenue Statistics and the National Accounts (see section 1.4 of chapter 1 for more information); the supranational revenues which are included in total tax revenues of EU countries in Revenue Statistics; and for countries with fiscal years that differ between Revenue Statistics and the National Accounts.

Source: Revenue Statistics (OECD, 2017), National Accounts of OECD Countries (OECD, 2017, Issue 1).

StatLink http://dx.doi.org/10.1787/888933611639

Between 2000 and 2015, the unweighted average tax to expenditure ratio in the OECD experienced volatility, particularly during the crisis period. Following a drop from 84.5% to 78.7% between 2000 and 2003, the ratio then rose to 83.7% in 2007. However, during the crisis, there was a fall of 12.9 p.p., to the low point of 70.8% in 2009, which was driven by an increase in government expenditure as a percentage of GDP (Figure 2.5). Since 2009, the tax to expenditure ratio has been increasing steadily, but has not recovered to its pre-crisis levels. In

2015, the ratio was 79.0%, which remained lower than at any point between 2004 and 2009, indicating that in the post-crisis period, tax revenues fund a smaller percentage, on an average basis, of government expenditures than they did prior to the crisis. However, the increase in the tax to expenditure ratio since 2009 was driven by a decrease in total expenditures as a percentage of GDP, whereas the tax-to-GDP ratio increased slowly over this period (Figure 2.5).

This drop in the tax to expenditure ratio during the financial crisis, and the lack of recovery in the level of the ratio since the crisis, was mirrored in almost all OECD countries. Measuring between the highest pre-crisis point and the lowest point following the crisis, the largest fall was seen in Ireland: between 2006 and 2010 the tax to expenditure ratio fell by 50.1 p.p. Iceland experienced the sharpest decline, falling 35.2 p.p. between 2006 and 2008 to 63.3%. By contrast, the smallest decrease was seen in Switzerland (4.0 p.p. between 2007 and 2010), with no other countries experiencing a difference in their pre- and post-crisis ratios of less than five percentage points.

In 2015, the tax to expenditure ratio had recovered to pre-crisis levels only in Austria, Germany, Greece, Mexico, and Portugal with all other countries having a lower ratio in 2015 than in 2007. Only Austria, Germany, Israel, the Slovak Republic, and Switzerland had a higher tax to expenditure ratio in 2015 than in 2000.

2.3. Conclusion

The tax-to-GDP ratio is a fundamental and internationally-used indicator of the level of tax revenues collected by an economy, allowing comparisons of tax levels and changes to be made both across countries and over time. It will continue to be the primary indicator used by *Revenue Statistics*. The additional indicators presented in this Special Feature provide a complementary perspective on how the tax revenue data collected by *Revenue Statistics* relate to the economy in which they were generated, as well as to the fiscal position of governments.

- The tax-to-GNI ratio measures tax revenues against a country's gross income, rather than gross production (as in GDP). The tax-to-GNI ratio, which varies significantly across OECD countries, decreased on an unweighted average basis during the global financial crisis until 2010 and then increased to surpass pre-crisis peaks in 2014 and 2015.
- Tax per capita measures tax revenues against the resident population, thereby expressing tax revenues as a function of the individuals who receive government services and contribute to tax revenues. There is much diversity in tax per capita across OECD countries, some of which can be explained by differences in GDP per capita and the tax-to-GDP ratio.
- Tax revenue as a percentage of total revenue measures the proportion of government revenue that is derived from the tax base rather than from non-tax sources. OECD countries were relatively homogenous in this measure in 2015. After a steady but slight decline over the years preceding the global financial crisis, the unweighted OECD average dipped in 2008 and 2009, remaining relatively flat until 2013, and increasing slightly, although not back to pre-crisis levels, in 2014 and 2015.
- Tax revenue as a percentage of government expenditure measures the portion of public expenditure that is financed through the tax system. OECD countries were relatively homogenous in 2015, but there is more variation than when measuring tax revenue as a percentage of government revenue. The unweighted OECD average tax to expenditure ratio experienced a sharp decline during the crisis and subsequently increased, although remained below pre-crisis levels. However, this trend was driven by changes in total government expenditure, rather than by changes in tax revenues.

Notes

1. Caution is needed when interpreting the unweighted average as it is influenced by the number of small open economies in the OECD, which tend to have net financial outflows. On a weighted average basis, the tax-to-GDP and tax-to-GNI measures are at similar levels from 2009 onwards.
2. 2008 SNA, Section 19.10.
3. The high tax-per-capita figures in Luxembourg is affected by the number of non-resident workers, who pay income tax on their earnings in Luxembourg, but are resident and counted in the population in neighbouring countries. The Luxembourg Statistics Portal estimates that in the third quarter of 2016 there were 177 000 non-resident workers in Luxembourg, compared to a resident population of 576 000 in 2016. By contrast, this has a considerably smaller impact on the revenues of countries where these workers live due to their higher populations.
4. For consistency with the tax-to-GDP ratios shown in chapters 1 and 3 of this book, Figure 2.4 presents figures in market exchange rates, rather than as PPP-adjusted figures.

Chapter 3

Tax levels and tax structures, 1965-2016

In all of the following tables the symbol (..) indicates not available/or not applicable. The data in this chapter cover the years 1965 to 2016 (preliminary data). A selection of years are shown in this chapter because of lack of space. The complete series is available on line. Data for 1955 and 1960 (for nineteen OECD countries) are provided in part V of the 1998 edition of this Report.

The Gross Domestic Product (GDP) figures are based on the 2008 System of National Accounts (SNA) for all OECD countries.

Treatment of capital transfers. Footnotes to Tables 3.1 to 3.18 refer to the treatment of the capital transfers that some countries make to account for taxes that have been assessed but not collected. The capital transfer has been subtracted from the total tax revenue and this reduction has been allocated between tax headings in proportion to their tax revenues.

This applies to the following countries:

- Denmark from 1971.
- France from 1992.
- Greece for 1999 and 2000.
- Spain from 1995.

Table 3.1. **Total tax revenue as % of GDP**

	1965	1990	2000	2007	2010	2012	2013	2014	2015	2016p
Australia	20.6	28.0	30.4	29.5	25.4	27.1	27.3	27.6	28.2	..
Austria	33.6	39.4	42.4	40.8	41.1	42.0	42.8	43.1	43.7	42.7
Belgium	30.6	41.2	43.5	42.7	42.6	44.2	45.2	45.0	44.8	44.2
Canada	25.2	35.2	34.8	32.1	30.6	31.0	30.9	31.2	32.0	31.7
Chile	..	16.9	18.8	22.7	19.6	21.3	19.9	19.6	20.5	20.4
Czech Republic	..	..	32.4	34.2	32.5	33.7	34.1	33.1	33.3	34.0
Denmark[1]	29.1	44.4	46.9	46.4	44.8	45.5	45.9	48.6	45.9	45.9
Estonia	..	..	31.1	31.3	33.3	31.7	31.7	32.8	33.9	34.7
Finland	30.0	42.9	45.8	41.5	40.8	42.7	43.6	43.8	43.9	44.1
France[1]	33.6	41.0	43.1	42.4	42.0	44.3	45.2	45.3	45.2	45.3
Germany[2]	31.6	34.8	36.2	34.9	35.0	36.4	36.8	36.8	37.1	37.6
Greece[1]	17.1	25.2	33.4	31.2	32.0	35.5	35.5	35.9	36.4	38.6
Hungary	..	..	38.6	39.6	37.5	38.5	38.1	38.2	39.0	39.4
Iceland	25.5	30.2	36.2	39.0	33.3	35.2	35.8	38.6	36.7	36.4
Ireland	24.5	32.4	30.8	30.4	27.0	27.5	28.2	28.5	23.1	23.0
Israel[3]	..	..	34.9	34.2	30.7	30.0	30.7	31.1	31.3	31.2
Italy	24.7	36.4	40.6	41.7	41.9	43.9	44.1	43.5	43.3	42.9
Japan	17.6	28.2	25.8	27.5	26.5	28.2	28.9	30.3	30.7	..
Korea	..	18.8	21.5	24.8	23.4	24.8	24.3	24.6	25.2	26.3
Latvia	..	..	29.1	28.1	28.1	28.4	28.5	28.8	29.0	30.2
Luxembourg	26.4	33.5	36.9	36.1	37.4	38.4	38.2	37.4	36.8	37.1
Mexico[4]	..	12.4	13.1	12.6	13.4	13.1	13.8	14.2	16.2	17.2
Netherlands	30.9	40.2	37.2	36.0	36.1	36.0	36.5	37.5	37.4	38.8
New Zealand	23.2	36.2	32.5	33.9	30.3	32.1	31.1	32.4	33.0	32.1
Norway	29.4	40.2	41.9	42.1	42.0	41.5	39.9	38.9	38.3	38.0
Poland	..	..	32.9	34.6	31.4	32.1	31.9	32.0	32.4	33.6
Portugal	15.7	26.5	31.1	31.8	30.4	31.8	34.1	34.3	34.6	34.4
Slovak Republic	..	..	33.6	29.2	28.1	28.3	30.2	31.2	32.3	32.7
Slovenia	..	..	36.6	37.1	36.9	36.9	36.7	36.5	36.6	37.0
Spain[1]	14.3	31.6	33.2	36.4	31.2	32.2	33.1	33.7	33.8	33.5
Sweden	31.4	49.5	49.0	45.0	43.2	42.6	42.9	42.6	43.3	44.1
Switzerland	16.6	23.6	27.4	26.1	26.5	26.8	26.9	27.0	27.7	27.8
Turkey	10.6	14.5	23.6	23.1	24.8	24.9	25.3	24.6	25.1	25.5
United Kingdom	30.1	32.9	33.2	33.2	32.6	32.8	32.6	32.2	32.5	33.2
United States	23.5	26.0	28.2	26.7	23.5	24.1	25.7	25.9	26.2	26.0
Unweighted average										
OECD Average[5]	**24.8**	**31.9**	**33.9**	**33.7**	**32.5**	**33.3**	**33.6**	**33.9**	**34.0**	**34.3**

Note: Full time series can be accessed at http://oe.cd/full-time-series.

1. The total tax revenue has been reduced by the amount of any capital transfer that represents uncollected taxes. The capital transfer has been allocated between tax headings in proportion to the reported tax revenue.
2. From 1991 the figures relate to the united Germany.
3. Information on data for Israel: http://oe.cd/israel-disclaimer.
4. 2016: Secretariat estimate, including expected revenues collected by state and local governments.
5. 2016: calculated by applying the unweighted average percentage change for 2016 in the 33 countries providing data for that year to the overall average tax-to-GDP ratio in 2015.

StatLink http://dx.doi.org/10.1787/888933611810

Table 3.2. **Total tax revenue in billions of US dollars at market exchange rates**

	1965	1990	2000	2007	2010	2012	2013	2014	2015	2016p
Australia	5.6	90.9	124.2	291.0	328.8	428.8	419.2	400.8	348.0	..
Austria	..	68.6	83.2	157.6	160.5	171.1	183.3	188.7	164.6	164.9
Belgium	..	89.4	103.6	201.6	206.1	220.0	234.9	239.3	203.9	206.0
Canada	14.2	209.2	262.8	477.2	501.4	570.1	574.8	561.2	499.0	491.1
Chile	..	5.8	14.7	39.4	42.8	57.0	55.3	51.1	49.7	50.4
Czech Republic	..	..	20.0	64.8	67.4	70.0	71.4	68.8	62.3	66.5
Denmark[1]	3.0	61.4	76.9	148.3	144.2	149.0	157.6	171.0	138.4	140.9
Estonia	..	..	1.8	7.0	6.5	7.3	7.9	8.6	7.6	8.0
Finland	..	49.6	57.5	106.0	101.1	109.6	117.7	119.4	102.1	105.2
France[1]	..	550.7	589.3	1 129.0	1 111.0	1 188.9	1 270.2	1 291.9	1 100.6	1 115.9
Germany[2]	..	577.4	706.9	1 200.4	1 196.2	1 290.1	1 379.0	1 431.1	1 251.7	1 305.7
Greece[1]	..	14.6	43.4	99.3	95.9	87.3	85.0	84.7	70.9	75.0
Hungary	..	..	18.2	55.1	48.8	49.1	51.3	53.2	47.5	49.0
Iceland	0.1	2.0	3.2	8.3	4.4	5.0	5.5	6.6	6.2	7.3
Ireland	0.7	15.6	30.7	82.0	60.0	62.0	67.4	73.6	67.2	70.2
Israel[3]	..	..	46.2	61.2	72.0	77.4	90.1	96.1	93.7	99.6
Italy	..	336.6	463.6	918.8	889.5	910.2	938.3	935.1	790.1	792.8
Japan	17.1	903.6	1 263.4	1 242.0	1 509.6	1 749.1	1 500.1	1 482.2	1 351.6	..
Korea	..	52.6	120.5	278.2	256.2	303.2	317.2	347.0	347.9	371.1
Latvia	..	..	1.8	8.7	6.7	8.0	8.6	9.0	7.8	8.4
Luxembourg	..	4.7	7.9	18.4	19.9	21.8	23.6	24.8	21.4	22.2
Mexico	..	35.9	85.1	131.4	140.3	155.7	173.2	184.4	186.0	..
Netherlands	..	132.6	153.7	302.5	301.9	298.7	316.6	330.1	283.3	301.9
New Zealand	1.4	16.4	18.0	47.1	44.9	56.8	60.3	64.6	57.7	60.1
Norway	2.4	48.2	71.8	168.9	179.9	211.7	208.7	193.7	148.1	140.7
Poland	..	..	56.6	148.7	150.6	160.7	167.5	174.4	154.8	157.5
Portugal	..	18.8	36.8	76.4	72.5	68.8	77.0	78.7	68.8	70.3
Slovak Republic	..	..	9.8	25.2	25.1	26.5	29.8	31.4	28.2	29.3
Slovenia	..	..	6.4	17.8	17.7	17.1	17.5	18.1	15.6	16.3
Spain[1]	..	131.6	197.9	537.9	446.8	430.8	451.1	464.2	403.4	412.4
Sweden	7.8	127.7	127.3	219.4	211.2	231.7	248.4	244.4	214.7	225.6
Switzerland	2.6	60.8	74.6	124.8	153.8	178.2	184.1	189.7	185.7	183.7
Turkey	1.3	30.2	64.5	156.2	192.0	218.6	240.8	229.6	215.5	218.3
United Kingdom	30.6	359.5	542.8	1 016.7	791.5	869.4	885.7	965.5	930.8	869.4
United States	167.0	1 552.4	2 900.5	3 867.4	3 515.8	3 888.5	4 281.9	4 518.4	4 752.4	4 846.3
Unweighted average										
OECD Average	..	**205.4**	**239.6**	**383.8**	**373.5**	**409.9**	**425.8**	**438.0**	**410.8**	..

Note: Full time series can be accessed at http://oe.cd/full-time-series.

1. The total tax revenue has been reduced by the amount of any capital transfer that represents uncollected taxes. The capital transfer has been allocated between tax headings in proportion to the reported tax revenue.
2. From 1991 the figures relate to the united Germany.
3. Information on data for Israel: http://oe.cd/israel-disclaimer.

StatLink http://dx.doi.org/10.1787/888933611829

Table 3.3. Tax revenue of main headings as % of GDP, 2015

	1000 Income & profits	2000 Social security	3000 Payroll	4000 Property	5000 Goods and services	6000 Others	EU Custom Duties
Australia	16.0	0.0	1.4	3.0	7.8	0.0	..
Austria	13.2	14.7	3.0	0.6	11.9	0.2	0.1
Belgium	16.0	14.3	0.0	3.5	10.7	0.0	0.3
Canada	15.3	4.8	0.7	3.8	7.4	0.0	..
Chile	7.5	1.4	0.0	0.9	11.1	-0.4	..
Czech Republic	7.2	14.4	0.0	0.5	11.2	0.0	0.2
Denmark[1]	29.0	0.1	0.3	1.9	14.5	0.0	0.2
Estonia	7.9	11.3	0.0	0.3	14.2	0.0	0.2
Finland	15.4	12.7	0.0	1.4	14.2	0.0	0.1
France[1]	10.6	16.8	1.6	4.0	11.0	1.1	0.1
Germany[2]	11.6	14.0	0.0	1.1	10.3	0.0	0.2
Greece	8.2	10.7	0.0	3.1	14.3	0.0	0.1
Hungary	7.1	12.6	0.6	1.3	17.1	0.2	0.1
Iceland	17.2	3.6	0.3	2.0	11.9	1.7	..
Ireland	9.9	3.9	0.1	1.5	7.5	0.0	0.1
Israel	9.8	5.1	1.2	3.3	11.9	0.0	..
Italy	13.8	13.0	0.0	2.8	11.8	1.7	0.1
Japan	9.6	12.1	0.0	2.5	6.4	0.1	..
Korea	7.6	6.7	0.1	3.1	7.1	0.6	..
Latvia	7.5	8.3	0.0	1.0	12.0	0.0	0.2
Luxembourg	13.4	10.7	0.0	3.3	9.4	0.1	0.0
Mexico	6.8	2.2	0.4	0.3	6.3	0.2	..
Netherlands	10.4	14.1	0.0	1.4	11.1	0.1	0.3
New Zealand	18.3	0.0	0.0	2.0	12.7	0.0	..
Norway	15.1	10.5	0.0	1.1	11.6	0.0	..
Poland	6.5	12.5	0.2	1.4	11.7	0.0	0.2
Portugal	10.4	9.0	0.0	1.3	13.3	0.5	0.1
Slovak Republic	7.0	13.8	0.0	0.4	10.9	0.0	0.2
Slovenia	6.6	14.5	0.1	0.6	14.6	0.0	0.1
Spain[1]	9.6	11.4	0.0	2.6	10.0	0.0	0.2
Sweden	15.5	9.7	4.6	1.0	12.2	0.0	0.1
Switzerland	12.9	6.8	0.0	1.9	6.0	0.1	..
Turkey	5.1	7.3	0.0	1.2	11.1	0.4	..
United Kingdom	11.5	6.1	0.0	4.1	10.7	0.0	0.2
United States	12.9	6.2	0.0	2.7	4.5	0.0	..
Unweighted average							
OECD Average	**11.5**	**9.0**	**0.4**	**1.9**	**10.9**	**0.2**	**0.2**

1. The total tax revenue has been reduced by the amount of any capital transfer that represents uncollected taxes. The capital transfer has been allocated between tax headings in proportion to the reported tax revenue.
2. From 1991 the figures relate to the united Germany.

StatLink http://dx.doi.org/10.1787/888933611848

Table 3.4. **Tax revenue of main headings as % of total tax revenue, 2015**

	1000 Income & profits	2000 Social security	3000 Payroll	4000 Property	5000 Goods and services	6000 Others	EU Custom Duties
Australia	56.7	0.0	5.0	10.7	27.5	0.0	..
Austria	30.2	33.6	6.8	1.3	27.3	0.5	0.3
Belgium	35.7	31.9	0.0	7.8	23.8	0.0	0.7
Canada	47.9	15.1	2.0	11.8	23.1	0.1	..
Chile	36.4	6.9	0.0	4.4	54.1	-1.8	..
Czech Republic	21.5	43.1	0.0	1.4	33.5	0.0	0.5
Denmark[1]	63.1	0.1	0.6	4.1	31.6	0.0	0.4
Estonia	23.4	33.4	0.0	0.8	41.8	0.0	0.5
Finland	35.2	28.9	0.0	3.3	32.4	0.1	0.2
France[1]	23.5	37.1	3.5	9.0	24.3	2.5	0.2
Germany[2]	31.2	37.6	0.0	2.9	27.8	0.0	0.5
Greece	22.5	29.4	0.0	8.5	39.4	0.0	0.3
Hungary	18.3	32.4	1.5	3.3	43.8	0.4	0.3
Iceland	46.9	9.8	0.8	5.4	32.4	4.7	..
Ireland	43.0	16.8	0.6	6.4	32.6	0.0	0.5
Israel	31.2	16.4	3.8	10.6	38.0	0.0	..
Italy	31.8	30.1	0.0	6.5	27.3	3.9	0.3
Japan	31.2	39.4	0.0	8.2	21.0	0.3	..
Korea	30.3	26.6	0.3	12.4	28.0	2.5	..
Latvia	25.9	28.7	0.0	3.4	41.3	0.0	0.6
Luxembourg	36.4	29.0	0.0	8.9	25.5	0.1	0.1
Mexico	41.7	13.9	2.4	2.0	38.6	1.5	..
Netherlands	27.7	37.8	0.0	3.8	29.6	0.2	0.9
New Zealand	55.5	0.0	0.0	6.1	38.4	0.0	..
Norway	39.4	27.3	0.0	2.9	30.4	0.0	..
Poland	20.1	38.5	0.7	4.2	35.9	0.1	0.5
Portugal	30.2	26.1	0.0	3.7	38.4	1.3	0.3
Slovak Republic	21.8	42.7	0.0	1.3	33.7	0.0	0.5
Slovenia	18.1	39.7	0.1	1.7	40.0	0.0	0.4
Spain[1]	28.3	33.8	0.0	7.7	29.7	0.0	0.5
Sweden	35.9	22.4	10.7	2.4	28.1	0.1	0.3
Switzerland	46.5	24.6	0.0	6.7	21.8	0.4	..
Turkey	20.3	29.0	0.0	4.9	44.3	1.5	..
United Kingdom	35.3	18.7	0.0	12.6	32.9	0.0	0.5
United States	49.1	23.7	0.0	10.3	17.0	0.0	..
Unweighted average							
OECD Average	**34.1**	**25.8**	**1.1**	**5.8**	**32.4**	**0.5**	**0.4**

1. The total tax revenue has been reduced by the amount of any capital transfer that represents uncollected taxes. The capital transfer has been allocated between tax headings in proportion to the reported tax revenue.
2. From 1991 the figures relate to the united Germany.

StatLink http://dx.doi.org/10.1787/888933611867

Table 3.5. **Tax revenue of main headings as % of GDP, 2016p**

	1000 Income & profits	2000 Social security	3000 Payroll	4000 Property	5000 Goods and services	6000 Others	EU Custom Duties
Australia	..	..	..	..	..	..	..
Austria	11.9	14.9	3.0	0.6	12.0	0.2	0.1
Belgium	15.7	13.7	0.0	3.5	10.8	0.0	0.4
Canada	15.1	4.8	0.7	3.8	7.4	0.0	..
Chile	6.8	1.5	0.0	1.0	11.1	-0.1	..
Czech Republic	7.4	14.7	0.0	0.5	11.3	0.0	0.2
Denmark[1]	28.7	0.1	0.3	1.9	14.9	0.0	0.1
Estonia	7.8	11.6	0.0	0.3	14.9	0.0	0.2
Finland	15.3	12.8	0.0	1.4	14.5	0.0	0.1
France[1]	10.6	16.7	1.6	4.1	11.1	1.1	0.1
Germany[2]	12.0	14.1	0.0	1.1	10.2	0.0	0.2
Greece	9.1	11.0	0.0	2.6	15.8	0.0	0.1
Hungary	7.1	13.6	0.6	1.1	16.7	0.1	0.1
Iceland	17.8	3.6	0.3	1.9	12.1	0.6	..
Ireland	10.0	3.9	0.1	1.3	7.5	0.0	0.1
Israel	9.8	5.2	1.2	3.3	11.8	0.0	..
Italy	13.7	13.0	0.0	2.8	12.1	1.2	0.1
Japan	9.5	..	0.0	2.5	6.2	0.1	..
Korea	8.2	6.9	0.1	3.0	7.4	0.7	..
Latvia	8.0	8.3	0.0	1.1	12.6	0.0	0.2
Luxembourg	13.7	10.6	0.0	3.5	9.1	0.1	0.0
Mexico	7.3	2.2	..	..	..	..	..
Netherlands	10.6	14.8	0.0	1.5	11.5	0.0	0.3
New Zealand	17.8	0.0	0.0	2.0	12.3	0.0	..
Norway	14.0	10.6	0.0	1.2	12.1	0.0	..
Poland	6.7	12.8	0.0	1.4	10.7	1.8	0.2
Portugal	9.9	9.2	0.0	1.3	13.6	0.4	0.1
Slovak Republic	7.3	14.1	0.0	0.4	10.7	0.0	0.2
Slovenia	6.9	14.7	0.1	0.6	14.6	0.0	0.1
Spain[1]	9.4	11.4	0.0	2.6	9.8	0.1	0.2
Sweden	15.7	10.0	4.7	1.1	12.4	0.0	0.1
Switzerland	13.0	6.8	0.0	1.9	6.0	0.1	..
Turkey	5.4	7.3	0.0	1.2	11.1	0.4	..
United Kingdom	11.9	6.3	0.0	4.2	10.7	0.0	0.2
United States	12.7	6.2	0.0	2.7	4.4	0.0	..

1. The total tax revenue has been reduced by the amount of any capital transfer that represents uncollected taxes. The capital transfer has been allocated between tax headings in proportion to the reported tax revenue.
2. From 1991 the figures relate to the united Germany.

StatLink http://dx.doi.org/10.1787/888933611886

Table 3.6. **Tax revenue of main headings as % of total tax revenue, 2016p**

	1000 Income & profits	2000 Social security	3000 Payroll	4000 Property	5000 Goods and services	6000 Others	EU Custom Duties
Australia	..	..	..	..	..	..	..
Austria	28.0	34.8	7.0	1.3	28.1	0.5	0.3
Belgium	35.6	31.0	0.0	8.0	24.5	0.0	0.8
Canada	47.5	15.0	2.1	11.9	23.3	0.1	..
Chile	33.6	7.2	0.0	5.0	54.6	-0.3	..
Czech Republic	21.8	43.1	0.0	1.4	33.2	0.0	0.5
Denmark[1]	62.5	0.1	0.6	4.0	32.3	0.0	0.3
Estonia	22.4	33.4	0.0	0.8	42.9	0.0	0.5
Finland	34.6	29.0	0.0	3.2	32.9	0.1	0.2
France[1]	23.5	37.0	3.4	9.1	24.5	2.4	0.2
Germany[2]	31.9	37.7	0.0	2.8	27.1	0.0	0.4
Greece	23.6	28.5	0.0	6.7	40.9	0.0	0.3
Hungary	17.9	34.6	1.6	2.9	42.4	0.4	0.3
Iceland	49.1	9.9	0.8	5.3	33.2	1.7	..
Ireland	43.3	17.0	0.6	5.8	32.5	0.0	0.5
Israel	31.5	16.6	3.7	10.5	37.7	0.0	..
Italy	32.0	30.2	0.0	6.5	28.1	2.9	0.3
Japan	..	..	..	..	..	..	..
Korea	31.2	26.2	0.3	11.6	28.1	2.6	..
Latvia	26.6	27.6	0.0	3.5	41.7	0.0	0.6
Luxembourg	37.1	28.7	0.0	9.3	24.7	0.2	0.1
Mexico	..	..	..	..	..	..	..
Netherlands	27.3	38.2	0.0	3.9	29.6	0.1	0.9
New Zealand	55.6	0.0	0.0	6.1	38.3	0.0	..
Norway	36.8	28.0	0.0	3.2	32.0	0.0	..
Poland	20.0	38.1	0.0	4.1	31.8	5.4	0.5
Portugal	28.8	26.6	0.0	3.7	39.5	1.0	0.3
Slovak Republic	22.4	43.1	0.0	1.3	32.7	0.0	0.5
Slovenia	18.6	39.7	0.1	1.7	39.4	0.0	0.4
Spain[1]	28.2	34.1	0.0	7.7	29.3	0.2	0.5
Sweden	35.7	22.8	10.6	2.4	28.2	0.1	0.3
Switzerland	46.6	24.6	0.0	6.7	21.7	0.4	..
Turkey	21.2	28.8	0.0	4.8	43.6	1.6	..
United Kingdom	35.7	18.9	0.0	12.6	32.2	0.0	0.5
United States	48.8	24.0	0.0	10.2	17.0	0.0	..

1. The total tax revenue has been reduced by the amount of any capital transfer that represents uncollected taxes. The capital transfer has been allocated between tax headings in proportion to the reported tax revenue.
2. From 1991 the figures relate to the united Germany.

StatLink http://dx.doi.org/10.1787/888933611905

Table 3.7. **Taxes on income and profits (1000) as % of GDP and as % of total tax revenue**

	% of GDP					% of total tax revenue				
	1990	2000	2010	2014	2015	1990	2000	2010	2014	2015
Australia	16.0	17.6	14.3	15.9	16.0	57.1	58.0	56.4	57.6	56.7
Austria	10.1	12.0	11.5	12.6	13.2	25.5	28.3	28.1	29.3	30.2
Belgium	15.2	16.8	14.6	16.1	16.0	36.9	38.6	34.2	35.8	35.7
Canada	17.1	17.4	14.3	15.0	15.3	48.6	50.1	46.6	48.2	47.9
Chile	3.9	4.4	7.5	6.5	7.5	23.2	23.3	38.1	33.0	36.4
Czech Republic	..	7.4	6.6	7.1	7.2	..	22.8	20.2	21.4	21.5
Denmark[1]	27.1	28.8	27.5	31.7	29.0	61.2	61.4	61.5	65.2	63.1
Estonia	..	7.7	6.6	7.5	7.9	..	24.8	19.8	22.8	23.4
Finland	16.8	19.7	14.5	15.3	15.4	39.2	43.1	35.5	35.0	35.2
France[1]	6.6	10.7	9.5	10.8	10.6	16.1	24.9	22.7	23.8	23.5
Germany[2]	11.3	10.9	10.0	11.4	11.6	32.4	30.1	28.5	30.9	31.2
Greece[1]	5.0	9.0	7.0	8.5	8.2	19.9	26.8	22.0	23.7	22.5
Hungary	..	9.4	7.7	6.9	7.1	..	24.3	20.7	18.1	18.3
Iceland	9.0	14.4	14.8	18.0	17.2	29.7	39.9	44.4	46.6	46.9
Ireland	12.3	13.4	10.5	11.5	9.9	38.0	43.6	38.7	40.3	43.0
Israel	..	13.8	9.0	9.5	9.8	..	39.6	29.1	30.6	31.2
Italy	13.3	13.5	13.7	13.9	13.8	36.5	33.2	32.6	31.9	31.8
Japan	14.2	9.0	8.0	9.6	9.6	50.2	34.8	30.2	31.8	31.2
Korea	6.2	6.2	6.6	7.2	7.6	32.8	28.8	28.0	29.1	30.3
Latvia	..	7.0	7.2	7.5	7.5	..	24.1	25.6	25.9	25.9
Luxembourg	13.5	13.5	13.6	12.9	13.4	40.2	36.5	36.4	34.6	36.4
Mexico	4.2	4.5	5.2	5.7	6.8	34.0	34.4	38.6	39.9	41.7
Netherlands	13.0	9.7	10.1	9.6	10.4	32.3	25.9	27.9	25.6	27.7
New Zealand	21.6	19.5	16.3	17.9	18.3	59.6	60.0	53.8	55.4	55.5
Norway	14.2	18.8	19.8	16.5	15.1	35.2	45.0	47.1	42.4	39.4
Poland	..	6.7	6.3	6.3	6.5	..	20.4	20.0	19.8	20.1
Portugal	6.8	9.1	8.1	10.5	10.4	25.7	29.3	26.8	30.8	30.2
Slovak Republic	..	6.9	5.3	6.5	7.0	..	20.5	19.0	20.9	21.8
Slovenia	..	6.8	7.4	6.5	6.6	..	18.5	20.1	17.9	18.1
Spain[1]	9.7	9.4	8.8	9.6	9.6	30.6	28.3	28.1	28.6	28.3
Sweden	20.6	20.0	15.3	14.9	15.5	41.6	40.8	35.5	34.9	35.9
Switzerland	11.2	12.2	12.1	12.3	12.9	47.4	44.3	45.6	45.7	46.5
Turkey	4.9	7.0	5.3	5.2	5.1	33.5	29.5	21.3	21.1	20.3
United Kingdom	12.9	13.2	12.2	11.3	11.5	39.3	39.7	37.6	35.1	35.3
United States	11.7	14.1	10.0	12.5	12.9	45.2	50.1	42.4	48.1	49.1
Unweighted average										
OECD Average	**12.2**	**12.0**	**10.8**	**11.5**	**11.5**	**37.5**	**35.0**	**33.2**	**33.8**	**34.1**

Note: Full time series can be accessed at http://oe.cd/full-time-series.

1. The total tax revenue has been reduced by the amount of any capital transfer that represents uncollected taxes. The capital transfer has been allocated between tax headings in proportion to the reported tax revenue.
2. From 1991 the figures relate to the united Germany.

StatLink http://dx.doi.org/10.1787/888933611924

Table 3.8. **Taxes on personal income (1100) as % of GDP and as % of total tax revenue**

	% of GDP					% of total tax revenue				
	1990	2000	2010	2014	2015	1990	2000	2010	2014	2015
Australia	12.1	11.5	9.8	11.4	11.7	43.0	37.8	38.5	41.2	41.5
Austria	8.3	9.3	9.2	10.1	10.5	21.0	22.0	22.4	23.5	24.1
Belgium	13.2	13.7	12.0	13.0	12.7	32.0	31.4	28.2	28.8	28.3
Canada	14.4	12.8	10.7	11.4	11.8	40.8	36.8	35.0	36.5	36.9
Chile	0.9	1.4	1.3	1.4	2.0	5.6	7.6	6.8	7.3	9.8
Czech Republic	..	4.2	3.3	3.6	3.6	..	12.9	10.2	10.8	10.7
Denmark[1]	24.0	24.7	23.2	26.3	25.3	54.0	52.7	51.9	54.1	55.2
Estonia	..	6.8	5.3	5.7	5.8	..	22.0	15.9	17.5	17.2
Finland	14.9	14.0	12.1	13.4	13.3	34.7	30.6	29.5	30.6	30.2
France[1]	4.4	7.8	7.2	8.5	8.5	10.7	18.0	17.1	18.7	18.9
Germany[2]	9.6	9.2	8.5	9.6	9.8	27.6	25.3	24.3	26.2	26.5
Greece[1]	3.6	4.8	4.0	5.9	5.5	14.1	14.5	12.4	16.5	15.0
Hungary	..	7.2	6.5	5.3	5.3	..	18.6	17.4	13.8	13.7
Iceland	8.1	12.6	12.2	13.5	13.5	26.9	34.8	36.5	34.9	36.7
Ireland	10.7	9.8	8.1	9.1	7.3	33.1	31.9	30.0	32.0	31.6
Israel	..	10.1	5.5	5.7	6.1	..	29.1	18.0	18.3	19.4
Italy	9.6	10.1	11.2	11.2	11.3	26.3	24.8	26.8	25.8	26.0
Japan	7.8	5.4	4.9	5.7	5.8	27.8	21.1	18.6	18.9	18.9
Korea	3.8	3.1	3.3	4.0	4.3	20.0	14.6	14.2	16.3	17.2
Latvia	..	5.5	6.2	5.9	5.9	..	18.8	22.2	20.5	20.4
Luxembourg	8.1	6.8	7.9	8.7	9.0	24.1	18.5	21.0	23.1	24.5
Mexico	..	..	2.4	3.0	3.3	..	..	17.7	21.0	20.6
Netherlands	9.9	5.6	7.8	7.0	7.7	24.7	15.1	21.5	18.7	20.5
New Zealand	17.4	14.0	11.4	12.5	12.6	48.0	43.1	37.7	38.6	38.1
Norway	10.5	10.1	9.9	9.9	10.7	26.2	24.1	23.6	25.4	27.9
Poland	..	4.3	4.4	4.6	4.7	..	13.2	13.9	14.3	14.4
Portugal	4.2	5.4	5.4	7.7	7.3	15.9	17.4	17.6	22.5	21.2
Slovak Republic	..	3.3	2.6	3.0	3.1	..	9.9	9.4	9.6	9.7
Slovenia	..	5.5	5.6	5.1	5.1	..	15.0	15.1	14.0	14.0
Spain[1]	6.9	6.4	6.8	7.6	7.2	21.7	19.2	21.9	22.4	21.3
Sweden	19.1	16.3	12.0	12.2	12.6	38.5	33.2	27.9	28.6	29.1
Switzerland	7.7	8.2	8.4	8.4	8.6	32.8	29.8	31.9	31.0	31.1
Turkey	3.9	5.2	3.5	3.6	3.7	26.8	22.2	14.0	14.7	14.6
United Kingdom	9.7	9.6	9.4	8.8	9.0	29.4	29.0	28.7	27.3	27.7
United States	9.8	11.9	8.2	10.2	10.6	37.7	42.2	34.8	39.3	40.5
Unweighted average										
OECD Average	**9.7**	**8.7**	**7.7**	**8.4**	**8.4**	**28.6**	**24.6**	**23.2**	**24.1**	**24.4**

Note: Full time series can be accessed at http://oe.cd/full-time-series.

1. The total tax revenue has been reduced by the amount of any capital transfer that represents uncollected taxes. The capital transfer has been allocated between tax headings in proportion to the reported tax revenue.
2. From 1991 the figures relate to the united Germany.

StatLink http://dx.doi.org/10.1787/888933611943

Table 3.9. **Taxes on corporate income (1200) as % of GDP and as % of total tax revenue**

	% of GDP					% of total tax revenue				
	1990	2000	2010	2014	2015	1990	2000	2010	2014	2015
Australia	4.0	6.2	4.5	4.5	4.3	14.1	20.3	17.9	16.4	15.3
Austria	1.4	2.0	1.9	2.1	2.3	3.6	4.6	4.6	4.9	5.2
Belgium	2.0	3.1	2.5	3.1	3.3	4.8	7.2	5.9	7.0	7.4
Canada	2.5	4.2	3.2	3.3	3.2	7.0	12.2	10.5	10.6	9.9
Chile	2.1	2.1	4.0	4.2	4.3	12.4	11.2	20.4	21.3	21.0
Czech Republic	..	3.2	3.2	3.5	3.6	..	9.9	10.0	10.6	10.8
Denmark[1]	1.7	3.2	2.3	2.8	2.6	3.8	6.8	5.0	5.7	5.6
Estonia	..	0.9	1.3	1.7	2.1	..	2.8	4.0	5.3	6.2
Finland	1.9	5.7	2.4	1.9	2.2	4.5	12.5	6.0	4.4	4.9
France[1]	2.2	3.0	2.3	2.3	2.1	5.3	6.9	5.6	5.1	4.6
Germany[2]	1.7	1.8	1.5	1.7	1.7	4.8	4.8	4.3	4.7	4.7
Greece[1]	1.4	4.0	2.5	1.9	2.2	5.5	12.0	7.9	5.2	5.9
Hungary	..	2.2	1.2	1.7	1.8	..	5.7	3.3	4.3	4.6
Iceland	0.8	1.2	0.9	3.3	2.4	2.8	3.3	2.7	8.6	6.5
Ireland	1.6	3.6	2.4	2.4	2.6	4.9	11.7	8.7	8.3	11.3
Israel	..	3.3	2.6	3.2	3.0	..	9.6	8.6	10.2	9.5
Italy	3.7	2.8	2.3	2.2	2.0	10.0	6.9	5.5	5.0	4.7
Japan	6.3	3.5	3.1	3.9	3.8	22.4	13.7	11.6	12.9	12.3
Korea	2.4	3.0	3.2	3.2	3.3	12.8	14.1	13.8	12.8	13.1
Latvia	..	1.5	1.0	1.5	1.6	..	5.3	3.5	5.3	5.5
Luxembourg	5.4	6.6	5.8	4.3	4.4	16.1	18.0	15.4	11.4	11.9
Mexico	..	..	1.9	2.6	3.3	..	..	13.9	18.0	20.1
Netherlands	3.0	4.0	2.3	2.6	2.7	7.5	10.9	6.4	6.9	7.2
New Zealand	2.3	4.0	3.7	4.3	4.6	6.5	12.4	12.2	13.1	13.8
Norway	3.6	8.8	9.9	6.6	4.4	9.0	20.9	23.5	17.1	11.5
Poland	..	2.4	1.9	1.7	1.8	..	7.3	6.2	5.5	5.7
Portugal	2.1	3.7	2.7	2.8	3.1	8.0	11.9	9.0	8.3	9.0
Slovak Republic	..	2.6	2.5	3.3	3.7	..	7.7	8.7	10.6	11.5
Slovenia	..	1.1	1.8	1.4	1.5	..	3.1	5.0	3.9	4.0
Spain[1]	2.8	3.0	1.9	2.1	2.4	8.8	9.1	6.2	6.2	7.0
Sweden	1.5	3.7	3.3	2.7	3.0	3.1	7.5	7.6	6.3	6.9
Switzerland	1.8	2.4	2.7	2.8	3.0	7.4	8.9	10.1	10.4	10.8
Turkey	1.0	1.7	1.8	1.6	1.4	6.7	7.3	7.3	6.4	5.7
United Kingdom	3.3	3.5	2.9	2.5	2.5	9.9	10.6	8.9	7.8	7.5
United States	2.0	2.2	1.8	2.3	2.2	7.5	7.9	7.6	8.8	8.5
Unweighted average										
OECD Average	**2.5**	**3.2**	**2.7**	**2.8**	**2.8**	**8.1**	**9.6**	**8.8**	**8.8**	**8.9**

Note: Full time series can be accessed at http://oe.cd/full-time-series.

1. The total tax revenue has been reduced by the amount of any capital transfer that represents uncollected taxes. The capital transfer has been allocated between tax headings in proportion to the reported tax revenue.
2. From 1991 the figures relate to the united Germany.

StatLink http://dx.doi.org/10.1787/888933611962

Table 3.10. **Social security contributions (2000) as % of GDP and as % of total tax revenue**

	% of GDP					% of total tax revenue				
	1990	2000	2010	2014	2015	1990	2000	2010	2014	2015
Australia	0.0	0.0	0.0	0.0	0.0	0.0	0.0	0.0	0.0	0.0
Austria	12.9	14.3	14.1	14.6	14.7	32.9	33.8	34.2	34.0	33.6
Belgium	13.7	13.4	13.8	14.2	14.3	33.2	30.8	32.4	31.7	31.9
Canada	4.3	4.7	4.6	4.7	4.8	12.1	13.6	14.9	15.1	15.1
Chile	1.5	1.4	1.3	1.4	1.4	9.0	7.3	6.8	7.2	6.9
Czech Republic	..	14.4	14.5	14.5	14.4	..	44.3	44.8	43.8	43.1
Denmark[1]	0.0	0.6	0.1	0.1	0.1	0.0	1.4	0.2	0.1	0.1
Estonia	..	10.9	12.8	11.0	11.3	..	35.1	38.4	33.6	33.4
Finland	11.0	11.6	12.1	12.7	12.7	25.6	25.2	29.7	28.9	28.9
France[1]	18.1	15.5	16.1	16.9	16.8	44.1	36.0	38.4	37.4	37.1
Germany[2]	13.0	14.1	13.7	13.9	14.0	37.5	39.0	39.2	37.8	37.6
Greece[1]	7.6	10.1	10.9	10.4	10.7	30.2	30.3	34.2	29.1	29.4
Hungary	..	11.3	11.8	12.4	12.6	..	29.3	31.4	32.6	32.4
Iceland	0.9	2.8	3.9	3.7	3.6	3.1	7.7	11.8	9.5	9.8
Ireland	4.6	3.6	5.0	4.9	3.9	14.1	11.8	18.6	17.3	16.8
Israel	..	5.1	5.2	5.1	5.1	..	14.6	16.9	16.3	16.4
Italy	12.0	11.6	13.0	12.9	13.0	32.9	28.5	31.1	29.8	30.1
Japan	7.5	9.1	10.9	12.0	12.1	26.5	35.2	41.1	39.7	39.4
Korea	1.9	3.6	5.5	6.6	6.7	10.1	16.7	23.3	26.9	26.6
Latvia	..	9.8	8.7	8.4	8.3	..	33.5	30.8	29.1	28.7
Luxembourg	9.2	9.6	10.8	10.7	10.7	27.5	26.1	29.0	28.5	29.0
Mexico	2.1	2.3	2.1	2.2	2.2	16.8	17.2	15.7	15.4	13.9
Netherlands	15.0	14.4	13.1	14.9	14.1	37.4	38.7	36.3	39.6	37.8
New Zealand	0.0	0.0	0.0	0.0	0.0	0.0	0.0	0.0	0.0	0.0
Norway	10.6	8.8	9.4	10.0	10.5	26.3	20.9	22.4	25.6	27.3
Poland	..	12.9	10.8	12.2	12.5	..	39.2	34.4	38.2	38.5
Portugal	7.2	7.9	8.6	9.0	9.0	27.2	25.5	28.3	26.3	26.1
Slovak Republic	..	14.0	12.1	13.4	13.8	..	41.5	43.0	43.0	42.7
Slovenia	..	13.9	14.8	14.4	14.5	..	38.0	40.2	39.4	39.7
Spain[1]	11.2	11.6	11.7	11.6	11.4	35.4	34.9	37.5	34.5	33.8
Sweden	13.5	12.9	10.9	9.9	9.7	27.2	26.3	25.3	23.2	22.4
Switzerland	5.6	6.7	6.3	6.7	6.8	23.5	24.3	23.9	24.9	24.6
Turkey	2.9	4.4	6.2	7.0	7.3	19.7	18.7	24.9	28.5	29.0
United Kingdom	5.6	5.6	6.2	6.0	6.1	17.0	16.8	19.0	18.6	18.7
United States	6.6	6.6	6.1	6.2	6.2	25.6	23.6	26.1	23.9	23.7
Unweighted average										
OECD Average	**7.4**	**8.6**	**8.8**	**9.0**	**9.0**	**22.0**	**24.7**	**26.4**	**26.0**	**25.8**

Note: Full time series can be accessed at http://oe.cd/full-time-series.

1. The total tax revenue has been reduced by the amount of any capital transfer that represents uncollected taxes. The capital transfer has been allocated between tax headings in proportion to the reported tax revenue.
2. From 1991 the figures relate to the united Germany.

StatLink http://dx.doi.org/10.1787/888933611981

Table 3.11. **Taxes on payroll and workforce (3000) as % of GDP and as % of total tax revenue**

	% of GDP					% of total tax revenue				
	1990	2000	2010	2014	2015	1990	2000	2010	2014	2015
Australia	1.7	1.4	1.3	1.4	1.4	6.1	4.5	5.2	5.1	5.0
Austria	2.4	2.7	2.8	3.0	3.0	6.0	6.4	6.9	6.9	6.8
Belgium	0.0	0.0	0.0	0.0	0.0	0.0	0.0	0.0	0.0	0.0
Canada	0.8	0.7	0.6	0.6	0.7	2.3	2.1	2.1	2.1	2.0
Chile	0.0	0.0	0.0	0.0	0.0	0.0	0.0	0.0	0.0	0.0
Czech Republic	..	0.0	0.0	0.0	0.0	..	0.0	0.0	0.0	0.0
Denmark[1]	0.3	0.2	0.2	0.3	0.3	0.7	0.4	0.5	0.6	0.6
Estonia	..	0.0	0.0	0.0	0.0	..	0.0	0.0	0.0	0.0
Finland	0.0	0.0	0.0	0.0	0.0	0.0	0.0	0.0	0.0	0.0
France[1]	0.8	1.0	1.3	1.6	1.6	1.9	2.3	3.2	3.5	3.5
Germany[2]	0.0	0.0	0.0	0.0	0.0	0.0	0.0	0.0	0.0	0.0
Greece[1]	0.2	0.0	0.0	0.0	0.0	0.7	0.0	0.0	0.0	0.0
Hungary	..	1.4	0.4	0.6	0.6	..	3.6	1.1	1.5	1.5
Iceland	1.1	0.0	0.2	0.3	0.3	3.5	0.1	0.5	0.9	0.8
Ireland	0.4	0.0	0.2	0.2	0.1	1.3	0.0	0.7	0.6	0.6
Israel	..	1.3	1.2	1.2	1.2	..	3.6	3.8	3.9	3.8
Italy	0.1	0.0	0.0	0.0	0.0	0.3	0.0	0.0	0.0	0.0
Japan	0.0	0.0	0.0	0.0	0.0	0.0	0.0	0.0	0.0	0.0
Korea	0.1	0.0	0.1	0.1	0.1	0.4	0.2	0.2	0.3	0.3
Latvia	..	0.0	0.0	0.0	0.0	..	0.0	0.1	0.0	0.0
Luxembourg	0.0	0.0	0.0	0.0	0.0	0.0	0.0	0.0	0.0	0.0
Mexico	0.2	0.2	0.3	0.4	0.4	1.8	1.4	2.1	2.6	2.4
Netherlands	0.0	0.0	0.0	0.0	0.0	0.0	0.0	0.0	0.0	0.0
New Zealand	0.0	0.0	0.0	0.0	0.0	0.0	0.0	0.0	0.0	0.0
Norway	0.0	0.0	0.0	0.0	0.0	0.0	0.0	0.0	0.0	0.0
Poland	..	0.2	0.3	0.2	0.2	..	0.7	0.8	0.7	0.7
Portugal	0.0	0.0	0.0	0.0	0.0	0.0	0.0	0.0	0.0	0.0
Slovak Republic	..	0.0	0.0	0.0	0.0	..	0.0	0.0	0.0	0.0
Slovenia	..	1.5	0.1	0.1	0.1	..	4.2	0.2	0.1	0.1
Spain[1]	0.0	0.0	0.0	0.0	0.0	0.0	0.0	0.0	0.0	0.0
Sweden	1.2	2.1	3.1	4.5	4.6	2.5	4.3	7.1	10.6	10.7
Switzerland	0.0	0.0	0.0	0.0	0.0	0.0	0.0	0.0	0.0	0.0
Turkey	0.0	0.0	0.0	0.0	0.0	0.0	0.0	0.0	0.0	0.0
United Kingdom	0.0	0.0	0.0	0.0	0.0	0.0	0.0	0.0	0.0	0.0
United States	0.0	0.0	0.0	0.0	0.0	0.0	0.0	0.0	0.0	0.0
Unweighted average										
OECD Average	**0.3**	**0.4**	**0.3**	**0.4**	**0.4**	**1.0**	**1.0**	**1.0**	**1.1**	**1.1**

Note: Full time series can be accessed at http://oe.cd/full-time-series.

1. The total tax revenue has been reduced by the amount of any capital transfer that represents uncollected taxes. The capital transfer has been allocated between tax headings in proportion to the reported tax revenue.
2. From 1991 the figures relate to the united Germany.

StatLink http://dx.doi.org/10.1787/888933612000

Table 3.12. **Taxes on property (4000) as % of GDP and as % of total tax revenue**

	% of GDP					% of total tax revenue				
	1990	2000	2010	2014	2015	1990	2000	2010	2014	2015
Australia	2.5	2.7	2.4	2.8	3.0	9.0	8.8	9.3	10.2	10.7
Austria	1.1	0.6	0.5	0.6	0.6	2.7	1.3	1.3	1.4	1.3
Belgium	1.6	2.0	3.1	3.6	3.5	3.8	4.7	7.2	7.9	7.8
Canada	3.5	3.3	3.8	3.7	3.8	10.0	9.5	12.3	11.7	11.8
Chile	1.0	1.3	0.8	0.8	0.9	6.2	7.0	4.1	4.2	4.4
Czech Republic	..	0.5	0.4	0.5	0.5	..	1.4	1.3	1.4	1.4
Denmark[1]	1.9	1.6	1.8	1.8	1.9	4.3	3.3	4.1	3.7	4.1
Estonia	..	0.4	0.3	0.3	0.3	..	1.2	1.0	0.9	0.8
Finland	1.1	1.1	1.1	1.3	1.4	2.4	2.4	2.7	3.0	3.3
France[1]	2.6	2.9	3.5	3.9	4.0	6.3	6.9	8.4	8.6	9.0
Germany[2]	1.2	0.8	0.8	1.0	1.1	3.4	2.3	2.3	2.6	2.9
Greece[1]	1.2	2.0	1.7	2.9	3.1	4.6	6.1	5.2	8.0	8.5
Hungary	..	0.7	1.2	1.3	1.3	..	1.7	3.1	3.4	3.3
Iceland	2.5	2.8	2.3	2.5	2.0	8.4	7.9	7.0	6.4	5.4
Ireland	1.5	1.8	1.4	2.2	1.5	4.6	5.7	5.3	7.6	6.4
Israel	..	3.1	3.3	3.1	3.3	..	9.0	10.7	10.0	10.6
Italy	0.8	1.9	2.0	2.9	2.8	2.3	4.6	4.8	6.6	6.5
Japan	2.7	2.7	2.6	2.6	2.5	9.4	10.5	9.7	8.5	8.2
Korea	2.2	2.7	2.6	2.7	3.1	11.8	12.4	11.3	11.0	12.4
Latvia	..	1.1	0.9	1.0	1.0	..	3.8	3.1	3.6	3.4
Luxembourg	2.8	3.9	2.6	2.9	3.3	8.4	10.7	7.1	7.8	8.9
Mexico	0.2	0.2	0.3	0.3	0.3	1.9	1.7	2.2	2.2	2.0
Netherlands	1.5	2.0	1.4	1.4	1.4	3.7	5.3	3.8	3.9	3.8
New Zealand	2.5	1.7	2.0	2.0	2.0	6.8	5.3	6.6	6.1	6.1
Norway	1.2	1.0	1.2	1.2	1.1	2.9	2.3	2.8	3.2	2.9
Poland	..	1.4	1.3	1.4	1.4	..	4.3	4.2	4.4	4.2
Portugal	0.7	1.1	1.1	1.2	1.3	2.7	3.7	3.5	3.6	3.7
Slovak Republic	..	0.6	0.4	0.4	0.4	..	1.8	1.5	1.4	1.3
Slovenia	..	0.6	0.6	0.6	0.6	..	1.7	1.7	1.7	1.7
Spain[1]	1.7	2.1	2.1	2.5	2.6	5.5	6.4	6.6	7.4	7.7
Sweden	1.7	1.7	1.0	1.1	1.0	3.5	3.4	2.4	2.5	2.4
Switzerland	1.9	2.5	1.9	1.8	1.9	8.1	9.0	7.0	6.6	6.7
Turkey	0.3	0.7	1.0	1.2	1.2	2.3	3.2	4.1	4.9	4.9
United Kingdom	2.7	3.8	3.9	4.1	4.1	8.2	11.5	12.0	12.7	12.6
United States	3.0	2.9	3.1	2.8	2.7	11.6	10.2	13.1	10.7	10.3
Unweighted average										
OECD Average	**1.8**	**1.8**	**1.7**	**1.9**	**1.9**	**5.7**	**5.5**	**5.5**	**5.7**	**5.8**

Note: Full time series can be accessed at http://oe.cd/full-time-series.

1. The total tax revenue has been reduced by the amount of any capital transfer that represents uncollected taxes. The capital transfer has been allocated between tax headings in proportion to the reported tax revenue.
2. From 1991 the figures relate to the united Germany.

StatLink http://dx.doi.org/10.1787/888933612019

Table 3.13. **Taxes on goods and services (5000) as % of GDP and as % of total tax revenue**

	% of GDP					% of total tax revenue				
	1990	2000	2010	2014	2015	1990	2000	2010	2014	2015
Australia	7.8	8.7	7.4	7.5	7.8	27.8	28.7	29.1	27.1	27.5
Austria	12.4	12.3	11.7	11.9	11.9	31.5	28.9	28.4	27.6	27.3
Belgium	10.7	10.9	10.8	10.8	10.7	26.1	25.0	25.3	23.9	23.8
Canada	9.1	8.4	7.3	7.1	7.4	25.8	24.2	24.0	22.8	23.1
Chile	10.6	12.0	10.0	10.8	11.1	62.9	63.8	51.2	55.3	54.1
Czech Republic	..	10.2	10.8	10.9	11.2	..	31.5	33.2	32.9	33.5
Denmark[1]	15.1	15.5	14.9	14.5	14.5	33.9	33.1	33.3	29.9	31.6
Estonia	..	12.1	13.4	13.8	14.2	..	38.8	40.2	42.1	41.8
Finland	14.0	13.3	13.0	14.4	14.2	32.5	29.0	31.8	32.8	32.4
France[1]	11.6	11.1	10.5	10.9	11.0	28.4	25.9	24.9	24.1	24.3
Germany[2]	9.3	10.2	10.3	10.4	10.3	26.7	28.1	29.5	28.2	27.8
Greece[1]	11.2	12.1	12.3	14.0	14.3	44.5	36.3	38.3	38.9	39.4
Hungary	..	15.6	16.1	16.7	17.1	..	40.5	42.9	43.7	43.8
Iceland	15.5	16.0	11.7	12.0	11.9	51.3	44.1	35.2	31.0	32.4
Ireland	13.6	11.7	9.8	9.6	7.5	41.9	38.2	36.2	33.7	32.6
Israel	..	11.6	12.1	12.2	11.9	..	33.1	39.4	39.1	38.0
Italy	10.2	11.3	11.0	11.8	11.8	28.0	27.9	26.3	27.1	27.3
Japan	3.9	5.0	5.0	6.0	6.4	13.7	19.3	18.7	19.8	21.0
Korea	8.3	8.2	7.9	7.4	7.1	44.3	38.4	33.7	30.0	28.0
Latvia	..	11.2	11.2	11.8	12.0	..	38.6	39.9	40.9	41.3
Luxembourg	7.9	9.7	10.2	10.8	9.4	23.6	26.3	27.3	28.9	25.5
Mexico	5.4	5.8	5.3	5.5	6.3	44.0	44.3	39.9	38.3	38.6
Netherlands	10.6	10.7	11.1	11.1	11.1	26.4	28.9	30.8	29.6	29.6
New Zealand	12.1	11.3	12.0	12.5	12.7	33.6	34.7	39.6	38.5	38.4
Norway	14.3	13.3	11.6	11.2	11.6	35.5	31.8	27.7	28.8	30.4
Poland	..	11.6	12.6	11.6	11.7	..	35.3	40.1	36.3	35.9
Portugal	11.7	12.5	12.2	13.0	13.3	44.2	40.3	40.2	38.0	38.4
Slovak Republic	..	12.2	10.1	10.6	10.9	..	36.2	35.8	34.1	33.7
Slovenia	..	13.8	13.8	14.7	14.6	..	37.6	37.3	40.4	40.0
Spain[1]	9.0	10.0	8.5	9.8	10.0	28.4	30.0	27.2	29.0	29.7
Sweden	12.4	12.1	12.7	12.1	12.2	25.0	24.8	29.3	28.4	28.1
Switzerland	4.9	6.1	6.1	6.0	6.0	20.8	22.1	23.1	22.4	21.8
Turkey	4.1	9.9	11.8	10.8	11.1	27.9	42.0	47.7	44.1	44.3
United Kingdom	10.2	10.5	10.0	10.7	10.7	31.0	31.6	30.8	33.1	32.9
United States	4.6	4.6	4.3	4.5	4.5	17.6	16.1	18.3	17.3	17.0
Unweighted average										
OECD Average	**10.0**	**10.9**	**10.6**	**10.8**	**10.9**	**32.5**	**33.0**	**33.0**	**32.5**	**32.4**

Note: Full time series can be accessed at http://oe.cd/full-time-series.

1. The total tax revenue has been reduced by the amount of any capital transfer that represents uncollected taxes. The capital transfer has been allocated between tax headings in proportion to the reported tax revenue.
2. From 1991 the figures relate to the united Germany.

StatLink http://dx.doi.org/10.1787/888933612038

Table 3.14. **Value added taxes (5111) as % of GDP and as % of total tax revenue**

	% of GDP					% of total tax revenue				
	1990	2000	2010	2014	2015	1990	2000	2010	2014	2015
Australia	0.0	3.4	3.4	3.5	3.7	0.0	11.1	13.4	12.7	13.0
Austria	8.2	7.9	7.7	7.7	7.7	20.8	18.7	18.7	17.9	17.7
Belgium	6.8	7.0	6.9	6.9	6.7	16.4	16.1	16.2	15.3	15.0
Canada	0.0	3.2	4.2	4.1	4.2	0.0	9.2	13.7	13.2	13.2
Chile	6.3	7.9	7.5	8.2	8.4	37.4	41.8	38.5	41.6	40.8
Czech Republic	..	5.9	6.6	7.4	7.3	..	18.3	20.5	22.4	21.7
Denmark[1]	8.4	9.2	9.4	9.2	9.2	18.9	19.5	21.1	19.0	20.0
Estonia	..	8.4	8.5	8.7	9.2	..	27.1	25.7	26.4	27.3
Finland	8.3	8.0	8.3	9.2	9.1	19.3	17.4	20.4	21.0	20.6
France[1]	7.6	7.2	6.8	6.9	6.9	18.4	16.7	16.1	15.2	15.3
Germany[2]	5.8	6.7	7.0	6.9	7.0	16.6	18.4	20.0	18.9	18.8
Greece[1]	6.2	6.9	7.1	7.1	7.3	24.6	20.8	22.0	19.9	20.1
Hungary	..	8.7	8.6	9.3	9.7	..	22.4	22.9	24.4	24.9
Iceland	8.6	10.3	7.6	8.0	8.3	28.5	28.5	22.7	20.8	22.6
Ireland	6.6	7.1	6.0	5.9	4.6	20.4	22.9	22.2	20.8	19.7
Israel	..	7.4	7.5	7.9	7.8	..	21.1	24.4	25.5	24.9
Italy	5.3	6.3	6.1	6.0	6.1	14.7	15.4	14.5	13.8	14.2
Japan	1.2	2.3	2.5	3.7	4.2	4.4	9.1	9.6	12.2	13.7
Korea	3.5	3.7	4.1	4.2	3.8	18.7	17.0	17.5	17.2	15.3
Latvia	..	7.0	6.7	7.6	7.7	..	23.9	23.9	26.3	26.5
Luxembourg	4.0	4.9	6.4	7.4	6.5	12.1	13.4	17.0	19.7	17.6
Mexico	3.2	3.1	3.8	3.9	3.9	26.1	23.6	28.5	27.2	23.9
Netherlands	6.6	6.4	6.8	6.4	6.6	16.5	17.3	18.7	17.2	17.6
New Zealand	8.1	8.1	9.3	9.7	9.8	22.4	24.9	30.7	29.9	29.7
Norway	7.6	8.2	7.8	7.8	8.2	18.8	19.7	18.5	20.0	21.4
Poland	..	6.9	7.6	7.1	7.0	..	21.0	24.2	22.3	21.6
Portugal	5.2	7.6	7.5	8.5	8.6	19.6	24.4	24.7	24.8	24.8
Slovak Republic	..	6.9	6.2	6.6	6.9	..	20.4	22.0	21.2	21.3
Slovenia	..	8.5	8.1	8.5	8.4	..	23.3	21.9	23.2	22.9
Spain[1]	5.0	5.9	5.3	6.2	6.4	15.7	17.7	16.9	18.3	19.0
Sweden	7.4	8.3	9.2	9.0	9.1	14.9	16.9	21.2	21.1	20.9
Switzerland	2.8	3.6	3.4	3.5	3.4	11.7	13.2	12.8	12.9	12.4
Turkey	2.7	5.7	5.4	5.0	5.2	18.3	24.2	21.7	20.4	20.6
United Kingdom	5.5	5.9	6.1	6.8	6.9	16.9	17.9	18.7	21.2	21.2
United States	0.0	0.0	0.0	0.0	0.0	0.0	0.0	0.0	0.0	0.0
Unweighted average										
OECD Average	**5.2**	**6.4**	**6.4**	**6.7**	**6.7**	**16.7**	**19.2**	**20.0**	**20.1**	**20.0**

Note: Full time series can be accessed at http://oe.cd/full-time-series.

1. The total tax revenue has been reduced by the amount of any capital transfer that represents uncollected taxes. The capital transfer has been allocated between tax headings in proportion to the reported tax revenue.
2. From 1991 the figures relate to the united Germany.

StatLink http://dx.doi.org/10.1787/888933612057

Table 3.15. **Tax revenues of sub-sectors of general government as % of total tax revenue**

	Supranational			Central government			State or Regional government			Local government			Social Security Funds		
	1975	1995	2015	1975	1995	2015	1975	1995	2015	1975	1995	2015	1975	1995	2015
Federal countries															
Australia	..	..	..	80.1	77.5	79.3	15.7	19.0	17.1	4.2	3.4	3.6	0.0	0.0	0.0
Austria	..	0.0	0.4	51.7	65.1	67.0	10.6	1.8	1.5	12.4	4.1	3.0	25.3	29.0	28.0
Belgium	1.4	1.0	0.9	65.3	60.1	54.3	..	1.8	7.7	4.4	4.8	4.9	28.8	32.2	32.2
Canada	..	..	..	47.6	39.1	40.9	32.5	37.1	39.5	9.9	9.8	10.3	10.0	14.0	9.2
Germany	1.2	0.6	0.5	33.5	31.4	30.6	22.3	21.6	23.0	9.0	7.4	8.3	34.0	39.0	37.6
Mexico	..	..	..	..	73.9	80.4	..	2.8	4.2	..	1.5	1.6	..	21.8	13.9
Switzerland	..	..	..	30.7	31.6	35.8	27.0	23.8	24.5	20.3	17.6	15.2	22.0	27.0	24.6
United States	..	..	..	45.4	41.4	43.3	19.5	20.0	19.4	14.7	13.3	13.6	20.5	25.2	23.7
Unweighted average	1.3	0.6	0.6	50.6	52.5	54.0	21.3	16.0	17.1	10.7	7.7	7.5	20.1	23.5	21.1
Regional country															
Spain[1,2]	..	0.5	0.5	48.2	51.3	42.5	..	4.8	14.0	4.3	8.8	9.9	47.5	34.6	33.1
Unitary countries															
Chile	..	..	..	..	89.9	86.9	..	..	..	..	6.5	7.6	..	3.6	5.6
Czech Republic	..	..	0.5	..	57.7	55.3	..	..	..	..	0.9	1.2	..	41.4	43.1
Denmark[2]	1.1	0.5	0.4	68.9	68.2	72.8	..	..	..	30.0	31.3	26.8	0.1	0.0	0.1
Estonia	..	..	0.5	..	84.3	82.3	..	..	..	..	0.8	1.0	..	14.9	16.2
Finland	..	0.4	0.3	56.0	46.6	47.1	..	..	..	23.5	22.3	23.7	20.4	30.8	28.9
France[2]	0.7	0.4	0.2	51.2	42.3	33.3	..	..	..	7.6	11.0	13.2	40.6	46.3	53.3
Greece[2]	..	0.6	0.3	67.1	66.8	68.6	..	..	..	3.4	0.9	2.4	29.5	31.7	28.7
Hungary	..	..	0.3	..	63.8	60.8	..	..	..	..	2.5	5.8	..	33.6	33.1
Iceland	..	..	..	81.3	79.2	74.4	..	..	..	18.7	20.8	25.6	0.0	0.0	0.0
Ireland	2.3	1.5	0.5	77.4	83.1	83.0	..	..	..	7.3	2.7	2.4	13.1	12.7	14.0
Israel	..	..	..	..	79.6	75.5	..	..	..	..	6.4	8.1	..	14.0	16.4
Italy	..	0.4	0.3	53.2	62.7	53.1	..	..	..	0.9	5.4	16.5	45.9	31.5	30.1
Japan	..	..	..	45.5	41.2	36.7	..	..	..	25.6	25.2	23.9	29.0	33.6	39.4
Korea	..	..	..	89.0	69.2	55.4	..	..	..	10.1	18.7	18.0	0.9	12.1	26.6
Latvia	..	..	0.6	..	43.5	51.3	..	..	..	..	19.5	19.4	..	36.9	28.7
Luxembourg	0.8	0.4	0.1	63.6	66.5	68.3	..	..	..	6.7	6.5	3.5	29.0	26.6	28.1
Netherlands	1.5	1.3	1.0	58.9	56.0	57.4	..	..	..	1.2	3.1	3.8	38.4	39.5	37.8
New Zealand	..	..	..	92.3	94.7	93.2	..	..	..	7.7	5.3	6.8	0.0	0.0	0.0
Norway	..	..	..	50.6	58.4	84.7	..	..	..	22.4	19.6	15.3	27.0	22.0	0.0
Poland	..	..	0.5	..	61.9	48.1	..	..	..	..	8.3	12.9	..	29.8	38.5
Portugal	..	0.8	0.3	65.4	72.3	67.8	..	..	..	0.0	5.4	7.2	34.6	21.5	24.7
Slovak Republic	..	..	0.5	..	62.5	55.8	..	..	..	..	1.3	2.0	..	36.2	41.7
Slovenia	..	..	0.4	..	51.8	50.7	..	..	..	..	6.3	9.6	..	41.9	39.3
Sweden	..	0.4	0.3	51.3	46.9	51.3	..	..	..	29.2	30.9	36.0	19.5	21.8	12.4
Turkey	..	..	..	..	75.1	61.3	..	..	..	..	12.8	9.6	..	12.1	29.0
United Kingdom	1.0	1.0	0.5	70.5	77.5	75.9	..	..	..	11.1	3.7	4.9	17.5	17.8	18.7
Unweighted average	1.2	0.7	0.4	65.1	65.5	63.5	..	..	..	12.8	10.7	11.8	21.6	23.5	24.4

1. Spain is constitutionally a non-federal country but has a highly decentralised political structure.
2. The total tax revenue has been reduced by the amount of any capital transfer that represents uncollected taxes.

StatLink http://dx.doi.org/10.1787/888933612076

Table 3.16. **Main central government taxes as % of total tax revenues of central government, 2015**

	1000 Income & profits	2000 Social security[2]	3000 Payroll	4000 Property	5000 Goods and services	6000 Others
Federal countries						
Australia	71.5	0.0	0.2	0.0	28.3	0.0
Austria	43.9	7.6	6.9	1.3	39.8	0.5
Belgium	57.2	2.3	0.0	1.9	38.6	0.0
Canada	71.1	9.1	0.0	0.0	19.8	0.0
Germany	41.7	0.0	0.0	0.6	57.8	0.0
Mexico	51.8	0.0	0.0	0.0	47.0	1.2
Switzerland	41.2	0.0	0.0	2.6	56.2	0.0
United States	92.2	0.0	0.0	1.0	6.8	0.0
Unweighted average	58.8	2.4	0.9	0.9	36.8	0.2
Regional country						
Spain[1]	40.3	2.2	0.0	0.7	56.7	0.1
Unitary countries						
Chile	41.9	1.5	0.0	1.3	57.3	-2.1
Czech Republic	38.9	0.0	0.0	1.4	59.6	0.0
Denmark[1]	54.4	0.1	0.8	1.6	43.0	0.0
Estonia	28.5	20.9	0.0	0.0	50.6	0.0
Finland	28.0	0.0	0.0	3.3	68.6	0.2
France[1]	36.6	2.4	1.4	6.1	52.9	0.6
Greece	32.7	1.7	0.0	9.0	56.6	0.0
Hungary	28.7	1.8	2.3	3.6	63.0	0.5
Iceland	34.9	13.2	1.1	1.5	43.0	6.4
Ireland	51.8	3.1	0.7	5.0	39.3	0.0
Israel	41.4	0.0	5.0	3.9	49.8	0.0
Italy	51.9	0.0	0.0	5.9	42.2	0.0
Japan	52.7	0.0	0.0	5.0	42.3	0.0
Korea	48.7	0.0	0.0	7.0	42.7	1.6
Latvia	18.7	0.0	0.1	1.2	80.0	0.0
Luxembourg	48.6	1.3	0.0	12.6	37.2	0.2
Netherlands	48.3	0.0	0.0	3.2	48.2	0.3
New Zealand	59.5	0.0	0.0	0.1	40.3	0.0
Norway	30.7	32.2	0.0	1.4	35.7	0.0
Poland	25.4	0.0	1.4	0.0	73.2	0.0
Portugal	41.6	5.0	0.0	0.5	51.1	1.9
Slovak Republic	39.1	1.8	0.0	0.0	59.1	0.0
Slovenia	21.4	0.8	0.3	0.0	77.5	0.0
Sweden	1.5	19.5	20.9	3.0	54.9	0.1
Turkey	29.1	0.0	0.0	5.6	64.2	1.1
United Kingdom	46.5	0.0	0.0	10.1	43.4	0.0
Unweighted average	37.7	4.1	1.3	3.6	52.9	0.4

Note: Excluding social security contributions accruing to social security funds.

1. The total tax revenue has been reduced by the amount of any capital transfer that represents uncollected taxes. The capital transfer has been allocated between tax headings in proportion to the reported tax revenue.
2. These comprise only social security contributions accruing to central government.

StatLink http://dx.doi.org/10.1787/888933612095

Table 3.17. **Main state government taxes as % of total tax revenues of state government, 2015**

	1000 Income & profits	2000 Social security	3000 Payroll	4000 Property	5000 Goods and services	6000 Others
Federal countries						
Australia	0.0	0.0	28.7	41.7	29.6	0.0
Austria[1]	47.2	22.2	8.9	1.9	15.1	4.7
Belgium[1]	31.0	0.1	0.0	50.0	18.6	0.3
Canada	47.4	5.5	5.2	4.6	37.4	0.0
Germany[1]	51.7	0.0	0.0	6.8	41.6	0.0
Mexico	0.0	0.0	56.8	18.2	19.7	5.2
Switzerland	78.4	0.0	0.0	14.5	6.6	0.5
United States	42.3	0.0	0.0	2.0	55.6	0.0
Unweighted average	37.3	3.5	12.4	17.5	28.0	1.3
Regional country						
Spain[1,2,3]	68.1	0.0	0.0	20.7	11.2	0.0
Unitary countries						
Chile	..	..	..	..	..	..
Czech Republic	..	..	..	..	..	..
Denmark	..	..	..	..	..	..
Estonia	..	..	..	..	..	..
Finland	..	..	..	..	..	..
France	..	..	..	..	..	..
Greece	..	..	..	..	..	..
Hungary	..	..	..	..	..	..
Iceland	..	..	..	..	..	..
Ireland	..	..	..	..	..	..
Israel	..	..	..	..	..	..
Italy	..	..	..	..	..	..
Japan	..	..	..	..	..	..
Korea	..	..	..	..	..	..
Latvia	..	..	..	..	..	..
Luxembourg	..	..	..	..	..	..
Netherlands	..	..	..	..	..	..
New Zealand	..	..	..	..	..	..
Norway	..	..	..	..	..	..
Poland	..	..	..	..	..	..
Portugal	..	..	..	..	..	..
Slovak Republic	..	..	..	..	..	..
Slovenia	..	..	..	..	..	..
Sweden	..	..	..	..	..	..
Turkey	..	..	..	..	..	..
United Kingdom	..	..	..	..	..	..
Unweighted average	..	..	..	..	..	..

1. Payments to the European Union are excluded from these comparisons.
2. The total tax revenue has been reduced by the amount of any capital transfer that represents uncollected taxes. The capital transfer has been allocated between tax headings in proportion to the reported tax revenue.
3. Spain is constitutionally a non-federal country but has a highly decentralised political structure.

StatLink http://dx.doi.org/10.1787/888933612114

Table 3.18. Main local government taxes as % of total tax revenues of local government, 2015

	1000 Income & profits	2000 Social security	3000 Payroll	4000 Property	5000 Goods and services	6000 Others
Federal countries						
Australia	0.0	0.0	0.0	100.0	0.0	0.0
Austria[1]	0.0	6.1	67.7	15.3	8.0	2.9
Belgium[1]	34.2	0.3	0.0	57.6	8.0	0.0
Canada	0.0	0.0	0.0	97.2	1.7	1.1
Germany[1]	79.2	0.0	0.0	14.2	6.4	0.2
Mexico	0.0	0.0	0.0	75.3	1.7	23.0
Switzerland	82.8	0.0	0.0	14.7	0.5	2.1
United States	6.3	0.0	0.0	69.8	23.8	0.0
Unweighted average	25.3	0.8	8.5	55.5	6.3	3.7
Regional country						
Spain[1,2]	15.6	0.0	0.0	46.0	38.2	0.2
Unitary countries						
Chile	0.0	0.0	0.0	42.4	57.6	0.0
Czech Republic[1]	0.0	0.0	0.0	57.1	42.9	0.0
Denmark[1,3]	88.7	0.0	0.0	11.3	0.0	0.0
Estonia[1]	0.0	0.0	0.0	83.8	16.2	0.0
Finland[1]	92.6	0.1	0.0	7.3	0.0	0.0
France[1,3]	0.0	0.0	7.1	52.5	23.6	16.8
Greece[1]	0.0	0.0	0.0	93.8	6.2	0.0
Hungary[1]	0.0	0.0	0.0	18.9	81.1	0.0
Iceland	82.0	0.0	0.0	16.7	1.4	0.0
Ireland[1]	0.0	8.6	0.0	91.4	0.0	0.0
Israel	0.0	0.0	0.0	95.1	4.9	0.0
Italy[1]	25.8	0.0	0.0	20.3	29.9	23.9
Japan	49.5	0.0	0.0	26.6	22.9	1.1
Korea	18.3	0.0	1.6	47.1	24.2	8.7
Latvia[1]	84.3	0.0	0.0	14.4	1.3	0.0
Luxembourg[1]	90.3	0.0	0.0	8.1	1.4	0.2
Netherlands[1]	0.0	0.0	0.0	52.2	47.8	0.0
New Zealand	0.0	0.0	0.0	88.9	11.1	0.0
Norway	87.4	0.0	0.0	11.5	1.1	0.0
Poland[1]	60.8	0.0	0.0	32.8	5.5	0.9
Portugal[1]	27.7	0.4	0.0	46.5	25.1	0.3
Slovak Republic[1]	0.0	0.0	0.0	64.8	35.2	0.0
Slovenia[1]	75.2	0.0	0.0	17.7	7.1	0.0
Sweden[1]	97.6	0.0	0.0	2.4	0.0	0.0
Turkey	25.6	0.0	0.0	14.8	50.8	8.8
United Kingdom[1]	0.0	0.0	0.0	100.0	0.0	0.0
Unweighted average	34.8	0.3	0.3	43.0	19.1	2.3

1. Payments to the European Union are excluded from these comparisons.
2. Spain is constitutionally a non-federal country but has a highly decentralised political structure.
3. The total tax revenue has been reduced by the amount of any capital transfer that represents uncollected taxes. The capital transfer has been allocated between tax headings in proportion to the reported tax revenue.

StatLink http://dx.doi.org/10.1787/888933612133

Table 3.19. **Gross domestic product for tax reporting years at market prices, in billions of national currency**

		1965	1990	2000	2007	2010	2012	2013	2014	2015	2016p
Australia[1]	AUD	24.4	415.4	706.0	1 178.8	1 410.4	1 527.5	1 589.9	1 610.8	1 640.9	1 742.3
Austria	EUR	18.5	137.2	213.2	282.3	294.6	317.1	322.5	330.4	339.9	349.3
Belgium	EUR	21.0	171.0	258.2	344.7	365.1	387.5	391.7	400.8	410.2	421.6
Canada[1]	CAD	60.7	693.5	1 122.2	1 596.1	1 685.6	1 838.2	1 918.5	1 988.9	1 992.5	2 054.7
Chile	CLP	..	10 522.7	42 005.2	90 702.9	111 508.6	129 947.3	137 876.2	148 855.3	158 636.8	167 227.4
Czech Republic	CZK	..	..	2 379.4	3 840.1	3 962.5	4 059.9	4 098.1	4 313.8	4 595.8	4 773.2
Denmark	DKK	71.5	855.6	1 326.9	1 738.8	1 810.9	1 895.0	1 929.7	1 977.3	2 027.2	2 064.8
Estonia	EUR	..	..	6.2	16.2	14.7	17.9	18.9	19.8	20.3	20.9
Finland	EUR	4.5	91.0	136.3	186.6	187.1	199.8	203.3	205.5	209.6	215.6
France	EUR	76.6	1 058.6	1 485.3	1 945.7	1 998.5	2 086.9	2 115.3	2 147.6	2 194.2	2 228.9
Germany	EUR	234.8	1 306.7	2 116.5	2 513.2	2 580.1	2 758.3	2 826.2	2 932.5	3 043.7	3 144.1
Greece	EUR	0.7	45.5	141.2	232.7	226.0	191.2	180.7	177.9	175.7	175.9
Hungary	HUF	..	..	13 321.5	25 560.4	27 085.9	28 660.5	30 127.3	32 400.1	33 999.0	35 005.4
Iceland	ISK	0.2	380.1	703.3	1 364.1	1 620.3	1 778.5	1 891.2	2 005.9	2 214.1	2 422.0
Ireland	EUR	1.3	37.9	108.4	197.2	167.6	175.6	180.3	194.5	262.0	275.6
Israel	ILS	..	..	539.5	734.3	874.0	993.4	1 059.1	1 104.7	1 163.8	1 224.2
Italy	EUR	22.3	728.5	1 239.3	1 609.6	1 604.5	1 613.3	1 604.6	1 621.8	1 645.4	1 672.4
Japan[1]	JPY	35 113.5	463 770.8	528 621.2	531 013.5	499 194.9	494 674.4	507 401.1	517 754.7	531 977.3	537 935.3
Korea	KRW	..	197 712.3	635 184.6	1 043 257.8	1 265 308.0	1 377 456.7	1 429 445.4	1 486 079.3	1 564 123.9	1 637 420.8
Latvia	EUR	..	..	6.9	22.6	17.9	21.9	22.8	23.6	24.4	25.0
Luxembourg	EUR	1.0	11.0	23.1	37.2	40.2	44.1	46.6	50.0	52.3	54.2
Mexico	MXN	..	825.1	6 132.4	11 399.5	13 266.9	15 599.3	16 079.0	17 217.0	18 194.8	19 472.1
Netherlands	EUR	35.2	259.7	448.1	613.3	631.5	645.2	652.7	663.0	683.5	702.6
New Zealand[1]	NZD	4.3	75.9	122.2	189.0	205.9	218.7	236.3	240.8	250.6	269.4
Norway	NOK	57.2	749.9	1 507.9	2 349.9	2 590.1	2 965.2	3 071.1	3 140.4	3 117.4	3 112.7
Poland	PLN	..	..	747.0	1 187.6	1 445.3	1 629.4	1 656.8	1 719.7	1 799.3	1 851.2
Portugal	EUR	0.6	56.0	128.5	175.5	179.9	168.4	170.3	173.1	179.5	184.9
Slovak Republic	EUR	..	..	31.6	63.1	67.6	72.7	74.2	75.9	78.7	81.0
Slovenia	EUR	..	..	18.9	35.2	36.3	36.0	35.9	37.3	38.6	39.8
Spain	EUR	8.7	327.8	646.3	1 080.8	1 080.9	1 039.8	1 025.6	1 037.0	1 075.6	1 113.9
Sweden	SEK	127.5	1 528.0	2 380.4	3 297.1	3 520.0	3 684.8	3 769.9	3 936.8	4 181.1	4 375.2
Switzerland	CHF	67.9	357.6	458.8	573.1	606.1	623.6	634.8	643.8	645.6	650.2
Turkey	TRY	0.0	0.5	170.7	880.5	1 160.0	1 569.7	1 809.7	2 044.5	2 337.5	2 590.5
United Kingdom	GBP	36.4	615.7	1 080.9	1 530.9	1 572.4	1 675.0	1 739.6	1 822.5	1 872.7	1 939.6
United States	USD	710.7	5 979.6	10 284.8	14 477.6	14 964.4	16 155.3	16 691.5	17 427.6	18 120.7	18 624.5

1. GDP is fiscal year. The year Y is calculated (at annual rate) as the average of: Q2(Y) to Q1(Y+1) for Canada and Japan; and Q3(Y) to Q2(Y+1) for Australia and New Zealand.

Source: OECD National Accounts.

StatLink http://dx.doi.org/10.1787/888933612152

Table 3.20. **Exchange rates used, national currency per US dollar at market exchange rates**

		1965	1990	2000	2007	2010	2012	2013	2014	2015	2016p
Australia	AUD	0.893	1.282	1.727	1.195	1.090	0.966	1.036	1.109	1.331	1.345
Austria	EUR	..	0.788	1.085	0.730	0.755	0.778	0.753	0.754	0.901	0.904
Belgium	EUR	..	0.788	1.085	0.730	0.755	0.778	0.753	0.754	0.901	0.904
Canada	CAD	1.078	1.167	1.485	1.074	1.030	0.999	1.030	1.105	1.278	1.325
Chile	CLP	..	304.903	539.388	522.228	509.982	485.984	495.282	570.636	654.322	676.540
Czech Republic	CZK	..	..	38.637	20.289	19.080	19.538	19.560	20.758	24.593	24.441
Denmark	DKK	6.915	6.186	8.088	5.443	5.622	5.790	5.618	5.619	6.725	6.731
Estonia	EUR	..	..	1.085	0.730	0.755	0.778	0.753	0.754	0.901	0.904
Finland	EUR	..	0.788	1.085	0.730	0.755	0.778	0.753	0.754	0.901	0.904
France	EUR	..	0.788	1.085	0.730	0.755	0.778	0.753	0.754	0.901	0.904
Germany	EUR	..	0.788	1.085	0.730	0.755	0.778	0.753	0.754	0.901	0.904
Greece	EUR	..	0.788	1.085	0.730	0.755	0.778	0.753	0.754	0.901	0.904
Hungary	HUF	..	..	282.286	183.595	207.764	224.823	223.582	232.619	279.194	281.521
Iceland	ISK	0.431	58.378	78.845	64.075	122.242	125.118	122.167	116.688	131.896	120.835
Ireland	EUR	0.454	0.788	1.085	0.730	0.755	0.778	0.753	0.754	0.901	0.904
Israel	ILS	..	..	4.077	4.109	3.731	3.850	3.609	3.577	3.887	3.839
Italy	EUR	..	0.788	1.085	0.730	0.755	0.778	0.753	0.754	0.901	0.904
Japan	JPY	361.491	144.796	107.835	117.755	87.761	79.814	97.598	105.848	121.002	108.803
Korea	KRW	..	707.995	1 130.640	929.450	1 155.431	1 125.935	1 094.926	1 053.064	1 131.309	1 160.589
Latvia	EUR	..	..	1.085	0.730	0.755	0.778	0.753	0.754	0.901	0.904
Luxembourg	EUR	..	0.788	1.085	0.730	0.755	0.778	0.753	0.754	0.901	0.904
Mexico	MXN	..	2.841	9.453	10.929	12.632	13.150	12.770	13.305	15.874	18.627
Netherlands	EUR	..	0.788	1.085	0.730	0.755	0.778	0.753	0.754	0.901	0.904
New Zealand	NZD	0.722	1.678	2.205	1.361	1.388	1.235	1.220	1.206	1.434	1.437
Norway	NOK	7.151	6.258	8.797	5.858	6.042	5.815	5.877	6.302	8.064	8.400
Poland	PLN	..	..	4.346	2.765	3.015	3.252	3.160	3.154	3.770	3.944
Portugal	EUR	..	0.788	1.085	0.730	0.755	0.778	0.753	0.754	0.901	0.904
Slovak Republic	EUR	..	..	1.085	0.730	0.755	0.778	0.753	0.754	0.901	0.904
Slovenia	EUR	..	..	1.085	0.730	0.755	0.778	0.753	0.754	0.901	0.904
Spain	EUR	..	0.788	1.085	0.730	0.755	0.778	0.753	0.754	0.901	0.904
Sweden	SEK	5.158	5.918	9.161	6.758	7.202	6.769	6.513	6.860	8.429	8.556
Switzerland	CHF	4.328	1.389	1.688	1.200	1.043	0.937	0.927	0.915	0.962	0.985
Turkey	TRY	0.000	0.003	0.624	1.300	1.499	1.792	1.905	2.189	2.723	3.022
United Kingdom	GBP	0.358	0.563	0.661	0.500	0.647	0.631	0.640	0.607	0.654	0.741
United States	USD	1.000	1.000	1.000	1.000	1.000	1.000	1.000	1.000	1.000	1.000

Source: OECD Financial indicators data.

StatLink http://dx.doi.org/10.1787/888933612171

Revenue Statistics 1965-2016

Chapter 4

Country tables, 1990-2015

4.1. Tax revenue and % of GDP by selected tax category and by level of government

In all of the following tables the symbol (..) indicates not available/or not applicable. The data in this chapter cover the years 1990 to 2015. Figures referring to 1965-1989, 1991-1999, 2001-2009 and 2011-2013 have been omitted because of lack of space. A complete series is, however, available on line. Data for 1955 and 1960 (for nineteen OECD countries) are provided in part V of the 1998 edition of this Report.

The Gross Domestic Product (GDP) figures are based on the 2008 System of National Accounts (SNA) for all OECD countries.

Treatment of capital transfers. Some tables refer to the treatment of the capital transfers that some countries make to account for taxes that have been assessed but not collected. The capital transfer has been subtracted from the total tax revenue and this reduction has been allocated between tax headings in proportion to their tax revenues.

This applies to the following countries:

- Denmark from 1971.
- France from 1992.
- Greece for 1999 and 2000.
- Spain from 1995.

Table 4.1. **Australia, tax revenue and % of GDP by selected tax category**

	Billion AUD					% of GDP				
	1990	2000	2010	2014	2015	1990	2000	2010	2014	2015
Total tax revenue	**116.5**	**214.5**	**358.5**	**444.6**	**463.1**	**28.0**	**30.4**	**25.4**	**27.6**	**28.2**
1000 Taxes on income, profits and capital gains	**66.5**	**124.4**	**202.2**	**256.3**	**262.6**	**16.0**	**17.6**	**14.3**	**15.9**	**16.0**
1100 Of individuals	50.1	81.0	138.2	183.3	192.0	12.1	11.5	9.8	11.4	11.7
1200 Corporate	16.5	43.4	64.0	73.0	70.7	4.0	6.2	4.5	4.5	4.3
1300 Unallocable between 1100 and 1200	0.0	0.0	0.0	0.0	0.0	0.0	0.0	0.0	0.0	0.0
2000 Social security contributions	**0.0**	**0.0**	**0.0**	**0.0**	**0.0**	**0.0**	**0.0**	**0.0**	**0.0**	**0.0**
2100 Employees	0.0	0.0	0.0	0.0	0.0	0.0	0.0	0.0	0.0	0.0
2200 Employers	0.0	0.0	0.0	0.0	0.0	0.0	0.0	0.0	0.0	0.0
2300 Self-employed or non-employed	0.0	0.0	0.0	0.0	0.0	0.0	0.0	0.0	0.0	0.0
2400 Unallocable between 2100, 2200 and 2300	0.0	0.0	0.0	0.0	0.0	0.0	0.0	0.0	0.0	0.0
3000 Taxes on payroll and workforce	**7.1**	**9.6**	**18.5**	**22.8**	**23.4**	**1.7**	**1.4**	**1.3**	**1.4**	**1.4**
4000 Taxes on property	**10.4**	**18.8**	**33.5**	**45.3**	**49.6**	**2.5**	**2.7**	**2.4**	**2.8**	**3.0**
4100 Recurrent taxes on immovable property	6.1	9.1	19.9	25.1	27.1	1.5	1.3	1.4	1.6	1.7
4200 Recurrent taxes on net wealth	0.0	0.0	0.0	0.0	0.0	0.0	0.0	0.0	0.0	0.0
4300 Estate, inheritance and gift taxes	0.0	0.0	0.0	0.0	0.0	0.0	0.0	0.0	0.0	0.0
4400 Taxes on financial and capital transactions	4.3	9.8	13.6	20.2	22.5	1.0	1.4	1.0	1.3	1.4
4500 Non-recurrent taxes	0.0	0.0	0.0	0.0	0.0	0.0	0.0	0.0	0.0	0.0
4600 Other recurrent taxes on property	0.0	0.0	0.0	0.0	0.0	0.0	0.0	0.0	0.0	0.0
5000 Taxes on goods and services	**32.4**	**61.6**	**104.3**	**120.3**	**127.5**	**7.8**	**8.7**	**7.4**	**7.5**	**7.8**
5100 Taxes on production, sale, transfer, etc	27.2	56.2	92.0	104.5	110.2	6.6	8.0	6.5	6.5	6.7
5110 General taxes	9.4	25.8	49.3	57.8	61.8	2.3	3.7	3.5	3.6	3.8
5111 Value added taxes	0.0	23.9	48.1	56.5	60.3	0.0	3.4	3.4	3.5	3.7
5120 Taxes on specific goods and services	17.8	30.4	42.7	46.7	48.4	4.3	4.3	3.0	2.9	2.9
5121 Excises	12.0	19.8	26.7	24.5	22.5	2.9	2.8	1.9	1.5	1.4
5200 Taxes on use of goods and perform activities	5.2	5.4	12.3	15.8	17.3	1.3	0.8	0.9	1.0	1.1
5300 Unallocable between 5100 and 5200	0.0	0.0	0.0	0.0	0.0	0.0	0.0	0.0	0.0	0.0
6000 Other taxes	**0.0**	**0.0**	**0.0**	**0.0**	**0.0**	**0.0**	**0.0**	**0.0**	**0.0**	**0.0**
Non-wastable tax credits										
Non-wastable tax credits against 1000	..	0.2	6.7	8.8	9.3	..	0.0	0.5	0.5	0.6
Transfer component	..	0.0	4.4	6.5	6.8	..	0.0	0.3	0.4	0.4
Tax expenditure component	..	0.2	2.4	2.3	2.5	..	0.0	0.2	0.1	0.2

Note: More detailed country data and country notes are available in online chapter 5: http://dx.doi.org/10.1787/9789264283183-en. Full time series can be accessed at http://oe.cd/full-time-series.

Source: Australian Bureau of Statistics.

StatLink http://dx.doi.org/10.1787/888933612190

Table 4.2. **Australia, tax revenue and % of GDP by level of government and main taxes**

	Billion AUD					% of GDP				
	1990	2000	2010	2014	2015	1990	2000	2010	2014	2015
Federal or Central government										
Total tax revenue	**92.6**	**175.4**	**287.7**	**355.1**	**367.4**	**22.3**	**24.8**	**20.4**	**22.0**	**22.4**
1000 Taxes on income, profits and capital gains	66.5	124.4	202.2	256.3	262.6	16.0	17.6	14.3	15.9	16.0
2000 Social security contributions	0.0	0.0	0.0	0.0	0.0	0.0	0.0	0.0	0.0	0.0
3000 Taxes on payroll and workforce	1.3	0.1	0.5	0.7	0.7	0.3	0.0	0.0	0.0	0.0
4000 Taxes on property	0.2	0.0	0.0	0.0	0.0	0.1	0.0	0.0	0.0	0.0
5000 Taxes on goods and services	24.5	50.8	85.0	98.1	104.1	5.9	7.2	6.0	6.1	6.3
6000 Other taxes	0.0	0.0	0.0	0.0	0.0	0.0	0.0	0.0	0.0	0.0
State/Regional										
Total tax revenue	**19.7**	**32.7**	**58.4**	**73.7**	**79.1**	**4.7**	**4.6**	**4.1**	**4.6**	**4.8**
1000 Taxes on income, profits and capital gains	0.0	0.0	0.0	0.0	0.0	0.0	0.0	0.0	0.0	0.0
2000 Social security contributions	0.0	0.0	0.0	0.0	0.0	0.0	0.0	0.0	0.0	0.0
3000 Taxes on payroll and workforce	5.8	9.5	18.0	22.1	22.7	1.4	1.3	1.3	1.4	1.4
4000 Taxes on property	6.0	12.4	21.0	29.5	33.0	1.4	1.8	1.5	1.8	2.0
5000 Taxes on goods and services	7.9	10.8	19.3	22.2	23.4	1.9	1.5	1.4	1.4	1.4
6000 Other taxes	0.0	0.0	0.0	0.0	0.0	0.0	0.0	0.0	0.0	0.0
Local government										
Total tax revenue	**4.2**	**6.4**	**12.4**	**15.8**	**16.6**	**1.0**	**0.9**	**0.9**	**1.0**	**1.0**
1000 Taxes on income, profits and capital gains	0.0	0.0	0.0	0.0	0.0	0.0	0.0	0.0	0.0	0.0
2000 Social security contributions	0.0	0.0	0.0	0.0	0.0	0.0	0.0	0.0	0.0	0.0
3000 Taxes on payroll and workforce	0.0	0.0	0.0	0.0	0.0	0.0	0.0	0.0	0.0	0.0
4000 Taxes on property	4.2	6.4	12.4	15.8	16.6	1.0	0.9	0.9	1.0	1.0
5000 Taxes on goods and services	0.0	0.0	0.0	0.0	0.0	0.0	0.0	0.0	0.0	0.0
6000 Other taxes	0.0	0.0	0.0	0.0	0.0	0.0	0.0	0.0	0.0	0.0
Social Security Funds										
Total tax revenue	**0.0**	**0.0**	**0.0**	**0.0**	**0.0**	**0.0**	**0.0**	**0.0**	**0.0**	**0.0**
1000 Taxes on income, profits and capital gains	0.0	0.0	0.0	0.0	0.0	0.0	0.0	0.0	0.0	0.0
2000 Social security contributions	0.0	0.0	0.0	0.0	0.0	0.0	0.0	0.0	0.0	0.0
3000 Taxes on payroll and workforce	0.0	0.0	0.0	0.0	0.0	0.0	0.0	0.0	0.0	0.0
4000 Taxes on property	0.0	0.0	0.0	0.0	0.0	0.0	0.0	0.0	0.0	0.0
5000 Taxes on goods and services	0.0	0.0	0.0	0.0	0.0	0.0	0.0	0.0	0.0	0.0
6000 Other taxes	0.0	0.0	0.0	0.0	0.0	0.0	0.0	0.0	0.0	0.0

Note: More detailed country data and country notes are available in online chapter 6: http://dx.doi.org/10.1787/9789264283183-en. Full time series can be accessed at http://oe.cd/full-time-series.
Source: Australian Bureau of Statistics.

StatLink http://dx.doi.org/10.1787/888933612209

Table 4.3. **Austria, tax revenue and % of GDP by selected tax category**

	Billion EUR					% of GDP				
	1990	2000	2010	2014	2015	1990	2000	2010	2014	2015
Total tax revenue	**54.0**	**90.3**	**121.2**	**142.3**	**148.4**	**39.4**	**42.4**	**41.1**	**43.1**	**43.7**
1000 Taxes on income, profits and capital gains	**13.8**	**25.6**	**34.0**	**41.7**	**44.8**	**10.1**	**12.0**	**11.5**	**12.6**	**13.2**
1100 Of individuals	11.3	19.9	27.1	33.4	35.8	8.3	9.3	9.2	10.1	10.5
1200 Corporate	1.9	4.2	5.5	7.0	7.7	1.4	2.0	1.9	2.1	2.3
1300 Unallocable between 1100 and 1200	0.5	1.5	1.4	1.3	1.3	0.4	0.7	0.5	0.4	0.4
2000 Social security contributions	**17.8**	**30.5**	**41.4**	**48.3**	**49.9**	**12.9**	**14.3**	**14.1**	**14.6**	**14.7**
2100 Employees	7.5	12.5	16.8	19.4	20.1	5.5	5.9	5.7	5.9	5.9
2200 Employers	8.8	14.7	19.4	22.6	23.3	6.4	6.9	6.6	6.8	6.9
2300 Self-employed or non-employed	1.5	3.4	5.2	6.2	6.5	1.1	1.6	1.8	1.9	1.9
2400 Unallocable between 2100, 2200 and 2300	0.0	0.0	0.0	0.0	0.0	0.0	0.0	0.0	0.0	0.0
3000 Taxes on payroll and workforce	**3.3**	**5.8**	**8.4**	**9.8**	**10.0**	**2.4**	**2.7**	**2.8**	**3.0**	**3.0**
4000 Taxes on property	**1.5**	**1.2**	**1.6**	**2.0**	**2.0**	**1.1**	**0.6**	**0.5**	**0.6**	**0.6**
4100 Recurrent taxes on immovable property	0.4	0.5	0.7	0.7	0.8	0.3	0.2	0.2	0.2	0.2
4200 Recurrent taxes on net wealth	0.6	0.0	0.0	0.0	0.0	0.5	0.0	0.0	0.0	0.0
4300 Estate, inheritance and gift taxes	0.1	0.1	0.0	0.0	0.0	0.1	0.1	0.0	0.0	0.0
4400 Taxes on financial and capital transactions	0.4	0.6	0.8	0.9	1.1	0.3	0.3	0.3	0.3	0.3
4500 Non-recurrent taxes	0.0	0.0	0.0	0.3	0.1	0.0	0.0	0.0	0.1	0.0
4600 Other recurrent taxes on property	0.0	0.0	0.0	0.0	0.0	0.0	0.0	0.0	0.0	0.0
5000 Taxes on goods and services	**17.0**	**26.1**	**34.4**	**39.3**	**40.5**	**12.4**	**12.3**	**11.7**	**11.9**	**11.9**
5100 Taxes on production, sale, transfer, etc	16.2	24.3	31.8	35.9	37.1	11.8	11.4	10.8	10.9	10.9
5110 General taxes	11.2	16.9	22.7	25.4	26.3	8.2	7.9	7.7	7.7	7.7
5111 Value added taxes	11.2	16.9	22.7	25.4	26.3	8.2	7.9	7.7	7.7	7.7
5120 Taxes on specific goods and services	4.9	7.4	9.1	10.5	10.8	3.6	3.5	3.1	3.2	3.2
5121 Excises	3.3	5.5	6.9	7.5	7.7	2.4	2.6	2.3	2.3	2.3
5200 Taxes on use of goods and perform activities	0.9	1.9	2.6	3.4	3.4	0.6	0.9	0.9	1.0	1.0
5300 Unallocable between 5100 and 5200	0.0	0.0	0.0	0.0	0.0	0.0	0.0	0.0	0.0	0.0
6000 Other taxes	**0.7**	**0.8**	**1.1**	**0.8**	**0.8**	**0.5**	**0.4**	**0.4**	**0.2**	**0.2**
Non-wastable tax credits										
Non-wastable tax credits against 1000	..	0.7	0.7	0.6	0.5	..	0.3	0.2	0.2	0.2
Transfer component	..	0.1	0.2	0.2	0.2	..	0.0	0.1	0.1	0.1
Tax expenditure component	..	0.6	0.4	0.3	0.3	..	0.3	0.1	0.1	0.1

Note: More detailed country data and country notes are available in online chapter 5: http://dx.doi.org/10.1787/9789264283183-en. Full time series can be accessed at http://oe.cd/full-time-series.

Source: Statistics Austria.

StatLink http://dx.doi.org/10.1787/888933612228

Table 4.4. Austria, tax revenue and % of GDP by level of government and main taxes

	Billion EUR					% of GDP				
	1990	2000	2010	2014	2015	1990	2000	2010	2014	2015
Federal or Central government										
Total tax revenue	**27.2**	**60.5**	**80.7**	**95.0**	**99.5**	**19.8**	**28.4**	**27.4**	**28.7**	**29.3**
1000 Taxes on income, profits and capital gains	8.6	24.9	33.1	40.7	43.7	6.3	11.7	11.2	12.3	12.9
2000 Social security contributions	2.4	5.1	6.3	7.3	7.5	1.7	2.4	2.1	2.2	2.2
3000 Taxes on payroll and workforce	2.6	3.9	5.8	6.7	6.9	1.9	1.8	2.0	2.0	2.0
4000 Taxes on property	0.9	0.7	0.9	1.3	1.2	0.6	0.3	0.3	0.4	0.4
5000 Taxes on goods and services	12.3	25.3	33.7	38.5	39.6	8.9	11.9	11.4	11.6	11.7
6000 Other taxes	0.5	0.6	0.9	0.6	0.5	0.4	0.3	0.3	0.2	0.2
State/Regional										
Total tax revenue	**5.8**	**1.4**	**2.0**	**2.2**	**2.3**	**4.2**	**0.7**	**0.7**	**0.7**	**0.7**
1000 Taxes on income, profits and capital gains	2.8	0.6	0.9	1.0	1.1	2.0	0.3	0.3	0.3	0.3
2000 Social security contributions	0.2	0.4	0.5	0.5	0.5	0.2	0.2	0.2	0.1	0.1
3000 Taxes on payroll and workforce	0.0	0.1	0.2	0.2	0.2	0.0	0.1	0.1	0.1	0.1
4000 Taxes on property	0.1	0.0	0.0	0.0	0.0	0.0	0.0	0.0	0.0	0.0
5000 Taxes on goods and services	2.7	0.2	0.3	0.4	0.3	2.0	0.1	0.1	0.1	0.1
6000 Other taxes	0.0	0.1	0.1	0.1	0.1	0.0	0.0	0.0	0.0	0.0
Local government										
Total tax revenue	**6.1**	**3.2**	**3.8**	**4.4**	**4.4**	**4.4**	**1.5**	**1.3**	**1.3**	**1.3**
1000 Taxes on income, profits and capital gains	2.4	0.0	0.0	0.0	0.0	1.8	0.0	0.0	0.0	0.0
2000 Social security contributions	0.2	0.3	0.3	0.3	0.3	0.1	0.1	0.1	0.1	0.1
3000 Taxes on payroll and workforce	0.7	1.8	2.4	2.9	3.0	0.5	0.8	0.8	0.9	0.9
4000 Taxes on property	0.5	0.5	0.6	0.7	0.7	0.4	0.2	0.2	0.2	0.2
5000 Taxes on goods and services	2.1	0.6	0.4	0.4	0.4	1.5	0.3	0.1	0.1	0.1
6000 Other taxes	0.2	0.1	0.1	0.1	0.1	0.1	0.0	0.0	0.0	0.0
Social Security Funds										
Total tax revenue	**15.0**	**24.8**	**34.4**	**40.3**	**41.6**	**10.9**	**11.6**	**11.7**	**12.2**	**12.2**
1000 Taxes on income, profits and capital gains	0.0	0.0	0.0	0.0	0.0	0.0	0.0	0.0	0.0	0.0
2000 Social security contributions	15.0	24.8	34.4	40.3	41.6	10.9	11.6	11.7	12.2	12.2
3000 Taxes on payroll and workforce	0.0	0.0	0.0	0.0	0.0	0.0	0.0	0.0	0.0	0.0
4000 Taxes on property	0.0	0.0	0.0	0.0	0.0	0.0	0.0	0.0	0.0	0.0
5000 Taxes on goods and services	0.0	0.0	0.0	0.0	0.0	0.0	0.0	0.0	0.0	0.0
6000 Other taxes	0.0	0.0	0.0	0.0	0.0	0.0	0.0	0.0	0.0	0.0

Note: More detailed country data and country notes are available in online chapter 6: http://dx.doi.org/10.1787/9789264283183-en. Full time series can be accessed at http://oe.cd/full-time-series.
Source: Statistics Austria.

StatLink http://dx.doi.org/10.1787/888933612247

Table 4.5. **Belgium, tax revenue and % of GDP by selected tax category**

	Billion EUR					% of GDP				
	1990	2000	2010	2014	2015	1990	2000	2010	2014	2015
Total tax revenue	**70.4**	**112.4**	**155.6**	**180.3**	**183.8**	**41.2**	**43.5**	**42.6**	**45.0**	**44.8**
1000 Taxes on income, profits and capital gains	**26.0**	**43.4**	**53.2**	**64.6**	**65.7**	**15.2**	**16.8**	**14.6**	**16.1**	**16.0**
1100 Of individuals	22.5	35.3	44.0	51.9	52.1	13.2	13.7	12.0	13.0	12.7
1200 Corporate	3.4	8.1	9.2	12.6	13.6	2.0	3.1	2.5	3.1	3.3
1300 Unallocable between 1100 and 1200	0.0	0.1	0.0	0.1	0.1	0.0	0.0	0.0	0.0	0.0
2000 Social security contributions	**23.4**	**34.6**	**50.4**	**57.1**	**58.6**	**13.7**	**13.4**	**13.8**	**14.2**	**14.3**
2100 Employees	7.2	10.9	15.0	16.7	17.0	4.2	4.2	4.1	4.2	4.1
2200 Employers	14.7	20.8	30.8	35.2	36.2	8.6	8.1	8.4	8.8	8.8
2300 Self-employed or non-employed	1.5	2.9	4.6	5.2	5.5	0.9	1.1	1.3	1.3	1.3
2400 Unallocable between 2100, 2200 and 2300	0.0	0.0	0.0	0.0	0.0	0.0	0.0	0.0	0.0	0.0
3000 Taxes on payroll and workforce	**0.0**	**0.0**	**0.0**	**0.0**	**0.0**	**0.0**	**0.0**	**0.0**	**0.0**	**0.0**
4000 Taxes on property	**2.7**	**5.3**	**11.3**	**14.3**	**14.4**	**1.6**	**2.0**	**3.1**	**3.6**	**3.5**
4100 Recurrent taxes on immovable property	0.6	1.2	4.6	5.3	5.4	0.4	0.5	1.3	1.3	1.3
4200 Recurrent taxes on net wealth	0.0	0.1	0.2	0.6	0.7	0.0	0.0	0.1	0.2	0.2
4300 Estate, inheritance and gift taxes	0.5	1.1	2.3	2.8	3.0	0.3	0.4	0.6	0.7	0.7
4400 Taxes on financial and capital transactions	1.5	2.7	3.5	4.1	4.4	0.9	1.0	1.0	1.0	1.1
4500 Non-recurrent taxes	0.0	0.1	0.3	1.1	0.6	0.0	0.0	0.1	0.3	0.2
4600 Other recurrent taxes on property	0.1	0.2	0.3	0.3	0.3	0.1	0.1	0.1	0.1	0.1
5000 Taxes on goods and services	**18.4**	**28.1**	**39.4**	**43.1**	**43.8**	**10.7**	**10.9**	**10.8**	**10.8**	**10.7**
5100 Taxes on production, sale, transfer, etc	17.4	26.0	37.0	40.7	41.3	10.2	10.1	10.1	10.1	10.1
5110 General taxes	11.6	18.2	25.5	27.7	27.8	6.8	7.1	7.0	6.9	6.8
5111 Value added taxes	11.5	18.1	25.3	27.5	27.5	6.8	7.0	6.9	6.9	6.7
5120 Taxes on specific goods and services	5.8	7.8	11.5	12.9	13.5	3.4	3.0	3.1	3.2	3.3
5121 Excises	3.5	5.7	7.8	8.2	8.6	2.0	2.2	2.1	2.0	2.1
5200 Taxes on use of goods and perform activities	1.0	2.1	2.4	2.5	2.5	0.6	0.8	0.7	0.6	0.6
5300 Unallocable between 5100 and 5200	0.0	0.0	0.0	0.0	0.0	0.0	0.0	0.0	0.0	0.0
6000 Other taxes	**0.0**	**0.0**	**0.0**	**0.0**	**0.0**	**0.0**	**0.0**	**0.0**	**0.0**	**0.0**
Non-wastable tax credits										
Non-wastable tax credits against 1000	..	..	1.0	1.1	0.7	..	..	0.3	0.3	0.2
Transfer component	..	..	0.4	0.3	0.3	..	..	0.1	0.1	0.1
Tax expenditure component	..	..	0.6	0.7	0.4	..	..	0.2	0.2	0.1

Note: More detailed country data and country notes are available in online chapter 5: http://dx.doi.org/10.1787/9789264283183-en. Full time series can be accessed at http://oe.cd/full-time-series.

Source: Federal Ministry of Finance.

StatLink http://dx.doi.org/10.1787/888933612266

Table 4.6. **Belgium, tax revenue and % of GDP by level of government and main taxes**

	Billion EUR					% of GDP				
	1990	2000	2010	2014	2015	1990	2000	2010	2014	2015
Federal or Central government										
Total tax revenue	**42.5**	**69.4**	**87.8**	**103.5**	**99.9**	**24.9**	**26.9**	**24.0**	**25.8**	**24.4**
1000 Taxes on income, profits and capital gains	23.9	39.6	49.3	60.9	57.1	13.9	15.3	13.5	15.2	13.9
2000 Social security contributions	0.9	1.3	2.5	2.3	2.3	0.5	0.5	0.7	0.6	0.6
3000 Taxes on payroll and workforce	0.0	0.0	0.0	0.0	0.0	0.0	0.0	0.0	0.0	0.0
4000 Taxes on property	1.1	2.3	0.9	2.0	1.9	0.6	0.9	0.3	0.5	0.5
5000 Taxes on goods and services	16.7	26.3	35.0	38.3	38.6	9.8	10.2	9.6	9.6	9.4
6000 Other taxes	0.0	0.0	0.0	0.0	0.0	0.0	0.0	0.0	0.0	0.0
State/Regional										
Total tax revenue	**1.2**	**2.4**	**8.1**	**9.6**	**14.2**	**0.7**	**0.9**	**2.2**	**2.4**	**3.5**
1000 Taxes on income, profits and capital gains	0.0	0.1	0.0	0.0	4.4	0.0	0.0	0.0	0.0	1.1
2000 Social security contributions	0.0	0.0	0.0	0.0	0.0	0.0	0.0	0.0	0.0	0.0
3000 Taxes on payroll and workforce	0.0	0.0	0.0	0.0	0.0	0.0	0.0	0.0	0.0	0.0
4000 Taxes on property	0.9	1.9	5.6	6.9	7.1	0.5	0.7	1.5	1.7	1.7
5000 Taxes on goods and services	0.2	0.5	2.4	2.6	2.6	0.1	0.2	0.7	0.6	0.6
6000 Other taxes	0.0	0.0	0.0	0.0	0.0	0.0	0.0	0.0	0.0	0.0
Local government										
Total tax revenue	**3.1**	**4.6**	**7.9**	**8.3**	**8.9**	**1.8**	**1.8**	**2.2**	**2.1**	**2.2**
1000 Taxes on income, profits and capital gains	2.1	3.1	2.9	2.6	3.1	1.2	1.2	0.8	0.6	0.7
2000 Social security contributions	0.1	0.0	0.0	0.0	0.0	0.1	0.0	0.0	0.0	0.0
3000 Taxes on payroll and workforce	0.0	0.0	0.0	0.0	0.0	0.0	0.0	0.0	0.0	0.0
4000 Taxes on property	0.6	1.0	4.4	5.1	5.1	0.3	0.4	1.2	1.3	1.3
5000 Taxes on goods and services	0.3	0.4	0.6	0.7	0.7	0.2	0.2	0.2	0.2	0.2
6000 Other taxes	0.0	0.0	0.0	0.0	0.0	0.0	0.0	0.0	0.0	0.0
Social Security Funds										
Total tax revenue	**22.7**	**34.9**	**50.6**	**57.7**	**59.2**	**13.3**	**13.5**	**13.9**	**14.4**	**14.4**
1000 Taxes on income, profits and capital gains	0.0	0.6	1.0	1.1	1.1	0.0	0.2	0.3	0.3	0.3
2000 Social security contributions	22.4	33.3	47.9	54.7	56.2	13.1	12.9	13.1	13.7	13.7
3000 Taxes on payroll and workforce	0.0	0.0	0.0	0.0	0.0	0.0	0.0	0.0	0.0	0.0
4000 Taxes on property	0.1	0.2	0.3	0.3	0.3	0.1	0.1	0.1	0.1	0.1
5000 Taxes on goods and services	0.2	0.8	1.3	1.5	1.6	0.1	0.3	0.4	0.4	0.4
6000 Other taxes	0.0	0.0	0.0	0.0	0.0	0.0	0.0	0.0	0.0	0.0

Note: More detailed country data and country notes are available in online chapter 6: http://dx.doi.org/10.1787/9789264283183-en. Full time series can be accessed at http://oe.cd/full-time-series.
Source: Federal Ministry of Finance.

StatLink http://dx.doi.org/10.1787/888933612285

Table 4.7. **Canada, tax revenue and % of GDP by selected tax category**

	Billion CAD					% of GDP				
	1990	2000	2010	2014	2015	1990	2000	2010	2014	2015
Total tax revenue	**244.2**	**390.2**	**516.6**	**620.0**	**637.9**	**35.2**	**34.8**	**30.6**	**31.2**	**32.0**
1000 Taxes on income, profits and capital gains	**118.6**	**195.3**	**241.0**	**298.8**	**305.2**	**17.1**	**17.4**	**14.3**	**15.0**	**15.3**
1100 Of individuals	99.7	143.7	180.9	226.2	235.2	14.4	12.8	10.7	11.4	11.8
1200 Corporate	17.2	47.6	54.1	65.9	63.3	2.5	4.2	3.2	3.3	3.2
1300 Unallocable between 1100 and 1200	1.7	4.0	6.0	6.6	6.7	0.2	0.4	0.4	0.3	0.3
2000 Social security contributions	**29.7**	**53.1**	**76.8**	**93.4**	**96.2**	**4.3**	**4.7**	**4.6**	**4.7**	**4.8**
2100 Employees	10.6	21.4	30.6	37.4	38.7	1.5	1.9	1.8	1.9	1.9
2200 Employers	18.4	30.3	43.5	52.8	54.3	2.7	2.7	2.6	2.7	2.7
2300 Self-employed or non-employed	0.6	1.4	2.6	3.2	3.3	0.1	0.1	0.2	0.2	0.2
2400 Unallocable between 2100, 2200 and 2300	0.0	0.0	0.0	0.0	0.0	0.0	0.0	0.0	0.0	0.0
3000 Taxes on payroll and workforce	**5.5**	**8.0**	**10.8**	**12.8**	**13.0**	**0.8**	**0.7**	**0.6**	**0.6**	**0.7**
4000 Taxes on property	**24.5**	**37.2**	**63.7**	**72.8**	**75.6**	**3.5**	**3.3**	**3.8**	**3.7**	**3.8**
4100 Recurrent taxes on immovable property	20.2	30.2	51.7	59.7	61.1	2.9	2.7	3.1	3.0	3.1
4200 Recurrent taxes on net wealth	1.9	4.2	1.5	0.4	0.4	0.3	0.4	0.1	0.0	0.0
4300 Estate, inheritance and gift taxes	0.0	0.0	0.2	0.2	0.3	0.0	0.0	0.0	0.0	0.0
4400 Taxes on financial and capital transactions	0.0	0.0	3.1	4.1	5.0	0.0	0.0	0.2	0.2	0.3
4500 Non-recurrent taxes	2.4	2.7	7.3	8.5	8.9	0.3	0.2	0.4	0.4	0.4
4600 Other recurrent taxes on property	0.0	0.0	0.0	0.0	0.0	0.0	0.0	0.0	0.0	0.0
5000 Taxes on goods and services	**63.1**	**94.5**	**123.8**	**141.5**	**147.1**	**9.1**	**8.4**	**7.3**	**7.1**	**7.4**
5100 Taxes on production, sale, transfer, etc	59.6	88.9	116.2	133.0	138.4	8.6	7.9	6.9	6.7	6.9
5110 General taxes	34.5	55.3	72.1	84.4	87.4	5.0	4.9	4.3	4.2	4.4
5111 Value added taxes	0.0	35.9	70.7	81.6	84.2	0.0	3.2	4.2	4.1	4.2
5120 Taxes on specific goods and services	25.2	33.6	44.0	48.6	51.0	3.6	3.0	2.6	2.4	2.6
5121 Excises	14.5	18.4	23.3	25.6	26.4	2.1	1.6	1.4	1.3	1.3
5200 Taxes on use of goods and perform activities	3.5	5.6	7.6	8.5	8.7	0.5	0.5	0.5	0.4	0.4
5300 Unallocable between 5100 and 5200	0.0	0.0	0.0	0.0	0.0	0.0	0.0	0.0	0.0	0.0
6000 Other taxes	**2.9**	**2.2**	**0.6**	**0.7**	**0.7**	**0.4**	**0.2**	**0.0**	**0.0**	**0.0**
Non-wastable tax credits										
Non-wastable tax credits against 1000	..	3.4	11.1	11.2	11.1	..	0.3	0.7	0.6	0.6
Transfer component	..	3.1	10.2	10.2	10.1	..	0.3	0.6	0.5	0.5
Tax expenditure component	..	0.3	0.9	1.0	1.0	..	0.0	0.1	0.1	0.1

Note: More detailed country data and country notes are available in online chapter 5: http://dx.doi.org/10.1787/9789264283183-en. Full time series can be accessed at http://oe.cd/full-time-series.

Source: Statistics Canada.

StatLink http://dx.doi.org/10.1787/888933612304

Table 4.8. **Canada, tax revenue and % of GDP by level of government and main taxes**

	Billion CAD					% of GDP				
	1990	2000	2010	2014	2015	1990	2000	2010	2014	2015
Federal or Central government										
Total tax revenue	**101.7**	**184.4**	**212.8**	**256.2**	**261.1**	**14.7**	**16.4**	**12.6**	**12.9**	**13.1**
1000 Taxes on income, profits and capital gains	73.6	126.3	148.7	182.5	185.7	10.6	11.3	8.8	9.2	9.3
2000 Social security contributions	0.0	18.8	17.9	22.9	23.7	0.0	1.7	1.1	1.2	1.2
3000 Taxes on payroll and workforce	0.0	0.0	0.0	0.0	0.0	0.0	0.0	0.0	0.0	0.0
4000 Taxes on property	0.0	0.0	0.0	0.0	0.0	0.0	0.0	0.0	0.0	0.0
5000 Taxes on goods and services	28.1	39.4	46.2	50.8	51.8	4.0	3.5	2.7	2.6	2.6
6000 Other taxes	0.0	0.0	0.0	0.0	0.0	0.0	0.0	0.0	0.0	0.0
State/Regional										
Total tax revenue	**89.3**	**148.2**	**201.1**	**242.5**	**252.1**	**12.9**	**13.2**	**11.9**	**12.2**	**12.7**
1000 Taxes on income, profits and capital gains	44.9	69.0	92.2	116.3	119.6	6.5	6.2	5.5	5.8	6.0
2000 Social security contributions	0.0	8.3	11.7	13.6	13.8	0.0	0.7	0.7	0.7	0.7
3000 Taxes on payroll and workforce	5.5	8.0	10.8	12.8	13.0	0.8	0.7	0.6	0.6	0.7
4000 Taxes on property	4.2	8.4	9.8	10.2	11.5	0.6	0.7	0.6	0.5	0.6
5000 Taxes on goods and services	34.6	54.5	76.7	89.6	94.2	5.0	4.9	4.5	4.5	4.7
6000 Other taxes	0.0	0.0	0.0	0.0	0.0	0.0	0.0	0.0	0.0	0.0
Local government										
Total tax revenue	**23.5**	**31.5**	**55.4**	**64.4**	**65.9**	**3.4**	**2.8**	**3.3**	**3.2**	**3.3**
1000 Taxes on income, profits and capital gains	0.0	0.0	0.0	0.0	0.0	0.0	0.0	0.0	0.0	0.0
2000 Social security contributions	0.0	0.0	0.0	0.0	0.0	0.0	0.0	0.0	0.0	0.0
3000 Taxes on payroll and workforce	0.0	0.0	0.0	0.0	0.0	0.0	0.0	0.0	0.0	0.0
4000 Taxes on property	20.3	28.8	53.9	62.6	64.1	2.9	2.6	3.2	3.1	3.2
5000 Taxes on goods and services	0.4	0.6	0.9	1.1	1.1	0.1	0.1	0.1	0.1	0.1
6000 Other taxes	2.9	2.2	0.6	0.7	0.7	0.4	0.2	0.0	0.0	0.0
Social Security Funds										
Total tax revenue	**29.7**	**26.0**	**47.2**	**56.9**	**58.8**	**4.3**	**2.3**	**2.8**	**2.9**	**3.0**
1000 Taxes on income, profits and capital gains	0.0	0.0	0.0	0.0	0.0	0.0	0.0	0.0	0.0	0.0
2000 Social security contributions	29.7	26.0	47.2	56.9	58.8	4.3	2.3	2.8	2.9	3.0
3000 Taxes on payroll and workforce	0.0	0.0	0.0	0.0	0.0	0.0	0.0	0.0	0.0	0.0
4000 Taxes on property	0.0	0.0	0.0	0.0	0.0	0.0	0.0	0.0	0.0	0.0
5000 Taxes on goods and services	0.0	0.0	0.0	0.0	0.0	0.0	0.0	0.0	0.0	0.0
6000 Other taxes	0.0	0.0	0.0	0.0	0.0	0.0	0.0	0.0	0.0	0.0

Note: More detailed country data and country notes are available in online chapter 6: http://dx.doi.org/10.1787/9789264283183-en. Full time series can be accessed at http://oe.cd/full-time-series.

Source: Statistics Canada.

StatLink http://dx.doi.org/10.1787/888933612323

Table 4.9. **Chile, tax revenue and % of GDP by selected tax category**

	Billion CLP					% of GDP				
	1990	2000	2010	2014	2015	1990	2000	2010	2014	2015
Total tax revenue	**1 777.2**	**7 902.0**	**21 845.7**	**29 145.2**	**32 532.4**	**16.9**	**18.8**	**19.6**	**19.6**	**20.5**
1000 Taxes on income, profits and capital gains	**413.0**	**1 841.6**	**8 329.1**	**9 628.0**	**11 840.5**	**3.9**	**4.4**	**7.5**	**6.5**	**7.5**
1100 Of individuals	99.2	604.1	1 492.8	2 114.3	3 199.9	0.9	1.4	1.3	1.4	2.0
1200 Corporate	219.6	882.9	4 448.7	6 196.1	6 839.1	2.1	2.1	4.0	4.2	4.3
1300 Unallocable between 1100 and 1200	94.2	354.6	2 387.5	1 317.7	1 801.5	0.9	0.8	2.1	0.9	1.1
2000 Social security contributions	**159.6**	**576.8**	**1 494.0**	**2 110.1**	**2 252.5**	**1.5**	**1.4**	**1.3**	**1.4**	**1.4**
2100 Employees	154.0	553.9	1 433.2	2 044.4	2 188.6	1.5	1.3	1.3	1.4	1.4
2200 Employers	5.5	22.8	60.8	65.7	63.9	0.1	0.1	0.1	0.0	0.0
2300 Self-employed or non-employed	0.0	0.0	0.0	0.0	0.0	0.0	0.0	0.0	0.0	0.0
2400 Unallocable between 2100, 2200 and 2300	0.0	0.0	0.0	0.0	0.0	0.0	0.0	0.0	0.0	0.0
3000 Taxes on payroll and workforce	**0.0**	**0.0**	**0.0**	**0.0**	**0.0**	**0.0**	**0.0**	**0.0**	**0.0**	**0.0**
4000 Taxes on property	**109.3**	**554.0**	**898.6**	**1 229.0**	**1 421.3**	**1.0**	**1.3**	**0.8**	**0.8**	**0.9**
4100 Recurrent taxes on immovable property	60.0	302.2	662.4	924.1	1 056.9	0.6	0.7	0.6	0.6	0.7
4200 Recurrent taxes on net wealth	0.0	0.0	0.0	0.0	0.0	0.0	0.0	0.0	0.0	0.0
4300 Estate, inheritance and gift taxes	3.4	10.9	39.3	31.3	92.2	0.0	0.0	0.0	0.0	0.1
4400 Taxes on financial and capital transactions	45.9	240.9	196.9	273.6	272.1	0.4	0.6	0.2	0.2	0.2
4500 Non-recurrent taxes	0.0	0.0	0.0	0.0	0.0	0.0	0.0	0.0	0.0	0.0
4600 Other recurrent taxes on property	0.0	0.0	0.0	0.0	0.0	0.0	0.0	0.0	0.0	0.0
5000 Taxes on goods and services	**1 118.7**	**5 041.8**	**11 185.2**	**16 127.9**	**17 597.4**	**10.6**	**12.0**	**10.0**	**10.8**	**11.1**
5100 Taxes on production, sale, transfer, etc	1 074.0	4 789.8	10 532.9	15 131.7	16 515.5	10.2	11.4	9.4	10.2	10.4
5110 General taxes	664.4	3 306.4	8 399.9	12 133.7	13 274.0	6.3	7.9	7.5	8.2	8.4
5111 Value added taxes	664.4	3 306.4	8 399.9	12 133.7	13 274.0	6.3	7.9	7.5	8.2	8.4
5120 Taxes on specific goods and services	409.6	1 483.5	2 133.0	2 998.0	3 241.5	3.9	3.5	1.9	2.0	2.0
5121 Excises	166.0	816.2	1 561.2	2 224.2	2 412.8	1.6	1.9	1.4	1.5	1.5
5200 Taxes on use of goods and perform activities	44.7	251.9	652.3	996.2	1 081.9	0.4	0.6	0.6	0.7	0.7
5300 Unallocable between 5100 and 5200	0.0	0.0	0.0	0.0	0.0	0.0	0.0	0.0	0.0	0.0
6000 Other taxes	**-23.4**	**-112.2**	**-61.1**	**50.3**	**-579.3**	**-0.2**	**-0.3**	**-0.1**	**0.0**	**-0.4**
Non-wastable tax credits										
Non-wastable tax credits against 1000	0.0	0.0	0.0	184.3	175.5	0.0	0.0	0.0	0.1	0.1
Transfer component	..	..	..	140.6	129.7	..	..	..	0.1	0.1
Tax expenditure component	..	..	..	43.7	45.8	..	..	..	0.0	0.0

Note: More detailed country data and country notes are available in online chapter 5: http://dx.doi.org/10.1787/9789264283183-en. Full time series can be accessed at http://oe.cd/full-time-series.

Source: Servicio de Impuestos internos (Chile's Tax Service).

StatLink http://dx.doi.org/10.1787/888933612342

Table 4.10. **Chile, tax revenue and % of GDP by level of government and main taxes**

	Billion CLP					% of GDP				
	1990	2000	2010	2014	2015	1990	2000	2010	2014	2015
Federal or Central government										
Total tax revenue	**1 579.7**	**6 936.8**	**19 214.8**	**25 263.9**	**28 257.2**	**15.0**	**16.5**	**17.2**	**17.0**	**17.8**
1000 Taxes on income, profits and capital gains	413.0	1 841.6	8 329.1	9 628.0	11 840.5	3.9	4.4	7.5	6.5	7.5
2000 Social security contributions	66.7	232.7	371.4	431.0	434.7	0.6	0.6	0.3	0.3	0.3
3000 Taxes on payroll and workforce	0.0	0.0	0.0	0.0	0.0	0.0	0.0	0.0	0.0	0.0
4000 Taxes on property	59.7	255.4	245.0	318.7	379.6	0.6	0.6	0.2	0.2	0.2
5000 Taxes on goods and services	1 063.7	4 719.3	10 330.4	14 835.9	16 181.7	10.1	11.2	9.3	10.0	10.2
6000 Other taxes	-23.4	-112.2	-61.1	50.3	-579.3	-0.2	-0.3	-0.1	0.0	-0.4
State/Regional										
Total tax revenue	..	..	..	..	..	..	..	..	..	..
1000 Taxes on income, profits and capital gains	..	..	..	..	..	..	..	..	..	..
2000 Social security contributions	..	..	..	..	..	..	..	..	..	..
3000 Taxes on payroll and workforce	..	..	..	..	..	..	..	..	..	..
4000 Taxes on property	..	..	..	..	..	..	..	..	..	..
5000 Taxes on goods and services	..	..	..	..	..	..	..	..	..	..
6000 Other taxes	..	..	..	..	..	..	..	..	..	..
Local government										
Total tax revenue	**104.7**	**621.2**	**1 508.3**	**2 202.2**	**2 457.3**	**1.0**	**1.5**	**1.4**	**1.5**	**1.5**
1000 Taxes on income, profits and capital gains	0.0	0.0	0.0	0.0	0.0	0.0	0.0	0.0	0.0	0.0
2000 Social security contributions	0.0	0.0	0.0	0.0	0.0	0.0	0.0	0.0	0.0	0.0
3000 Taxes on payroll and workforce	0.0	0.0	0.0	0.0	0.0	0.0	0.0	0.0	0.0	0.0
4000 Taxes on property	49.6	298.7	653.6	910.2	1 041.7	0.5	0.7	0.6	0.6	0.7
5000 Taxes on goods and services	55.0	322.5	854.8	1 292.0	1 415.7	0.5	0.8	0.8	0.9	0.9
6000 Other taxes	0.0	0.0	0.0	0.0	0.0	0.0	0.0	0.0	0.0	0.0
Social Security Funds										
Total tax revenue	**92.8**	**344.0**	**1 122.6**	**1 679.1**	**1 817.8**	**0.9**	**0.8**	**1.0**	**1.1**	**1.1**
1000 Taxes on income, profits and capital gains	0.0	0.0	0.0	0.0	0.0	0.0	0.0	0.0	0.0	0.0
2000 Social security contributions	92.8	344.0	1 122.6	1 679.1	1 817.8	0.9	0.8	1.0	1.1	1.1
3000 Taxes on payroll and workforce	0.0	0.0	0.0	0.0	0.0	0.0	0.0	0.0	0.0	0.0
4000 Taxes on property	0.0	0.0	0.0	0.0	0.0	0.0	0.0	0.0	0.0	0.0
5000 Taxes on goods and services	0.0	0.0	0.0	0.0	0.0	0.0	0.0	0.0	0.0	0.0
6000 Other taxes	0.0	0.0	0.0	0.0	0.0	0.0	0.0	0.0	0.0	0.0

Note: More detailed country data and country notes are available in online chapter 6: http://dx.doi.org/10.1787/9789264283183-en. Full time series can be accessed at http://oe.cd/full-time-series.

Source: Servicio de Impuestos internos (Chile's Tax Service).

StatLink http://dx.doi.org/10.1787/888933612361

Table 4.11. Czech Republic, tax revenue and % of GDP by selected tax category

	Billion CZK					% of GDP				
	1990	2000	2010	2014	2015	1990	2000	2010	2014	2015
Total tax revenue	..	**771.6**	**1 286.9**	**1 427.6**	**1 532.5**	..	**32.4**	**32.5**	**33.1**	**33.3**
1000 Taxes on income, profits and capital gains	..	**175.8**	**259.9**	**305.7**	**329.8**	..	**7.4**	**6.6**	**7.1**	**7.2**
1100 Of individuals	..	99.7	131.7	153.8	164.7	..	4.2	3.3	3.6	3.6
1200 Corporate	..	76.2	128.2	151.9	165.1	..	3.2	3.2	3.5	3.6
1300 Unallocable between 1100 and 1200	..	0.0	0.0	0.0	0.0	..	0.0	0.0	0.0	0.0
2000 Social security contributions	..	**341.5**	**576.0**	**625.5**	**659.7**	..	**14.4**	**14.5**	**14.5**	**14.4**
2100 Employees	..	77.3	116.8	126.9	133.9	..	3.2	2.9	2.9	2.9
2200 Employers	..	220.2	363.1	396.0	417.8	..	9.3	9.2	9.2	9.1
2300 Self-employed or non-employed	..	44.1	96.1	102.6	108.1	..	1.9	2.4	2.4	2.4
2400 Unallocable between 2100, 2200 and 2300	..	0.0	0.0	0.0	0.0	..	0.0	0.0	0.0	0.0
3000 Taxes on payroll and workforce	..	**0.0**	**0.0**	**0.0**	**0.0**	..	**0.0**	**0.0**	**0.0**	**0.0**
4000 Taxes on property	..	**10.9**	**16.4**	**19.5**	**21.9**	..	**0.5**	**0.4**	**0.5**	**0.5**
4100 Recurrent taxes on immovable property	..	4.5	8.8	9.9	10.3	..	0.2	0.2	0.2	0.2
4200 Recurrent taxes on net wealth	..	0.0	0.0	0.0	0.0	..	0.0	0.0	0.0	0.0
4300 Estate, inheritance and gift taxes	..	0.6	0.2	0.0	0.0	..	0.0	0.0	0.0	0.0
4400 Taxes on financial and capital transactions	..	5.8	7.4	9.6	11.6	..	0.2	0.2	0.2	0.3
4500 Non-recurrent taxes	..	0.0	0.0	0.0	0.0	..	0.0	0.0	0.0	0.0
4600 Other recurrent taxes on property	..	0.0	0.0	0.0	0.0	..	0.0	0.0	0.0	0.0
5000 Taxes on goods and services	..	**243.0**	**427.8**	**469.8**	**512.8**	..	**10.2**	**10.8**	**10.9**	**11.2**
5100 Taxes on production, sale, transfer, etc	..	226.4	402.1	444.7	487.4	..	9.5	10.1	10.3	10.6
5110 General taxes	..	141.2	263.5	319.5	333.3	..	5.9	6.6	7.4	7.3
5111 Value added taxes	..	141.2	263.5	319.5	333.3	..	5.9	6.6	7.4	7.3
5120 Taxes on specific goods and services	..	85.1	138.6	125.2	154.1	..	3.6	3.5	2.9	3.4
5121 Excises	..	71.4	138.4	124.9	153.8	..	3.0	3.5	2.9	3.3
5200 Taxes on use of goods and perform activities	..	16.6	25.7	25.2	25.5	..	0.7	0.7	0.6	0.6
5300 Unallocable between 5100 and 5200	..	0.0	0.0	0.0	0.0	..	0.0	0.0	0.0	0.0
6000 Other taxes	..	**0.4**	**0.1**	**0.1**	**0.4**	..	**0.0**	**0.0**	**0.0**	**0.0**
Non-wastable tax credits										
Non-wastable tax credits against 1000	..	0.0	28.5	29.0	32.1	..	0.0	0.7	0.7	0.7
Transfer component	..	..	7.8	8.3	8.9	..	..	0.2	0.2	0.2
Tax expenditure component	..	..	20.7	20.7	23.2	..	..	0.5	0.5	0.5

Note: More detailed country data and country notes are available in online chapter 5: http://dx.doi.org/10.1787/9789264283183-en. Full time series can be accessed at http://oe.cd/full-time-series.

Source: Ministry of Finance, Economic Department.

StatLink http://dx.doi.org/10.1787/888933612380

Table 4.12. **Czech Republic, tax revenue and % of GDP by level of government and main taxes**

	Billion CZK					% of GDP				
	1990	2000	2010	2014	2015	1990	2000	2010	2014	2015
Federal or Central government										
Total tax revenue	..	**423.4**	**687.3**	**777.4**	**846.8**	..	**17.8**	**17.3**	**18.0**	**18.4**
1000 Taxes on income, profits and capital gains	..	175.8	259.9	305.7	329.8	..	7.4	6.6	7.1	7.2
2000 Social security contributions	..	0.0	0.0	0.0	0.0	..	0.0	0.0	0.0	0.0
3000 Taxes on payroll and workforce	..	0.0	0.0	0.0	0.0	..	0.0	0.0	0.0	0.0
4000 Taxes on property	..	6.4	7.6	9.6	11.6	..	0.3	0.2	0.2	0.3
5000 Taxes on goods and services	..	241.0	419.6	462.0	505.1	..	10.1	10.6	10.7	11.0
6000 Other taxes	..	0.1	0.1	0.1	0.4	..	0.0	0.0	0.0	0.0
State/Regional										
Total tax revenue	..	..	..	..	..	..	..	..	..	..
1000 Taxes on income, profits and capital gains	..	..	..	..	..	..	..	..	..	..
2000 Social security contributions	..	..	..	..	..	..	..	..	..	..
3000 Taxes on payroll and workforce	..	..	..	..	..	..	..	..	..	..
4000 Taxes on property	..	..	..	..	..	..	..	..	..	..
5000 Taxes on goods and services	..	..	..	..	..	..	..	..	..	..
6000 Other taxes	..	..	..	..	..	..	..	..	..	..
Local government										
Total tax revenue	..	**6.7**	**17.0**	**17.7**	**18.1**	..	**0.3**	**0.4**	**0.4**	**0.4**
1000 Taxes on income, profits and capital gains	..	0.0	0.0	0.0	0.0	..	0.0	0.0	0.0	0.0
2000 Social security contributions	..	0.0	0.0	0.0	0.0	..	0.0	0.0	0.0	0.0
3000 Taxes on payroll and workforce	..	0.0	0.0	0.0	0.0	..	0.0	0.0	0.0	0.0
4000 Taxes on property	..	4.5	8.7	9.9	10.3	..	0.2	0.2	0.2	0.2
5000 Taxes on goods and services	..	2.0	8.2	7.8	7.7	..	0.1	0.2	0.2	0.2
6000 Other taxes	..	0.3	0.0	0.0*	0.0	..	0.0	0.0	0.0	0.0
Social Security Funds										
Total tax revenue	..	**341.5**	**576.0**	**625.5**	**659.7**	..	**14.4**	**14.5**	**14.5**	**14.4**
1000 Taxes on income, profits and capital gains	..	0.0	0.0	0.0	0.0	..	0.0	0.0	0.0	0.0
2000 Social security contributions	..	341.5	576.0	625.5	659.7	..	14.4	14.5	14.5	14.4
3000 Taxes on payroll and workforce	..	0.0	0.0	0.0	0.0	..	0.0	0.0	0.0	0.0
4000 Taxes on property	..	0.0	0.0	0.0	0.0	..	0.0	0.0	0.0	0.0
5000 Taxes on goods and services	..	0.0	0.0	0.0	0.0	..	0.0	0.0	0.0	0.0
6000 Other taxes	..	0.0	0.0	0.0	0.0	..	0.0	0.0	0.0	0.0

Note: More detailed country data and country notes are available in online chapter 6: http://dx.doi.org/10.1787/9789264283183-en. Full time series can be accessed at http://oe.cd/full-time-series.
Source: Ministry of Finance, Economic Department.

StatLink http://dx.doi.org/10.1787/888933612399

Table 4.13. **Denmark, tax revenue and % of GDP by selected tax category**

	Billion DKK					% of GDP				
	1990	2000	2010	2014	2015	1990	2000	2010	2014	2015
Total tax revenue	**379.8**	**622.0**	**810.5**	**960.6**	**930.6**	**44.4**	**46.9**	**44.8**	**48.6**	**45.9**
1000 Taxes on income, profits and capital gains	**232.3**	**382.1**	**498.1**	**626.5**	**587.6**	**27.1**	**28.8**	**27.5**	**31.7**	**29.0**
1100 Of individuals	205.2	327.5	420.9	519.7	513.2	24.0	24.7	23.2	26.3	25.3
1200 Corporate	14.6	42.1	40.9	54.8	52.0	1.7	3.2	2.3	2.8	2.6
1300 Unallocable between 1100 and 1200	12.5	12.4	36.4	52.1	22.4	1.5	0.9	2.0	2.6	1.1
2000 Social security contributions	**0.1**	**8.4**	**1.8**	**1.4**	**1.3**	**0.0**	**0.6**	**0.1**	**0.1**	**0.1**
2100 Employees	0.1	8.2	0.9	0.7	0.8	0.0	0.6	0.1	0.0	0.0
2200 Employers	0.0	0.2	0.9	0.7	0.5	0.0	0.0	0.1	0.0	0.0
2300 Self-employed or non-employed	0.0	0.0	0.0	0.0	0.0	0.0	0.0	0.0	0.0	0.0
2400 Unallocable between 2100, 2200 and 2300	0.0	0.0	0.0	0.0	0.0	0.0	0.0	0.0	0.0	0.0
3000 Taxes on payroll and workforce	**2.5**	**2.3**	**4.1**	**6.2**	**5.8**	**0.3**	**0.2**	**0.2**	**0.3**	**0.3**
4000 Taxes on property	**16.2**	**20.7**	**33.4**	**35.6**	**38.4**	**1.9**	**1.6**	**1.8**	**1.8**	**1.9**
4100 Recurrent taxes on immovable property	8.8	13.5	24.1	26.7	27.5	1.0	1.0	1.3	1.3	1.4
4200 Recurrent taxes on net wealth	0.9	0.0	0.0	0.0	0.0	0.1	0.0	0.0	0.0	0.0
4300 Estate, inheritance and gift taxes	2.2	2.9	3.6	3.8	5.1	0.3	0.2	0.2	0.2	0.3
4400 Taxes on financial and capital transactions	4.1	4.2	5.7	5.2	5.8	0.5	0.3	0.3	0.3	0.3
4500 Non-recurrent taxes	0.1	0.1	0.0	0.0	0.0	0.0	0.0	0.0	0.0	0.0
4600 Other recurrent taxes on property	0.0	0.0	0.0	0.0	0.0	0.0	0.0	0.0	0.0	0.0
5000 Taxes on goods and services	**128.8**	**205.9**	**269.6**	**287.6**	**293.9**	**15.1**	**15.5**	**14.9**	**14.5**	**14.5**
5100 Taxes on production, sale, transfer, etc	122.9	195.1	250.0	265.2	270.7	14.4	14.7	13.8	13.4	13.4
5110 General taxes	80.1	121.6	170.8	182.6	186.1	9.4	9.2	9.4	9.2	9.2
5111 Value added taxes	71.7	121.6	170.8	182.6	186.1	8.4	9.2	9.4	9.2	9.2
5120 Taxes on specific goods and services	42.7	73.5	79.1	82.7	84.6	5.0	5.5	4.4	4.2	4.2
5121 Excises	38.1	68.8	73.7	78.4	80.2	4.5	5.2	4.1	4.0	4.0
5200 Taxes on use of goods and perform activities	4.4	7.4	14.7	15.7	16.2	0.5	0.6	0.8	0.8	0.8
5300 Unallocable between 5100 and 5200	1.6	3.4	4.9	6.7	7.0	0.2	0.3	0.3	0.3	0.3
6000 Other taxes	**0.0**	**0.4**	**0.2**	**0.2**	**0.3**	**0.0**	**0.0**	**0.0**	**0.0**	**0.0**
Non-wastable tax credits										
Non-wastable tax credits against 1000	..	..	5.0	5.5	4.2	..	..	0.3	0.3	0.2
Transfer component	..	..	0.2	0.3	0.2	..	..	0.0	0.0	0.0
Tax expenditure component	..	..	4.7	5.3	4.0	..	..	0.3	0.3	0.2

Note: More detailed country data and country notes are available in online chapter 5: http://dx.doi.org/10.1787/9789264283183-en. Full time series can be accessed at http://oe.cd/full-time-series.

The total tax revenue has been reduced by the amount of any capital transfer that represents uncollected taxes. The capital transfer has been allocated between tax headings in proportion to the reported tax revenue. Therefore, the tax revenue amounts are different to those reported in the detailed country data available in online chapter 5.

Source: Danmarks Statistik.

StatLink http://dx.doi.org/10.1787/888933612418

Table 4.14. **Denmark, tax revenue and % of GDP by level of government and main taxes**

	Billion DKK					% of GDP				
	1990	2000	2010	2014	2015	1990	2000	2010	2014	2015
Federal or Central government										
Total tax revenue	**259.5**	**420.6**	**589.0**	**715.7**	**677.7**	**30.3**	**31.7**	**32.5**	**36.2**	**33.4**
1000 Taxes on income, profits and capital gains	123.7	204.2	305.4	413.9	368.4	14.5	15.4	16.9	20.9	18.2
2000 Social security contributions	0.1	1.4	0.9	0.7	0.8	0.0	0.1	0.1	0.0	0.0
3000 Taxes on payroll and workforce	2.5	2.2	4.1	6.2	5.7	0.3	0.2	0.2	0.3	0.3
4000 Taxes on property	7.5	7.1	9.3	8.9	10.8	0.9	0.5	0.5	0.5	0.5
5000 Taxes on goods and services	125.8	205.3	269.1	285.8	291.7	14.7	15.5	14.9	14.5	14.4
6000 Other taxes	0.0	0.4	0.2	0.2	0.3	0.0	0.0	0.0	0.0	0.0
State/Regional										
Total tax revenue	..	..	..	..	..	..	..	..	..	..
1000 Taxes on income, profits and capital gains	..	..	..	..	..	..	..	..	..	..
2000 Social security contributions	..	..	..	..	..	..	..	..	..	..
3000 Taxes on payroll and workforce	..	..	..	..	..	..	..	..	..	..
4000 Taxes on property	..	..	..	..	..	..	..	..	..	..
5000 Taxes on goods and services	..	..	..	..	..	..	..	..	..	..
6000 Other taxes	..	..	..	..	..	..	..	..	..	..
Local government										
Total tax revenue	**117.6**	**191.7**	**217.3**	**241.2**	**249.0**	**13.8**	**14.4**	**12.0**	**12.2**	**12.3**
1000 Taxes on income, profits and capital gains	108.9	178.1	193.1	214.0	220.9	12.7	13.4	10.7	10.8	10.9
2000 Social security contributions	0.0	0.0	0.0	0.0	0.0	0.0	0.0	0.0	0.0	0.0
3000 Taxes on payroll and workforce	0.0	0.0	0.0	0.0	0.0	0.0	0.0	0.0	0.0	0.0
4000 Taxes on property	8.7	13.6	24.2	27.2	28.1	1.0	1.0	1.3	1.4	1.4
5000 Taxes on goods and services	0.0	0.0	0.0	0.0	0.0	0.0	0.0	0.0	0.0	0.0
6000 Other taxes	0.0	0.0	0.0	0.0	0.0	0.0	0.0	0.0	0.0	0.0
Social Security Funds										
Total tax revenue	**0.0**	**7.1**	**0.9**	**0.7**	**0.5**	**0.0**	**0.5**	**0.1**	**0.0**	**0.0**
1000 Taxes on income, profits and capital gains	0.0	0.0	0.0	0.0	0.0	0.0	0.0	0.0	0.0	0.0
2000 Social security contributions	0.0	7.1	0.9	0.7	0.5	0.0	0.5	0.1	0.0	0.0
3000 Taxes on payroll and workforce	0.0	0.0	0.0	0.0	0.0	0.0	0.0	0.0	0.0	0.0
4000 Taxes on property	0.0	0.0	0.0	0.0	0.0	0.0	0.0	0.0	0.0	0.0
5000 Taxes on goods and services	0.0	0.0	0.0	0.0	0.0	0.0	0.0	0.0	0.0	0.0
6000 Other taxes	0.0	0.0	0.0	0.0	0.0	0.0	0.0	0.0	0.0	0.0

Note: More detailed country data and country notes are available in online chapter 6: http://dx.doi.org/10.1787/9789264283183-en. Full time series can be accessed at http://oe.cd/full-time-series.

The total tax revenue has been reduced by the amount of any capital transfer that represents uncollected taxes. The capital transfer has been allocated between tax headings in proportion to the reported tax revenue. Therefore, the tax revenue amounts are different to those reported in the detailed country data available in online chapter 6.

Source: Danmarks Statistik.

StatLink http://dx.doi.org/10.1787/888933612437

Table 4.15. **Estonia, tax revenue and % of GDP by selected tax category**

	Billion EUR					% of GDP				
	1990	2000	2010	2014	2015	1990	2000	2010	2014	2015
Total tax revenue	..	**1.9**	**4.9**	**6.5**	**6.9**	..	**31.1**	**33.3**	**32.8**	**33.9**
1000 Taxes on income, profits and capital gains	..	**0.5**	**1.0**	**1.5**	**1.6**	..	**7.7**	**6.6**	**7.5**	**7.9**
1100 Of individuals	..	0.4	0.8	1.1	1.2	..	6.8	5.3	5.7	5.8
1200 Corporate	..	0.1	0.2	0.3	0.4	..	0.9	1.3	1.7	2.1
1300 Unallocable between 1100 and 1200	..	0.0	0.0	0.0	0.0	..	0.0	0.0	0.0	0.0
2000 Social security contributions	..	**0.7**	**1.9**	**2.2**	**2.3**	..	**10.9**	**12.8**	**11.0**	**11.3**
2100 Employees	..	0.0	0.1	0.1	0.1	..	0.0	0.8	0.6	0.5
2200 Employers	..	0.7	1.7	2.0	2.2	..	10.7	11.8	10.3	10.7
2300 Self-employed or non-employed	..	0.0	0.0	0.0	0.0	..	0.2	0.1	0.1	0.1
2400 Unallocable between 2100, 2200 and 2300	..	0.0	0.0	0.0	0.0	..	0.0	0.0	0.0	0.0
3000 Taxes on payroll and workforce	..	**0.0**	**0.0**	**0.0**	**0.0**	..	**0.0**	**0.0**	**0.0**	**0.0**
4000 Taxes on property	..	**0.0**	**0.1**	**0.1**	**0.1**	..	**0.4**	**0.3**	**0.3**	**0.3**
4100 Recurrent taxes on immovable property	..	0.0	0.1	0.1	0.1	..	0.4	0.3	0.3	0.3
4200 Recurrent taxes on net wealth	..	0.0	0.0	0.0	0.0	..	0.0	0.0	0.0	0.0
4300 Estate, inheritance and gift taxes	..	0.0	0.0	0.0	0.0	..	0.0	0.0	0.0	0.0
4400 Taxes on financial and capital transactions	..	0.0	0.0	0.0	0.0	..	0.0	0.0	0.0	0.0
4500 Non-recurrent taxes	..	0.0	0.0	0.0	0.0	..	0.0	0.0	0.0	0.0
4600 Other recurrent taxes on property	..	0.0	0.0	0.0	0.0	..	0.0	0.0	0.0	0.0
5000 Taxes on goods and services	..	**0.7**	**2.0**	**2.7**	**2.9**	..	**12.1**	**13.4**	**13.8**	**14.2**
5100 Taxes on production, sale, transfer, etc	..	0.7	1.9	2.6	2.8	..	11.7	13.0	13.2	13.8
5110 General taxes	..	0.5	1.3	1.7	1.9	..	8.4	8.6	8.7	9.2
5111 Value added taxes	..	0.5	1.3	1.7	1.9	..	8.4	8.5	8.7	9.2
5120 Taxes on specific goods and services	..	0.2	0.7	0.9	0.9	..	3.3	4.4	4.5	4.6
5121 Excises	..	0.2	0.6	0.8	0.9	..	3.0	4.2	4.3	4.3
5200 Taxes on use of goods and perform activities	..	0.0	0.1	0.1	0.1	..	0.4	0.4	0.6	0.4
5300 Unallocable between 5100 and 5200	..	0.0	0.0	0.0	0.0	..	0.0	0.0	0.0	0.0
6000 Other taxes	..	**0.0**	**0.0**	**0.0**	**0.0**	..	**0.0**	**0.0**	**0.0**	**0.0**
Non-wastable tax credits										
Non-wastable tax credits against 1000	..	..	..	..	..	..	..	..	..	..
Transfer component	..	..	..	..	..	..	..	..	..	..
Tax expenditure component	..	..	..	..	..	..	..	..	..	..

Note: More detailed country data and country notes are available in online chapter 5: http://dx.doi.org/10.1787/9789264283183-en. Full time series can be accessed at http://oe.cd/full-time-series.
Source: Statistics Estonia.

StatLink http://dx.doi.org/10.1787/888933612456

Table 4.16. **Estonia, tax revenue and % of GDP by level of government and main taxes**

	Billion EUR					% of GDP				
	1990	2000	2010	2014	2015	1990	2000	2010	2014	2015
Federal or Central government										
Total tax revenue	..	**1.6**	**3.9**	**5.3**	**5.6**	..	**26.3**	**26.7**	**26.9**	**27.9**
1000 Taxes on income, profits and capital gains	..	0.5	1.0	1.5	1.6	..	7.7	6.6	7.5	7.9
2000 Social security contributions	..	0.4	1.0	1.1	1.2	..	6.6	6.8	5.6	5.8
3000 Taxes on payroll and workforce	..	0.0	0.0	0.0	0.0	..	0.0	0.0	0.0	0.0
4000 Taxes on property	..	0.0	0.0	0.0	0.0	..	0.0	0.0	0.0	0.0
5000 Taxes on goods and services	..	0.7	2.0	2.7	2.9	..	12.0	13.3	13.8	14.1
6000 Other taxes	..	0.0	0.0	0.0	0.0	..	0.0	0.0	0.0	0.0
State/Regional										
Total tax revenue	..	..	..	..	..	..	..	..	..	..
1000 Taxes on income, profits and capital gains	..	..	..	..	..	..	..	..	..	..
2000 Social security contributions	..	..	..	..	..	..	..	..	..	..
3000 Taxes on payroll and workforce	..	..	..	..	..	..	..	..	..	..
4000 Taxes on property	..	..	..	..	..	..	..	..	..	..
5000 Taxes on goods and services	..	..	..	..	..	..	..	..	..	..
6000 Other taxes	..	..	..	..	..	..	..	..	..	..
Local government										
Total tax revenue	..	**0.0**	**0.1**	**0.1**	**0.1**	..	**0.5**	**0.5**	**0.4**	**0.3**
1000 Taxes on income, profits and capital gains	..	0.0	0.0	0.0	0.0	..	0.0	0.0	0.0	0.0
2000 Social security contributions	..	0.0	0.0	0.0	0.0	..	0.0	0.0	0.0	0.0
3000 Taxes on payroll and workforce	..	0.0	0.0	0.0	0.0	..	0.0	0.0	0.0	0.0
4000 Taxes on property	..	0.0	0.1	0.1	0.1	..	0.4	0.3	0.3	0.3
5000 Taxes on goods and services	..	0.0	0.0	0.0	0.0	..	0.1	0.1	0.1	0.1
6000 Other taxes	..	0.0	0.0	0.0	0.0	..	0.0	0.0	0.0	0.0
Social Security Funds										
Total tax revenue	..	**0.3**	**0.9**	**1.1**	**1.1**	..	**4.3**	**5.9**	**5.4**	**5.5**
1000 Taxes on income, profits and capital gains	..	0.0	0.0	0.0	0.0	..	0.0	0.0	0.0	0.0
2000 Social security contributions	..	0.3	0.9	1.1	1.1	..	4.3	5.9	5.4	5.5
3000 Taxes on payroll and workforce	..	0.0	0.0	0.0	0.0	..	0.0	0.0	0.0	0.0
4000 Taxes on property	..	0.0	0.0	0.0	0.0	..	0.0	0.0	0.0	0.0
5000 Taxes on goods and services	..	0.0	0.0	0.0	0.0	..	0.0	0.0	0.0	0.0
6000 Other taxes	..	0.0	0.0	0.0	0.0	..	0.0	0.0	0.0	0.0

Note: More detailed country data and country notes are available in online chapter 6: http://dx.doi.org/10.1787/9789264283183-en. Full time series can be accessed at http://oe.cd/full-time-series.

Source: Statistics Estonia.

StatLink http://dx.doi.org/10.1787/888933612475

Table 4.17. **Finland, tax revenue and % of GDP by selected tax category**

	Billion EUR					% of GDP				
	1990	2000	2010	2014	2015	1990	2000	2010	2014	2015
Total tax revenue	**39.1**	**62.4**	**76.3**	**90.0**	**92.1**	**42.9**	**45.8**	**40.8**	**43.8**	**43.9**
1000 Taxes on income, profits and capital gains	**15.3**	**26.9**	**27.1**	**31.5**	**32.4**	**16.8**	**19.7**	**14.5**	**15.3**	**15.4**
1100 Of individuals	13.6	19.1	22.5	27.5	27.8	14.9	14.0	12.1	13.4	13.3
1200 Corporate	1.8	7.8	4.6	4.0	4.5	1.9	5.7	2.4	1.9	2.2
1300 Unallocable between 1100 and 1200	0.0	0.0	0.0	0.0	0.0	0.0	0.0	0.0	0.0	0.0
2000 Social security contributions	**10.0**	**15.8**	**22.6**	**26.0**	**26.6**	**11.0**	**11.6**	**12.1**	**12.7**	**12.7**
2100 Employees	1.2	2.9	4.7	6.1	6.4	1.3	2.1	2.5	3.0	3.0
2200 Employers	8.1	11.6	16.0	17.9	18.2	8.9	8.5	8.6	8.7	8.7
2300 Self-employed or non-employed	0.7	1.3	1.9	2.0	2.0	0.8	0.9	1.0	1.0	1.0
2400 Unallocable between 2100, 2200 and 2300	0.0	0.0	0.0	0.0	0.0	0.0	0.0	0.0	0.0	0.0
3000 Taxes on payroll and workforce	**0.0**	**0.0**	**0.0**	**0.0**	**0.0**	**0.0**	**0.0**	**0.0**	**0.0**	**0.0**
4000 Taxes on property	**1.0**	**1.5**	**2.1**	**2.7**	**3.0**	**1.1**	**1.1**	**1.1**	**1.3**	**1.4**
4100 Recurrent taxes on immovable property	0.1	0.6	1.2	1.5	1.6	0.1	0.4	0.6	0.7	0.8
4200 Recurrent taxes on net wealth	0.0	0.2	0.0	0.0	0.0	0.0	0.1	0.0	0.0	0.0
4300 Estate, inheritance and gift taxes	0.1	0.4	0.4	0.5	0.6	0.2	0.3	0.2	0.2	0.3
4400 Taxes on financial and capital transactions	0.7	0.4	0.5	0.7	0.8	0.8	0.3	0.3	0.3	0.4
4500 Non-recurrent taxes	0.0	0.0	0.0	0.0	0.0	0.0	0.0	0.0	0.0	0.0
4600 Other recurrent taxes on property	0.0	0.0	0.0	0.0	0.0	0.0	0.0	0.0	0.0	0.0
5000 Taxes on goods and services	**12.7**	**18.1**	**24.3**	**29.6**	**29.8**	**14.0**	**13.3**	**13.0**	**14.4**	**14.2**
5100 Taxes on production, sale, transfer, etc	12.6	17.7	23.5	28.5	28.7	13.8	13.0	12.6	13.9	13.7
5110 General taxes	7.5	10.9	15.5	18.9	19.0	8.3	8.0	8.3	9.2	9.1
5111 Value added taxes	7.5	10.9	15.5	18.9	19.0	8.3	8.0	8.3	9.2	9.1
5120 Taxes on specific goods and services	5.0	6.8	8.0	9.6	9.8	5.5	5.0	4.3	4.7	4.7
5121 Excises	3.8	5.6	6.3	7.4	7.7	4.2	4.1	3.4	3.6	3.7
5200 Taxes on use of goods and perform activities	0.2	0.4	0.8	1.1	1.1	0.2	0.3	0.4	0.5	0.5
5300 Unallocable between 5100 and 5200	0.0	0.0	0.0	0.0	0.0	0.0	0.0	0.0	0.0	0.0
6000 Other taxes	**0.0**	**0.0**	**0.1**	**0.1**	**0.1**	**0.1**	**0.0**	**0.0**	**0.0**	**0.0**
Non-wastable tax credits										
Non-wastable tax credits against 1000	..	..	..	..	..	..	..	..	..	..
Transfer component	..	..	..	..	..	..	..	..	..	..
Tax expenditure component	..	..	..	..	..	..	..	..	..	..

Note: More detailed country data and country notes are available in online chapter 5: http://dx.doi.org/10.1787/9789264283183-en. Full time series can be accessed at http://oe.cd/full-time-series.

Source: Bulletin of Statistics; Central Statistical Office (for Central Government revenues); the Annual report of the National Pension Institute and Official Statistics of Finland Series XXIIA published by the Ministry and Social Affairs (for the Social Security and private pension respectively); supplementary information from unpublished sources.

StatLink http://dx.doi.org/10.1787/888933612494

Table 4.18. Finland, tax revenue and % of GDP by level of government and main taxes

	Billion EUR					% of GDP				
	1990	2000	2010	2014	2015	1990	2000	2010	2014	2015
Federal or Central government										
Total tax revenue	**20.7**	**33.1**	**35.0**	**42.7**	**43.3**	**22.7**	**24.3**	**18.7**	**20.8**	**20.7**
1000 Taxes on income, profits and capital gains	7.0	14.0	9.8	11.8	12.1	7.7	10.3	5.2	5.8	5.8
2000 Social security contributions	0.0	0.0	0.0	0.0	0.0	0.0	0.0	0.0	0.0	0.0
3000 Taxes on payroll and workforce	0.0	0.0	0.0	0.0	0.0	0.0	0.0	0.0	0.0	0.0
4000 Taxes on property	0.9	0.9	0.9	1.2	1.4	1.0	0.7	0.5	0.6	0.7
5000 Taxes on goods and services	12.7	18.1	24.3	29.6	29.7	14.0	13.3	13.0	14.4	14.2
6000 Other taxes	0.0	0.0	0.1	0.1	0.1	0.1	0.0	0.0	0.0	0.0
State/Regional										
Total tax revenue	..	..	..	..	..	..	..	..	..	..
1000 Taxes on income, profits and capital gains	..	..	..	..	..	..	..	..	..	..
2000 Social security contributions	..	..	..	..	..	..	..	..	..	..
3000 Taxes on payroll and workforce	..	..	..	..	..	..	..	..	..	..
4000 Taxes on property	..	..	..	..	..	..	..	..	..	..
5000 Taxes on goods and services	..	..	..	..	..	..	..	..	..	..
6000 Other taxes	..	..	..	..	..	..	..	..	..	..
Local government										
Total tax revenue	**8.4**	**13.5**	**18.5**	**21.2**	**21.9**	**9.2**	**9.9**	**9.9**	**10.3**	**10.4**
1000 Taxes on income, profits and capital gains	8.3	12.9	17.3	19.6	20.2	9.1	9.5	9.3	9.6	9.7
2000 Social security contributions	0.0	0.0	0.0	0.0	0.0	0.0	0.0	0.0	0.0	0.0
3000 Taxes on payroll and workforce	0.0	0.0	0.0	0.0	0.0	0.0	0.0	0.0	0.0	0.0
4000 Taxes on property	0.1	0.6	1.2	1.5	1.6	0.1	0.4	0.6	0.7	0.8
5000 Taxes on goods and services	0.0	0.0	0.0	0.0	0.0	0.0	0.0	0.0	0.0	0.0
6000 Other taxes	0.0	0.0	0.0	0.0	0.0	0.0	0.0	0.0	0.0	0.0
Social Security Funds										
Total tax revenue	**10.0**	**15.7**	**22.6**	**26.0**	**26.6**	**11.0**	**11.6**	**12.1**	**12.7**	**12.7**
1000 Taxes on income, profits and capital gains	0.0	0.0	0.0	0.0	0.0	0.0	0.0	0.0	0.0	0.0
2000 Social security contributions	10.0	15.7	22.6	26.0	26.6	11.0	11.6	12.1	12.7	12.7
3000 Taxes on payroll and workforce	0.0	0.0	0.0	0.0	0.0	0.0	0.0	0.0	0.0	0.0
4000 Taxes on property	0.0	0.0	0.0	0.0	0.0	0.0	0.0	0.0	0.0	0.0
5000 Taxes on goods and services	0.0	0.0	0.0	0.0	0.0	0.0	0.0	0.0	0.0	0.0
6000 Other taxes	0.0	0.0	0.0	0.0	0.0	0.0	0.0	0.0	0.0	0.0

Note: More detailed country data and country notes are available in online chapter 6: http://dx.doi.org/10.1787/9789264283183-en. Full time series can be accessed at http://oe.cd/full-time-series.

Source: Bulletin of Statistics; Central Statistical Office (for Central Government revenues); the Annual report of the National Pension Institute and Official Statistics of Finland Series XXIIA published by the Ministry and Social Affairs (for the Social Security and private pension respectively); supplementary information from unpublished sources.

StatLink http://dx.doi.org/10.1787/888933612513

Table 4.19. **France, tax revenue and % of GDP by selected tax category**

	Billion EUR					% of GDP				
	1990	2000	2010	2014	2015	1990	2000	2010	2014	2015
Total tax revenue	**433.8**	**639.4**	**838.8**	**973.7**	**992.1**	**41.0**	**43.1**	**42.0**	**45.3**	**45.2**
1000 Taxes on income, profits and capital gains	**69.6**	**159.4**	**190.0**	**232.1**	**233.2**	**6.6**	**10.7**	**9.5**	**10.8**	**10.6**
1100 Of individuals	46.3	115.2	143.4	182.4	187.3	4.4	7.8	7.2	8.5	8.5
1200 Corporate	23.1	44.2	46.7	49.6	45.9	2.2	3.0	2.3	2.3	2.1
1300 Unallocable between 1100 and 1200	0.3	0.0	0.0	0.0	0.0	0.0	0.0	0.0	0.0	0.0
2000 Social security contributions	**191.1**	**230.5**	**322.0**	**363.8**	**367.9**	**18.1**	**15.5**	**16.1**	**16.9**	**16.8**
2100 Employees	57.3	57.3	77.8	90.4	93.1	5.4	3.9	3.9	4.2	4.2
2200 Employers	118.1	158.5	218.4	244.6	246.5	11.2	10.7	10.9	11.4	11.2
2300 Self-employed or non-employed	15.7	14.6	25.7	28.7	28.3	1.5	1.0	1.3	1.3	1.3
2400 Unallocable between 2100, 2200 and 2300	0.0	0.0	0.0	0.0	0.0	0.0	0.0	0.0	0.0	0.0
3000 Taxes on payroll and workforce	**8.3**	**14.8**	**26.8**	**34.2**	**34.4**	**0.8**	**1.0**	**1.3**	**1.6**	**1.6**
4000 Taxes on property	**27.4**	**43.8**	**70.2**	**83.3**	**88.8**	**2.6**	**2.9**	**3.5**	**3.9**	**4.0**
4100 Recurrent taxes on immovable property	14.8	27.2	47.3	55.1	57.1	1.4	1.8	2.4	2.6	2.6
4200 Recurrent taxes on net wealth	2.6	2.4	4.4	5.3	5.2	0.2	0.2	0.2	0.2	0.2
4300 Estate, inheritance and gift taxes	4.1	6.9	7.7	10.3	12.2	0.4	0.5	0.4	0.5	0.6
4400 Taxes on financial and capital transactions	5.9	7.3	10.8	12.6	14.3	0.6	0.5	0.5	0.6	0.7
4500 Non-recurrent taxes	0.0	0.0	0.0	0.0	0.0	0.0	0.0	0.0	0.0	0.0
4600 Other recurrent taxes on property	0.0	0.0	0.0	0.0	0.0	0.0	0.0	0.0	0.0	0.0
5000 Taxes on goods and services	**123.2**	**165.6**	**208.9**	**234.9**	**241.5**	**11.6**	**11.1**	**10.5**	**10.9**	**11.0**
5100 Taxes on production, sale, transfer, etc	119.2	161.0	202.6	228.1	234.6	11.3	10.8	10.1	10.6	10.7
5110 General taxes	81.3	109.6	140.4	153.7	156.0	7.7	7.4	7.0	7.2	7.1
5111 Value added taxes	80.0	106.9	135.4	148.3	151.6	7.6	7.2	6.8	6.9	6.9
5120 Taxes on specific goods and services	37.9	51.4	62.2	74.4	78.6	3.6	3.5	3.1	3.5	3.6
5121 Excises	26.8	39.6	45.5	52.7	56.4	2.5	2.7	2.3	2.5	2.6
5200 Taxes on use of goods and perform activities	4.0	4.6	6.3	6.8	6.9	0.4	0.3	0.3	0.3	0.3
5300 Unallocable between 5100 and 5200	0.0	0.0	0.0	0.0	0.0	0.0	0.0	0.0	0.0	0.0
6000 Other taxes	**14.1**	**23.8**	**19.2**	**23.6**	**24.4**	**1.3**	**1.6**	**1.0**	**1.1**	**1.1**
Non-wastable tax credits										
Non-wastable tax credits against 1000	..	0.5	17.4	21.3	25.8	..	0.0	0.9	1.0	1.2
Transfer component	..	..	7.9	8.4	10.4	..	..	0.4	0.4	0.5
Tax expenditure component	..	..	9.5	12.9	15.4	..	..	0.5	0.6	0.7

Note: More detailed country data and country notes are available in online chapter 5: http://dx.doi.org/10.1787/9789264283183-en. Full time series can be accessed at http://oe.cd/full-time-series.

The total tax revenue has been reduced by the amount of any capital transfer that represents uncollected taxes. The capital transfer has been allocated between tax headings in proportion to the reported tax revenue. Therefore, the tax revenue amounts are different to those reported in the detailed country data available in online chapter 5.

Source: General Account of the Administration of finances for the figures of fiscal receipts. OSCE for the figures of Social Security from 1965 to 1969, and ESA for the following years.

StatLink http://dx.doi.org/10.1787/888933612532

Table 4.20. **France, tax revenue and % of GDP by level of government and main taxes**

	Billion EUR					% of GDP				
	1990	2000	2010	2014	2015	1990	2000	2010	2014	2015
Federal or Central government										
Total tax revenue	**200.1**	**267.6**	**297.2**	**322.4**	**330.2**	**18.9**	**18.0**	**14.9**	**15.0**	**15.0**
1000 Taxes on income, profits and capital gains	69.6	94.3	97.1	124.2	120.9	6.6	6.3	4.9	5.8	5.5
2000 Social security contributions	3.2	5.4	7.6	7.7	7.9	0.3	0.4	0.4	0.4	0.4
3000 Taxes on payroll and workforce	6.2	10.5	4.2	4.8	4.8	0.6	0.7	0.2	0.2	0.2
4000 Taxes on property	8.6	11.3	13.4	18.1	20.3	0.8	0.8	0.7	0.8	0.9
5000 Taxes on goods and services	112.1	143.1	157.4	166.5	174.5	10.6	9.6	7.9	7.8	8.0
6000 Other taxes	0.4	3.0	17.4	1.1	1.9	0.0	0.2	0.9	0.1	0.1
State/Regional										
Total tax revenue	..	..	..	..	..	..	..	..	..	..
1000 Taxes on income, profits and capital gains	..	..	..	..	..	..	..	..	..	..
2000 Social security contributions	..	..	..	..	..	..	..	..	..	..
3000 Taxes on payroll and workforce	..	..	..	..	..	..	..	..	..	..
4000 Taxes on property	..	..	..	..	..	..	..	..	..	..
5000 Taxes on goods and services	..	..	..	..	..	..	..	..	..	..
6000 Other taxes	..	..	..	..	..	..	..	..	..	..
Local government										
Total tax revenue	**40.2**	**64.7**	**89.3**	**126.7**	**131.3**	**3.8**	**4.4**	**4.5**	**5.9**	**6.0**
1000 Taxes on income, profits and capital gains	0.0	0.0	0.1	0.0	0.0	0.0	0.0	0.0	0.0	0.0
2000 Social security contributions	0.0	0.0	0.0	0.0	0.0	0.0	0.0	0.0	0.0	0.0
3000 Taxes on payroll and workforce	1.7	3.9	7.5	9.1	9.3	0.2	0.3	0.4	0.4	0.4
4000 Taxes on property	18.8	32.7	57.1	65.6	68.9	1.8	2.2	2.9	3.1	3.1
5000 Taxes on goods and services	6.0	7.3	23.0	29.8	31.0	0.6	0.5	1.2	1.4	1.4
6000 Other taxes	13.7	20.9	1.6	22.2	22.1	1.3	1.4	0.1	1.0	1.0
Social Security Funds										
Total tax revenue	**190.9**	**305.2**	**450.3**	**522.6**	**528.4**	**18.0**	**20.5**	**22.5**	**24.3**	**24.1**
1000 Taxes on income, profits and capital gains	0.0	65.0	92.7	107.5	112.2	0.0	4.4	4.6	5.0	5.1
2000 Social security contributions	187.9	224.8	313.9	356.1	359.4	17.8	15.1	15.7	16.6	16.4
3000 Taxes on payroll and workforce	0.4	0.4	15.1	20.4	20.4	0.0	0.0	0.8	0.9	0.9
4000 Taxes on property	0.0	0.0	0.0	0.0	0.0	0.0	0.0	0.0	0.0	0.0
5000 Taxes on goods and services	2.5	14.9	28.4	38.2	35.9	0.2	1.0	1.4	1.8	1.6
6000 Other taxes	0.0	0.1	0.2	0.5	0.6	0.0	0.0	0.0	0.0	0.0

Note: More detailed country data and country notes are available in online chapter 6: http://dx.doi.org/10.1787/9789264283183-en. Full time series can be accessed at http://oe.cd/full-time-series.

The total tax revenue has been reduced by the amount of any capital transfer that represents uncollected taxes. The capital transfer has been allocated between tax headings in proportion to the reported tax revenue. Therefore, the tax revenue amounts are different to those reported in the detailed country data available in online chapter 6.

Source: General Account of the Administration of finances for the figures of fiscal receipts. OSCE for the figures of Social Security from 1965 to 1969, and ESA for the following years.

StatLink http://dx.doi.org/10.1787/888933612551

Table 4.21. **Germany, tax revenue and % of GDP by selected tax category**

	Billion EUR					% of GDP				
	1990	2000	2010	2014	2015	1990	2000	2010	2014	2015
Total tax revenue	**454.8**	**767.0**	**903.2**	**1 078.6**	**1 128.4**	**34.8**	**36.2**	**35.0**	**36.8**	**37.1**
1000 Taxes on income, profits and capital gains	**147.3**	**231.2**	**257.8**	**333.6**	**352.3**	**11.3**	**10.9**	**10.0**	**11.4**	**11.6**
1100 Of individuals	125.3	194.2	219.4	282.8	299.6	9.6	9.2	8.5	9.6	9.8
1200 Corporate	22.0	37.1	38.4	50.8	52.7	1.7	1.8	1.5	1.7	1.7
1300 Unallocable between 1100 and 1200	0.0	0.0	0.0	0.0	0.0	0.0	0.0	0.0	0.0	0.0
2000 Social security contributions	**170.4**	**299.4**	**354.0**	**407.7**	**424.6**	**13.0**	**14.1**	**13.7**	**13.9**	**14.0**
2100 Employees	73.6	131.6	155.3	181.6	188.9	5.6	6.2	6.0	6.2	6.2
2200 Employers	86.7	147.4	167.2	191.4	199.2	6.6	7.0	6.5	6.5	6.5
2300 Self-employed or non-employed	10.2	20.4	31.5	34.7	36.5	0.8	1.0	1.2	1.2	1.2
2400 Unallocable between 2100, 2200 and 2300	0.0	0.0	0.0	0.0	0.0	0.0	0.0	0.0	0.0	0.0
3000 Taxes on payroll and workforce	**0.0**	**0.0**	**0.0**	**0.0**	**0.0**	**0.0**	**0.0**	**0.0**	**0.0**	**0.0**
4000 Taxes on property	**15.3**	**17.5**	**21.0**	**28.2**	**32.7**	**1.2**	**0.8**	**0.8**	**1.0**	**1.1**
4100 Recurrent taxes on immovable property	4.5	8.8	11.3	12.7	13.2	0.3	0.4	0.4	0.4	0.4
4200 Recurrent taxes on net wealth	6.2	0.4	0.0	0.7	1.9	0.5	0.0	0.0	0.0	0.1
4300 Estate, inheritance and gift taxes	1.5	3.0	4.4	5.5	6.3	0.1	0.1	0.2	0.2	0.2
4400 Taxes on financial and capital transactions	3.1	5.2	5.3	9.3	11.2	0.2	0.2	0.2	0.3	0.4
4500 Non-recurrent taxes	0.0	0.0	0.0	0.0	0.0	0.0	0.0	0.0	0.0	0.0
4600 Other recurrent taxes on property	0.0	0.0	0.0	0.0	0.0	0.0	0.0	0.0	0.0	0.0
5000 Taxes on goods and services	**121.6**	**215.3**	**266.1**	**304.4**	**313.4**	**9.3**	**10.2**	**10.3**	**10.4**	**10.3**
5100 Taxes on production, sale, transfer, etc	117.2	208.1	256.9	285.4	294.3	9.0	9.8	10.0	9.7	9.7
5110 General taxes	75.5	140.9	180.5	203.4	211.9	5.8	6.7	7.0	6.9	7.0
5111 Value added taxes	75.5	140.9	180.5	203.4	211.9	5.8	6.7	7.0	6.9	7.0
5120 Taxes on specific goods and services	41.7	67.2	76.1	81.7	82.0	3.2	3.2	2.9	2.8	2.7
5121 Excises	31.2	57.2	63.5	65.1	65.3	2.4	2.7	2.5	2.2	2.1
5200 Taxes on use of goods and perform activities	4.4	7.2	9.2	19.0	19.1	0.3	0.3	0.4	0.6	0.6
5300 Unallocable between 5100 and 5200	0.0	0.0	0.0	0.0	0.0	0.0	0.0	0.0	0.0	0.0
6000 Other taxes	**0.2**	**0.2**	**0.1**	**0.2**	**0.2**	**0.0**	**0.0**	**0.0**	**0.0**	**0.0**
Non-wastable tax credits										
Non-wastable tax credits against 1000	..	39.3	46.3	41.5	42.2	..	1.9	1.8	1.4	1.4
Transfer component	..	..	17.7	15.8	15.7	..	..	0.7	0.5	0.5
Tax expenditure component	..	..	28.6	25.8	26.4	..	..	1.1	0.9	0.9

Note: More detailed country data and country notes are available in online chapter 5: http://dx.doi.org/10.1787/9789264283183-en. Full time series can be accessed at http://oe.cd/full-time-series.

Source: Finanzbericht, Bonn; Tax Statistics. Unpublished estimates by the Ministry of Finance.

StatLink http://dx.doi.org/10.1787/888933612570

Table 4.22. **Germany, tax revenue and % of GDP by level of government and main taxes**

	Billion EUR					% of GDP				
	1990	2000	2010	2014	2015	1990	2000	2010	2014	2015
Federal or Central government										
Total tax revenue	**143.9**	**234.8**	**283.0**	**334.5**	**345.4**	**11.0**	**11.1**	**11.0**	**11.4**	**11.4**
1000 Taxes on income, profits and capital gains	58.2	97.9	104.5	136.5	144.0	4.5	4.6	4.1	4.7	4.7
2000 Social security contributions	0.0	0.0	0.0	0.0	0.0	0.0	0.0	0.0	0.0	0.0
3000 Taxes on payroll and workforce	0.0	0.0	0.0	0.0	0.0	0.0	0.0	0.0	0.0	0.0
4000 Taxes on property	1.2	0.0	0.0	0.7	1.9	0.1	0.0	0.0	0.0	0.1
5000 Taxes on goods and services	84.6	136.9	178.5	197.4	199.5	6.5	6.5	6.9	6.7	6.6
6000 Other taxes	0.0	0.0	0.0	0.0	0.0	0.0	0.0	0.0	0.0	0.0
State/Regional										
Total tax revenue	**97.8**	**172.1**	**190.6**	**243.9**	**259.7**	**7.5**	**8.1**	**7.4**	**8.3**	**8.5**
1000 Taxes on income, profits and capital gains	58.2	88.9	97.6	127.3	134.2	4.5	4.2	3.8	4.3	4.4
2000 Social security contributions	0.0	0.0	0.0	0.0	0.0	0.0	0.0	0.0	0.0	0.0
3000 Taxes on payroll and workforce	0.0	0.0	0.0	0.0	0.0	0.0	0.0	0.0	0.0	0.0
4000 Taxes on property	7.0	8.5	9.7	14.8	17.5	0.5	0.4	0.4	0.5	0.6
5000 Taxes on goods and services	32.6	74.6	83.4	101.8	107.9	2.5	3.5	3.2	3.5	3.5
6000 Other taxes	0.0	0.0	0.0	0.0	0.0	0.0	0.0	0.0	0.0	0.0
Local government										
Total tax revenue	**38.4**	**57.0**	**71.4**	**88.0**	**93.4**	**2.9**	**2.7**	**2.8**	**3.0**	**3.1**
1000 Taxes on income, profits and capital gains	30.9	44.4	55.7	69.9	74.0	2.4	2.1	2.2	2.4	2.4
2000 Social security contributions	0.0	0.0	0.0	0.0	0.0	0.0	0.0	0.0	0.0	0.0
3000 Taxes on payroll and workforce	0.0	0.0	0.0	0.0	0.0	0.0	0.0	0.0	0.0	0.0
4000 Taxes on property	7.2	9.0	11.3	12.7	13.2	0.5	0.4	0.4	0.4	0.4
5000 Taxes on goods and services	0.3	3.4	4.3	5.2	5.9	0.0	0.2	0.2	0.2	0.2
6000 Other taxes	0.2	0.1	0.1	0.2	0.2	0.0	0.0	0.0	0.0	0.0
Social Security Funds										
Total tax revenue	**170.4**	**299.4**	**354.0**	**407.7**	**424.6**	**13.0**	**14.1**	**13.7**	**13.9**	**14.0**
1000 Taxes on income, profits and capital gains	0.0	0.0	0.0	0.0	0.0	0.0	0.0	0.0	0.0	0.0
2000 Social security contributions	170.4	299.4	354.0	407.7	424.6	13.0	14.1	13.7	13.9	14.0
3000 Taxes on payroll and workforce	0.0	0.0	0.0	0.0	0.0	0.0	0.0	0.0	0.0	0.0
4000 Taxes on property	0.0	0.0	0.0	0.0	0.0	0.0	0.0	0.0	0.0	0.0
5000 Taxes on goods and services	0.0	0.0	0.0	0.0	0.0	0.0	0.0	0.0	0.0	0.0
6000 Other taxes	0.0	0.0	0.0	0.0	0.0	0.0	0.0	0.0	0.0	0.0

Note: More detailed country data and country notes are available in online chapter 6: http://dx.doi.org/10.1787/9789264283183-en. Full time series can be accessed at http://oe.cd/full-time-series.

Source: Finanzbericht, Bonn; Tax Statistics. Unpublished estimates by the Ministry of Finance.

StatLink http://dx.doi.org/10.1787/888933612589

Table 4.23. **Greece, tax revenue and % of GDP by selected tax category**

	Billion EUR					% of GDP				
	1990	2000	2010	2014	2015	1990	2000	2010	2014	2015
Total tax revenue	**11.5**	**47.1**	**72.4**	**63.8**	**64.0**	**25.2**	**33.4**	**32.0**	**35.9**	**36.4**
1000 Taxes on income, profits and capital gains	**2.3**	**12.6**	**15.9**	**15.1**	**14.4**	**5.0**	**9.0**	**7.0**	**8.5**	**8.2**
1100 Of individuals	1.6	6.8	9.0	10.6	9.6	3.6	4.8	4.0	5.9	5.5
1200 Corporate	0.6	5.6	5.7	3.3	3.8	1.4	4.0	2.5	1.9	2.2
1300 Unallocable between 1100 and 1200	0.0	0.2	1.2	1.2	0.9	0.1	0.1	0.5	0.7	0.5
2000 Social security contributions	**3.5**	**14.3**	**24.7**	**18.6**	**18.8**	**7.6**	**10.1**	**10.9**	**10.4**	**10.7**
2100 Employees	1.7	5.6	13.3	10.6	11.1	3.8	4.0	5.9	6.0	6.3
2200 Employers	1.7	6.7	11.5	8.0	7.7	3.8	4.7	5.1	4.5	4.4
2300 Self-employed or non-employed	0.0	2.0	0.0	0.0	0.0	0.0	1.4	0.0	0.0	0.0
2400 Unallocable between 2100, 2200 and 2300	0.0	0.0	0.0	0.0	0.0	0.0	0.0	0.0	0.0	0.0
3000 Taxes on payroll and workforce	**0.1**	**0.0**	**0.0**	**0.0**	**0.0**	**0.2**	**0.0**	**0.0**	**0.0**	**0.0**
4000 Taxes on property	**0.5**	**2.9**	**3.7**	**5.1**	**5.4**	**1.2**	**2.0**	**1.7**	**2.9**	**3.1**
4100 Recurrent taxes on immovable property	0.0	0.2	0.6	3.3	3.6	0.0	0.2	0.2	1.9	2.0
4200 Recurrent taxes on net wealth	0.0	0.1	1.3	1.0	1.1	0.0	0.0	0.6	0.6	0.6
4300 Estate, inheritance and gift taxes	0.1	0.4	0.2	0.1	0.1	0.3	0.3	0.1	0.1	0.1
4400 Taxes on financial and capital transactions	0.4	2.0	1.1	0.6	0.5	0.8	1.4	0.5	0.3	0.3
4500 Non-recurrent taxes	0.0	0.0	0.0	0.0	0.0	0.0	0.0	0.0	0.0	0.0
4600 Other recurrent taxes on property	0.0	0.2	0.6	0.1	0.1	0.0	0.1	0.3	0.1	0.0
5000 Taxes on goods and services	**5.1**	**17.1**	**27.7**	**24.8**	**25.2**	**11.2**	**12.1**	**12.3**	**14.0**	**14.3**
5100 Taxes on production, sale, transfer, etc	4.9	15.6	25.2	21.3	21.3	10.7	11.0	11.2	12.0	12.1
5110 General taxes	3.0	10.1	16.8	13.3	13.4	6.7	7.2	7.4	7.5	7.6
5111 Value added taxes	2.8	9.8	16.0	12.7	12.9	6.2	6.9	7.1	7.1	7.3
5120 Taxes on specific goods and services	1.8	5.4	8.4	7.9	7.8	3.9	3.8	3.7	4.4	4.5
5121 Excises	1.4	4.2	7.3	6.8	6.7	3.0	3.0	3.2	3.8	3.8
5200 Taxes on use of goods and perform activities	0.2	1.3	1.7	3.0	3.2	0.5	0.9	0.7	1.7	1.8
5300 Unallocable between 5100 and 5200	0.0	0.3	0.8	0.4	0.7	0.0	0.2	0.3	0.3	0.4
6000 Other taxes	**0.0**	**0.0**	**0.0**	**0.0**	**0.0**	**0.0**	**0.0**	**0.0**	**0.0**	**0.0**
Non-wastable tax credits										
Non-wastable tax credits against 1000	..	..	..	..	..	..	..	..	..	..
Transfer component	..	..	..	..	..	..	..	..	..	..
Tax expenditure component	..	..	..	..	..	..	..	..	..	..

Note: More detailed country data and country notes are available in online chapter 5: http://dx.doi.org/10.1787/9789264283183-en. Full time series can be accessed at http://oe.cd/full-time-series.

The total tax revenue has been reduced by the amount of any capital transfer that represents uncollected taxes. The capital transfer has been allocated between tax headings in proportion to the reported tax revenue. Therefore, the tax revenue amounts are different to those reported in the detailed country data available in online chapter 5.

Source: Ministry of Finance, General accounting Office, 20th Directorate of Budget except the heading 2000 provided by the National Statistics Bureau.

StatLink http://dx.doi.org/10.1787/888933612608

Table 4.24. **Greece, tax revenue and % of GDP by level of government and main taxes**

	Billion EUR					% of GDP				
	1990	2000	2010	2014	2015	1990	2000	2010	2014	2015
Federal or Central government										
Total tax revenue	**7.8**	**32.4**	**46.5**	**43.8**	**43.9**	**17.1**	**23.0**	**20.6**	**24.6**	**25.0**
1000 Taxes on income, profits and capital gains	2.3	12.7	15.9	15.1	14.4	5.0	9.0	7.0	8.5	8.2
2000 Social security contributions	0.0	0.7	1.3	0.7	0.7	0.1	0.5	0.6	0.4	0.4
3000 Taxes on payroll and workforce	0.0	0.0	0.0	0.0	0.0	0.0	0.0	0.0	0.0	0.0
4000 Taxes on property	0.5	2.4	2.1	3.7	3.9	1.2	1.7	0.9	2.1	2.2
5000 Taxes on goods and services	4.9	16.7	27.1	24.3	24.9	10.9	11.8	12.0	13.7	14.1
6000 Other taxes	0.0	0.0	0.0	0.0	0.0	0.0	0.0	0.0	0.0	0.0
State/Regional										
Total tax revenue	..	..	..	..	..	..	..	..	..	..
1000 Taxes on income, profits and capital gains	..	..	..	..	..	..	..	..	..	..
2000 Social security contributions	..	..	..	..	..	..	..	..	..	..
3000 Taxes on payroll and workforce	..	..	..	..	..	..	..	..	..	..
4000 Taxes on property	..	..	..	..	..	..	..	..	..	..
5000 Taxes on goods and services	..	..	..	..	..	..	..	..	..	..
6000 Other taxes	..	..	..	..	..	..	..	..	..	..
Local government										
Total tax revenue	**0.1**	**0.4**	**1.7**	**1.6**	**1.5**	**0.3**	**0.3**	**0.8**	**0.9**	**0.9**
1000 Taxes on income, profits and capital gains	0.0	0.0	0.0	0.0	0.0	0.0	0.0	0.0	0.0	0.0
2000 Social security contributions	0.0	0.0	0.0	0.0	0.0	0.0	0.0	0.0	0.0	0.0
3000 Taxes on payroll and workforce	0.1	0.0	0.0	0.0	0.0	0.2	0.0	0.0	0.0	0.0
4000 Taxes on property	0.0	0.3	1.5	1.4	1.4	0.0	0.2	0.7	0.8	0.8
5000 Taxes on goods and services	0.1	0.1	0.2	0.1	0.1	0.1	0.1	0.1	0.1	0.1
6000 Other taxes	0.0	0.0	0.0	0.0	0.0	0.0	0.0	0.0	0.0	0.0
Social Security Funds										
Total tax revenue	**3.4**	**14.1**	**24.0**	**18.3**	**18.3**	**7.5**	**10.0**	**10.6**	**10.3**	**10.4**
1000 Taxes on income, profits and capital gains	0.0	0.0	0.0	0.0	0.0	0.0	0.0	0.0	0.0	0.0
2000 Social security contributions	3.4	13.6	23.4	17.8	18.1	7.5	9.6	10.4	10.0	10.3
3000 Taxes on payroll and workforce	0.0	0.0	0.0	0.0	0.0	0.0	0.0	0.0	0.0	0.0
4000 Taxes on property	0.0	0.2	0.1	0.0	0.0	0.0	0.1	0.1	0.0	0.0
5000 Taxes on goods and services	0.0	0.3	0.4	0.4	0.2	0.0	0.2	0.2	0.2	0.1
6000 Other taxes	0.0	0.0	0.0	0.0	0.0	0.0	0.0	0.0	0.0	0.0

Note: More detailed country data and country notes are available in online chapter 6: http://dx.doi.org/10.1787/9789264283183-en. Full time series can be accessed at http://oe.cd/full-time-series.

The total tax revenue has been reduced by the amount of any capital transfer that represents uncollected taxes. The capital transfer has been allocated between tax headings in proportion to the reported tax revenue. Therefore, the tax revenue amounts are different to those reported in the detailed country data available in online chapter 6.

Source: Ministry of Finance, General accounting Office, 20th Directorate of Budget except the heading 2000 provided by the National Statistics Bureau.

StatLink http://dx.doi.org/10.1787/888933612627

Table 4.25. **Hungary, tax revenue and % of GDP by selected tax category**

	Billion HUF					% of GDP				
	1990	2000	2010	2014	2015	1990	2000	2010	2014	2015
Total tax revenue	..	**5 140.6**	**10 145.5**	**12 364.5**	**13 261.9**	..	**38.6**	**37.5**	**38.2**	**39.0**
1000 Taxes on income, profits and capital gains	..	**1 247.4**	**2 098.6**	**2 239.8**	**2 428.4**	..	**9.4**	**7.7**	**6.9**	**7.1**
1100 Of individuals	..	954.7	1 768.8	1 705.1	1 814.9	..	7.2	6.5	5.3	5.3
1200 Corporate	..	292.7	329.7	534.7	613.5	..	2.2	1.2	1.7	1.8
1300 Unallocable between 1100 and 1200	..	0.0	0.0	0.0	0.0	..	0.0	0.0	0.0	0.0
2000 Social security contributions	..	**1 506.8**	**3 184.2**	**4 025.3**	**4 293.7**	..	**11.3**	**11.8**	**12.4**	**12.6**
2100 Employees	..	275.3	1 069.1	1 660.5	1 784.5	..	2.1	3.9	5.1	5.2
2200 Employers	..	1 213.2	2 047.6	2 337.1	2 480.1	..	9.1	7.6	7.2	7.3
2300 Self-employed or non-employed	..	0.9	21.2	0.0	0.0	..	0.0	0.1	0.0	0.0
2400 Unallocable between 2100, 2200 and 2300	..	17.4	46.3	27.7	29.1	..	0.1	0.2	0.1	0.1
3000 Taxes on payroll and workforce	..	**183.4**	**116.0**	**180.5**	**199.3**	..	**1.4**	**0.4**	**0.6**	**0.6**
4000 Taxes on property	..	**89.0**	**312.1**	**417.4**	**438.4**	..	**0.7**	**1.2**	**1.3**	**1.3**
4100 Recurrent taxes on immovable property	..	30.8	92.5	191.2	201.4	..	0.2	0.3	0.6	0.6
4200 Recurrent taxes on net wealth	..	0.0	135.7	138.1	136.3	..	0.0	0.5	0.4	0.4
4300 Estate, inheritance and gift taxes	..	5.5	6.3	6.2	7.4	..	0.0	0.0	0.0	0.0
4400 Taxes on financial and capital transactions	..	52.8	77.6	81.9	93.4	..	0.4	0.3	0.3	0.3
4500 Non-recurrent taxes	..	0.0	0.0	0.0	0.0	..	0.0	0.0	0.0	0.0
4600 Other recurrent taxes on property	..	0.0	0.0	0.0	0.0	..	0.0	0.0	0.0	0.0
5000 Taxes on goods and services	..	**2 081.1**	**4 350.3**	**5 408.8**	**5 806.2**	..	**15.6**	**16.1**	**16.7**	**17.1**
5100 Taxes on production, sale, transfer, etc	..	2 052.4	4 238.8	5 282.2	5 670.4	..	15.4	15.6	16.3	16.7
5110 General taxes	..	1 340.6	3 010.8	3 748.2	4 097.5	..	10.1	11.1	11.6	12.1
5111 Value added taxes	..	1 153.7	2 325.6	3 011.2	3 307.3	..	8.7	8.6	9.3	9.7
5120 Taxes on specific goods and services	..	711.8	1 228.0	1 534.0	1 572.9	..	5.3	4.5	4.7	4.6
5121 Excises	..	533.5	929.9	1 027.6	1 119.2	..	4.0	3.4	3.2	3.3
5200 Taxes on use of goods and perform activities	..	28.7	111.6	126.7	135.8	..	0.2	0.4	0.4	0.4
5300 Unallocable between 5100 and 5200	..	0.0	0.0	0.0	0.0	..	0.0	0.0	0.0	0.0
6000 Other taxes	..	**32.9**	**59.4**	**60.8**	**56.8**	..	**0.2**	**0.2**	**0.2**	**0.2**
Non-wastable tax credits										
Non-wastable tax credits against 1000	..	..	..	..	..	..	..	..	..	..
Transfer component	..	..	..	..	..	..	..	..	..	..
Tax expenditure component	..	..	..	..	..	..	..	..	..	..

Note: More detailed country data and country notes are available in online chapter 5: http://dx.doi.org/10.1787/9789264283183-en. Full time series can be accessed at http://oe.cd/full-time-series.

Source: Ministry of Finance, Economic Department.

StatLink http://dx.doi.org/10.1787/888933612646

Table 4.26. **Hungary, tax revenue and % of GDP by level of government and main taxes**

	Billion HUF					% of GDP				
	1990	2000	2010	2014	2015	1990	2000	2010	2014	2015
Federal or Central government										
Total tax revenue	..	**3 316.0**	**6 391.5**	**7 544.8**	**8 061.6**	..	**24.9**	**23.6**	**23.3**	**23.7**
1000 Taxes on income, profits and capital gains	..	1 230.8	2 064.3	2 132.6	2 311.9	..	9.2	7.6	6.6	6.8
2000 Social security contributions	..	136.6	182.0	155.6	148.0	..	1.0	0.7	0.5	0.4
3000 Taxes on payroll and workforce	..	15.4	103.1	170.7	189.1	..	0.1	0.4	0.5	0.6
4000 Taxes on property	..	29.1	182.8	281.2	293.0	..	0.2	0.7	0.9	0.9
5000 Taxes on goods and services	..	1 878.3	3 799.9	4 759.2	5 076.8	..	14.1	14.0	14.7	14.9
6000 Other taxes	..	25.8	59.4	45.4	42.8	..	0.2	0.2	0.1	0.1
State/Regional										
Total tax revenue	..	..	..	..	..	..	..	..	..	..
1000 Taxes on income, profits and capital gains	..	..	..	..	..	..	..	..	..	..
2000 Social security contributions	..	..	..	..	..	..	..	..	..	..
3000 Taxes on payroll and workforce	..	..	..	..	..	..	..	..	..	..
4000 Taxes on property	..	..	..	..	..	..	..	..	..	..
5000 Taxes on goods and services	..	..	..	..	..	..	..	..	..	..
6000 Other taxes	..	..	..	..	..	..	..	..	..	..
Local government										
Total tax revenue	..	**266.0**	**652.2**	**698.5**	**771.0**	..	**2.0**	**2.4**	**2.2**	**2.3**
1000 Taxes on income, profits and capital gains	..	2.2	0.1	0.0	0.0	..	0.0	0.0	0.0	0.0
2000 Social security contributions	..	0.0	0.0	0.0	0.0	..	0.0	0.0	0.0	0.0
3000 Taxes on payroll and workforce	..	1.2	1.2	0.0	0.0	..	0.0	0.0	0.0	0.0
4000 Taxes on property	..	59.9	129.3	136.2	145.4	..	0.5	0.5	0.4	0.4
5000 Taxes on goods and services	..	202.8	521.6	562.3	625.6	..	1.5	1.9	1.7	1.8
6000 Other taxes	..	0.0	0.0	0.0	0.0	..	0.0	0.0	0.0	0.0
Social Security Funds										
Total tax revenue	..	**1 558.6**	**3 076.2**	**4 088.5**	**4 389.5**	..	**11.7**	**11.4**	**12.6**	**12.9**
1000 Taxes on income, profits and capital gains	..	14.5	34.2	107.1	116.5	..	0.1	0.1	0.3	0.3
2000 Social security contributions	..	1 370.2	3 002.2	3 869.7	4 145.7	..	10.3	11.1	11.9	12.2
3000 Taxes on payroll and workforce	..	166.9	11.7	9.7	10.3	..	1.3	0.0	0.0	0.0
4000 Taxes on property	..	0.0	0.0	0.0	0.0	..	0.0	0.0	0.0	0.0
5000 Taxes on goods and services	..	0.0	28.1	86.6	103.1	..	0.0	0.1	0.3	0.3
6000 Other taxes	..	7.0	0.0	15.4	14.0	..	0.1	0.0	0.0	0.0

Note: More detailed country data and country notes are available in online chapter 6: http://dx.doi.org/10.1787/9789264283183-en. Full time series can be accessed at http://oe.cd/full-time-series.

Source: Ministry of Finance, Economic Department.

StatLink http://dx.doi.org/10.1787/888933612665

Table 4.27. Iceland, tax revenue and % of GDP by selected tax category

	Billion ISK					% of GDP				
	1990	2000	2010	2014	2015	1990	2000	2010	2014	2015
Total tax revenue	**114.9**	**254.6**	**540.3**	**774.3**	**812.0**	**30.2**	**36.2**	**33.3**	**38.6**	**36.7**
1000 Taxes on income, profits and capital gains	**34.1**	**101.5**	**239.7**	**360.5**	**381.0**	**9.0**	**14.4**	**14.8**	**18.0**	**17.2**
1100 Of individuals	30.9	88.5	197.3	270.6	298.0	8.1	12.6	12.2	13.5	13.5
1200 Corporate	3.2	8.4	14.6	66.8	52.5	0.8	1.2	0.9	3.3	2.4
1300 Unallocable between 1100 and 1200	0.0	4.6	27.7	23.1	30.5	0.0	0.7	1.7	1.2	1.4
2000 Social security contributions	**3.6**	**19.7**	**63.6**	**73.4**	**79.7**	**0.9**	**2.8**	**3.9**	**3.7**	**3.6**
2100 Employees	0.3	..	..	..	..	0.1	..	..	..	..
2200 Employers	3.3	..	..	..	..	0.9	..	..	..	..
2300 Self-employed or non-employed	0.0	..	..	..	..	0.0	..	..	..	..
2400 Unallocable between 2100, 2200 and 2300	0.0	19.7	63.6	73.4	79.7	0.0	2.8	3.9	3.7	3.6
3000 Taxes on payroll and workforce	**4.1**	**0.2**	**2.8**	**7.0**	**6.6**	**1.1**	**0.0**	**0.2**	**0.3**	**0.3**
4000 Taxes on property	**9.7**	**20.0**	**38.1**	**49.6**	**43.5**	**2.5**	**2.8**	**2.3**	**2.5**	**2.0**
4100 Recurrent taxes on immovable property	4.1	10.1	28.5	32.3	34.9	1.1	1.4	1.8	1.6	1.6
4200 Recurrent taxes on net wealth	2.4	5.2	3.8	10.8	0.7	0.6	0.7	0.2	0.5	0.0
4300 Estate, inheritance and gift taxes	0.2	0.8	2.6	2.5	2.9	0.1	0.1	0.2	0.1	0.1
4400 Taxes on financial and capital transactions	2.9	3.1	2.7	3.5	4.3	0.8	0.4	0.2	0.2	0.2
4500 Non-recurrent taxes	0.0	0.1	0.1	0.2	0.4	0.0	0.0	0.0	0.0	0.0
4600 Other recurrent taxes on property	0.0	0.7	0.3	0.3	0.3	0.0	0.1	0.0	0.0	0.0
5000 Taxes on goods and services	**58.9**	**112.2**	**190.1**	**239.9**	**262.8**	**15.5**	**16.0**	**11.7**	**12.0**	**11.9**
5100 Taxes on production, sale, transfer, etc	56.6	100.7	179.0	228.7	250.1	14.9	14.3	11.0	11.4	11.3
5110 General taxes	37.1	72.7	122.4	160.9	183.7	9.8	10.3	7.6	8.0	8.3
5111 Value added taxes	32.7	72.7	122.4	160.9	183.7	8.6	10.3	7.6	8.0	8.3
5120 Taxes on specific goods and services	19.5	28.0	56.6	67.8	66.4	5.1	4.0	3.5	3.4	3.0
5121 Excises	2.3	23.6	46.7	57.5	56.9	0.6	3.4	2.9	2.9	2.6
5200 Taxes on use of goods and perform activities	2.4	11.6	11.1	11.2	12.7	0.6	1.6	0.7	0.6	0.6
5300 Unallocable between 5100 and 5200	0.0	0.0	0.0	0.0	0.0	0.0	0.0	0.0	0.0	0.0
6000 Other taxes	**4.5**	**1.0**	**6.0**	**43.8**	**38.4**	**1.2**	**0.1**	**0.4**	**2.2**	**1.7**
Non-wastable tax credits										
Non-wastable tax credits against 1000	..	..	..	1.2	1.2	..	..	..	0.1	0.1
Transfer component	..	..	..	1.0	1.0	..	..	..	0.1	0.0
Tax expenditure component	..	..	..	0.2	0.2	..	..	..	0.0	0.0

Note: More detailed country data and country notes are available in online chapter 5: http://dx.doi.org/10.1787/9789264283183-en. Full time series can be accessed at http://oe.cd/full-time-series.

Source: Ministry of Finance, Economic Department.

StatLink http://dx.doi.org/10.1787/888933612684

Table 4.28. Iceland, tax revenue and % of GDP by level of government and main taxes

	Billion ISK					% of GDP				
	1990	2000	2010	2014	2015	1990	2000	2010	2014	2015
Federal or Central government										
Total tax revenue	**91.6**	**195.1**	**402.3**	**584.4**	**604.0**	**24.1**	**27.7**	**24.8**	**29.1**	**27.3**
1000 Taxes on income, profits and capital gains	19.9	55.5	132.9	204.3	210.5	5.2	7.9	8.2	10.2	9.5
2000 Social security contributions	3.6	19.7	63.6	73.4	79.7	0.9	2.8	3.9	3.7	3.6
3000 Taxes on payroll and workforce	4.1	0.2	2.8	7.0	6.6	1.1	0.0	0.2	0.3	0.3
4000 Taxes on property	6.0	9.9	9.7	17.5	8.8	1.6	1.4	0.6	0.9	0.4
5000 Taxes on goods and services	57.7	108.9	187.4	238.5	260.0	15.2	15.5	11.6	11.9	11.7
6000 Other taxes	0.4	1.0	6.0	43.8	38.4	0.1	0.1	0.4	2.2	1.7
State/Regional										
Total tax revenue	..	..	..	..	..	..	..	..	..	..
1000 Taxes on income, profits and capital gains	..	..	..	..	..	..	..	..	..	..
2000 Social security contributions	..	..	..	..	..	..	..	..	..	..
3000 Taxes on payroll and workforce	..	..	..	..	..	..	..	..	..	..
4000 Taxes on property	..	..	..	..	..	..	..	..	..	..
5000 Taxes on goods and services	..	..	..	..	..	..	..	..	..	..
6000 Other taxes	..	..	..	..	..	..	..	..	..	..
Local government										
Total tax revenue	**23.3**	**59.4**	**138.0**	**189.8**	**208.0**	**6.1**	**8.5**	**8.5**	**9.5**	**9.4**
1000 Taxes on income, profits and capital gains	14.2	46.0	106.8	156.2	170.4	3.7	6.5	6.6	7.8	7.7
2000 Social security contributions	0.0	0.0	0.0	0.0	0.0	0.0	0.0	0.0	0.0	0.0
3000 Taxes on payroll and workforce	0.0	0.0	0.0	0.0	0.0	0.0	0.0	0.0	0.0	0.0
4000 Taxes on property	3.7	10.1	28.4	32.2	34.7	1.0	1.4	1.8	1.6	1.6
5000 Taxes on goods and services	1.2	3.3	2.8	1.4	2.8	0.3	0.5	0.2	0.1	0.1
6000 Other taxes	4.1	0.0	0.0	0.0	0.0	1.1	0.0	0.0	0.0	0.0
Social Security Funds										
Total tax revenue	**0.0**	**0.0**	**0.0**	**0.0**	**0.0**	**0.0**	**0.0**	**0.0**	**0.0**	**0.0**
1000 Taxes on income, profits and capital gains	0.0	0.0	0.0	0.0	0.0	0.0	0.0	0.0	0.0	0.0
2000 Social security contributions	0.0	0.0	0.0	0.0	0.0	0.0	0.0	0.0	0.0	0.0
3000 Taxes on payroll and workforce	0.0	0.0	0.0	0.0	0.0	0.0	0.0	0.0	0.0	0.0
4000 Taxes on property	0.0	0.0	0.0	0.0	0.0	0.0	0.0	0.0	0.0	0.0
5000 Taxes on goods and services	0.0	0.0	0.0	0.0	0.0	0.0	0.0	0.0	0.0	0.0
6000 Other taxes	0.0	0.0	0.0	0.0	0.0	0.0	0.0	0.0	0.0	0.0

Note: More detailed country data and country notes are available in online chapter 6: http://dx.doi.org/10.1787/9789264283183-en. Full time series can be accessed at http://oe.cd/full-time-series.

Source: Ministry of Finance, Economic Department.

StatLink http://dx.doi.org/10.1787/888933612703

Table 4.29. **Ireland, tax revenue and % of GDP by selected tax category**

	Billion EUR					% of GDP				
	1990	2000	2010	2014	2015	1990	2000	2010	2014	2015
Total tax revenue	**12.3**	**33.3**	**45.3**	**55.5**	**60.6**	**32.4**	**30.8**	**27.0**	**28.5**	**23.1**
1000 Taxes on income, profits and capital gains	**4.7**	**14.6**	**17.5**	**22.3**	**26.0**	**12.3**	**13.4**	**10.5**	**11.5**	**9.9**
1100 Of individuals	4.1	10.6	13.6	17.7	19.2	10.7	9.8	8.1	9.1	7.3
1200 Corporate	0.6	3.9	3.9	4.6	6.9	1.6	3.6	2.4	2.4	2.6
1300 Unallocable between 1100 and 1200	0.0	0.0	0.0	0.0	0.0	0.0	0.0	0.0	0.0	0.0
2000 Social security contributions	**1.7**	**3.9**	**8.4**	**9.6**	**10.2**	**4.6**	**3.6**	**5.0**	**4.9**	**3.9**
2100 Employees	0.6	0.9	3.2	3.4	3.5	1.5	0.9	1.9	1.7	1.3
2200 Employers	1.1	2.8	4.9	5.8	6.2	2.9	2.6	2.9	3.0	2.4
2300 Self-employed or non-employed	0.1	0.2	0.3	0.4	0.5	0.2	0.2	0.2	0.2	0.2
2400 Unallocable between 2100, 2200 and 2300	0.0	0.0	0.0	0.0	0.0	0.0	0.0	0.0	0.0	0.0
3000 Taxes on payroll and workforce	**0.2**	**0.0**	**0.3**	**0.3**	**0.4**	**0.4**	**0.0**	**0.2**	**0.2**	**0.1**
4000 Taxes on property	**0.6**	**1.9**	**2.4**	**4.2**	**3.9**	**1.5**	**1.8**	**1.4**	**2.2**	**1.5**
4100 Recurrent taxes on immovable property	0.3	0.6	1.3	1.9	1.8	0.8	0.5	0.8	1.0	0.7
4200 Recurrent taxes on net wealth	0.0	0.0	0.0	0.7	0.2	0.0	0.0	0.0	0.4	0.1
4300 Estate, inheritance and gift taxes	0.0	0.2	0.2	0.4	0.4	0.1	0.2	0.1	0.2	0.2
4400 Taxes on financial and capital transactions	0.2	1.1	0.8	1.2	1.5	0.6	1.0	0.5	0.6	0.6
4500 Non-recurrent taxes	0.0	0.0	0.0	0.0	0.0	0.0	0.0	0.0	0.0	0.0
4600 Other recurrent taxes on property	0.0	0.0	0.0	0.0	0.0	0.0	0.0	0.0	0.0	0.0
5000 Taxes on goods and services	**5.1**	**12.7**	**16.4**	**18.7**	**19.8**	**13.6**	**11.7**	**9.8**	**9.6**	**7.5**
5100 Taxes on production, sale, transfer, etc	4.9	12.2	15.1	17.0	17.8	13.0	11.2	9.0	8.8	6.8
5110 General taxes	2.5	7.6	10.1	11.5	12.0	6.6	7.1	6.0	5.9	4.6
5111 Value added taxes	2.5	7.6	10.1	11.5	12.0	6.6	7.1	6.0	5.9	4.6
5120 Taxes on specific goods and services	2.4	4.5	5.0	5.5	5.9	6.4	4.2	3.0	2.8	2.2
5121 Excises	2.1	4.4	4.9	5.2	5.5	5.5	4.1	2.9	2.7	2.1
5200 Taxes on use of goods and perform activities	0.2	0.6	1.3	1.6	1.9	0.5	0.5	0.8	0.8	0.7
5300 Unallocable between 5100 and 5200	0.0	0.0	0.0	0.0	0.0	0.0	0.0	0.0	0.0	0.0
6000 Other taxes	**0.0**	**0.0**	**0.0**	**0.0**	**0.0**	**0.0**	**0.0**	**0.0**	**0.0**	**0.0**
Non-wastable tax credits										
Non-wastable tax credits against 1000	..	..	1.1	0.7	0.5	..	..	0.6	0.3	0.2
Transfer component	..	..	..	..	..	..	..	..	..	..
Tax expenditure component	..	..	1.1	0.7	0.5	..	..	0.6	0.3	0.2

Note: More detailed country data and country notes are available in online chapter 5: http://dx.doi.org/10.1787/9789264283183-en. Full time series can be accessed at http://oe.cd/full-time-series.

Source: Annual Report of he Revenue Commissioners, Financial Accounts and National Income and Expenditure Accounts.

StatLink http://dx.doi.org/10.1787/888933612722

Table 4.30. **Ireland, tax revenue and % of GDP by level of government and main taxes**

	Billion EUR					% of GDP				
	1990	2000	2010	2014	2015	1990	2000	2010	2014	2015
Federal or Central government										
Total tax revenue	**10.1**	**28.7**	**36.8**	**45.7**	**50.3**	**26.7**	**26.5**	**22.0**	**23.5**	**19.2**
1000 Taxes on income, profits and capital gains	4.7	14.6	17.5	22.3	26.0	12.3	13.4	10.5	11.5	9.9
2000 Social security contributions	0.1	0.1	1.5	1.5	1.6	0.2	0.1	0.9	0.8	0.6
3000 Taxes on payroll and workforce	0.2	0.0	0.3	0.3	0.4	0.4	0.0	0.2	0.2	0.1
4000 Taxes on property	0.3	1.3	1.1	2.8	2.5	0.7	1.2	0.6	1.5	1.0
5000 Taxes on goods and services	5.0	12.7	16.4	18.7	19.8	13.1	11.7	9.8	9.6	7.5
6000 Other taxes	0.0	0.0	0.0	0.0	0.0	0.0	0.0	0.0	0.0	0.0
State/Regional										
Total tax revenue	..	..	..	..	..	..	..	..	..	..
1000 Taxes on income, profits and capital gains	..	..	..	..	..	..	..	..	..	..
2000 Social security contributions	..	..	..	..	..	..	..	..	..	..
3000 Taxes on payroll and workforce	..	..	..	..	..	..	..	..	..	..
4000 Taxes on property	..	..	..	..	..	..	..	..	..	..
5000 Taxes on goods and services	..	..	..	..	..	..	..	..	..	..
6000 Other taxes	..	..	..	..	..	..	..	..	..	..
Local government										
Total tax revenue	**0.3**	**0.7**	**1.5**	**1.5**	**1.5**	**0.9**	**0.6**	**0.9**	**0.8**	**0.6**
1000 Taxes on income, profits and capital gains	0.0	0.0	0.0	0.0	0.0	0.0	0.0	0.0	0.0	0.0
2000 Social security contributions	0.0	0.1	0.2	0.1	0.1	0.1	0.1	0.1	0.1	0.0
3000 Taxes on payroll and workforce	0.0	0.0	0.0	0.0	0.0	0.0	0.0	0.0	0.0	0.0
4000 Taxes on property	0.3	0.6	1.3	1.4	1.3	0.8	0.5	0.8	0.7	0.5
5000 Taxes on goods and services	0.0	0.0	0.0	0.0	0.0	0.0	0.0	0.0	0.0	0.0
6000 Other taxes	0.0	0.0	0.0	0.0	0.0	0.0	0.0	0.0	0.0	0.0
Social Security Funds										
Total tax revenue	**1.6**	**3.7**	**6.7**	**7.9**	**8.5**	**4.3**	**3.5**	**4.0**	**4.1**	**3.2**
1000 Taxes on income, profits and capital gains	0.0	0.0	0.0	0.0	0.0	0.0	0.0	0.0	0.0	0.0
2000 Social security contributions	1.6	3.7	6.7	7.9	8.5	4.3	3.5	4.0	4.1	3.2
3000 Taxes on payroll and workforce	0.0	0.0	0.0	0.0	0.0	0.0	0.0	0.0	0.0	0.0
4000 Taxes on property	0.0	0.0	0.0	0.0	0.0	0.0	0.0	0.0	0.0	0.0
5000 Taxes on goods and services	0.0	0.0	0.0	0.0	0.0	0.0	0.0	0.0	0.0	0.0
6000 Other taxes	0.0	0.0	0.0	0.0	0.0	0.0	0.0	0.0	0.0	0.0

Note: More detailed country data and country notes are available in online chapter 6: http://dx.doi.org/10.1787/9789264283183-en. Full time series can be accessed at http://oe.cd/full-time-series.

Source: Annual Report of he Revenue Commissioners, Financial Accounts and National Income and Expenditure Accounts.

StatLink http://dx.doi.org/10.1787/888933612741

Table 4.31. **Israel, tax revenue and % of GDP by selected tax category**

	Billion ILS					% of GDP				
	1990	2000	2010	2014	2015	1990	2000	2010	2014	2015
Total tax revenue	..	**188.3**	**268.5**	**343.8**	**364.1**	..	**34.9**	**30.7**	**31.1**	**31.3**
1000 Taxes on income, profits and capital gains	..	**74.6**	**78.3**	**105.0**	**113.7**	..	**13.8**	**9.0**	**9.5**	**9.8**
1100 Of individuals	..	54.8	48.2	62.8	70.6	..	10.1	5.5	5.7	6.1
1200 Corporate	..	18.0	23.1	35.0	34.7	..	3.3	2.6	3.2	3.0
1300 Unallocable between 1100 and 1200	..	1.8	6.9	7.3	8.4	..	0.3	0.8	0.7	0.7
2000 Social security contributions	..	**27.6**	**45.3**	**56.1**	**59.6**	..	**5.1**	**5.2**	**5.1**	**5.1**
2100 Employees	..	15.8	27.8	32.8	34.7	..	2.9	3.2	3.0	3.0
2200 Employers	..	8.2	11.4	16.2	17.2	..	1.5	1.3	1.5	1.5
2300 Self-employed or non-employed	..	3.6	6.1	7.2	7.6	..	0.7	0.7	0.7	0.7
2400 Unallocable between 2100, 2200 and 2300	..	0.0	0.0	0.0	0.0	..	0.0	0.0	0.0	0.0
3000 Taxes on payroll and workforce	..	**6.8**	**10.3**	**13.6**	**13.8**	..	**1.3**	**1.2**	**1.2**	**1.2**
4000 Taxes on property	..	**16.9**	**28.8**	**34.5**	**38.7**	..	**3.1**	**3.3**	**3.1**	**3.3**
4100 Recurrent taxes on immovable property	..	11.3	18.8	22.5	23.7	..	2.1	2.1	2.0	2.0
4200 Recurrent taxes on net wealth	..	0.0	0.0	0.0	0.0	..	0.0	0.0	0.0	0.0
4300 Estate, inheritance and gift taxes	..	0.0	0.0	0.0	0.0	..	0.0	0.0	0.0	0.0
4400 Taxes on financial and capital transactions	..	3.2	4.1	5.0	6.7	..	0.6	0.5	0.5	0.6
4500 Non-recurrent taxes	..	2.4	6.0	7.0	8.3	..	0.5	0.7	0.6	0.7
4600 Other recurrent taxes on property	..	0.0	0.0	0.0	0.0	..	0.0	0.0	0.0	0.0
5000 Taxes on goods and services	..	**62.4**	**105.9**	**134.6**	**138.3**	..	**11.6**	**12.1**	**12.2**	**11.9**
5100 Taxes on production, sale, transfer, etc	..	57.9	98.1	125.6	128.3	..	10.7	11.2	11.4	11.0
5110 General taxes	..	49.9	79.9	105.7	107.8	..	9.2	9.1	9.6	9.3
5111 Value added taxes	..	39.8	65.5	87.8	90.8	..	7.4	7.5	7.9	7.8
5120 Taxes on specific goods and services	..	8.0	18.1	19.9	20.5	..	1.5	2.1	1.8	1.8
5121 Excises	..	6.6	15.5	17.1	17.6	..	1.2	1.8	1.5	1.5
5200 Taxes on use of goods and perform activities	..	4.5	7.8	9.0	10.0	..	0.8	0.9	0.8	0.9
5300 Unallocable between 5100 and 5200	..	0.0	0.0	0.0	0.0	..	0.0	0.0	0.0	0.0
6000 Other taxes	..	**0.0**	**0.0**	**0.0**	**0.0**	..	**0.0**	**0.0**	**0.0**	**0.0**
Non-wastable tax credits										
Non-wastable tax credits against 1000	..	0.0	0.1	0.6	1.4	..	0.0	0.0	0.1	0.1
Transfer component	..	..	0.1	0.6	1.3	..	..	0.0	0.1	0.1
Tax expenditure component	..	..	0.0	0.0	0.1	..	..	0.0	0.0	0.0

Note: More detailed country data and country notes are available in online chapter 5: http://dx.doi.org/10.1787/9789264283183-en. Full time series can be accessed at http://oe.cd/full-time-series.

The data for Israel are supplied by and under the responsibility of the relevant Israeli authorities. The use of such data by the OECD is without prejudice to the status of the Golan Heights, East Jerusalem and Israeli settlements in the West Bank under the terms of international law.

Source: Israel Central Bureau of Statistics and Israel Ministry of Finance.

StatLink http://dx.doi.org/10.1787/888933612760

Table 4.32. **Israel, tax revenue and % of GDP by level of government and main taxes**

	Billion ILS					% of GDP				
	1990	2000	2010	2014	2015	1990	2000	2010	2014	2015
Federal or Central government										
Total tax revenue	..	**148.0**	**199.8**	**259.6**	**274.9**	..	**27.4**	**22.9**	**23.5**	**23.6**
1000 Taxes on income, profits and capital gains	..	74.6	78.3	105.0	113.7	..	13.8	9.0	9.5	9.8
2000 Social security contributions	..	0.0	0.0	0.0	0.0	..	0.0	0.0	0.0	0.0
3000 Taxes on payroll and workforce	..	6.8	10.3	13.6	13.8	..	1.3	1.2	1.2	1.2
4000 Taxes on property	..	4.8	6.6	7.8	10.6	..	0.9	0.8	0.7	0.9
5000 Taxes on goods and services	..	61.8	104.7	133.2	136.8	..	11.5	12.0	12.1	11.8
6000 Other taxes	..	0.0	0.0	0.0	0.0	..	0.0	0.0	0.0	0.0
State/Regional										
Total tax revenue	..	..	..	..	..	..	..	..	..	..
1000 Taxes on income, profits and capital gains	..	..	..	..	..	..	..	..	..	..
2000 Social security contributions	..	..	..	..	..	..	..	..	..	..
3000 Taxes on payroll and workforce	..	..	..	..	..	..	..	..	..	..
4000 Taxes on property	..	..	..	..	..	..	..	..	..	..
5000 Taxes on goods and services	..	..	..	..	..	..	..	..	..	..
6000 Other taxes	..	..	..	..	..	..	..	..	..	..
Local government										
Total tax revenue	..	**12.7**	**23.4**	**28.0**	**29.6**	..	**2.4**	**2.7**	**2.5**	**2.5**
1000 Taxes on income, profits and capital gains	..	0.0	0.0	0.0	0.0	..	0.0	0.0	0.0	0.0
2000 Social security contributions	..	0.0	0.0	0.0	0.0	..	0.0	0.0	0.0	0.0
3000 Taxes on payroll and workforce	..	0.0	0.0	0.0	0.0	..	0.0	0.0	0.0	0.0
4000 Taxes on property	..	12.1	22.2	26.7	28.1	..	2.2	2.5	2.4	2.4
5000 Taxes on goods and services	..	0.6	1.1	1.4	1.4	..	0.1	0.1	0.1	0.1
6000 Other taxes	..	0.0	0.0	0.0	0.0	..	0.0	0.0	0.0	0.0
Social Security Funds										
Total tax revenue	..	**27.6**	**45.3**	**56.1**	**59.6**	..	**5.1**	**5.2**	**5.1**	**5.1**
1000 Taxes on income, profits and capital gains	..	0.0	0.0	0.0	0.0	..	0.0	0.0	0.0	0.0
2000 Social security contributions	..	27.6	45.3	56.1	59.6	..	5.1	5.2	5.1	5.1
3000 Taxes on payroll and workforce	..	0.0	0.0	0.0	0.0	..	0.0	0.0	0.0	0.0
4000 Taxes on property	..	0.0	0.0	0.0	0.0	..	0.0	0.0	0.0	0.0
5000 Taxes on goods and services	..	0.0	0.0	0.0	0.0	..	0.0	0.0	0.0	0.0
6000 Other taxes	..	0.0	0.0	0.0	0.0	..	0.0	0.0	0.0	0.0

Note: More detailed country data and country notes are available in online chapter 6: http://dx.doi.org/10.1787/9789264283183-en. Full time series can be accessed at http://oe.cd/full-time-series.

The data for Israel are supplied by and under the responsibility of the relevant Israeli authorities. The use of such data by the OECD is without prejudice to the status of the Golan Heights, East Jerusalem and Israeli settlements in the West Bank under the terms of international law.

Source: Israel Central Bureau of Statistics and Israel Ministry of Finance.

StatLink http://dx.doi.org/10.1787/888933612779

Table 4.33. **Italy, tax revenue and % of GDP by selected tax category**

	Billion EUR					% of GDP				
	1990	2000	2010	2014	2015	1990	2000	2010	2014	2015
Total tax revenue	**265.1**	**503.1**	**671.6**	**704.8**	**712.3**	**36.4**	**40.6**	**41.9**	**43.5**	**43.3**
1000 Taxes on income, profits and capital gains	**96.7**	**166.9**	**219.3**	**225.0**	**226.6**	**13.3**	**13.5**	**13.7**	**13.9**	**13.8**
1100 Of individuals	69.7	124.9	180.2	182.1	185.2	9.6	10.1	11.2	11.2	11.3
1200 Corporate	26.6	34.7	36.7	35.2	33.6	3.7	2.8	2.3	2.2	2.0
1300 Unallocable between 1100 and 1200	0.4	7.3	2.3	7.7	7.8	0.1	0.6	0.1	0.5	0.5
2000 Social security contributions	**87.3**	**143.6**	**209.1**	**209.7**	**214.4**	**12.0**	**11.6**	**13.0**	**12.9**	**13.0**
2100 Employees	16.8	27.3	37.6	38.6	39.8	2.3	2.2	2.3	2.4	2.4
2200 Employers	62.5	99.9	144.3	141.2	143.3	8.6	8.1	9.0	8.7	8.7
2300 Self-employed or non-employed	8.0	16.4	27.2	29.9	31.3	1.1	1.3	1.7	1.8	1.9
2400 Unallocable between 2100, 2200 and 2300	0.0	0.0	0.0	0.0	0.0	0.0	0.0	0.0	0.0	0.0
3000 Taxes on payroll and workforce	**0.9**	**0.0**	**0.0**	**0.0**	**0.0**	**0.1**	**0.0**	**0.0**	**0.0**	**0.0**
4000 Taxes on property	**6.0**	**23.4**	**32.4**	**46.9**	**46.2**	**0.8**	**1.9**	**2.0**	**2.9**	**2.8**
4100 Recurrent taxes on immovable property	0.0	9.4	9.7	25.2	25.6	0.0	0.8	0.6	1.6	1.6
4200 Recurrent taxes on net wealth	0.0	0.0	2.1	0.8	0.2	0.0	0.0	0.1	0.1	0.0
4300 Estate, inheritance and gift taxes	0.4	1.0	0.5	0.6	0.7	0.1	0.1	0.0	0.0	0.0
4400 Taxes on financial and capital transactions	5.6	12.3	17.4	18.0	17.4	0.8	1.0	1.1	1.1	1.1
4500 Non-recurrent taxes	0.0	0.1	0.9	0.1	0.3	0.0	0.0	0.1	0.0	0.0
4600 Other recurrent taxes on property	0.0	0.6	1.9	2.1	2.0	0.0	0.0	0.1	0.1	0.1
5000 Taxes on goods and services	**74.3**	**140.3**	**176.6**	**190.9**	**194.7**	**10.2**	**11.3**	**11.0**	**11.8**	**11.8**
5100 Taxes on production, sale, transfer, etc	67.1	125.7	158.5	168.2	172.3	9.2	10.1	9.9	10.4	10.5
5110 General taxes	38.9	77.5	97.6	97.1	101.0	5.3	6.3	6.1	6.0	6.1
5111 Value added taxes	38.9	77.5	97.6	97.1	101.0	5.3	6.3	6.1	6.0	6.1
5120 Taxes on specific goods and services	28.0	48.3	61.0	71.2	71.3	3.9	3.9	3.8	4.4	4.3
5121 Excises	20.3	31.5	36.4	48.7	46.2	2.8	2.5	2.3	3.0	2.8
5200 Taxes on use of goods and perform activities	4.5	8.5	10.5	11.4	11.2	0.6	0.7	0.7	0.7	0.7
5300 Unallocable between 5100 and 5200	2.7	6.1	7.6	11.2	11.2	0.4	0.5	0.5	0.7	0.7
6000 Other taxes	**0.0**	**27.3**	**31.9**	**30.4**	**28.1**	**0.0**	**2.2**	**2.0**	**1.9**	**1.7**
Non-wastable tax credits										
Non-wastable tax credits against 1000	..	..	0.3	12.6	14.7	..	..	0.0	0.8	0.9
Transfer component	..	..	0.1	7.6	6.0	..	..	0.0	0.5	0.4
Tax expenditure component	..	..	0.2	5.0	8.6	..	..	0.0	0.3	0.5

Note: More detailed country data and country notes are available in online chapter 5: http://dx.doi.org/10.1787/9789264283183-en. Full time series can be accessed at http://oe.cd/full-time-series.

Source: Ministero dell'economia e delle finanze; Istituto nazionale di statistica.

StatLink http://dx.doi.org/10.1787/888933612798

Table 4.34. Italy, tax revenue and % of GDP by level of government and main taxes

	Billion EUR					% of GDP				
	1990	2000	2010	2014	2015	1990	2000	2010	2014	2015
Federal or Central government										
Total tax revenue	**168.9**	**280.8**	**357.0**	**376.5**	**378.2**	**23.2**	**22.7**	**22.3**	**23.2**	**23.0**
1000 Taxes on income, profits and capital gains	92.7	154.2	193.6	196.2	196.3	12.7	12.4	12.1	12.1	11.9
2000 Social security contributions	0.0	0.0	0.0	0.0	0.0	0.0	0.0	0.0	0.0	0.0
3000 Taxes on payroll and workforce	0.9	0.0	0.0	0.0	0.0	0.1	0.0	0.0	0.0	0.0
4000 Taxes on property	6.0	12.9	21.0	23.2	22.3	0.8	1.0	1.3	1.4	1.4
5000 Taxes on goods and services	69.3	113.6	142.5	157.0	159.6	9.5	9.2	8.9	9.7	9.7
6000 Other taxes	0.0	0.0	0.0	0.0	0.0	0.0	0.0	0.0	0.0	0.0
State/Regional										
Total tax revenue	..	..	..	..	..	..	..	..	..	..
1000 Taxes on income, profits and capital gains	..	..	..	..	..	..	..	..	..	..
2000 Social security contributions	..	..	..	..	..	..	..	..	..	..
3000 Taxes on payroll and workforce	..	..	..	..	..	..	..	..	..	..
4000 Taxes on property	..	..	..	..	..	..	..	..	..	..
5000 Taxes on goods and services	..	..	..	..	..	..	..	..	..	..
6000 Other taxes	..	..	..	..	..	..	..	..	..	..
Local government										
Total tax revenue	**7.7**	**77.2**	**103.2**	**116.6**	**117.4**	**1.1**	**6.2**	**6.4**	**7.2**	**7.1**
1000 Taxes on income, profits and capital gains	4.0	12.7	25.6	28.8	30.3	0.6	1.0	1.6	1.8	1.8
2000 Social security contributions	0.0	0.0	0.0	0.0	0.0	0.0	0.0	0.0	0.0	0.0
3000 Taxes on payroll and workforce	0.0	0.0	0.0	0.0	0.0	0.0	0.0	0.0	0.0	0.0
4000 Taxes on property	0.0	10.5	11.5	23.6	23.9	0.0	0.8	0.7	1.5	1.5
5000 Taxes on goods and services	3.7	26.7	34.2	33.9	35.1	0.5	2.2	2.1	2.1	2.1
6000 Other taxes	0.0	27.3	31.9	30.4	28.1	0.0	2.2	2.0	1.9	1.7
Social Security Funds										
Total tax revenue	**87.3**	**143.6**	**209.1**	**209.7**	**214.4**	**12.0**	**11.6**	**13.0**	**12.9**	**13.0**
1000 Taxes on income, profits and capital gains	0.0	0.0	0.0	0.0	0.0	0.0	0.0	0.0	0.0	0.0
2000 Social security contributions	87.3	143.6	209.1	209.7	214.4	12.0	11.6	13.0	12.9	13.0
3000 Taxes on payroll and workforce	0.0	0.0	0.0	0.0	0.0	0.0	0.0	0.0	0.0	0.0
4000 Taxes on property	0.0	0.0	0.0	0.0	0.0	0.0	0.0	0.0	0.0	0.0
5000 Taxes on goods and services	0.0	0.0	0.0	0.0	0.0	0.0	0.0	0.0	0.0	0.0
6000 Other taxes	0.0	0.0	0.0	0.0	0.0	0.0	0.0	0.0	0.0	0.0

Note: More detailed country data and country notes are available in online chapter 6: http://dx.doi.org/10.1787/9789264283183-en. Full time series can be accessed at http://oe.cd/full-time-series.

Source: Ministero dell'economia e delle finanze; Istituto nazionale di statistica.

StatLink http://dx.doi.org/10.1787/888933612817

Table 4.35. **Japan, tax revenue and % of GDP by selected tax category**

	Billion JPY					% of GDP				
	1990	2000	2010	2014	2015	1990	2000	2010	2014	2015
Total tax revenue	**130 842.7**	**136 235.8**	**132 484.3**	**156 886.4**	**163 545.1**	**28.2**	**25.8**	**26.5**	**30.3**	**30.7**
1000 Taxes on income, profits and capital gains	**65 681.6**	**47 398.2**	**40 034.3**	**49 939.2**	**50 968.7**	**14.2**	**9.0**	**8.0**	**9.6**	**9.6**
1100 Of individuals	36 393.6	28 677.3	24 662.7	29 655.0	30 862.5	7.8	5.4	4.9	5.7	5.8
1200 Corporate	29 288.0	18 720.9	15 371.6	20 284.2	20 106.2	6.3	3.5	3.1	3.9	3.8
1300 Unallocable between 1100 and 1200	0.0	0.0	0.0	0.0	0.0	0.0	0.0	0.0	0.0	0.0
2000 Social security contributions	**34 612.6**	**47 968.3**	**54 460.6**	**62 251.8**	**64 477.2**	**7.5**	**9.1**	**10.9**	**12.0**	**12.1**
2100 Employees	13 895.0	19 829.9	23 592.6	27 168.1	28 216.2	3.0	3.8	4.7	5.2	5.3
2200 Employers	16 648.8	22 455.5	24 674.2	28 373.9	29 527.8	3.6	4.2	4.9	5.5	5.6
2300 Self-employed or non-employed	4 068.8	5 682.9	6 193.8	6 709.8	6 733.2	0.9	1.1	1.2	1.3	1.3
2400 Unallocable between 2100, 2200 and 2300	0.0	0.0	0.0	0.0	0.0	0.0	0.0	0.0	0.0	0.0
3000 Taxes on payroll and workforce	**0.0**	**0.0**	**0.0**	**0.0**	**0.0**	**0.0**	**0.0**	**0.0**	**0.0**	**0.0**
4000 Taxes on property	**12 296.3**	**14 294.4**	**12 878.3**	**13 305.6**	**13 399.7**	**2.7**	**2.7**	**2.6**	**2.6**	**2.5**
4100 Recurrent taxes on immovable property	7 098.5	10 413.7	10 225.0	10 016.0	10 005.0	1.5	2.0	2.0	1.9	1.9
4200 Recurrent taxes on net wealth	0.0	0.0	0.0	0.0	0.0	0.0	0.0	0.0	0.0	0.0
4300 Estate, inheritance and gift taxes	1 918.0	1 782.2	1 250.4	1 882.9	1 968.4	0.4	0.3	0.3	0.4	0.4
4400 Taxes on financial and capital transactions	3 279.8	2 098.5	1 402.9	1 406.7	1 426.3	0.7	0.4	0.3	0.3	0.3
4500 Non-recurrent taxes	0.0	0.0	0.0	0.0	0.0	0.0	0.0	0.0	0.0	0.0
4600 Other recurrent taxes on property	0.0	0.0	0.0	0.0	0.0	0.0	0.0	0.0	0.0	0.0
5000 Taxes on goods and services	**17 916.8**	**26 227.2**	**24 730.2**	**30 991.3**	**34 286.4**	**3.9**	**5.0**	**5.0**	**6.0**	**6.4**
5100 Taxes on production, sale, transfer, etc	15 646.5	23 180.2	22 160.4	28 587.1	31 870.7	3.4	4.4	4.4	5.5	6.0
5110 General taxes	5 778.3	12 350.3	12 675.2	19 135.4	22 400.5	1.2	2.3	2.5	3.7	4.2
5111 Value added taxes	5 778.3	12 350.3	12 675.2	19 135.4	22 400.5	1.2	2.3	2.5	3.7	4.2
5120 Taxes on specific goods and services	9 868.2	10 829.9	9 485.2	9 451.7	9 470.2	2.1	2.0	1.9	1.8	1.8
5121 Excises	8 637.2	9 837.0	8 622.4	8 308.4	8 351.2	1.9	1.9	1.7	1.6	1.6
5200 Taxes on use of goods and perform activities	2 270.3	3 047.0	2 569.8	2 404.2	2 415.7	0.5	0.6	0.5	0.5	0.5
5300 Unallocable between 5100 and 5200	0.0	0.0	0.0	0.0	0.0	0.0	0.0	0.0	0.0	0.0
6000 Other taxes	**335.4**	**347.7**	**381.1**	**398.5**	**413.0**	**0.1**	**0.1**	**0.1**	**0.1**	**0.1**
Non-wastable tax credits										
Non-wastable tax credits against 1000	..	..	..	..	..	..	..	..	..	..
Transfer component	..	..	..	..	..	..	..	..	..	..
Tax expenditure component	..	..	..	..	..	..	..	..	..	..

Note: More detailed country data and country notes are available in online chapter 5: http://dx.doi.org/10.1787/9789264283183-en. Full time series can be accessed at http://oe.cd/full-time-series.

Source: Tax Bureau, Ministry of Finance.

StatLink http://dx.doi.org/10.1787/888933612836

Table 4.36. **Japan, tax revenue and % of GDP by level of government and main taxes**

	Billion JPY					% of GDP				
	1990	2000	2010	2014	2015	1990	2000	2010	2014	2015
Federal or Central government										
Total tax revenue	**62 779.7**	**52 720.8**	**43 707.4**	**57 849.2**	**59 969.4**	**13.5**	**10.0**	**8.8**	**11.2**	**11.3**
1000 Taxes on income, profits and capital gains	44 379.1	30 536.2	23 372.1	30 999.2	31 606.8	9.6	5.8	4.7	6.0	5.9
2000 Social security contributions	0.0	0.0	0.0	0.0	0.0	0.0	0.0	0.0	0.0	0.0
3000 Taxes on payroll and workforce	0.0	0.0	0.0	0.0	0.0	0.0	0.0	0.0	0.0	0.0
4000 Taxes on property	4 601.6	3 314.9	2 274.5	2 917.9	3 018.0	1.0	0.6	0.5	0.6	0.6
5000 Taxes on goods and services	13 799.0	18 869.7	18 060.9	23 932.1	25 344.5	3.0	3.6	3.6	4.6	4.8
6000 Other taxes	0.0	0.0	0.0	0.0	0.0	0.0	0.0	0.0	0.0	0.0
State/Regional										
Total tax revenue	..	..	..	..	..	..	..	..	..	..
1000 Taxes on income, profits and capital gains	..	..	..	..	..	..	..	..	..	..
2000 Social security contributions	..	..	..	..	..	..	..	..	..	..
3000 Taxes on payroll and workforce	..	..	..	..	..	..	..	..	..	..
4000 Taxes on property	..	..	..	..	..	..	..	..	..	..
5000 Taxes on goods and services	..	..	..	..	..	..	..	..	..	..
6000 Other taxes	..	..	..	..	..	..	..	..	..	..
Local government										
Total tax revenue	**33 450.4**	**35 546.7**	**34 316.3**	**36 785.4**	**39 098.5**	**7.2**	**6.7**	**6.9**	**7.1**	**7.4**
1000 Taxes on income, profits and capital gains	21 302.5	16 862.0	16 662.3	18 940.0	19 361.9	4.6	3.2	3.3	3.7	3.6
2000 Social security contributions	0.0	0.0	0.0	0.0	0.0	0.0	0.0	0.0	0.0	0.0
3000 Taxes on payroll and workforce	0.0	0.0	0.0	0.0	0.0	0.0	0.0	0.0	0.0	0.0
4000 Taxes on property	7 694.7	10 979.5	10 603.8	10 387.7	10 381.8	1.7	2.1	2.1	2.0	2.0
5000 Taxes on goods and services	4 117.8	7 357.5	6 669.2	7 059.2	8 941.9	0.9	1.4	1.3	1.4	1.7
6000 Other taxes	335.4	347.7	381.1	398.5	413.0	0.1	0.1	0.1	0.1	0.1
Social Security Funds										
Total tax revenue	**34 612.6**	**47 968.3**	**54 460.6**	**62 251.8**	**64 477.2**	**7.5**	**9.1**	**10.9**	**12.0**	**12.1**
1000 Taxes on income, profits and capital gains	0.0	0.0	0.0	0.0	0.0	0.0	0.0	0.0	0.0	0.0
2000 Social security contributions	34 612.6	47 968.3	54 460.6	62 251.8	64 477.2	7.5	9.1	10.9	12.0	12.1
3000 Taxes on payroll and workforce	0.0	0.0	0.0	0.0	0.0	0.0	0.0	0.0	0.0	0.0
4000 Taxes on property	0.0	0.0	0.0	0.0	0.0	0.0	0.0	0.0	0.0	0.0
5000 Taxes on goods and services	0.0	0.0	0.0	0.0	0.0	0.0	0.0	0.0	0.0	0.0
6000 Other taxes	0.0	0.0	0.0	0.0	0.0	0.0	0.0	0.0	0.0	0.0

Note: More detailed country data and country notes are available in online chapter 6: http://dx.doi.org/10.1787/9789264283183-en. Full time series can be accessed at http://oe.cd/full-time-series.

Source: Tax Bureau, Ministry of Finance.

StatLink http://dx.doi.org/10.1787/888933612855

Table 4.37. **Korea, tax revenue and % of GDP by selected tax category**

	Billion KRW					% of GDP				
	1990	2000	2010	2014	2015	1990	2000	2010	2014	2015
Total tax revenue	**37 261.7**	**136 295.0**	**295 968.0**	**365 428.0**	**393 559.0**	**18.8**	**21.5**	**23.4**	**24.6**	**25.2**
1000 Taxes on income, profits and capital gains	**12 203.5**	**39 254.0**	**82 905.0**	**106 353.0**	**119 151.0**	**6.2**	**6.2**	**6.6**	**7.2**	**7.6**
1100 Of individuals	7 440.4	19 950.0	42 098.0	59 457.0	67 600.0	3.8	3.1	3.3	4.0	4.3
1200 Corporate	4 756.6	19 271.0	40 807.0	46 896.0	51 551.0	2.4	3.0	3.2	3.2	3.3
1300 Unallocable between 1100 and 1200	6.5	33.0	0.0	0.0	0.0	0.0	0.0	0.0	0.0	0.0
2000 Social security contributions	**3 760.0**	**22 759.0**	**69 090.0**	**98 184.0**	**104 693.0**	**1.9**	**3.6**	**5.5**	**6.6**	**6.7**
2100 Employees	1 464.0	8 578.0	28 213.0	41 355.0	44 281.0	0.7	1.4	2.2	2.8	2.8
2200 Employers	1 694.0	9 409.0	30 856.0	44 806.0	47 846.0	0.9	1.5	2.4	3.0	3.1
2300 Self-employed or non-employed	602.0	4 772.0	10 021.0	12 023.0	12 566.0	0.3	0.8	0.8	0.8	0.8
2400 Unallocable between 2100, 2200 and 2300	0.0	0.0	0.0	0.0	0.0	0.0	0.0	0.0	0.0	0.0
3000 Taxes on payroll and workforce	**152.8**	**258.0**	**714.0**	**1 042.0**	**1 122.0**	**0.1**	**0.0**	**0.1**	**0.1**	**0.1**
4000 Taxes on property	**4 388.9**	**16 846.0**	**33 516.0**	**40 305.0**	**48 625.0**	**2.2**	**2.7**	**2.6**	**2.7**	**3.1**
4100 Recurrent taxes on immovable property	980.0	3 385.0	9 270.0	11 654.0	12 486.0	0.5	0.5	0.7	0.8	0.8
4200 Recurrent taxes on net wealth	0.0	0.0	0.0	0.0	0.0	0.0	0.0	0.0	0.0	0.0
4300 Estate, inheritance and gift taxes	353.9	989.0	3 076.0	4 625.0	5 044.0	0.2	0.2	0.2	0.3	0.3
4400 Taxes on financial and capital transactions	2 959.7	11 935.0	21 170.0	24 026.0	31 095.0	1.5	1.9	1.7	1.6	2.0
4500 Non-recurrent taxes	95.3	537.0	0.0	0.0	0.0	0.0	0.1	0.0	0.0	0.0
4600 Other recurrent taxes on property	0.0	0.0	0.0	0.0	0.0	0.0	0.0	0.0	0.0	0.0
5000 Taxes on goods and services	**16 497.5**	**52 271.0**	**99 769.0**	**109 451.0**	**110 326.0**	**8.3**	**8.2**	**7.9**	**7.4**	**7.1**
5100 Taxes on production, sale, transfer, etc	16 023.5	50 023.0	96 573.0	102 531.0	103 254.0	8.1	7.9	7.6	6.9	6.6
5110 General taxes	6 964.4	23 212.0	51 800.0	62 975.0	60 162.0	3.5	3.7	4.1	4.2	3.8
5111 Value added taxes	6 964.4	23 212.0	51 800.0	62 975.0	60 162.0	3.5	3.7	4.1	4.2	3.8
5120 Taxes on specific goods and services	9 059.1	26 811.0	44 773.0	39 556.0	43 092.0	4.6	4.2	3.5	2.7	2.8
5121 Excises	4 923.7	18 155.0	31 340.0	28 226.0	31 857.0	2.5	2.9	2.5	1.9	2.0
5200 Taxes on use of goods and perform activities	473.9	2 248.0	3 196.0	6 920.0	7 072.0	0.2	0.4	0.3	0.5	0.5
5300 Unallocable between 5100 and 5200	0.0	0.0	0.0	0.0	0.0	0.0	0.0	0.0	0.0	0.0
6000 Other taxes	**259.1**	**4 907.0**	**9 974.0**	**10 093.0**	**9 642.0**	**0.1**	**0.8**	**0.8**	**0.7**	**0.6**
Non-wastable tax credits										
Non-wastable tax credits against 1000	..	..	..	..	..	..	..	..	..	..
Transfer component	..	..	..	..	..	..	..	..	..	..
Tax expenditure component	..	..	..	..	..	..	..	..	..	..

Note: More detailed country data and country notes are available in online chapter 5: http://dx.doi.org/10.1787/9789264283183-en. Full time series can be accessed at http://oe.cd/full-time-series.

Source: Ministry of Finance and Economy, Ministry of Home Affairs.

StatLink http://dx.doi.org/10.1787/888933612874

Table 4.38. **Korea, tax revenue and % of GDP by level of government and main taxes**

	Billion KRW					% of GDP				
	1990	2000	2010	2014	2015	1990	2000	2010	2014	2015
Federal or Central government										
Total tax revenue	**27 140.8**	**92 935.0**	**177 718.0**	**205 519.0**	**217 888.0**	**13.7**	**14.6**	**14.0**	**13.8**	**13.9**
1000 Taxes on income, profits and capital gains	11 655.2	35 824.0	75 352.0	96 454.0	106 162.0	5.9	5.6	6.0	6.5	6.8
2000 Social security contributions	0.0	0.0	0.0	0.0	0.0	0.0	0.0	0.0	0.0	0.0
3000 Taxes on payroll and workforce	29.3	0.0	0.0	0.0	0.0	0.0	0.0	0.0	0.0	0.0
4000 Taxes on property	866.3	5 866.0	11 288.0	12 347.0	15 164.0	0.4	0.9	0.9	0.8	1.0
5000 Taxes on goods and services	14 377.5	46 812.0	86 629.0	92 669.0	93 127.0	7.3	7.4	6.8	6.2	6.0
6000 Other taxes	212.5	4 433.0	4 449.0	4 049.0	3 435.0	0.1	0.7	0.4	0.3	0.2
State/Regional										
Total tax revenue	..	..	..	..	..	..	..	..	..	..
1000 Taxes on income, profits and capital gains	..	..	..	..	..	..	..	..	..	..
2000 Social security contributions	..	..	..	..	..	..	..	..	..	..
3000 Taxes on payroll and workforce	..	..	..	..	..	..	..	..	..	..
4000 Taxes on property	..	..	..	..	..	..	..	..	..	..
5000 Taxes on goods and services	..	..	..	..	..	..	..	..	..	..
6000 Other taxes	..	..	..	..	..	..	..	..	..	..
Local government										
Total tax revenue	**6 360.9**	**20 601.0**	**49 160.0**	**61 725.0**	**70 978.0**	**3.2**	**3.2**	**3.9**	**4.2**	**4.5**
1000 Taxes on income, profits and capital gains	548.3	3 430.0	7 553.0	9 899.0	12 989.0	0.3	0.5	0.6	0.7	0.8
2000 Social security contributions	0.0	0.0	0.0	0.0	0.0	0.0	0.0	0.0	0.0	0.0
3000 Taxes on payroll and workforce	123.5	258.0	714.0	1 042.0	1 122.0	0.1	0.0	0.1	0.1	0.1
4000 Taxes on property	3 522.6	10 980.0	22 228.0	27 958.0	33 461.0	1.8	1.7	1.8	1.9	2.1
5000 Taxes on goods and services	2 120.0	5 459.0	13 140.0	16 782.0	17 199.0	1.1	0.9	1.0	1.1	1.1
6000 Other taxes	46.6	474.0	5 525.0	6 044.0	6 207.0	0.0	0.1	0.4	0.4	0.4
Social Security Funds										
Total tax revenue	**3 760.0**	**22 759.0**	**69 090.0**	**98 184.0**	**104 693.0**	**1.9**	**3.6**	**5.5**	**6.6**	**6.7**
1000 Taxes on income, profits and capital gains	0.0	0.0	0.0	0.0	0.0	0.0	0.0	0.0	0.0	0.0
2000 Social security contributions	3 760.0	22 759.0	69 090.0	98 184.0	104 693.0	1.9	3.6	5.5	6.6	6.7
3000 Taxes on payroll and workforce	0.0	0.0	0.0	0.0	0.0	0.0	0.0	0.0	0.0	0.0
4000 Taxes on property	0.0	0.0	0.0	0.0	0.0	0.0	0.0	0.0	0.0	0.0
5000 Taxes on goods and services	0.0	0.0	0.0	0.0	0.0	0.0	0.0	0.0	0.0	0.0
6000 Other taxes	0.0	0.0	0.0	0.0	0.0	0.0	0.0	0.0	0.0	0.0

Note: More detailed country data and country notes are available in online chapter 6: http://dx.doi.org/10.1787/9789264283183-en. Full time series can be accessed at http://oe.cd/full-time-series.

Source: Ministry of Finance and Economy, Ministry of Home Affairs.

StatLink http://dx.doi.org/10.1787/888933612893

Table 4.39. **Latvia, tax revenue and % of GDP by selected tax category**

	Billion EUR					% of GDP				
	1990	2000	2010	2014	2015	1990	2000	2010	2014	2015
Total tax revenue	..	**2.0**	**5.0**	**6.8**	**7.1**	..	**29.1**	**28.1**	**28.8**	**29.0**
1000 Taxes on income, profits and capital gains	..	**0.5**	**1.3**	**1.8**	**1.8**	..	**7.0**	**7.2**	**7.5**	**7.5**
1100 Of individuals	..	0.4	1.1	1.4	1.4	..	5.5	6.2	5.9	5.9
1200 Corporate	..	0.1	0.2	0.4	0.4	..	1.5	1.0	1.5	1.6
1300 Unallocable between 1100 and 1200	..	0.0	0.0	0.0	0.0	..	0.0	0.0	0.0	0.0
2000 Social security contributions	..	**0.7**	**1.6**	**2.0**	**2.0**	..	**9.8**	**8.7**	**8.4**	**8.3**
2100 Employees	..	0.2	0.4	0.6	0.6	..	2.4	2.3	2.6	2.6
2200 Employers	..	0.5	1.1	1.4	1.4	..	7.3	6.3	5.8	5.7
2300 Self-employed or non-employed	..	0.0	0.0	0.0	0.0	..	0.0	0.1	0.0	0.1
2400 Unallocable between 2100, 2200 and 2300	..	0.0	0.0	0.0	0.0	..	0.0	0.0	0.0	0.0
3000 Taxes on payroll and workforce	..	**0.0**	**0.0**	**0.0**	**0.0**	..	**0.0**	**0.0**	**0.0**	**0.0**
4000 Taxes on property	..	**0.1**	**0.2**	**0.2**	**0.2**	..	**1.1**	**0.9**	**1.0**	**1.0**
4100 Recurrent taxes on immovable property	..	0.1	0.1	0.2	0.2	..	0.9	0.7	0.8	0.8
4200 Recurrent taxes on net wealth	..	0.0	0.0	0.0	0.0	..	0.0	0.0	0.0	0.0
4300 Estate, inheritance and gift taxes	..	0.0	0.0	0.0	0.0	..	0.0	0.0	0.0	0.0
4400 Taxes on financial and capital transactions	..	0.0	0.0	0.0	0.0	..	0.2	0.1	0.2	0.2
4500 Non-recurrent taxes	..	0.0	0.0	0.0	0.0	..	0.0	0.0	0.0	0.0
4600 Other recurrent taxes on property	..	0.0	0.0	0.0	0.0	..	0.0	0.0	0.0	0.0
5000 Taxes on goods and services	..	**0.8**	**2.0**	**2.8**	**2.9**	..	**11.2**	**11.2**	**11.8**	**12.0**
5100 Taxes on production, sale, transfer, etc	..	0.7	1.9	2.6	2.8	..	10.8	10.5	11.1	11.3
5110 General taxes	..	0.5	1.2	1.8	1.9	..	7.0	6.7	7.7	7.8
5111 Value added taxes	..	0.5	1.2	1.8	1.9	..	7.0	6.7	7.6	7.7
5120 Taxes on specific goods and services	..	0.3	0.7	0.8	0.8	..	3.8	3.8	3.4	3.5
5121 Excises	..	0.2	0.6	0.8	0.8	..	3.4	3.6	3.2	3.3
5200 Taxes on use of goods and perform activities	..	0.0	0.1	0.2	0.2	..	0.5	0.7	0.7	0.7
5300 Unallocable between 5100 and 5200	..	0.0	0.0	0.0	0.0	..	0.0	0.0	0.0	0.0
6000 Other taxes	..	**0.0**	**0.0**	**0.0**	**0.0**	..	**0.0**	**0.0**	**0.0**	**0.0**
Non-wastable tax credits										
Non-wastable tax credits against 1000	..	..	..	..	..	..	..	..	..	..
Transfer component	..	..	..	..	..	..	..	..	..	..
Tax expenditure component	..	..	..	..	..	..	..	..	..	..

Note: More detailed country data and country notes are available in online chapter 5: http://dx.doi.org/10.1787/9789264283183-en. Full time series can be accessed at http://oe.cd/full-time-series.

Source: Ministry of Finance.

StatLink http://dx.doi.org/10.1787/888933612912

Table 4.40. **Latvia, tax revenue and % of GDP by level of government and main taxes**

	Billion EUR					% of GDP				
	1990	2000	2010	2014	2015	1990	2000	2010	2014	2015
Federal or Central government										
Total tax revenue	..	**1.0**	**2.4**	**3.5**	**3.6**	..	**14.4**	**13.5**	**14.6**	**14.9**
1000 Taxes on income, profits and capital gains	..	0.2	0.4	0.6	0.7	..	3.1	2.2	2.7	2.8
2000 Social security contributions	..	0.0	0.0	0.0	0.0	..	0.0	0.0	0.0	0.0
3000 Taxes on payroll and workforce	..	0.0	0.0	0.0	0.0	..	0.0	0.0	0.0	0.0
4000 Taxes on property	..	0.0	0.0	0.1	0.0	..	0.2	0.2	0.2	0.2
5000 Taxes on goods and services	..	0.8	2.0	2.8	2.9	..	11.2	11.1	11.7	11.9
6000 Other taxes	..	0.0	0.0	0.0	0.0	..	0.0	0.0	0.0	0.0
State/Regional										
Total tax revenue	..	..	..	..	..	..	..	..	..	..
1000 Taxes on income, profits and capital gains	..	..	..	..	..	..	..	..	..	..
2000 Social security contributions	..	..	..	..	..	..	..	..	..	..
3000 Taxes on payroll and workforce	..	..	..	..	..	..	..	..	..	..
4000 Taxes on property	..	..	..	..	..	..	..	..	..	..
5000 Taxes on goods and services	..	..	..	..	..	..	..	..	..	..
6000 Other taxes	..	..	..	..	..	..	..	..	..	..
Local government										
Total tax revenue	..	**0.3**	**1.0**	**1.3**	**1.4**	..	**4.9**	**5.8**	**5.6**	**5.6**
1000 Taxes on income, profits and capital gains	..	0.3	0.9	1.1	1.2	..	3.9	5.0	4.7	4.7
2000 Social security contributions	..	0.0	0.0	0.0	0.0	..	0.0	0.0	0.0	0.0
3000 Taxes on payroll and workforce	..	0.0	0.0	0.0	0.0	..	0.0	0.0	0.0	0.0
4000 Taxes on property	..	0.1	0.1	0.2	0.2	..	0.9	0.7	0.8	0.8
5000 Taxes on goods and services	..	0.0	0.0	0.0	0.0	..	0.1	0.1	0.1	0.1
6000 Other taxes	..	0.0	0.0	0.0	0.0	..	0.0	0.0	0.0	0.0
Social Security Funds										
Total tax revenue	..	**0.7**	**1.6**	**2.0**	**2.0**	..	**9.8**	**8.7**	**8.4**	**8.3**
1000 Taxes on income, profits and capital gains	..	0.0	0.0	0.0	0.0	..	0.0	0.0	0.0	0.0
2000 Social security contributions	..	0.7	1.6	2.0	2.0	..	9.8	8.7	8.4	8.3
3000 Taxes on payroll and workforce	..	0.0	0.0	0.0	0.0	..	0.0	0.0	0.0	0.0
4000 Taxes on property	..	0.0	0.0	0.0	0.0	..	0.0	0.0	0.0	0.0
5000 Taxes on goods and services	..	0.0	0.0	0.0	0.0	..	0.0	0.0	0.0	0.0
6000 Other taxes	..	0.0	0.0	0.0	0.0	..	0.0	0.0	0.0	0.0

Note: More detailed country data and country notes are available in online chapter 6: http://dx.doi.org/10.1787/9789264283183-en. Full time series can be accessed at http://oe.cd/full-time-series.

Source: Ministry of Finance.

StatLink http://dx.doi.org/10.1787/888933612931

Table 4.41. **Luxembourg, tax revenue and % of GDP by selected tax category**

	Billion EUR					% of GDP				
	1990	2000	2010	2014	2015	1990	2000	2010	2014	2015
Total tax revenue	**3.7**	**8.5**	**15.0**	**18.7**	**19.3**	**33.5**	**36.9**	**37.4**	**37.4**	**36.8**
1000 Taxes on income, profits and capital gains	**1.5**	**3.1**	**5.5**	**6.5**	**7.0**	**13.5**	**13.5**	**13.6**	**12.9**	**13.4**
1100 Of individuals	0.9	1.6	3.2	4.3	4.7	8.1	6.8	7.9	8.7	9.0
1200 Corporate	0.6	1.5	2.3	2.1	2.3	5.4	6.6	5.8	4.3	4.4
1300 Unallocable between 1100 and 1200	0.0	0.0	0.0	0.0	0.0	0.0	0.0	0.0	0.0	0.0
2000 Social security contributions	**1.0**	**2.2**	**4.4**	**5.3**	**5.6**	**9.2**	**9.6**	**10.8**	**10.7**	**10.7**
2100 Employees	0.4	1.0	2.0	2.4	2.6	3.5	4.3	5.0	4.9	4.9
2200 Employers	0.5	1.0	1.9	2.3	2.4	4.5	4.2	4.7	4.5	4.5
2300 Self-employed or non-employed	0.1	0.3	0.5	0.6	0.6	1.2	1.2	1.2	1.3	1.2
2400 Unallocable between 2100, 2200 and 2300	0.0	0.0	0.0	0.0	0.0	0.0	0.0	0.0	0.0	0.0
3000 Taxes on payroll and workforce	**0.0**	**0.0**	**0.0**	**0.0**	**0.0**	**0.0**	**0.0**	**0.0**	**0.0**	**0.0**
4000 Taxes on property	**0.3**	**0.9**	**1.1**	**1.5**	**1.7**	**2.8**	**3.9**	**2.6**	**2.9**	**3.3**
4100 Recurrent taxes on immovable property	0.0	0.0	0.0	0.0	0.0	0.1	0.1	0.1	0.1	0.1
4200 Recurrent taxes on net wealth	0.2	0.6	0.8	1.1	1.3	1.6	2.7	2.1	2.2	2.5
4300 Estate, inheritance and gift taxes	0.0	0.0	0.1	0.1	0.1	0.1	0.1	0.1	0.1	0.1
4400 Taxes on financial and capital transactions	0.1	0.2	0.2	0.3	0.3	1.0	1.0	0.4	0.5	0.5
4500 Non-recurrent taxes	0.0	0.0	0.0	0.0	0.0	0.0	0.0	0.0	0.0	0.0
4600 Other recurrent taxes on property	0.0	0.0	0.0	0.0	0.0	0.0	0.0	0.0	0.0	0.0
5000 Taxes on goods and services	**0.9**	**2.2**	**4.1**	**5.4**	**4.9**	**7.9**	**9.7**	**10.2**	**10.8**	**9.4**
5100 Taxes on production, sale, transfer, etc	0.8	2.2	4.0	5.3	4.8	7.7	9.6	10.0	10.7	9.2
5110 General taxes	0.4	1.1	2.6	3.7	3.4	4.0	4.9	6.4	7.4	6.5
5111 Value added taxes	0.4	1.1	2.6	3.7	3.4	4.0	4.9	6.4	7.4	6.5
5120 Taxes on specific goods and services	0.4	1.1	1.5	1.6	1.4	3.7	4.7	3.7	3.3	2.8
5121 Excises	0.4	1.0	1.4	1.6	1.4	3.3	4.5	3.5	3.1	2.6
5200 Taxes on use of goods and perform activities	0.0	0.0	0.1	0.1	0.1	0.2	0.1	0.2	0.2	0.2
5300 Unallocable between 5100 and 5200	0.0	0.0	0.0	0.0	0.0	0.0	0.0	0.0	0.0	0.0
6000 Other taxes	**0.0**	**0.0**	**0.0**	**0.0**	**0.0**	**0.1**	**0.1**	**0.1**	**0.0**	**0.1**
Non-wastable tax credits										
Non-wastable tax credits against 1000	..	..	..	0.2	0.2	..	..	..	0.4	0.4
Transfer component	..	..	..	..	..	..	..	..	..	..
Tax expenditure component	..	..	..	..	..	..	..	..	..	..

Note: More detailed country data and country notes are available in online chapter 5: http://dx.doi.org/10.1787/9789264283183-en. Full time series can be accessed at http://oe.cd/full-time-series.

Source: General account of the State.

StatLink http://dx.doi.org/10.1787/888933612950

Table 4.42. **Luxembourg, tax revenue and % of GDP by level of government and main taxes**

	Billion EUR					% of GDP				
	1990	2000	2010	2014	2015	1990	2000	2010	2014	2015
Federal or Central government										
Total tax revenue	**2.4**	**5.8**	**10.1**	**12.9**	**13.2**	**22.1**	**25.3**	**25.2**	**25.8**	**25.2**
1000 Taxes on income, profits and capital gains	1.3	2.6	4.9	5.9	6.4	11.6	11.5	12.1	11.9	12.2
2000 Social security contributions	0.0	0.1	0.1	0.2	0.2	0.1	0.3	0.3	0.3	0.3
3000 Taxes on payroll and workforce	0.0	0.0	0.0	0.0	0.0	0.0	0.0	0.0	0.0	0.0
4000 Taxes on property	0.3	0.9	1.0	1.4	1.7	2.6	3.8	2.5	2.8	3.2
5000 Taxes on goods and services	0.8	2.2	4.1	5.4	4.9	7.7	9.7	10.2	10.8	9.4
6000 Other taxes	0.0	0.0	0.0	0.0	0.0	0.1	0.0	0.0	0.0	0.1
State/Regional										
Total tax revenue	..	..	..	..	..	..	..	..	..	..
1000 Taxes on income, profits and capital gains	..	..	..	..	..	..	..	..	..	..
2000 Social security contributions	..	..	..	..	..	..	..	..	..	..
3000 Taxes on payroll and workforce	..	..	..	..	..	..	..	..	..	..
4000 Taxes on property	..	..	..	..	..	..	..	..	..	..
5000 Taxes on goods and services	..	..	..	..	..	..	..	..	..	..
6000 Other taxes	..	..	..	..	..	..	..	..	..	..
Local government										
Total tax revenue	**0.2**	**0.5**	**0.7**	**0.6**	**0.7**	**2.1**	**2.1**	**1.6**	**1.2**	**1.3**
1000 Taxes on income, profits and capital gains	0.2	0.5	0.6	0.5	0.6	1.9	2.0	1.5	1.1	1.2
2000 Social security contributions	0.0	0.0	0.0	0.0	0.0	0.0	0.0	0.0	0.0	0.0
3000 Taxes on payroll and workforce	0.0	0.0	0.0	0.0	0.0	0.0	0.0	0.0	0.0	0.0
4000 Taxes on property	0.0	0.0	0.0	0.1	0.1	0.2	0.1	0.1	0.1	0.1
5000 Taxes on goods and services	0.0	0.0	0.0	0.0	0.0	0.0	0.0	0.0	0.0	0.0
6000 Other taxes	0.0	0.0	0.0	0.0	0.0	0.0	0.0	0.0	0.0	0.0
Social Security Funds										
Total tax revenue	**1.0**	**2.2**	**4.2**	**5.2**	**5.4**	**9.1**	**9.3**	**10.5**	**10.3**	**10.3**
1000 Taxes on income, profits and capital gains	0.0	0.0	0.0	0.0	0.0	0.0	0.0	0.0	0.0	0.0
2000 Social security contributions	1.0	2.2	4.2	5.2	5.4	9.1	9.3	10.5	10.3	10.3
3000 Taxes on payroll and workforce	0.0	0.0	0.0	0.0	0.0	0.0	0.0	0.0	0.0	0.0
4000 Taxes on property	0.0	0.0	0.0	0.0	0.0	0.0	0.0	0.0	0.0	0.0
5000 Taxes on goods and services	0.0	0.0	0.0	0.0	0.0	0.0	0.0	0.0	0.0	0.0
6000 Other taxes	0.0	0.0	0.0	0.0	0.0	0.0	0.0	0.0	0.0	0.0

Note: More detailed country data and country notes are available in online chapter 6: http://dx.doi.org/10.1787/9789264283183-en. Full time series can be accessed at http://oe.cd/full-time-series.

Source: General account of the State.

StatLink http://dx.doi.org/10.1787/888933612969

Table 4.43. **Mexico, tax revenue and % of GDP by selected tax category**

	Billion MXN					% of GDP				
	1990	2000	2010	2014	2015	1990	2000	2010	2014	2015
Total tax revenue	**102.0**	**804.2**	**1 772.0**	**2 453.0**	**2 953.2**	**12.4**	**13.1**	**13.4**	**14.2**	**16.2**
1000 Taxes on income, profits and capital gains	**34.7**	**276.5**	**683.6**	**979.3**	**1 230.6**	**4.2**	**4.5**	**5.2**	**5.7**	**6.8**
1100 Of individuals	..	..	313.5	514.2	609.4	..	..	2.4	3.0	3.3
1200 Corporate	..	..	246.7	441.3	592.4	..	..	1.9	2.6	3.3
1300 Unallocable between 1100 and 1200	34.7	276.5	123.4	23.7	28.7	4.2	4.5	0.9	0.1	0.2
2000 Social security contributions	**17.2**	**138.2**	**277.5**	**378.4**	**409.2**	**2.1**	**2.3**	**2.1**	**2.2**	**2.2**
2100 Employees	..	..	..	..	..	..	..	..	..	..
2200 Employers	..	..	..	..	..	..	..	..	..	..
2300 Self-employed or non-employed	..	..	..	..	..	..	..	..	..	..
2400 Unallocable between 2100, 2200 and 2300	17.2	138.2	277.5	378.4	409.2	2.1	2.3	2.1	2.2	2.2
3000 Taxes on payroll and workforce	**1.8**	**11.2**	**36.9**	**64.7**	**70.2**	**0.2**	**0.2**	**0.3**	**0.4**	**0.4**
4000 Taxes on property	**1.9**	**14.0**	**39.0**	**55.0**	**57.7**	**0.2**	**0.2**	**0.3**	**0.3**	**0.3**
4100 Recurrent taxes on immovable property	1.0	9.9	25.7	37.8	38.0	0.1	0.2	0.2	0.2	0.2
4200 Recurrent taxes on net wealth	0.0	0.0	0.0	0.0	0.0	0.0	0.0	0.0	0.0	0.0
4300 Estate, inheritance and gift taxes	0.0	0.0	0.0	0.0	0.0	0.0	0.0	0.0	0.0	0.0
4400 Taxes on financial and capital transactions	0.9	4.0	13.2	17.2	19.7	0.1	0.1	0.1	0.1	0.1
4500 Non-recurrent taxes	0.0	0.0	0.0	0.0	0.0	0.0	0.0	0.0	0.0	0.0
4600 Other recurrent taxes on property	0.0	0.0	0.0	0.0	0.0	0.0	0.0	0.0	0.0	0.0
5000 Taxes on goods and services	**44.8**	**356.6**	**707.7**	**938.9**	**1 140.8**	**5.4**	**5.8**	**5.3**	**5.5**	**6.3**
5100 Taxes on production, sale, transfer, etc	44.2	310.3	630.1	859.3	1 120.6	5.4	5.1	4.8	5.0	6.2
5110 General taxes	26.6	189.6	504.5	667.1	707.2	3.2	3.1	3.8	3.9	3.9
5111 Value added taxes	26.6	189.6	504.5	667.1	707.2	3.2	3.1	3.8	3.9	3.9
5120 Taxes on specific goods and services	17.5	120.7	125.6	192.2	413.4	2.1	2.0	0.9	1.1	2.3
5121 Excises	10.1	86.2	86.1	160.8	361.5	1.2	1.4	0.6	0.9	2.0
5200 Taxes on use of goods and perform activities	0.7	46.3	77.5	79.6	20.2	0.1	0.8	0.6	0.5	0.1
5300 Unallocable between 5100 and 5200	0.0	0.0	0.0	0.0	0.0	0.0	0.0	0.0	0.0	0.0
6000 Other taxes	**1.6**	**7.7**	**27.4**	**36.8**	**44.6**	**0.2**	**0.1**	**0.2**	**0.2**	**0.2**
Non-wastable tax credits										
Non-wastable tax credits against 1000	..	..	40.3	43.7	43.8	..	..	0.3	0.3	0.2
Transfer component	..	..	9.7	2.4	1.0	..	..	0.1	0.0	0.0
Tax expenditure component	..	..	30.6	41.3	42.8	..	..	0.2	0.2	0.2

Note: More detailed country data and country notes are available in online chapter 5: http://dx.doi.org/10.1787/9789264283183-en. Full time series can be accessed at http://oe.cd/full-time-series.

Source: Ministry of Finance, Economic Department.

StatLink http://dx.doi.org/10.1787/888933612988

Table 4.44. **Mexico, tax revenue and % of GDP by level of government and main taxes**

	Billion MXN					% of GDP				
	1990	2000	2010	2014	2015	1990	2000	2010	2014	2015
Federal or Central government										
Total tax revenue	**81.4**	**637.5**	**1 407.2**	**1 917.1**	**2 373.6**	**9.9**	**10.4**	**10.6**	**11.1**	**13.0**
1000 Taxes on income, profits and capital gains	34.7	276.5	683.6	979.3	1 230.6	4.2	4.5	5.2	5.7	6.8
2000 Social security contributions	0.0	0.0	0.0	0.0	0.0	0.0	0.0	0.0	0.0	0.0
3000 Taxes on payroll and workforce	0.8	0.0	0.0	0.0	0.0	0.1	0.0	0.0	0.0	0.0
4000 Taxes on property	0.0	0.0	0.0	0.0	0.0	0.0	0.0	0.0	0.0	0.0
5000 Taxes on goods and services	44.6	355.1	701.4	913.6	1 115.7	5.4	5.8	5.3	5.3	6.1
6000 Other taxes	1.3	5.9	22.2	24.2	27.4	0.2	0.1	0.2	0.1	0.2
State/Regional										
Total tax revenue	**2.2**	**20.5**	**58.3**	**114.9**	**123.5**	**0.3**	**0.3**	**0.4**	**0.7**	**0.7**
1000 Taxes on income, profits and capital gains	0.0	0.0	0.0	0.0	0.0	0.0	0.0	0.0	0.0	0.0
2000 Social security contributions	0.0	0.0	0.0	0.0	0.0	0.0	0.0	0.0	0.0	0.0
3000 Taxes on payroll and workforce	1.0	11.2	36.8	64.7	70.2	0.1	0.2	0.3	0.4	0.4
4000 Taxes on property	0.9	7.0	13.1	19.4	22.5	0.1	0.1	0.1	0.1	0.1
5000 Taxes on goods and services	0.1	1.3	5.8	24.1	24.4	0.0	0.0	0.0	0.1	0.1
6000 Other taxes	0.2	0.9	2.5	6.8	6.5	0.0	0.0	0.0	0.0	0.0
Local government										
Total tax revenue	**1.3**	**8.0**	**29.0**	**42.7**	**46.7**	**0.2**	**0.1**	**0.2**	**0.2**	**0.3**
1000 Taxes on income, profits and capital gains	0.0	0.0	0.0	0.0	0.0	0.0	0.0	0.0	0.0	0.0
2000 Social security contributions	0.0	0.0	0.0	0.0	0.0	0.0	0.0	0.0	0.0	0.0
3000 Taxes on payroll and workforce	0.0	0.0	0.1	0.0	0.0	0.0	0.0	0.0	0.0	0.0
4000 Taxes on property	1.0	6.9	25.8	35.6	35.2	0.1	0.1	0.2	0.2	0.2
5000 Taxes on goods and services	0.1	0.2	0.5	1.3	0.8	0.0	0.0	0.0	0.0	0.0
6000 Other taxes	0.1	0.9	2.6	5.8	10.7	0.0	0.0	0.0	0.0	0.1
Social Security Funds										
Total tax revenue	**17.2**	**138.2**	**277.5**	**378.4**	**409.2**	**2.1**	**2.3**	**2.1**	**2.2**	**2.2**
1000 Taxes on income, profits and capital gains	0.0	0.0	0.0	0.0	0.0	0.0	0.0	0.0	0.0	0.0
2000 Social security contributions	17.2	138.2	277.5	378.4	409.2	2.1	2.3	2.1	2.2	2.2
3000 Taxes on payroll and workforce	0.0	0.0	0.0	0.0	0.0	0.0	0.0	0.0	0.0	0.0
4000 Taxes on property	0.0	0.0	0.0	0.0	0.0	0.0	0.0	0.0	0.0	0.0
5000 Taxes on goods and services	0.0	0.0	0.0	0.0	0.0	0.0	0.0	0.0	0.0	0.0
6000 Other taxes	0.0	0.0	0.0	0.0	0.0	0.0	0.0	0.0	0.0	0.0

Note: More detailed country data and country notes are available in online chapter 6: http://dx.doi.org/10.1787/9789264283183-en. Full time series can be accessed at http://oe.cd/full-time-series.

Source: Ministry of Finance, Economic Department.

StatLink http://dx.doi.org/10.1787/888933613007

Table 4.45. **Netherlands, tax revenue and % of GDP by selected tax category**

	Billion EUR					% of GDP				
	1990	2000	2010	2014	2015	1990	2000	2010	2014	2015
Total tax revenue	**104.4**	**166.8**	**227.9**	**248.8**	**255.3**	**40.2**	**37.2**	**36.1**	**37.5**	**37.4**
1000 Taxes on income, profits and capital gains	**33.7**	**43.3**	**63.6**	**63.7**	**70.8**	**13.0**	**9.7**	**10.1**	**9.6**	**10.4**
1100 Of individuals	25.8	25.1	49.0	46.6	52.4	9.9	5.6	7.8	7.0	7.7
1200 Corporate	7.9	18.1	14.6	17.1	18.4	3.0	4.0	2.3	2.6	2.7
1300 Unallocable between 1100 and 1200	0.0	0.0	0.0	0.0	0.0	0.0	0.0	0.0	0.0	0.0
2000 Social security contributions	**39.1**	**64.5**	**82.7**	**98.6**	**96.4**	**15.0**	**14.4**	**13.1**	**14.9**	**14.1**
2100 Employees	24.1	35.3	41.6	48.4	48.2	9.3	7.9	6.6	7.3	7.1
2200 Employers	7.8	18.7	29.4	35.0	34.6	3.0	4.2	4.6	5.3	5.1
2300 Self-employed or non-employed	7.1	10.5	11.7	15.3	13.6	2.7	2.4	1.9	2.3	2.0
2400 Unallocable between 2100, 2200 and 2300	0.0	0.0	0.0	0.0	0.0	0.0	0.0	0.0	0.0	0.0
3000 Taxes on payroll and workforce	**0.0**	**0.0**	**0.0**	**0.0**	**0.0**	**0.0**	**0.0**	**0.0**	**0.0**	**0.0**
4000 Taxes on property	**3.8**	**8.8**	**8.8**	**9.6**	**9.8**	**1.5**	**2.0**	**1.4**	**1.4**	**1.4**
4100 Recurrent taxes on immovable property	1.7	3.1	4.2	6.5	6.4	0.7	0.7	0.7	1.0	0.9
4200 Recurrent taxes on net wealth	0.6	0.8	0.0	0.0	0.0	0.2	0.2	0.0	0.0	0.0
4300 Estate, inheritance and gift taxes	0.5	1.5	1.7	1.5	1.6	0.2	0.3	0.3	0.2	0.2
4400 Taxes on financial and capital transactions	1.0	3.4	2.8	1.6	1.8	0.4	0.8	0.4	0.2	0.3
4500 Non-recurrent taxes	0.0	0.0	0.0	0.0	0.0	0.0	0.0	0.0	0.0	0.0
4600 Other recurrent taxes on property	0.0	0.0	0.0	0.0	0.0	0.0	0.0	0.0	0.0	0.0
5000 Taxes on goods and services	**27.6**	**48.2**	**70.1**	**73.6**	**75.6**	**10.6**	**10.7**	**11.1**	**11.1**	**11.1**
5100 Taxes on production, sale, transfer, etc	25.1	43.6	62.5	65.2	67.0	9.7	9.7	9.9	9.8	9.8
5110 General taxes	17.2	28.9	42.7	42.7	44.9	6.6	6.4	6.8	6.4	6.6
5111 Value added taxes	17.2	28.8	42.7	42.7	44.9	6.6	6.4	6.8	6.4	6.6
5120 Taxes on specific goods and services	7.9	14.7	19.8	22.5	22.1	3.0	3.3	3.1	3.4	3.2
5121 Excises	6.0	13.8	18.4	17.9	18.0	2.3	3.1	2.9	2.7	2.6
5200 Taxes on use of goods and perform activities	2.5	4.6	7.6	8.4	8.6	1.0	1.0	1.2	1.3	1.3
5300 Unallocable between 5100 and 5200	0.0	0.0	0.0	0.0	0.0	0.0	0.0	0.0	0.0	0.0
6000 Other taxes	**0.3**	**0.8**	**1.0**	**1.2**	**0.4**	**0.1**	**0.2**	**0.2**	**0.2**	**0.1**
Non-wastable tax credits										
Non-wastable tax credits against 1000	..	..	..	..	..	..	..	..	..	..
Transfer component	..	..	..	..	..	..	..	..	..	..
Tax expenditure component	..	..	..	..	..	..	..	..	..	..

Note: More detailed country data and country notes are available in online chapter 5: http://dx.doi.org/10.1787/9789264283183-en. Full time series can be accessed at http://oe.cd/full-time-series.

Source: Social security contributions and local taxes: Central Bureau of Statistics. Other taxes: Ministry of Finance.

StatLink http://dx.doi.org/10.1787/888933613026

Table 4.46. Netherlands, tax revenue and % of GDP by level of government and main taxes

	Billion EUR					% of GDP				
	1990	2000	2010	2014	2015	1990	2000	2010	2014	2015
Federal or Central government										
Total tax revenue	**61.4**	**95.1**	**135.1**	**138.4**	**146.7**	**23.6**	**21.2**	**21.4**	**20.9**	**21.5**
1000 Taxes on income, profits and capital gains	33.7	43.3	63.6	63.7	70.8	13.0	9.7	10.1	9.6	10.4
2000 Social security contributions	0.0	0.0	0.0	0.0	0.0	0.0	0.0	0.0	0.0	0.0
3000 Taxes on payroll and workforce	0.0	0.0	0.0	0.0	0.0	0.0	0.0	0.0	0.0	0.0
4000 Taxes on property	2.1	5.7	4.6	4.8	4.7	0.8	1.3	0.7	0.7	0.7
5000 Taxes on goods and services	25.3	45.4	66.2	68.7	70.7	9.8	10.1	10.5	10.4	10.3
6000 Other taxes	0.3	0.8	0.8	1.2	0.4	0.1	0.2	0.1	0.2	0.1
State/Regional										
Total tax revenue	..	..	..	..	..	..	..	..	..	..
1000 Taxes on income, profits and capital gains	..	..	..	..	..	..	..	..	..	..
2000 Social security contributions	..	..	..	..	..	..	..	..	..	..
3000 Taxes on payroll and workforce	..	..	..	..	..	..	..	..	..	..
4000 Taxes on property	..	..	..	..	..	..	..	..	..	..
5000 Taxes on goods and services	..	..	..	..	..	..	..	..	..	..
6000 Other taxes	..	..	..	..	..	..	..	..	..	..
Local government										
Total tax revenue	**2.5**	**5.6**	**8.1**	**9.3**	**9.6**	**1.0**	**1.2**	**1.3**	**1.4**	**1.4**
1000 Taxes on income, profits and capital gains	0.0	0.0	0.0	0.0	0.0	0.0	0.0	0.0	0.0	0.0
2000 Social security contributions	0.0	0.0	0.0	0.0	0.0	0.0	0.0	0.0	0.0	0.0
3000 Taxes on payroll and workforce	0.0	0.0	0.0	0.0	0.0	0.0	0.0	0.0	0.0	0.0
4000 Taxes on property	1.7	3.1	4.2	4.8	5.0	0.7	0.7	0.7	0.7	0.7
5000 Taxes on goods and services	0.8	2.5	3.7	4.5	4.6	0.3	0.6	0.6	0.7	0.7
6000 Other taxes	0.0	0.0	0.2	0.0	0.0	0.0	0.0	0.0	0.0	0.0
Social Security Funds										
Total tax revenue	**39.1**	**64.5**	**82.7**	**98.6**	**96.4**	**15.0**	**14.4**	**13.1**	**14.9**	**14.1**
1000 Taxes on income, profits and capital gains	0.0	0.0	0.0	0.0	0.0	0.0	0.0	0.0	0.0	0.0
2000 Social security contributions	39.1	64.5	82.7	98.6	96.4	15.0	14.4	13.1	14.9	14.1
3000 Taxes on payroll and workforce	0.0	0.0	0.0	0.0	0.0	0.0	0.0	0.0	0.0	0.0
4000 Taxes on property	0.0	0.0	0.0	0.0	0.0	0.0	0.0	0.0	0.0	0.0
5000 Taxes on goods and services	0.0	0.0	0.0	0.0	0.0	0.0	0.0	0.0	0.0	0.0
6000 Other taxes	0.0	0.0	0.0	0.0	0.0	0.0	0.0	0.0	0.0	0.0

Note: More detailed country data and country notes are available in online chapter 6: http://dx.doi.org/10.1787/9789264283183-en. Full time series can be accessed at http://oe.cd/full-time-series.

Source: Social security contributions and local taxes: Central Bureau of Statistics. Other taxes: Ministry of Finance.

StatLink http://dx.doi.org/10.1787/888933613045

Table 4.47. **New Zealand, tax revenue and % of GDP by selected tax category**

	Billion NZD					% of GDP				
	1990	2000	2010	2014	2015	1990	2000	2010	2014	2015
Total tax revenue	**27.5**	**39.8**	**62.3**	**78.0**	**82.8**	**36.2**	**32.5**	**30.3**	**32.4**	**33.0**
1000 Taxes on income, profits and capital gains	**16.4**	**23.9**	**33.5**	**43.2**	**46.0**	**21.6**	**19.5**	**16.3**	**17.9**	**18.3**
1100 Of individuals	13.2	17.1	23.5	30.1	31.6	17.4	14.0	11.4	12.5	12.6
1200 Corporate	1.8	4.9	7.6	10.3	11.4	2.3	4.0	3.7	4.3	4.6
1300 Unallocable between 1100 and 1200	1.4	1.8	2.4	2.8	3.0	1.9	1.5	1.1	1.2	1.2
2000 Social security contributions	**0.0**	**0.0**	**0.0**	**0.0**	**0.0**	**0.0**	**0.0**	**0.0**	**0.0**	**0.0**
2100 Employees	0.0	0.0	0.0	0.0	0.0	0.0	0.0	0.0	0.0	0.0
2200 Employers	0.0	0.0	0.0	0.0	0.0	0.0	0.0	0.0	0.0	0.0
2300 Self-employed or non-employed	0.0	0.0	0.0	0.0	0.0	0.0	0.0	0.0	0.0	0.0
2400 Unallocable between 2100, 2200 and 2300	0.0	0.0	0.0	0.0	0.0	0.0	0.0	0.0	0.0	0.0
3000 Taxes on payroll and workforce	**0.0**	**0.0**	**0.0**	**0.0**	**0.0**	**0.0**	**0.0**	**0.0**	**0.0**	**0.0**
4000 Taxes on property	**1.9**	**2.1**	**4.1**	**4.8**	**5.1**	**2.5**	**1.7**	**2.0**	**2.0**	**2.0**
4100 Recurrent taxes on immovable property	1.7	2.0	4.0	4.7	5.0	2.3	1.7	2.0	1.9	2.0
4200 Recurrent taxes on net wealth	0.0	0.0	0.0	0.0	0.0	0.0	0.0	0.0	0.0	0.0
4300 Estate, inheritance and gift taxes	0.1	0.0	0.0	0.0	0.0	0.1	0.0	0.0	0.0	0.0
4400 Taxes on financial and capital transactions	0.1	0.1	0.1	0.1	0.1	0.1	0.1	0.0	0.0	0.0
4500 Non-recurrent taxes	0.0	0.0	0.0	0.0	0.0	0.0	0.0	0.0	0.0	0.0
4600 Other recurrent taxes on property	0.0	0.0	0.0	0.0	0.0	0.0	0.0	0.0	0.0	0.0
5000 Taxes on goods and services	**9.2**	**13.8**	**24.7**	**30.0**	**31.8**	**12.1**	**11.3**	**12.0**	**12.5**	**12.7**
5100 Taxes on production, sale, transfer, etc	8.7	12.9	23.1	28.0	29.6	11.4	10.5	11.2	11.6	11.8
5110 General taxes	6.2	9.9	19.1	23.3	24.6	8.1	8.1	9.3	9.7	9.8
5111 Value added taxes	6.2	9.9	19.1	23.3	24.6	8.1	8.1	9.3	9.7	9.8
5120 Taxes on specific goods and services	2.5	3.0	4.0	4.7	5.0	3.3	2.5	1.9	2.0	2.0
5121 Excises	1.9	2.1	1.8	2.1	2.3	2.5	1.8	0.9	0.9	0.9
5200 Taxes on use of goods and perform activities	0.5	0.9	1.6	2.0	2.2	0.7	0.7	0.8	0.8	0.9
5300 Unallocable between 5100 and 5200	0.0	0.0	0.0	0.0	0.0	0.0	0.0	0.0	0.0	0.0
6000 Other taxes	**0.0**	**0.0**	**0.0**	**0.0**	**0.0**	**0.0**	**0.0**	**0.0**	**0.0**	**0.0**
Non-wastable tax credits										
Non-wastable tax credits against 1000	..	1.1	2.8	2.6	2.4	..	0.9	1.4	1.1	0.9
Transfer component	..	0.7	1.8	1.7	1.6	..	0.6	0.9	0.7	0.6
Tax expenditure component	..	0.3	1.0	0.9	0.8	..	0.3	0.5	0.4	0.3

Note: More detailed country data and country notes are available in online chapter 5: http://dx.doi.org/10.1787/9789264283183-en. Full time series can be accessed at http://oe.cd/full-time-series.

Source: Local Authorities Statistics, Department of Statistics, Wellington.

StatLink http://dx.doi.org/10.1787/888933613064

Table 4.48. **New Zealand, tax revenue and % of GDP by level of government and main taxes**

	Billion NZD					% of GDP				
	1990	2000	2010	2014	2015	1990	2000	2010	2014	2015
Federal or Central government										
Total tax revenue	**25.8**	**37.5**	**57.9**	**72.7**	**77.2**	**34.0**	**30.7**	**28.1**	**30.2**	**30.8**
1000 Taxes on income, profits and capital gains	16.4	23.9	33.5	43.2	46.0	21.6	19.5	16.3	17.9	18.3
2000 Social security contributions	0.0	0.0	0.0	0.0	0.0	0.0	0.0	0.0	0.0	0.0
3000 Taxes on payroll and workforce	0.0	0.0	0.0	0.0	0.0	0.0	0.0	0.0	0.0	0.0
4000 Taxes on property	0.3	0.1	0.1	0.1	0.1	0.4	0.1	0.0	0.0	0.0
5000 Taxes on goods and services	9.1	13.6	24.3	29.4	31.1	12.0	11.1	11.8	12.2	12.4
6000 Other taxes	0.0	0.0	0.0	0.0	0.0	0.0	0.0	0.0	0.0	0.0
State/Regional										
Total tax revenue	..	..	..	..	..	..	..	..	..	..
1000 Taxes on income, profits and capital gains	..	..	..	..	..	..	..	..	..	..
2000 Social security contributions	..	..	..	..	..	..	..	..	..	..
3000 Taxes on payroll and workforce	..	..	..	..	..	..	..	..	..	..
4000 Taxes on property	..	..	..	..	..	..	..	..	..	..
5000 Taxes on goods and services	..	..	..	..	..	..	..	..	..	..
6000 Other taxes	..	..	..	..	..	..	..	..	..	..
Local government										
Total tax revenue	**1.7**	**2.3**	**4.5**	**5.2**	**5.6**	**2.2**	**1.9**	**2.2**	**2.2**	**2.2**
1000 Taxes on income, profits and capital gains	0.0	0.0	0.0	0.0	0.0	0.0	0.0	0.0	0.0	0.0
2000 Social security contributions	0.0	0.0	0.0	0.0	0.0	0.0	0.0	0.0	0.0	0.0
3000 Taxes on payroll and workforce	0.0	0.0	0.0	0.0	0.0	0.0	0.0	0.0	0.0	0.0
4000 Taxes on property	1.6	2.0	4.0	4.7	5.0	2.0	1.7	2.0	1.9	2.0
5000 Taxes on goods and services	0.1	0.2	0.4	0.6	0.6	0.2	0.2	0.2	0.2	0.2
6000 Other taxes	0.0	0.0	0.0	0.0	0.0	0.0	0.0	0.0	0.0	0.0
Social Security Funds										
Total tax revenue	**0.0**	**0.0**	**0.0**	**0.0**	**0.0**	**0.0**	**0.0**	**0.0**	**0.0**	**0.0**
1000 Taxes on income, profits and capital gains	0.0	0.0	0.0	0.0	0.0	0.0	0.0	0.0	0.0	0.0
2000 Social security contributions	0.0	0.0	0.0	0.0	0.0	0.0	0.0	0.0	0.0	0.0
3000 Taxes on payroll and workforce	0.0	0.0	0.0	0.0	0.0	0.0	0.0	0.0	0.0	0.0
4000 Taxes on property	0.0	0.0	0.0	0.0	0.0	0.0	0.0	0.0	0.0	0.0
5000 Taxes on goods and services	0.0	0.0	0.0	0.0	0.0	0.0	0.0	0.0	0.0	0.0
6000 Other taxes	0.0	0.0	0.0	0.0	0.0	0.0	0.0	0.0	0.0	0.0

Note: More detailed country data and country notes are available in online chapter 6: http://dx.doi.org/10.1787/9789264283183-en. Full time series can be accessed at http://oe.cd/full-time-series.

Source: Local Authorities Statistics, Department of Statistics, Wellington.

StatLink http://dx.doi.org/10.1787/888933613083

Table 4.49. **Norway, tax revenue and % of GDP by selected tax category**

	Billion NOK					% of GDP				
	1990	2000	2010	2014	2015	1990	2000	2010	2014	2015
Total tax revenue	**301.8**	**631.6**	**1 086.7**	**1 220.7**	**1 194.2**	**40.2**	**41.9**	**42.0**	**38.9**	**38.3**
1000 Taxes on income, profits and capital gains	**106.3**	**284.2**	**512.0**	**517.9**	**470.6**	**14.2**	**18.8**	**19.8**	**16.5**	**15.1**
1100 Of individuals	79.1	152.0	256.5	309.6	333.7	10.5	10.1	9.9	9.9	10.7
1200 Corporate	27.2	132.2	255.5	208.3	136.9	3.6	8.8	9.9	6.6	4.4
1300 Unallocable between 1100 and 1200	0.0	0.0	0.0	0.0	0.0	0.0	0.0	0.0	0.0	0.0
2000 Social security contributions	**79.4**	**132.2**	**243.0**	**312.9**	**326.0**	**10.6**	**8.8**	**9.4**	**10.0**	**10.5**
2100 Employees	25.3	45.2	81.0	107.9	113.1	3.4	3.0	3.1	3.4	3.6
2200 Employers	50.1	79.2	148.1	186.5	191.4	6.7	5.3	5.7	5.9	6.1
2300 Self-employed or non-employed	3.9	7.8	13.9	18.6	21.5	0.5	0.5	0.5	0.6	0.7
2400 Unallocable between 2100, 2200 and 2300	0.0	0.0	0.0	0.0	0.0	0.0	0.0	0.0	0.0	0.0
3000 Taxes on payroll and workforce	**0.0**	**0.0**	**0.0**	**0.0**	**0.0**	**0.0**	**0.0**	**0.0**	**0.0**	**0.0**
4000 Taxes on property	**8.9**	**14.5**	**30.9**	**38.5**	**34.9**	**1.2**	**1.0**	**1.2**	**1.2**	**1.1**
4100 Recurrent taxes on immovable property	2.2	2.8	8.5	11.2	12.7	0.3	0.2	0.3	0.4	0.4
4200 Recurrent taxes on net wealth	5.1	7.7	14.1	17.8	13.4	0.7	0.5	0.5	0.6	0.4
4300 Estate, inheritance and gift taxes	0.4	1.3	2.4	1.9	0.3	0.1	0.1	0.1	0.1	0.0
4400 Taxes on financial and capital transactions	1.1	2.7	5.9	7.6	8.4	0.1	0.2	0.2	0.2	0.3
4500 Non-recurrent taxes	0.0	0.0	0.0	0.0	0.0	0.0	0.0	0.0	0.0	0.0
4600 Other recurrent taxes on property	0.0	0.0	0.0	0.0	0.0	0.0	0.0	0.0	0.0	0.0
5000 Taxes on goods and services	**107.3**	**200.7**	**300.7**	**351.3**	**362.7**	**14.3**	**13.3**	**11.6**	**11.2**	**11.6**
5100 Taxes on production, sale, transfer, etc	102.9	185.9	284.9	332.6	343.6	13.7	12.3	11.0	10.6	11.0
5110 General taxes	56.7	125.0	201.8	244.8	256.0	7.6	8.3	7.8	7.8	8.2
5111 Value added taxes	56.7	124.2	201.2	243.8	255.2	7.6	8.2	7.8	7.8	8.2
5120 Taxes on specific goods and services	46.2	60.9	83.1	87.9	87.6	6.2	4.0	3.2	2.8	2.8
5121 Excises	37.5	54.9	76.3	80.0	79.2	5.0	3.6	2.9	2.5	2.5
5200 Taxes on use of goods and perform activities	4.4	14.8	15.8	18.7	19.1	0.6	1.0	0.6	0.6	0.6
5300 Unallocable between 5100 and 5200	0.0	0.0	0.0	0.0	0.0	0.0	0.0	0.0	0.0	0.0
6000 Other taxes	**0.0**	**0.0**	**0.0**	**0.0**	**0.0**	**0.0**	**0.0**	**0.0**	**0.0**	**0.0**
Non-wastable tax credits										
Non-wastable tax credits against 1000	..	..	1.2	2.1	1.7	..	..	0.0	0.1	0.1
Transfer component	..	..	1.0	1.6	1.3	..	..	0.0	0.1	0.0
Tax expenditure component	..	..	0.3	0.5	0.4	..	..	0.0	0.0	0.0

Note: More detailed country data and country notes are available in online chapter 5: http://dx.doi.org/10.1787/9789264283183-en. Full time series can be accessed at http://oe.cd/full-time-series.

Source: Statistics Norway; National Accounts.

StatLink http://dx.doi.org/10.1787/888933613102

Table 4.50. **Norway, tax revenue and % of GDP by level of government and main taxes**

	Billion NOK					% of GDP				
	1990	2000	2010	2014	2015	1990	2000	2010	2014	2015
Federal or Central government										
Total tax revenue	**165.4**	**536.1**	**938.4**	**1 050.9**	**1 011.1**	**22.1**	**35.6**	**36.2**	**33.5**	**32.4**
1000 Taxes on income, profits and capital gains	50.6	198.4	380.8	369.5	310.7	6.8	13.2	14.7	11.8	10.0
2000 Social security contributions	4.7	132.2	243.0	312.9	326.0	0.6	8.8	9.4	10.0	10.5
3000 Taxes on payroll and workforce	0.0	0.0	0.0	0.0	0.0	0.0	0.0	0.0	0.0	0.0
4000 Taxes on property	3.4	7.0	16.0	19.3	13.8	0.5	0.5	0.6	0.6	0.4
5000 Taxes on goods and services	106.7	198.6	298.6	349.2	360.7	14.2	13.2	11.5	11.1	11.6
6000 Other taxes	0.0	0.0	0.0	0.0	0.0	0.0	0.0	0.0	0.0	0.0
State/Regional										
Total tax revenue	..	..	..	..	..	..	..	..	..	..
1000 Taxes on income, profits and capital gains	..	..	..	..	..	..	..	..	..	..
2000 Social security contributions	..	..	..	..	..	..	..	..	..	..
3000 Taxes on payroll and workforce	..	..	..	..	..	..	..	..	..	..
4000 Taxes on property	..	..	..	..	..	..	..	..	..	..
5000 Taxes on goods and services	..	..	..	..	..	..	..	..	..	..
6000 Other taxes	..	..	..	..	..	..	..	..	..	..
Local government										
Total tax revenue	**61.6**	**95.5**	**148.2**	**169.8**	**183.0**	**8.2**	**6.3**	**5.7**	**5.4**	**5.9**
1000 Taxes on income, profits and capital gains	55.7	85.8	131.2	148.4	159.9	7.4	5.7	5.1	4.7	5.1
2000 Social security contributions	0.0	0.0	0.0	0.0	0.0	0.0	0.0	0.0	0.0	0.0
3000 Taxes on payroll and workforce	0.0	0.0	0.0	0.0	0.0	0.0	0.0	0.0	0.0	0.0
4000 Taxes on property	5.5	7.6	14.9	19.2	21.1	0.7	0.5	0.6	0.6	0.7
5000 Taxes on goods and services	0.4	2.1	2.2	2.1	2.0	0.1	0.1	0.1	0.1	0.1
6000 Other taxes	0.0	0.0	0.0	0.0	0.0	0.0	0.0	0.0	0.0	0.0
Social Security Funds										
Total tax revenue	**74.8**	**0.0**	**0.0**	**0.0**	**0.0**	**10.0**	**0.0**	**0.0**	**0.0**	**0.0**
1000 Taxes on income, profits and capital gains	0.0	0.0	0.0	0.0	0.0	0.0	0.0	0.0	0.0	0.0
2000 Social security contributions	74.6	0.0	0.0	0.0	0.0	10.0	0.0	0.0	0.0	0.0
3000 Taxes on payroll and workforce	0.0	0.0	0.0	0.0	0.0	0.0	0.0	0.0	0.0	0.0
4000 Taxes on property	0.0	0.0	0.0	0.0	0.0	0.0	0.0	0.0	0.0	0.0
5000 Taxes on goods and services	0.2	0.0	0.0	0.0	0.0	0.0	0.0	0.0	0.0	0.0
6000 Other taxes	0.0	0.0	0.0	0.0	0.0	0.0	0.0	0.0	0.0	0.0

Note: More detailed country data and country notes are available in online chapter 6: http://dx.doi.org/10.1787/9789264283183-en. Full time series can be accessed at http://oe.cd/full-time-series.

Source: Statistics Norway; National Accounts.

StatLink http://dx.doi.org/10.1787/888933613121

Table 4.51. **Poland, tax revenue and % of GDP by selected tax category**

	Billion PLN					% of GDP				
	1990	2000	2010	2014	2015	1990	2000	2010	2014	2015
Total tax revenue	..	**246.0**	**454.0**	**550.0**	**583.7**	..	**32.9**	**31.4**	**32.0**	**32.4**
1000 Taxes on income, profits and capital gains	..	**50.3**	**91.0**	**108.8**	**117.1**	..	**6.7**	**6.3**	**6.3**	**6.5**
1100 Of individuals	..	32.4	62.9	78.7	84.0	..	4.3	4.4	4.6	4.7
1200 Corporate	..	17.9	28.1	30.0	33.1	..	2.4	1.9	1.7	1.8
1300 Unallocable between 1100 and 1200	..	0.0	0.0	0.0	0.0	..	0.0	0.0	0.0	0.0
2000 Social security contributions	..	**96.4**	**156.0**	**209.9**	**224.8**	..	**12.9**	**10.8**	**12.2**	**12.5**
2100 Employees	..	40.4	55.7	82.0	90.7	..	5.4	3.9	4.8	5.0
2200 Employers	..	42.8	71.8	89.9	93.3	..	5.7	5.0	5.2	5.2
2300 Self-employed or non-employed	..	13.2	28.5	38.0	40.9	..	1.8	2.0	2.2	2.3
2400 Unallocable between 2100, 2200 and 2300	..	0.0	0.0	0.0	0.0	..	0.0	0.0	0.0	0.0
3000 Taxes on payroll and workforce	..	**1.6**	**3.7**	**4.0**	**4.0**	..	**0.2**	**0.3**	**0.2**	**0.2**
4000 Taxes on property	..	**10.6**	**19.1**	**24.0**	**24.6**	..	**1.4**	**1.3**	**1.4**	**1.4**
4100 Recurrent taxes on immovable property	..	8.4	16.4	21.4	22.2	..	1.1	1.1	1.2	1.2
4200 Recurrent taxes on net wealth	..	0.0	0.0	0.0	0.0	..	0.0	0.0	0.0	0.0
4300 Estate, inheritance and gift taxes	..	0.2	0.3	0.3	0.2	..	0.0	0.0	0.0	0.0
4400 Taxes on financial and capital transactions	..	2.0	2.4	2.3	2.2	..	0.3	0.2	0.1	0.1
4500 Non-recurrent taxes	..	0.0	0.0	0.0	0.0	..	0.0	0.0	0.0	0.0
4600 Other recurrent taxes on property	..	0.0	0.0	0.0	0.0	..	0.0	0.0	0.0	0.0
5000 Taxes on goods and services	..	**86.9**	**182.0**	**199.9**	**209.7**	..	**11.6**	**12.6**	**11.6**	**11.7**
5100 Taxes on production, sale, transfer, etc	..	84.9	174.4	192.6	201.7	..	11.4	12.1	11.2	11.2
5110 General taxes	..	51.6	109.7	122.7	125.8	..	6.9	7.6	7.1	7.0
5111 Value added taxes	..	51.6	109.7	122.7	125.8	..	6.9	7.6	7.1	7.0
5120 Taxes on specific goods and services	..	33.3	64.6	69.9	75.8	..	4.5	4.5	4.1	4.2
5121 Excises	..	27.2	62.0	67.1	70.6	..	3.6	4.3	3.9	3.9
5200 Taxes on use of goods and perform activities	..	2.0	7.6	7.3	8.0	..	0.3	0.5	0.4	0.4
5300 Unallocable between 5100 and 5200	..	0.0	0.0	0.0	0.0	..	0.0	0.0	0.0	0.0
6000 Other taxes	..	**0.3**	**0.6**	**1.1**	**0.6**	..	**0.0**	**0.0**	**0.1**	**0.0**
Non-wastable tax credits										
Non-wastable tax credits against 1000	..	..	..	..	..	..	..	..	..	..
Transfer component	..	..	..	..	..	..	..	..	..	..
Tax expenditure component	..	..	..	..	..	..	..	..	..	..

Note: More detailed country data and country notes are available in online chapter 5: http://dx.doi.org/10.1787/9789264283183-en. Full time series can be accessed at http://oe.cd/full-time-series.

Source: Ministry of Finance, Economic Department.

StatLink http://dx.doi.org/10.1787/888933613140

Table 4.52. **Poland, tax revenue and % of GDP by level of government and main taxes**

	Billion PLN					% of GDP				
	1990	2000	2010	2014	2015	1990	2000	2010	2014	2015
Federal or Central government										
Total tax revenue	..	**126.9**	**239.2**	**266.6**	**280.9**	..	**17.0**	**16.6**	**15.5**	**15.6**
1000 Taxes on income, profits and capital gains	..	40.0	57.7	66.8	71.4	..	5.3	4.0	3.9	4.0
2000 Social security contributions	..	0.0	0.0	0.0	0.0	..	0.0	0.0	0.0	0.0
3000 Taxes on payroll and workforce	..	1.6	3.7	4.0	4.0	..	0.2	0.3	0.2	0.2
4000 Taxes on property	..	0.0	0.0	0.0	0.0	..	0.0	0.0	0.0	0.0
5000 Taxes on goods and services	..	85.3	177.8	195.7	205.5	..	11.4	12.3	11.4	11.4
6000 Other taxes	..	0.0	0.0	0.0	0.0	..	0.0	0.0	0.0	0.0
State/Regional										
Total tax revenue	..	..	..	..	..	..	..	..	..	..
1000 Taxes on income, profits and capital gains	..	..	..	..	..	..	..	..	..	..
2000 Social security contributions	..	..	..	..	..	..	..	..	..	..
3000 Taxes on payroll and workforce	..	..	..	..	..	..	..	..	..	..
4000 Taxes on property	..	..	..	..	..	..	..	..	..	..
5000 Taxes on goods and services	..	..	..	..	..	..	..	..	..	..
6000 Other taxes	..	..	..	..	..	..	..	..	..	..
Local government										
Total tax revenue	..	**22.7**	**57.1**	**71.1**	**75.1**	..	**3.0**	**4.0**	**4.1**	**4.2**
1000 Taxes on income, profits and capital gains	..	10.3	33.3	41.9	45.7	..	1.4	2.3	2.4	2.5
2000 Social security contributions	..	0.0	0.0	0.0	0.0	..	0.0	0.0	0.0	0.0
3000 Taxes on payroll and workforce	..	0.0	0.0	0.0	0.0	..	0.0	0.0	0.0	0.0
4000 Taxes on property	..	10.6	19.1	24.0	24.6	..	1.4	1.3	1.4	1.4
5000 Taxes on goods and services	..	1.5	4.1	4.1	4.1	..	0.2	0.3	0.2	0.2
6000 Other taxes	..	0.3	0.6	1.1	0.6	..	0.0	0.0	0.1	0.0
Social Security Funds										
Total tax revenue	..	**96.4**	**156.0**	**209.9**	**224.8**	..	**12.9**	**10.8**	**12.2**	**12.5**
1000 Taxes on income, profits and capital gains	..	0.0	0.0	0.0	0.0	..	0.0	0.0	0.0	0.0
2000 Social security contributions	..	96.4	156.0	209.9	224.8	..	12.9	10.8	12.2	12.5
3000 Taxes on payroll and workforce	..	0.0	0.0	0.0	0.0	..	0.0	0.0	0.0	0.0
4000 Taxes on property	..	0.0	0.0	0.0	0.0	..	0.0	0.0	0.0	0.0
5000 Taxes on goods and services	..	0.0	0.0	0.0	0.0	..	0.0	0.0	0.0	0.0
6000 Other taxes	..	0.0	0.0	0.0	0.0	..	0.0	0.0	0.0	0.0

Note: More detailed country data and country notes are available in online chapter 6: http://dx.doi.org/10.1787/9789264283183-en. Full time series can be accessed at http://oe.cd/full-time-series.

Source: Ministry of Finance, Economic Department.

StatLink http://dx.doi.org/10.1787/888933613159

Table 4.53. Portugal, tax revenue and % of GDP by selected tax category

	Billion EUR					% of GDP				
	1990	2000	2010	2014	2015	1990	2000	2010	2014	2015
Total tax revenue	**14.8**	**39.9**	**54.7**	**59.3**	**62.0**	**26.5**	**31.1**	**30.4**	**34.3**	**34.6**
1000 Taxes on income, profits and capital gains	**3.8**	**11.7**	**14.6**	**18.3**	**18.7**	**6.8**	**9.1**	**8.1**	**10.5**	**10.4**
1100 Of individuals	2.4	6.9	9.6	13.4	13.1	4.2	5.4	5.4	7.7	7.3
1200 Corporate	1.2	4.7	4.9	4.9	5.6	2.1	3.7	2.7	2.8	3.1
1300 Unallocable between 1100 and 1200	0.3	0.0	0.1	0.0	0.0	0.5	0.0	0.0	0.0	0.0
2000 Social security contributions	**4.0**	**10.2**	**15.5**	**15.6**	**16.2**	**7.2**	**7.9**	**8.6**	**9.0**	**9.0**
2100 Employees	1.5	4.3	6.7	6.8	7.0	2.6	3.3	3.7	3.9	3.9
2200 Employers	2.4	5.9	8.8	8.8	9.2	4.3	4.6	4.9	5.1	5.1
2300 Self-employed or non-employed	0.1	0.0	0.0	0.0	0.0	0.3	0.0	0.0	0.0	0.0
2400 Unallocable between 2100, 2200 and 2300	0.0	0.0	0.0	0.0	0.0	0.0	0.0	0.0	0.0	0.0
3000 Taxes on payroll and workforce	**0.0**	**0.0**	**0.0**	**0.0**	**0.0**	**0.0**	**0.0**	**0.0**	**0.0**	**0.0**
4000 Taxes on property	**0.4**	**1.5**	**1.9**	**2.1**	**2.3**	**0.7**	**1.1**	**1.1**	**1.2**	**1.3**
4100 Recurrent taxes on immovable property	0.1	0.5	1.1	1.4	1.5	0.2	0.4	0.6	0.8	0.8
4200 Recurrent taxes on net wealth	0.0	0.0	0.0	0.0	0.0	0.0	0.0	0.0	0.0	0.0
4300 Estate, inheritance and gift taxes	0.1	0.1	0.0	0.0	0.0	0.1	0.1	0.0	0.0	0.0
4400 Taxes on financial and capital transactions	0.2	0.9	0.8	0.7	0.8	0.3	0.7	0.5	0.4	0.4
4500 Non-recurrent taxes	0.0	0.0	0.0	0.0	0.0	0.0	0.0	0.0	0.0	0.0
4600 Other recurrent taxes on property	0.0	0.0	0.0	0.0	0.0	0.0	0.0	0.0	0.0	0.0
5000 Taxes on goods and services	**6.6**	**16.1**	**22.0**	**22.5**	**23.8**	**11.7**	**12.5**	**12.2**	**13.0**	**13.3**
5100 Taxes on production, sale, transfer, etc	6.4	15.6	21.2	21.5	22.8	11.5	12.2	11.8	12.4	12.7
5110 General taxes	2.9	9.7	13.5	14.7	15.4	5.2	7.6	7.5	8.5	8.6
5111 Value added taxes	2.9	9.7	13.5	14.7	15.4	5.2	7.6	7.5	8.5	8.6
5120 Taxes on specific goods and services	3.5	5.9	7.7	6.9	7.4	6.3	4.6	4.3	4.0	4.1
5121 Excises	2.1	4.5	5.7	4.8	5.2	3.7	3.5	3.1	2.8	2.9
5200 Taxes on use of goods and perform activities	0.1	0.4	0.7	1.0	1.0	0.2	0.3	0.4	0.6	0.6
5300 Unallocable between 5100 and 5200	0.0	0.1	0.0	0.0	0.0	0.0	0.0	0.0	0.0	0.0
6000 Other taxes	**0.0**	**0.3**	**0.5**	**0.6**	**0.8**	**0.1**	**0.2**	**0.3**	**0.4**	**0.5**
Non-wastable tax credits										
Non-wastable tax credits against 1000	..	..	..	..	..	..	..	..	..	..
Transfer component	..	..	..	..	..	..	..	..	..	..
Tax expenditure component	..	..	..	..	..	..	..	..	..	..

Note: More detailed country data and country notes are available in online chapter 5: http://dx.doi.org/10.1787/9789264283183-en. Full time series can be accessed at http://oe.cd/full-time-series.

Source: Instituto Nacionale de Estatistica; Conta do Estado, Contas de Gerência dos Fundos e Serviços Autonomos da Administraçao Central; Estatisticas das Financas publicas; Relatorio do Instituto de Gestao Financeira da Seguranta Social, Contas de Gerência das Regioes Autonomas da Madeira e dos Atores.

StatLink http://dx.doi.org/10.1787/888933613178

Table 4.54. Portugal, tax revenue and % of GDP by level of government and main taxes

	Billion EUR					% of GDP				
	1990	2000	2010	2014	2015	1990	2000	2010	2014	2015
Federal or Central government										
Total tax revenue	**9.8**	**27.8**	**36.5**	**40.2**	**42.1**	**17.6**	**21.6**	**20.3**	**23.2**	**23.4**
1000 Taxes on income, profits and capital gains	3.6	11.1	13.6	17.1	17.5	6.4	8.7	7.5	9.9	9.7
2000 Social security contributions	0.0	1.3	1.9	2.1	2.1	0.0	1.0	1.1	1.2	1.2
3000 Taxes on payroll and workforce	0.0	0.0	0.0	0.0	0.0	0.0	0.0	0.0	0.0	0.0
4000 Taxes on property	0.1	0.3	0.2	0.2	0.2	0.1	0.2	0.1	0.1	0.1
5000 Taxes on goods and services	6.1	14.8	20.3	20.3	21.5	10.9	11.5	11.3	11.7	12.0
6000 Other taxes	0.0	0.3	0.5	0.6	0.8	0.1	0.2	0.3	0.4	0.4
State/Regional										
Total tax revenue	..	..	..	..	..	..	..	..	..	..
1000 Taxes on income, profits and capital gains	..	..	..	..	..	..	..	..	..	..
2000 Social security contributions	..	..	..	..	..	..	..	..	..	..
3000 Taxes on payroll and workforce	..	..	..	..	..	..	..	..	..	..
4000 Taxes on property	..	..	..	..	..	..	..	..	..	..
5000 Taxes on goods and services	..	..	..	..	..	..	..	..	..	..
6000 Other taxes	..	..	..	..	..	..	..	..	..	..
Local government										
Total tax revenue	**0.8**	**2.5**	**3.6**	**4.3**	**4.5**	**1.5**	**2.0**	**2.0**	**2.5**	**2.5**
1000 Taxes on income, profits and capital gains	0.2	0.6	1.1	1.2	1.2	0.4	0.4	0.6	0.7	0.7
2000 Social security contributions	0.0	0.0	0.0	0.0	0.0	0.0	0.0	0.0	0.0	0.0
3000 Taxes on payroll and workforce	0.0	0.0	0.0	0.0	0.0	0.0	0.0	0.0	0.0	0.0
4000 Taxes on property	0.3	1.2	1.7	1.9	2.1	0.6	0.9	0.9	1.1	1.2
5000 Taxes on goods and services	0.3	0.7	0.8	1.1	1.1	0.5	0.6	0.5	0.6	0.6
6000 Other taxes	0.0	0.0	0.0	0.0	0.0	0.0	0.0	0.0	0.0	0.0
Social Security Funds										
Total tax revenue	**4.0**	**9.4**	**14.4**	**14.7**	**15.3**	**7.2**	**7.3**	**8.0**	**8.5**	**8.5**
1000 Taxes on income, profits and capital gains	0.0	0.0	0.0	0.0	0.0	0.0	0.0	0.0	0.0	0.0
2000 Social security contributions	4.0	8.8	13.5	13.5	14.1	7.2	6.9	7.5	7.8	7.9
3000 Taxes on payroll and workforce	0.0	0.0	0.0	0.0	0.0	0.0	0.0	0.0	0.0	0.0
4000 Taxes on property	0.0	0.0	0.0	0.0	0.0	0.0	0.0	0.0	0.0	0.0
5000 Taxes on goods and services	0.0	0.5	0.8	1.2	1.2	0.0	0.4	0.5	0.7	0.7
6000 Other taxes	0.0	0.0	0.0	0.0	0.0	0.0	0.0	0.0	0.0	0.0

Note: More detailed country data and country notes are available in online chapter 6: http://dx.doi.org/10.1787/9789264283183-en. Full time series can be accessed at http://oe.cd/full-time-series.

Source: Instituto Nacionale de Estatistica; Conta do Estado, Contas de Gerência dos Fundos e Serviços Autonomos da Administraçao Central; Estatisticas das Financas publicas; Relatorio do Instituto de Gestao Financeira da Seguranta Social, Contas de Gerência das Regioes Autonomas da Madeira e dos Atores.

StatLink http://dx.doi.org/10.1787/888933613197

Table 4.55. **Slovak Republic, tax revenue and % of GDP by selected tax category**

	Billion EUR					% of GDP				
	1990	2000	2010	2014	2015	1990	2000	2010	2014	2015
Total tax revenue	..	**10.6**	**19.0**	**23.7**	**25.4**	..	**33.6**	**28.1**	**31.2**	**32.3**
1000 Taxes on income, profits and capital gains	..	**2.2**	**3.6**	**4.9**	**5.5**	..	**6.9**	**5.3**	**6.5**	**7.0**
1100 Of individuals	..	1.1	1.8	2.3	2.5	..	3.3	2.6	3.0	3.1
1200 Corporate	..	0.8	1.7	2.5	2.9	..	2.6	2.5	3.3	3.7
1300 Unallocable between 1100 and 1200	..	0.3	0.2	0.2	0.2	..	1.0	0.2	0.2	0.2
2000 Social security contributions	..	**4.4**	**8.2**	**10.2**	**10.9**	..	**14.0**	**12.1**	**13.4**	**13.8**
2100 Employees	..	0.9	2.1	2.3	2.4	..	2.9	3.1	3.0	3.1
2200 Employers	..	2.9	4.6	5.8	6.3	..	9.0	6.8	7.7	8.0
2300 Self-employed or non-employed	..	0.7	1.5	2.1	2.2	..	2.1	2.2	2.7	2.8
2400 Unallocable between 2100, 2200 and 2300	..	0.0	0.0	0.0	0.0	..	0.0	0.0	0.0	0.0
3000 Taxes on payroll and workforce	..	**0.0**	**0.0**	**0.0**	**0.0**	..	**0.0**	**0.0**	**0.0**	**0.0**
4000 Taxes on property	..	**0.2**	**0.3**	**0.3**	**0.3**	..	**0.6**	**0.4**	**0.4**	**0.4**
4100 Recurrent taxes on immovable property	..	0.1	0.3	0.3	0.3	..	0.5	0.4	0.4	0.4
4200 Recurrent taxes on net wealth	..	0.0	0.0	0.0	0.0	..	0.0	0.0	0.0	0.0
4300 Estate, inheritance and gift taxes	..	0.0	0.0	0.0	0.0	..	0.0	0.0	0.0	0.0
4400 Taxes on financial and capital transactions	..	0.0	0.0	0.0	0.0	..	0.1	0.0	0.0	0.0
4500 Non-recurrent taxes	..	0.0	0.0	0.0	0.0	..	0.0	0.0	0.0	0.0
4600 Other recurrent taxes on property	..	0.0	0.0	0.0	0.0	..	0.0	0.0	0.0	0.0
5000 Taxes on goods and services	..	**3.8**	**6.8**	**8.1**	**8.6**	..	**12.2**	**10.1**	**10.6**	**10.9**
5100 Taxes on production, sale, transfer, etc	..	3.6	6.3	7.4	7.9	..	11.5	9.3	9.7	10.0
5110 General taxes	..	2.2	4.2	5.0	5.4	..	6.9	6.2	6.6	6.9
5111 Value added taxes	..	2.2	4.2	5.0	5.4	..	6.9	6.2	6.6	6.9
5120 Taxes on specific goods and services	..	1.5	2.1	2.3	2.5	..	4.6	3.1	3.1	3.1
5121 Excises	..	1.0	1.9	2.0	2.1	..	3.1	2.9	2.7	2.7
5200 Taxes on use of goods and perform activities	..	0.2	0.4	0.6	0.5	..	0.7	0.6	0.7	0.7
5300 Unallocable between 5100 and 5200	..	0.0	0.1	0.1	0.2	..	0.0	0.2	0.2	0.2
6000 Other taxes	..	**0.0**	**0.0**	**0.0**	**0.0**	..	**0.0**	**0.0**	**0.0**	**0.0**
Non-wastable tax credits										
Non-wastable tax credits against 1000	..	..	0.3	0.3	0.3	..	..	0.4	0.3	0.3
Transfer component	..	..	..	..	..	..	..	..	..	..
Tax expenditure component	..	..	..	..	..	..	..	..	..	..

Note: More detailed country data and country notes are available in online chapter 5: http://dx.doi.org/10.1787/9789264283183-en. Full time series can be accessed at http://oe.cd/full-time-series.

Source: Ministry of Finance.

StatLink http://dx.doi.org/10.1787/888933613216

Table 4.56. **Slovak Republic, tax revenue and % of GDP by level of government and main taxes**

	Billion EUR					% of GDP				
	1990	2000	2010	2014	2015	1990	2000	2010	2014	2015
Federal or Central government										
Total tax revenue	..	**6.2**	**10.3**	**13.0**	**14.2**	..	**19.5**	**15.3**	**17.1**	**18.0**
1000 Taxes on income, profits and capital gains	..	2.2	3.6	4.9	5.5	..	6.9	5.3	6.5	7.0
2000 Social security contributions	..	0.1	0.2	0.2	0.3	..	0.3	0.3	0.3	0.3
3000 Taxes on payroll and workforce	..	0.0	0.0	0.0	0.0	..	0.0	0.0	0.0	0.0
4000 Taxes on property	..	0.1	0.0	0.0	0.0	..	0.2	0.0	0.0	0.0
5000 Taxes on goods and services	..	3.8	6.5	7.8	8.4	..	12.1	9.7	10.2	10.7
6000 Other taxes	..	0.0	0.0	0.0	0.0	..	0.0	0.0	0.0	0.0
State/Regional										
Total tax revenue	..	..	..	..	..	..	..	..	..	..
1000 Taxes on income, profits and capital gains	..	..	..	..	..	..	..	..	..	..
2000 Social security contributions	..	..	..	..	..	..	..	..	..	..
3000 Taxes on payroll and workforce	..	..	..	..	..	..	..	..	..	..
4000 Taxes on property	..	..	..	..	..	..	..	..	..	..
5000 Taxes on goods and services	..	..	..	..	..	..	..	..	..	..
6000 Other taxes	..	..	..	..	..	..	..	..	..	..
Local government										
Total tax revenue	..	**0.1**	**0.5**	**0.6**	**0.5**	..	**0.5**	**0.8**	**0.8**	**0.7**
1000 Taxes on income, profits and capital gains	..	0.0	0.0	0.0	0.0	..	0.0	0.0	0.0	0.0
2000 Social security contributions	..	0.0	0.0	0.0	0.0	..	0.0	0.0	0.0	0.0
3000 Taxes on payroll and workforce	..	0.0	0.0	0.0	0.0	..	0.0	0.0	0.0	0.0
4000 Taxes on property	..	0.1	0.3	0.3	0.3	..	0.4	0.4	0.4	0.4
5000 Taxes on goods and services	..	0.0	0.3	0.3	0.2	..	0.0	0.4	0.4	0.2
6000 Other taxes	..	0.0	0.0	0.0	0.0	..	0.0	0.0	0.0	0.0
Social Security Funds										
Total tax revenue	..	**4.3**	**7.9**	**9.9**	**10.6**	..	**13.7**	**11.7**	**13.1**	**13.5**
1000 Taxes on income, profits and capital gains	..	0.0	0.0	0.0	0.0	..	0.0	0.0	0.0	0.0
2000 Social security contributions	..	4.3	7.9	9.9	10.6	..	13.7	11.7	13.1	13.5
3000 Taxes on payroll and workforce	..	0.0	0.0	0.0	0.0	..	0.0	0.0	0.0	0.0
4000 Taxes on property	..	0.0	0.0	0.0	0.0	..	0.0	0.0	0.0	0.0
5000 Taxes on goods and services	..	0.0	0.0	0.0	0.0	..	0.0	0.0	0.0	0.0
6000 Other taxes	..	0.0	0.0	0.0	0.0	..	0.0	0.0	0.0	0.0

Note: More detailed country data and country notes are available in online chapter 6: http://dx.doi.org/10.1787/9789264283183-en. Full time series can be accessed at http://oe.cd/full-time-series.

Source: Ministry of Finance.

StatLink http://dx.doi.org/10.1787/888933613235

Table 4.57. **Slovenia, tax revenue and % of GDP by selected tax category**

	Billion EUR					% of GDP				
	1990	2000	2010	2014	2015	1990	2000	2010	2014	2015
Total tax revenue	..	**6.9**	**13.4**	**13.6**	**14.1**	..	**36.6**	**36.9**	**36.5**	**36.6**
1000 Taxes on income, profits and capital gains	..	**1.3**	**2.7**	**2.4**	**2.5**	..	**6.8**	**7.4**	**6.5**	**6.6**
1100 Of individuals	..	1.0	2.0	1.9	2.0	..	5.5	5.6	5.1	5.1
1200 Corporate	..	0.2	0.7	0.5	0.6	..	1.1	1.8	1.4	1.5
1300 Unallocable between 1100 and 1200	..	0.0	0.0	0.0	0.0	..	0.1	0.0	0.0	0.0
2000 Social security contributions	..	**2.6**	**5.4**	**5.4**	**5.6**	..	**13.9**	**14.8**	**14.4**	**14.5**
2100 Employees	..	1.4	2.8	2.8	2.9	..	7.7	7.7	7.4	7.5
2200 Employers	..	1.0	2.1	2.0	2.1	..	5.3	5.7	5.4	5.5
2300 Self-employed or non-employed	..	0.2	0.5	0.6	0.6	..	0.9	1.5	1.5	1.5
2400 Unallocable between 2100, 2200 and 2300	..	0.0	0.0	0.0	0.0	..	0.0	0.0	0.0	0.0
3000 Taxes on payroll and workforce	..	**0.3**	**0.0**	**0.0**	**0.0**	..	**1.5**	**0.1**	**0.1**	**0.1**
4000 Taxes on property	..	**0.1**	**0.2**	**0.2**	**0.2**	..	**0.6**	**0.6**	**0.6**	**0.6**
4100 Recurrent taxes on immovable property	..	0.1	0.2	0.2	0.2	..	0.4	0.5	0.5	0.5
4200 Recurrent taxes on net wealth	..	0.0	0.0	0.0	0.0	..	0.0	0.0	0.0	0.0
4300 Estate, inheritance and gift taxes	..	0.0	0.0	0.0	0.0	..	0.0	0.0	0.0	0.0
4400 Taxes on financial and capital transactions	..	0.0	0.0	0.0	0.0	..	0.1	0.1	0.1	0.1
4500 Non-recurrent taxes	..	0.0	0.0	0.0	0.0	..	0.1	0.0	0.0	0.0
4600 Other recurrent taxes on property	..	0.0	0.0	0.0	0.0	..	0.0	0.0	0.0	0.0
5000 Taxes on goods and services	..	**2.6**	**5.0**	**5.5**	**5.6**	..	**13.8**	**13.8**	**14.7**	**14.6**
5100 Taxes on production, sale, transfer, etc	..	2.5	4.8	5.2	5.3	..	13.1	13.2	13.8	13.6
5110 General taxes	..	1.6	2.9	3.2	3.2	..	8.7	8.1	8.5	8.4
5111 Value added taxes	..	1.6	2.9	3.2	3.2	..	8.5	8.1	8.5	8.4
5120 Taxes on specific goods and services	..	0.8	1.9	2.0	2.0	..	4.4	5.1	5.3	5.3
5121 Excises	..	0.6	1.6	1.6	1.6	..	3.1	4.3	4.3	4.2
5200 Taxes on use of goods and perform activities	..	0.1	0.2	0.3	0.4	..	0.6	0.6	0.9	1.0
5300 Unallocable between 5100 and 5200	..	0.0	0.0	0.0	0.0	..	0.0	0.0	0.0	0.0
6000 Other taxes	..	**0.0**	**0.0**	**0.0**	**0.0**	..	**0.0**	**0.0**	**0.0**	**0.0**
Non-wastable tax credits										
Non-wastable tax credits against 1000	..	..	..	..	..	..	..	..	..	..
Transfer component	..	..	..	..	..	..	..	..	..	..
Tax expenditure component	..	..	..	..	..	..	..	..	..	..

Note: More detailed country data and country notes are available in online chapter 5: http://dx.doi.org/10.1787/9789264283183-en. Full time series can be accessed at http://oe.cd/full-time-series.

Source: Statistical Office of the Republic of Slovenia.

StatLink http://dx.doi.org/10.1787/888933613254

Table 4.58. Slovenia, tax revenue and % of GDP by level of government and main taxes

	Billion EUR					% of GDP				
	1990	2000	2010	2014	2015	1990	2000	2010	2014	2015
Federal or Central government										
Total tax revenue	..	**3.8**	**6.5**	**6.8**	**7.2**	..	**20.2**	**18.0**	**18.2**	**18.5**
1000 Taxes on income, profits and capital gains	..	0.9	1.6	1.3	1.5	..	4.8	4.3	3.5	4.0
2000 Social security contributions	..	0.0	0.1	0.1	0.1	..	0.1	0.2	0.2	0.2
3000 Taxes on payroll and workforce	..	0.3	0.0	0.0	0.0	..	1.5	0.1	0.1	0.1
4000 Taxes on property	..	0.0	0.0	0.0	0.0	..	0.1	0.0	0.0	0.0
5000 Taxes on goods and services	..	2.6	4.9	5.4	5.5	..	13.7	13.5	14.5	14.4
6000 Other taxes	..	0.0	0.0	0.0	0.0	..	0.0	0.0	0.0	0.0
State/Regional										
Total tax revenue	..	..	..	..	..	..	..	..	..	..
1000 Taxes on income, profits and capital gains	..	..	..	..	..	..	..	..	..	..
2000 Social security contributions	..	..	..	..	..	..	..	..	..	..
3000 Taxes on payroll and workforce	..	..	..	..	..	..	..	..	..	..
4000 Taxes on property	..	..	..	..	..	..	..	..	..	..
5000 Taxes on goods and services	..	..	..	..	..	..	..	..	..	..
6000 Other taxes	..	..	..	..	..	..	..	..	..	..
Local government										
Total tax revenue	..	**0.5**	**1.5**	**1.4**	**1.4**	..	**2.7**	**4.0**	**3.9**	**3.5**
1000 Taxes on income, profits and capital gains	..	0.4	1.1	1.1	1.0	..	2.0	3.1	3.0	2.6
2000 Social security contributions	..	0.0	0.0	0.0	0.0	..	0.0	0.0	0.0	0.0
3000 Taxes on payroll and workforce	..	0.0	0.0	0.0	0.0	..	0.0	0.0	0.0	0.0
4000 Taxes on property	..	0.1	0.2	0.2	0.2	..	0.6	0.6	0.6	0.6
5000 Taxes on goods and services	..	0.0	0.1	0.1	0.1	..	0.1	0.3	0.2	0.2
6000 Other taxes	..	0.0	0.0	0.0	0.0	..	0.0	0.0	0.0	0.0
Social Security Funds										
Total tax revenue	..	**2.6**	**5.3**	**5.3**	**5.5**	..	**13.8**	**14.7**	**14.2**	**14.4**
1000 Taxes on income, profits and capital gains	..	0.0	0.0	0.0	0.0	..	0.0	0.0	0.0	0.0
2000 Social security contributions	..	2.6	5.3	5.3	5.5	..	13.8	14.7	14.2	14.4
3000 Taxes on payroll and workforce	..	0.0	0.0	0.0	0.0	..	0.0	0.0	0.0	0.0
4000 Taxes on property	..	0.0	0.0	0.0	0.0	..	0.0	0.0	0.0	0.0
5000 Taxes on goods and services	..	0.0	0.0	0.0	0.0	..	0.0	0.0	0.0	0.0
6000 Other taxes	..	0.0	0.0	0.0	0.0	..	0.0	0.0	0.0	0.0

Note: More detailed country data and country notes are available in online chapter 6: http://dx.doi.org/10.1787/9789264283183-en. Full time series can be accessed at http://oe.cd/full-time-series.

Source: Statistical Office of the Republic of Slovenia.

StatLink http://dx.doi.org/10.1787/888933613273

Table 4.59. **Spain, tax revenue and % of GDP by selected tax category**

	Billion EUR					% of GDP				
	1990	2000	2010	2014	2015	1990	2000	2010	2014	2015
Total tax revenue	**103.7**	**214.7**	**337.4**	**349.8**	**363.7**	**31.6**	**33.2**	**31.2**	**33.7**	**33.8**
1000 Taxes on income, profits and capital gains	**31.8**	**60.8**	**94.8**	**100.0**	**102.9**	**9.7**	**9.4**	**8.8**	**9.6**	**9.6**
1100 Of individuals	22.5	41.2	73.9	78.4	77.3	6.9	6.4	6.8	7.6	7.2
1200 Corporate	9.1	19.6	21.0	21.6	25.6	2.8	3.0	1.9	2.1	2.4
1300 Unallocable between 1100 and 1200	0.1	0.0	0.0	0.0	0.0	0.0	0.0	0.0	0.0	0.0
2000 Social security contributions	**36.7**	**74.8**	**126.5**	**120.7**	**122.9**	**11.2**	**11.6**	**11.7**	**11.6**	**11.4**
2100 Employees	6.0	12.1	20.0	19.1	19.7	1.8	1.9	1.9	1.8	1.8
2200 Employers	26.4	53.9	88.5	84.4	87.1	8.0	8.3	8.2	8.1	8.1
2300 Self-employed or non-employed	4.4	8.8	18.1	17.2	16.1	1.3	1.4	1.7	1.7	1.5
2400 Unallocable between 2100, 2200 and 2300	0.0	0.0	0.0	0.0	0.0	0.0	0.0	0.0	0.0	0.0
3000 Taxes on payroll and workforce	**0.0**	**0.0**	**0.0**	**0.0**	**0.0**	**0.0**	**0.0**	**0.0**	**0.0**	**0.0**
4000 Taxes on property	**5.7**	**13.8**	**22.3**	**26.0**	**28.0**	**1.7**	**2.1**	**2.1**	**2.5**	**2.6**
4100 Recurrent taxes on immovable property	1.5	3.9	9.4	12.2	12.7	0.5	0.6	0.9	1.2	1.2
4200 Recurrent taxes on net wealth	0.6	1.4	0.7	1.9	1.9	0.2	0.2	0.1	0.2	0.2
4300 Estate, inheritance and gift taxes	0.4	1.4	2.4	2.7	2.7	0.1	0.2	0.2	0.3	0.3
4400 Taxes on financial and capital transactions	2.5	6.0	8.0	6.3	7.2	0.8	0.9	0.7	0.6	0.7
4500 Non-recurrent taxes	0.6	1.1	1.8	2.9	3.5	0.2	0.2	0.2	0.3	0.3
4600 Other recurrent taxes on property	0.0	0.0	0.0	0.0	0.0	0.0	0.0	0.0	0.0	0.0
5000 Taxes on goods and services	**29.4**	**64.3**	**91.7**	**101.4**	**107.9**	**9.0**	**10.0**	**8.5**	**9.8**	**10.0**
5100 Taxes on production, sale, transfer, etc	26.7	58.3	84.6	93.5	99.8	8.2	9.0	7.8	9.0	9.3
5110 General taxes	16.6	37.9	57.3	64.3	69.2	5.1	5.9	5.3	6.2	6.4
5111 Value added taxes	16.3	37.9	57.0	64.1	69.0	5.0	5.9	5.3	6.2	6.4
5120 Taxes on specific goods and services	10.1	20.4	27.3	29.3	30.6	3.1	3.2	2.5	2.8	2.8
5121 Excises	6.0	17.7	23.8	24.4	25.6	1.8	2.7	2.2	2.4	2.4
5200 Taxes on use of goods and perform activities	2.6	6.0	7.2	7.9	8.1	0.8	0.9	0.7	0.8	0.8
5300 Unallocable between 5100 and 5200	0.1	0.0	0.0	0.0	0.0	0.0	0.0	0.0	0.0	0.0
6000 Other taxes	**0.0**	**0.0**	**0.5**	**0.2**	**0.2**	**0.0**	**0.0**	**0.0**	**0.0**	**0.0**
Non-wastable tax credits										
Non-wastable tax credits against 1000	..	0.0	1.9	0.8	1.0	..	0.0	0.2	0.1	0.1
Transfer component	..	..	1.2	0.3	0.2	..	..	0.1	0.0	0.0
Tax expenditure component	..	..	0.7	0.4	0.8	..	..	0.1	0.0	0.1

Note: More detailed country data and country notes are available in online chapter 5: http://dx.doi.org/10.1787/9789264283183-en. Full time series can be accessed at http://oe.cd/full-time-series.

The total tax revenue has been reduced by the amount of any capital transfer that represents uncollected taxes. The capital transfer has been allocated between tax headings in proportion to the reported tax revenue. Therefore, the tax revenue amounts are different to those reported in the detailed country data available in online chapter 5.

Source: Informacion Estatistica del Ministerio de Hacienda (for national taxes). Cuentas de las Administraciones Publicas (for local taxes and social security) both published by Secretaria General Tecnica del Ministerio de Hacienda.

StatLink http://dx.doi.org/10.1787/888933613292

Table 4.60. **Spain, tax revenue and % of GDP by level of government and main taxes**

	Billion EUR					% of GDP				
	1990	2000	2010	2014	2015	1990	2000	2010	2014	2015
Federal or Central government										
Total tax revenue	**53.7**	**105.2**	**136.4**	**147.8**	**154.7**	**16.4**	**16.3**	**12.6**	**14.2**	**14.4**
1000 Taxes on income, profits and capital gains	29.5	51.6	61.0	61.8	62.3	9.0	8.0	5.6	6.0	5.8
2000 Social security contributions	0.4	2.2	3.4	3.2	3.4	0.1	0.3	0.3	0.3	0.3
3000 Taxes on payroll and workforce	0.0	0.0	0.0	0.0	0.0	0.0	0.0	0.0	0.0	0.0
4000 Taxes on property	0.4	0.3	0.1	0.9	1.2	0.1	0.1	0.0	0.1	0.1
5000 Taxes on goods and services	23.4	51.0	71.4	81.8	87.7	7.2	7.9	6.6	7.9	8.2
6000 Other taxes	0.0	0.0	0.5	0.1	0.1	0.0	0.0	0.0	0.0	0.0
State/Regional										
Total tax revenue	**5.0**	**16.5**	**43.6**	**47.6**	**50.8**	**1.5**	**2.5**	**4.0**	**4.6**	**4.7**
1000 Taxes on income, profits and capital gains	0.4	5.5	27.6	32.4	34.6	0.1	0.9	2.5	3.1	3.2
2000 Social security contributions	0.0	0.0	0.0	0.0	0.0	0.0	0.0	0.0	0.0	0.0
3000 Taxes on payroll and workforce	0.0	0.0	0.0	0.0	0.0	0.0	0.0	0.0	0.0	0.0
4000 Taxes on property	3.0	7.8	10.1	9.6	10.5	0.9	1.2	0.9	0.9	1.0
5000 Taxes on goods and services	1.6	3.2	5.9	5.6	5.7	0.5	0.5	0.5	0.5	0.5
6000 Other taxes	0.0	0.0	0.0	0.0	0.0	0.0	0.0	0.0	0.0	0.0
Local government										
Total tax revenue	**8.1**	**19.5**	**30.8**	**34.9**	**36.1**	**2.5**	**3.0**	**2.9**	**3.4**	**3.4**
1000 Taxes on income, profits and capital gains	1.9	3.5	5.2	5.5	5.6	0.6	0.5	0.5	0.5	0.5
2000 Social security contributions	0.0	0.0	0.0	0.0	0.0	0.0	0.0	0.0	0.0	0.0
3000 Taxes on payroll and workforce	0.0	0.0	0.0	0.0	0.0	0.0	0.0	0.0	0.0	0.0
4000 Taxes on property	2.3	5.8	12.4	15.7	16.6	0.7	0.9	1.1	1.5	1.5
5000 Taxes on goods and services	3.9	10.1	13.3	13.6	13.8	1.2	1.6	1.2	1.3	1.3
6000 Other taxes	0.0	0.0	0.0	0.1	0.1	0.0	0.0	0.0	0.0	0.0
Social Security Funds										
Total tax revenue	**36.4**	**72.6**	**125.1**	**118.0**	**120.3**	**11.1**	**11.2**	**11.6**	**11.4**	**11.2**
1000 Taxes on income, profits and capital gains	0.0	0.0	0.0	0.0	0.0	0.0	0.0	0.0	0.0	0.0
2000 Social security contributions	36.4	72.6	125.1	118.0	120.3	11.1	11.2	11.6	11.4	11.2
3000 Taxes on payroll and workforce	0.0	0.0	0.0	0.0	0.0	0.0	0.0	0.0	0.0	0.0
4000 Taxes on property	0.0	0.0	0.0	0.0	0.0	0.0	0.0	0.0	0.0	0.0
5000 Taxes on goods and services	0.0	0.0	0.0	0.0	0.0	0.0	0.0	0.0	0.0	0.0
6000 Other taxes	0.0	0.0	0.0	0.0	0.0	0.0	0.0	0.0	0.0	0.0

Note: More detailed country data and country notes are available in online chapter 6: http://dx.doi.org/10.1787/9789264283183-en. Full time series can be accessed at http://oe.cd/full-time-series.

The total tax revenue has been reduced by the amount of any capital transfer that represents uncollected taxes. The capital transfer has been allocated between tax headings in proportion to the reported tax revenue. Therefore, the tax revenue amounts are different to those reported in the detailed country data available in online chapter 6.

Source: Informacion Estatistica del Ministerio de Hacienda (for national taxes). Cuentas de las Administraciones Publicas (for local taxes and social security) both published by Secretaria General Tecnica del Ministerio de Hacienda.

StatLink http://dx.doi.org/10.1787/888933613311

Table 4.61. **Sweden, tax revenue and % of GDP by selected tax category**

	Billion SEK					% of GDP				
	1990	2000	2010	2014	2015	1990	2000	2010	2014	2015
Total tax revenue	**756.0**	**1 166.0**	**1 521.4**	**1 676.4**	**1 809.6**	**49.5**	**49.0**	**43.2**	**42.6**	**43.3**
1000 Taxes on income, profits and capital gains	**314.8**	**475.3**	**539.7**	**585.6**	**650.0**	**20.6**	**20.0**	**15.3**	**14.9**	**15.5**
1100 Of individuals	291.1	387.5	423.9	479.5	525.8	19.1	16.3	12.0	12.2	12.6
1200 Corporate	23.7	87.8	115.8	106.1	124.2	1.5	3.7	3.3	2.7	3.0
1300 Unallocable between 1100 and 1200	0.0	0.0	0.0	0.0	0.0	0.0	0.0	0.0	0.0	0.0
2000 Social security contributions	**205.9**	**307.0**	**384.7**	**388.7**	**404.9**	**13.5**	**12.9**	**10.9**	**9.9**	**9.7**
2100 Employees	0.8	63.1	89.2	104.0	108.4	0.1	2.7	2.5	2.6	2.6
2200 Employers	196.9	237.5	288.4	280.1	291.6	12.9	10.0	8.2	7.1	7.0
2300 Self-employed or non-employed	8.1	5.6	7.5	5.0	5.1	0.5	0.2	0.2	0.1	0.1
2400 Unallocable between 2100, 2200 and 2300	0.0	0.8	-0.4	-0.4	-0.2	0.0	0.0	0.0	0.0	0.0
3000 Taxes on payroll and workforce	**18.7**	**50.1**	**107.5**	**177.4**	**194.1**	**1.2**	**2.1**	**3.1**	**4.5**	**4.6**
4000 Taxes on property	**26.6**	**39.9**	**36.5**	**41.9**	**43.9**	**1.7**	**1.7**	**1.0**	**1.1**	**1.0**
4100 Recurrent taxes on immovable property	8.9	23.3	26.4	32.0	32.4	0.6	1.0	0.8	0.8	0.8
4200 Recurrent taxes on net wealth	3.2	8.2	0.0	0.0	0.0	0.2	0.3	0.0	0.0	0.0
4300 Estate, inheritance and gift taxes	1.4	2.5	0.0	0.0	0.0	0.1	0.1	0.0	0.0	0.0
4400 Taxes on financial and capital transactions	13.1	5.8	10.1	9.9	11.4	0.9	0.2	0.3	0.3	0.3
4500 Non-recurrent taxes	0.0	0.0	0.0	0.0	0.0	0.0	0.0	0.0	0.0	0.0
4600 Other recurrent taxes on property	0.0	0.0	0.0	0.0	0.0	0.0	0.0	0.0	0.0	0.0
5000 Taxes on goods and services	**188.7**	**288.8**	**446.2**	**475.7**	**509.2**	**12.4**	**12.1**	**12.7**	**12.1**	**12.2**
5100 Taxes on production, sale, transfer, etc	181.6	281.4	429.8	458.9	490.4	11.9	11.8	12.2	11.7	11.7
5110 General taxes	112.4	199.6	326.7	357.4	382.7	7.4	8.4	9.3	9.1	9.2
5111 Value added taxes	112.4	197.5	322.6	353.4	378.8	7.4	8.3	9.2	9.0	9.1
5120 Taxes on specific goods and services	69.2	81.8	103.1	101.5	107.7	4.5	3.4	2.9	2.6	2.6
5121 Excises	55.3	70.3	91.6	86.9	91.6	3.6	3.0	2.6	2.2	2.2
5200 Taxes on use of goods and perform activities	7.1	7.4	16.4	16.8	18.8	0.5	0.3	0.5	0.4	0.4
5300 Unallocable between 5100 and 5200	0.0	0.0	0.0	0.0	0.0	0.0	0.0	0.0	0.0	0.0
6000 Other taxes	**1.3**	**1.5**	**1.4**	**1.4**	**1.4**	**0.1**	**0.1**	**0.0**	**0.0**	**0.0**
Non-wastable tax credits										
Non-wastable tax credits against 1000	..	..	..	..	..	..	..	..	..	..
Transfer component	..	..	..	..	..	..	..	..	..	..
Tax expenditure component	..	..	..	..	..	..	..	..	..	..

Note: More detailed country data and country notes are available in online chapter 5: http://dx.doi.org/10.1787/9789264283183-en. Full time series can be accessed at http://oe.cd/full-time-series.

Source: Monthly reports of central Government Revenues (unpublished) National Audit Bureau, Stockholm. Local Government Finance (SOS), Tax assessment statistics (SOS) , National Central Bureau of Statistics, Stockholm.National Accounts (Statistical Reports), National Bureau of Statistics, Stockholm.

StatLink http://dx.doi.org/10.1787/888933613330

Table 4.62. Sweden, tax revenue and % of GDP by level of government and main taxes

	Billion SEK					% of GDP				
	1990	2000	2010	2014	2015	1990	2000	2010	2014	2015
Federal or Central government										
Total tax revenue	**383.9**	**699.1**	**795.3**	**838.7**	**927.5**	**25.1**	**29.4**	**22.6**	**21.3**	**22.2**
1000 Taxes on income, profits and capital gains	94.7	139.0	16.9	-17.1	14.3	6.2	5.8	0.5	-0.4	0.3
2000 Social security contributions	54.8	180.2	201.2	175.0	180.7	3.6	7.6	5.7	4.4	4.3
3000 Taxes on payroll and workforce	18.7	50.1	107.5	177.4	194.1	1.2	2.1	3.1	4.5	4.6
4000 Taxes on property	26.6	39.9	22.4	26.4	27.9	1.7	1.7	0.6	0.7	0.7
5000 Taxes on goods and services	187.8	288.5	445.9	475.6	509.1	12.3	12.1	12.7	12.1	12.2
6000 Other taxes	1.3	1.5	1.4	1.4	1.4	0.1	0.1	0.0	0.0	0.0
State/Regional										
Total tax revenue	..	..	..	..	..	..	..	..	..	..
1000 Taxes on income, profits and capital gains	..	..	..	..	..	..	..	..	..	..
2000 Social security contributions	..	..	..	..	..	..	..	..	..	..
3000 Taxes on payroll and workforce	..	..	..	..	..	..	..	..	..	..
4000 Taxes on property	..	..	..	..	..	..	..	..	..	..
5000 Taxes on goods and services	..	..	..	..	..	..	..	..	..	..
6000 Other taxes	..	..	..	..	..	..	..	..	..	..
Local government										
Total tax revenue	**221.0**	**336.3**	**537.0**	**618.2**	**651.7**	**14.5**	**14.1**	**15.3**	**15.7**	**15.6**
1000 Taxes on income, profits and capital gains	220.1	336.3	522.9	602.7	635.7	14.4	14.1	14.9	15.3	15.2
2000 Social security contributions	0.0	0.0	0.0	0.0	0.0	0.0	0.0	0.0	0.0	0.0
3000 Taxes on payroll and workforce	0.0	0.0	0.0	0.0	0.0	0.0	0.0	0.0	0.0	0.0
4000 Taxes on property	0.0	0.0	14.1	15.6	15.9	0.0	0.0	0.4	0.4	0.4
5000 Taxes on goods and services	0.9	0.0	0.0	0.0	0.0	0.1	0.0	0.0	0.0	0.0
6000 Other taxes	0.0	0.0	0.0	0.0	0.0	0.0	0.0	0.0	0.0	0.0
Social Security Funds										
Total tax revenue	**151.1**	**126.8**	**183.5**	**213.7**	**224.1**	**9.9**	**5.3**	**5.2**	**5.4**	**5.4**
1000 Taxes on income, profits and capital gains	0.0	0.0	0.0	0.0	0.0	0.0	0.0	0.0	0.0	0.0
2000 Social security contributions	151.1	126.8	183.5	213.7	224.1	9.9	5.3	5.2	5.4	5.4
3000 Taxes on payroll and workforce	0.0	0.0	0.0	0.0	0.0	0.0	0.0	0.0	0.0	0.0
4000 Taxes on property	0.0	0.0	0.0	0.0	0.0	0.0	0.0	0.0	0.0	0.0
5000 Taxes on goods and services	0.0	0.0	0.0	0.0	0.0	0.0	0.0	0.0	0.0	0.0
6000 Other taxes	0.0	0.0	0.0	0.0	0.0	0.0	0.0	0.0	0.0	0.0

Note: More detailed country data and country notes are available in online chapter 6: http://dx.doi.org/10.1787/9789264283183-en. Full time series can be accessed at http://oe.cd/full-time-series.

Source: Monthly reports of central Government Revenues (unpublished) National Audit Bureau, Stockholm. Local Government Finance (SOS), Tax assessment statistics (SOS) , National Central Bureau of Statistics, Stockholm.National Accounts (Statistical Reports), National Bureau of Statistics, Stockholm.

StatLink http://dx.doi.org/10.1787/888933613349

Table 4.63. **Switzerland, tax revenue and % of GDP by selected tax category**

	Billion CHF					% of GDP				
	1990	2000	2010	2014	2015	1990	2000	2010	2014	2015
Total tax revenue	**84.4**	**125.9**	**160.4**	**173.6**	**178.7**	**23.6**	**27.4**	**26.5**	**27.0**	**27.7**
1000 Taxes on income, profits and capital gains	**40.0**	**55.8**	**73.2**	**79.3**	**83.0**	**11.2**	**12.2**	**12.1**	**12.3**	**12.9**
1100 Of individuals	27.7	37.5	51.2	53.8	55.6	7.7	8.2	8.4	8.4	8.6
1200 Corporate	6.3	11.2	16.2	18.0	19.3	1.8	2.4	2.7	2.8	3.0
1300 Unallocable between 1100 and 1200	6.1	7.1	5.8	7.5	8.1	1.7	1.6	1.0	1.2	1.3
2000 Social security contributions	**19.9**	**30.6**	**38.3**	**43.2**	**43.9**	**5.6**	**6.7**	**6.3**	**6.7**	**6.8**
2100 Employees	9.3	14.4	17.5	20.0	20.5	2.6	3.1	2.9	3.1	3.2
2200 Employers	9.3	14.4	17.6	20.0	20.3	2.6	3.1	2.9	3.1	3.1
2300 Self-employed or non-employed	1.2	1.9	3.2	3.1	3.1	0.3	0.4	0.5	0.5	0.5
2400 Unallocable between 2100, 2200 and 2300	0.0	0.0	0.0	0.0	0.0	0.0	0.0	0.0	0.0	0.0
3000 Taxes on payroll and workforce	**0.0**	**0.0**	**0.0**	**0.0**	**0.0**	**0.0**	**0.0**	**0.0**	**0.0**	**0.0**
4000 Taxes on property	**6.9**	**11.4**	**11.3**	**11.5**	**12.0**	**1.9**	**2.5**	**1.9**	**1.8**	**1.9**
4100 Recurrent taxes on immovable property	0.4	0.7	1.0	1.0	1.1	0.1	0.2	0.2	0.2	0.2
4200 Recurrent taxes on net wealth	3.4	5.3	7.1	7.8	8.1	0.9	1.1	1.2	1.2	1.2
4300 Estate, inheritance and gift taxes	0.9	1.2	1.0	1.2	1.1	0.2	0.3	0.2	0.2	0.2
4400 Taxes on financial and capital transactions	2.1	4.2	2.3	1.5	1.7	0.6	0.9	0.4	0.2	0.3
4500 Non-recurrent taxes	0.0	0.0	0.0	0.0	0.0	0.0	0.0	0.0	0.0	0.0
4600 Other recurrent taxes on property	0.0	0.0	0.0	0.0	0.0	0.0	0.0	0.0	0.0	0.0
5000 Taxes on goods and services	**17.5**	**27.9**	**37.1**	**38.9**	**38.9**	**4.9**	**6.1**	**6.1**	**6.0**	**6.0**
5100 Taxes on production, sale, transfer, etc	16.0	25.3	32.1	33.8	33.6	4.5	5.5	5.3	5.2	5.2
5110 General taxes	9.9	16.9	20.9	22.7	22.6	2.8	3.7	3.4	3.5	3.5
5111 Value added taxes	9.9	16.6	20.5	22.4	22.2	2.8	3.6	3.4	3.5	3.4
5120 Taxes on specific goods and services	6.1	8.3	11.2	11.0	10.9	1.7	1.8	1.8	1.7	1.7
5121 Excises	1.5	6.8	8.3	8.1	8.1	0.4	1.5	1.4	1.3	1.2
5200 Taxes on use of goods and perform activities	1.6	2.6	4.9	5.2	5.3	0.4	0.6	0.8	0.8	0.8
5300 Unallocable between 5100 and 5200	0.0	0.0	0.0	0.0	0.0	0.0	0.0	0.0	0.0	0.0
6000 Other taxes	**0.1**	**0.2**	**0.6**	**0.8**	**0.8**	**0.0**	**0.0**	**0.1**	**0.1**	**0.1**
Non-wastable tax credits										
Non-wastable tax credits against 1000	..	..	..	..	..	..	..	..	..	..
Transfer component	..	..	..	..	..	..	..	..	..	..
Tax expenditure component	..	..	..	..	..	..	..	..	..	..

Note: More detailed country data and country notes are available in online chapter 5: http://dx.doi.org/10.1787/9789264283183-en. Full time series can be accessed at http://oe.cd/full-time-series.

Source: Financial Statistics, Federal Finance Administration.

StatLink http://dx.doi.org/10.1787/888933613368

Table 4.64. Switzerland, tax revenue and % of GDP by level of government and main taxes

	Billion CHF					% of GDP				
	1990	2000	2010	2014	2015	1990	2000	2010	2014	2015
Federal or Central government										
Total tax revenue	**29.0**	**46.9**	**58.8**	**61.1**	**63.9**	**8.1**	**10.2**	**9.7**	**9.5**	**9.9**
1000 Taxes on income, profits and capital gains	10.9	17.0	22.3	23.7	26.3	3.0	3.7	3.7	3.7	4.1
2000 Social security contributions	0.0	0.0	0.0	0.0	0.0	0.0	0.0	0.0	0.0	0.0
3000 Taxes on payroll and workforce	0.0	0.0	0.0	0.0	0.0	0.0	0.0	0.0	0.0	0.0
4000 Taxes on property	2.1	4.1	2.2	1.4	1.7	0.6	0.9	0.4	0.2	0.3
5000 Taxes on goods and services	16.0	25.7	34.2	36.0	35.9	4.5	5.6	5.6	5.6	5.6
6000 Other taxes	0.0	0.0	0.0	0.0	0.0	0.0	0.0	0.0	0.0	0.0
State/Regional										
Total tax revenue	**20.8**	**28.2**	**39.0**	**42.8**	**43.7**	**5.8**	**6.1**	**6.4**	**6.7**	**6.8**
1000 Taxes on income, profits and capital gains	16.4	21.7	30.8	33.7	34.3	4.6	4.7	5.1	5.2	5.3
2000 Social security contributions	0.0	0.0	0.0	0.0	0.0	0.0	0.0	0.0	0.0	0.0
3000 Taxes on payroll and workforce	0.0	0.0	0.0	0.0	0.0	0.0	0.0	0.0	0.0	0.0
4000 Taxes on property	3.0	4.4	5.5	6.1	6.3	0.8	1.0	0.9	1.0	1.0
5000 Taxes on goods and services	1.4	2.1	2.7	2.8	2.9	0.4	0.5	0.4	0.4	0.4
6000 Other taxes	0.0	0.0	0.0	0.2	0.2	0.0	0.0	0.0	0.0	0.0
Local government										
Total tax revenue	**14.7**	**20.2**	**24.4**	**26.5**	**27.1**	**4.1**	**4.4**	**4.0**	**4.1**	**4.2**
1000 Taxes on income, profits and capital gains	12.7	17.1	20.1	21.9	22.4	3.6	3.7	3.3	3.4	3.5
2000 Social security contributions	0.0	0.0	0.0	0.0	0.0	0.0	0.0	0.0	0.0	0.0
3000 Taxes on payroll and workforce	0.0	0.0	0.0	0.0	0.0	0.0	0.0	0.0	0.0	0.0
4000 Taxes on property	1.8	2.9	3.6	3.9	4.0	0.5	0.6	0.6	0.6	0.6
5000 Taxes on goods and services	0.1	0.1	0.1	0.1	0.1	0.0	0.0	0.0	0.0	0.0
6000 Other taxes	0.1	0.2	0.6	0.5	0.6	0.0	0.0	0.1	0.1	0.1
Social Security Funds										
Total tax revenue	**19.9**	**30.6**	**38.3**	**43.2**	**43.9**	**5.6**	**6.7**	**6.3**	**6.7**	**6.8**
1000 Taxes on income, profits and capital gains	0.0	0.0	0.0	0.0	0.0	0.0	0.0	0.0	0.0	0.0
2000 Social security contributions	19.9	30.6	38.3	43.2	43.9	5.6	6.7	6.3	6.7	6.8
3000 Taxes on payroll and workforce	0.0	0.0	0.0	0.0	0.0	0.0	0.0	0.0	0.0	0.0
4000 Taxes on property	0.0	0.0	0.0	0.0	0.0	0.0	0.0	0.0	0.0	0.0
5000 Taxes on goods and services	0.0	0.0	0.0	0.0	0.0	0.0	0.0	0.0	0.0	0.0
6000 Other taxes	0.0	0.0	0.0	0.0	0.0	0.0	0.0	0.0	0.0	0.0

Note: More detailed country data and country notes are available in online chapter 6: http://dx.doi.org/10.1787/9789264283183-en. Full time series can be accessed at http://oe.cd/full-time-series.

Source: Financial Statistics, Federal Finance Administration.

StatLink http://dx.doi.org/10.1787/888933613387

Table 4.65. Turkey, tax revenue and % of GDP by selected tax category

	Billion TRY					% of GDP				
	1990	2000	2010	2014	2015	1990	2000	2010	2014	2015
Total tax revenue	**0.1**	**40.3**	**287.9**	**502.6**	**586.7**	**14.5**	**23.6**	**24.8**	**24.6**	**25.1**
1000 Taxes on income, profits and capital gains	**0.0**	**11.9**	**61.3**	**106.2**	**119.1**	**4.9**	**7.0**	**5.3**	**5.2**	**5.1**
1100 Of individuals	0.0	9.0	40.4	73.9	85.8	3.9	5.2	3.5	3.6	3.7
1200 Corporate	0.0	2.9	20.9	32.3	33.4	1.0	1.7	1.8	1.6	1.4
1300 Unallocable between 1100 and 1200	0.0	0.0	0.0	0.0	0.0	0.0	0.0	0.0	0.0	0.0
2000 Social security contributions	**0.0**	**7.5**	**71.7**	**143.4**	**170.3**	**2.9**	**4.4**	**6.2**	**7.0**	**7.3**
2100 Employees	0.0	2.7	26.9	54.3	64.2	1.1	1.6	2.3	2.7	2.7
2200 Employers	0.0	3.6	39.4	80.0	95.1	1.6	2.1	3.4	3.9	4.1
2300 Self-employed or non-employed	0.0	1.2	5.4	9.1	11.0	0.2	0.7	0.5	0.4	0.5
2400 Unallocable between 2100, 2200 and 2300	0.0	0.0	0.0	0.0	0.0	0.0	0.0	0.0	0.0	0.0
3000 Taxes on payroll and workforce	**0.0**	**0.0**	**0.0**	**0.0**	**0.0**	**0.0**	**0.0**	**0.0**	**0.0**	**0.0**
4000 Taxes on property	**0.0**	**1.3**	**11.7**	**24.5**	**28.6**	**0.3**	**0.7**	**1.0**	**1.2**	**1.2**
4100 Recurrent taxes on immovable property	0.0	0.2	2.7	5.0	5.9	0.0	0.1	0.2	0.2	0.3
4200 Recurrent taxes on net wealth	0.0	0.0	0.0	0.0	0.0	0.0	0.0	0.0	0.0	0.0
4300 Estate, inheritance and gift taxes	0.0	0.0	0.2	0.4	0.4	0.0	0.0	0.0	0.0	0.0
4400 Taxes on financial and capital transactions	0.0	1.1	8.8	19.1	22.3	0.3	0.6	0.8	0.9	1.0
4500 Non-recurrent taxes	0.0	0.0	0.0	0.0	0.0	0.0	0.0	0.0	0.0	0.0
4600 Other recurrent taxes on property	0.0	0.0	0.0	0.0	0.0	0.0	0.0	0.0	0.0	0.0
5000 Taxes on goods and services	**0.0**	**16.9**	**137.3**	**221.6**	**260.0**	**4.1**	**9.9**	**11.8**	**10.8**	**11.1**
5100 Taxes on production, sale, transfer, etc	0.0	16.3	131.9	213.3	250.3	4.0	9.6	11.4	10.4	10.7
5110 General taxes	0.0	9.7	62.5	102.5	121.1	2.9	5.7	5.4	5.0	5.2
5111 Value added taxes	0.0	9.7	62.5	102.5	121.1	2.7	5.7	5.4	5.0	5.2
5120 Taxes on specific goods and services	0.0	6.6	69.3	110.7	129.2	1.1	3.9	6.0	5.4	5.5
5121 Excises	0.0	4.7	57.3	91.1	105.9	0.1	2.8	4.9	4.5	4.5
5200 Taxes on use of goods and perform activities	0.0	0.6	5.4	8.4	9.7	0.1	0.3	0.5	0.4	0.4
5300 Unallocable between 5100 and 5200	0.0	0.0	0.0	0.0	0.0	0.0	0.0	0.0	0.0	0.0
6000 Other taxes	**0.0**	**2.7**	**5.9**	**6.8**	**8.7**	**2.4**	**1.6**	**0.5**	**0.3**	**0.4**
Non-wastable tax credits										
Non-wastable tax credits against 1000	..	..	..	..	..	..	..	..	..	..
Transfer component	..	..	..	..	..	..	..	..	..	..
Tax expenditure component	..	..	..	..	..	..	..	..	..	..

Note: More detailed country data and country notes are available in online chapter 5: http://dx.doi.org/10.1787/9789264283183-en. Full time series can be accessed at http://oe.cd/full-time-series.

Source: Bulletin of national accounts and the Budget revenue Bulletin.

StatLink http://dx.doi.org/10.1787/888933613406

Table 4.66. **Turkey, tax revenue and % of GDP by level of government and main taxes**

	Billion TRY					% of GDP				
	1990	2000	2010	2014	2015	1990	2000	2010	2014	2015
Federal or Central government										
Total tax revenue	**0.1**	**29.1**	**189.4**	**311.7**	**359.9**	**10.4**	**17.1**	**16.3**	**15.2**	**15.4**
1000 Taxes on income, profits and capital gains	0.0	10.5	54.6	93.9	104.7	4.3	6.2	4.7	4.6	4.5
2000 Social security contributions	0.0	0.0	0.0	0.0	0.0	0.0	0.0	0.0	0.0	0.0
3000 Taxes on payroll and workforce	0.0	0.0	0.0	0.0	0.0	0.0	0.0	0.0	0.0	0.0
4000 Taxes on property	0.0	0.9	8.1	17.5	20.2	0.3	0.5	0.7	0.9	0.9
5000 Taxes on goods and services	0.0	15.2	124.0	197.8	231.2	3.6	8.9	10.7	9.7	9.9
6000 Other taxes	0.0	2.5	2.7	2.6	3.8	2.2	1.5	0.2	0.1	0.2
State/Regional										
Total tax revenue	..	..	..	..	..	..	..	..	..	..
1000 Taxes on income, profits and capital gains	..	..	..	..	..	..	..	..	..	..
2000 Social security contributions	..	..	..	..	..	..	..	..	..	..
3000 Taxes on payroll and workforce	..	..	..	..	..	..	..	..	..	..
4000 Taxes on property	..	..	..	..	..	..	..	..	..	..
5000 Taxes on goods and services	..	..	..	..	..	..	..	..	..	..
6000 Other taxes	..	..	..	..	..	..	..	..	..	..
Local government										
Total tax revenue	**0.0**	**3.6**	**26.8**	**47.5**	**56.5**	**1.3**	**2.1**	**2.3**	**2.3**	**2.4**
1000 Taxes on income, profits and capital gains	0.0	1.4	6.7	12.3	14.4	0.6	0.8	0.6	0.6	0.6
2000 Social security contributions	0.0	0.0	0.0	0.0	0.0	0.0	0.0	0.0	0.0	0.0
3000 Taxes on payroll and workforce	0.0	0.0	0.0	0.0	0.0	0.0	0.0	0.0	0.0	0.0
4000 Taxes on property	0.0	0.3	3.6	7.0	8.4	0.0	0.2	0.3	0.3	0.4
5000 Taxes on goods and services	0.0	1.7	13.3	23.8	28.7	0.5	1.0	1.1	1.2	1.2
6000 Other taxes	0.0	0.2	3.2	4.3	5.0	0.2	0.1	0.3	0.2	0.2
Social Security Funds										
Total tax revenue	**0.0**	**7.5**	**71.7**	**143.4**	**170.3**	**2.9**	**4.4**	**6.2**	**7.0**	**7.3**
1000 Taxes on income, profits and capital gains	0.0	0.0	0.0	0.0	0.0	0.0	0.0	0.0	0.0	0.0
2000 Social security contributions	0.0	7.5	71.7	143.4	170.3	2.9	4.4	6.2	7.0	7.3
3000 Taxes on payroll and workforce	0.0	0.0	0.0	0.0	0.0	0.0	0.0	0.0	0.0	0.0
4000 Taxes on property	0.0	0.0	0.0	0.0	0.0	0.0	0.0	0.0	0.0	0.0
5000 Taxes on goods and services	0.0	0.0	0.0	0.0	0.0	0.0	0.0	0.0	0.0	0.0
6000 Other taxes	0.0	0.0	0.0	0.0	0.0	0.0	0.0	0.0	0.0	0.0

Note: More detailed country data and country notes are available in online chapter 6: http://dx.doi.org/10.1787/9789264283183-en. Full time series can be accessed at http://oe.cd/full-time-series.

Source: Bulletin of national accounts and the Budget revenue Bulletin.

StatLink http://dx.doi.org/10.1787/888933613425

Table 4.67. **United Kingdom, tax revenue and % of GDP by selected tax category**

	Billion GBP					% of GDP				
	1990	2000	2010	2014	2015	1990	2000	2010	2014	2015
Total tax revenue	**202.4**	**358.6**	**512.5**	**586.4**	**609.2**	**32.9**	**33.2**	**32.6**	**32.2**	**32.5**
1000 Taxes on income, profits and capital gains	**79.6**	**142.2**	**192.6**	**205.7**	**214.8**	**12.9**	**13.2**	**12.2**	**11.3**	**11.5**
1100 Of individuals	59.5	104.1	147.0	160.1	168.9	9.7	9.6	9.4	8.8	9.0
1200 Corporate	20.1	38.1	45.6	45.6	45.9	3.3	3.5	2.9	2.5	2.5
1300 Unallocable between 1100 and 1200	0.0	0.0	0.0	0.0	0.0	0.0	0.0	0.0	0.0	0.0
2000 Social security contributions	**34.5**	**60.3**	**97.3**	**109.1**	**114.1**	**5.6**	**5.6**	**6.2**	**6.0**	**6.1**
2100 Employees	13.3	24.2	38.7	42.6	44.5	2.2	2.2	2.5	2.3	2.4
2200 Employers	20.0	34.0	55.9	63.8	66.5	3.2	3.1	3.6	3.5	3.6
2300 Self-employed or non-employed	1.2	2.0	2.8	2.7	3.1	0.2	0.2	0.2	0.1	0.2
2400 Unallocable between 2100, 2200 and 2300	0.0	0.0	0.0	0.0	0.0	0.0	0.0	0.0	0.0	0.0
3000 Taxes on payroll and workforce	**0.0**	**0.0**	**0.0**	**0.0**	**0.0**	**0.0**	**0.0**	**0.0**	**0.0**	**0.0**
4000 Taxes on property	**16.5**	**41.1**	**61.7**	**74.3**	**76.6**	**2.7**	**3.8**	**3.9**	**4.1**	**4.1**
4100 Recurrent taxes on immovable property	13.5	30.6	49.9	56.3	58.3	2.2	2.8	3.2	3.1	3.1
4200 Recurrent taxes on net wealth	0.0	0.0	0.0	0.0	0.0	0.0	0.0	0.0	0.0	0.0
4300 Estate, inheritance and gift taxes	1.3	2.2	2.6	3.9	4.4	0.2	0.2	0.2	0.2	0.2
4400 Taxes on financial and capital transactions	1.8	8.4	9.1	14.1	13.8	0.3	0.8	0.6	0.8	0.7
4500 Non-recurrent taxes	0.0	0.0	0.0	0.1	0.2	0.0	0.0	0.0	0.0	0.0
4600 Other recurrent taxes on property	0.0	0.0	0.0	0.0	0.0	0.0	0.0	0.0	0.0	0.0
5000 Taxes on goods and services	**62.8**	**113.2**	**157.9**	**194.3**	**200.6**	**10.2**	**10.5**	**10.0**	**10.7**	**10.7**
5100 Taxes on production, sale, transfer, etc	59.4	108.2	151.0	187.1	193.5	9.7	10.0	9.6	10.3	10.3
5110 General taxes	34.1	64.2	95.9	124.2	129.3	5.5	5.9	6.1	6.8	6.9
5111 Value added taxes	34.1	64.2	95.9	124.2	129.3	5.5	5.9	6.1	6.8	6.9
5120 Taxes on specific goods and services	25.3	44.0	55.0	62.9	64.2	4.1	4.1	3.5	3.5	3.4
5121 Excises	19.7	37.3	45.4	47.1	47.3	3.2	3.4	2.9	2.6	2.5
5200 Taxes on use of goods and perform activities	3.4	5.0	7.0	7.2	7.1	0.6	0.5	0.4	0.4	0.4
5300 Unallocable between 5100 and 5200	0.0	0.0	0.0	0.0	0.0	0.0	0.0	0.0	0.0	0.0
6000 Other taxes	**9.0**	**0.0**	**0.0**	**0.0**	**0.0**	**1.5**	**0.0**	**0.0**	**0.0**	**0.0**
Non-wastable tax credits										
Non-wastable tax credits against 1000	7.5	4.7	30.1	31.6	30.8	1.2	0.4	1.9	1.7	1.6
Transfer component	0.5	3.4	23.7	28.0	27.4	0.1	0.3	1.5	1.5	1.5
Tax expenditure component	7.0	1.2	6.5	3.6	3.4	1.1	0.1	0.4	0.2	0.2

Note: More detailed country data and country notes are available in online chapter 5: http://dx.doi.org/10.1787/9789264283183-en. Full time series can be accessed at http://oe.cd/full-time-series.

Source: National Income and Expenditure; Central Statistical Office; Annual reports of Her Majesty's Revenue and Customs.

StatLink http://dx.doi.org/10.1787/888933613444

Table 4.68. **United Kingdom, tax revenue and % of GDP by level of government and main taxes**

	Billion GBP					% of GDP				
	1990	2000	2010	2014	2015	1990	2000	2010	2014	2015
Federal or Central government										
Total tax revenue	**151.9**	**282.0**	**386.0**	**445.3**	**462.1**	**24.7**	**26.1**	**24.5**	**24.4**	**24.7**
1000 Taxes on income, profits and capital gains	79.6	142.2	192.6	205.7	214.8	12.9	13.2	12.2	11.3	11.5
2000 Social security contributions	0.0	0.0	0.0	0.0	0.0	0.0	0.0	0.0	0.0	0.0
3000 Taxes on payroll and workforce	0.0	0.0	0.0	0.0	0.0	0.0	0.0	0.0	0.0	0.0
4000 Taxes on property	11.4	26.9	35.4	45.3	46.7	1.9	2.5	2.3	2.5	2.5
5000 Taxes on goods and services	60.9	112.8	157.9	194.3	200.6	9.9	10.4	10.0	10.7	10.7
6000 Other taxes	0.0	0.0	0.0	0.0	0.0	0.0	0.0	0.0	0.0	0.0
State/Regional										
Total tax revenue	..	..	..	..	..	..	..	..	..	..
1000 Taxes on income, profits and capital gains	..	..	..	..	..	..	..	..	..	..
2000 Social security contributions	..	..	..	..	..	..	..	..	..	..
3000 Taxes on payroll and workforce	..	..	..	..	..	..	..	..	..	..
4000 Taxes on property	..	..	..	..	..	..	..	..	..	..
5000 Taxes on goods and services	..	..	..	..	..	..	..	..	..	..
6000 Other taxes	..	..	..	..	..	..	..	..	..	..
Local government										
Total tax revenue	**14.1**	**14.2**	**26.2**	**29.0**	**29.9**	**2.3**	**1.3**	**1.7**	**1.6**	**1.6**
1000 Taxes on income, profits and capital gains	0.0	0.0	0.0	0.0	0.0	0.0	0.0	0.0	0.0	0.0
2000 Social security contributions	0.0	0.0	0.0	0.0	0.0	0.0	0.0	0.0	0.0	0.0
3000 Taxes on payroll and workforce	0.0	0.0	0.0	0.0	0.0	0.0	0.0	0.0	0.0	0.0
4000 Taxes on property	5.1	14.2	26.2	29.0	29.9	0.8	1.3	1.7	1.6	1.6
5000 Taxes on goods and services	0.0	0.0	0.0	0.0	0.0	0.0	0.0	0.0	0.0	0.0
6000 Other taxes	9.0	0.0	0.0	0.0	0.0	1.5	0.0	0.0	0.0	0.0
Social Security Funds										
Total tax revenue	**34.5**	**60.3**	**97.3**	**109.1**	**114.1**	**5.6**	**5.6**	**6.2**	**6.0**	**6.1**
1000 Taxes on income, profits and capital gains	0.0	0.0	0.0	0.0	0.0	0.0	0.0	0.0	0.0	0.0
2000 Social security contributions	34.5	60.3	97.3	109.1	114.1	5.6	5.6	6.2	6.0	6.1
3000 Taxes on payroll and workforce	0.0	0.0	0.0	0.0	0.0	0.0	0.0	0.0	0.0	0.0
4000 Taxes on property	0.0	0.0	0.0	0.0	0.0	0.0	0.0	0.0	0.0	0.0
5000 Taxes on goods and services	0.0	0.0	0.0	0.0	0.0	0.0	0.0	0.0	0.0	0.0
6000 Other taxes	0.0	0.0	0.0	0.0	0.0	0.0	0.0	0.0	0.0	0.0

Note: More detailed country data and country notes are available in online chapter 6: http://dx.doi.org/10.1787/9789264283183-en. Full time series can be accessed at http://oe.cd/full-time-series.

Source: National Income and Expenditure; Central Statistical Office; Annual reports of Her Majesty's Revenue and Customs.

StatLink http://dx.doi.org/10.1787/888933613463

Table 4.69. **United States, tax revenue and % of GDP by selected tax category**

	Billion USD					% of GDP				
	1990	2000	2010	2014	2015	1990	2000	2010	2014	2015
Total tax revenue	**1 552.4**	**2 900.5**	**3 515.8**	**4 518.4**	**4 752.4**	**26.0**	**28.2**	**23.5**	**25.9**	**26.2**
1000 Taxes on income, profits and capital gains	**701.7**	**1 453.9**	**1 491.5**	**2 173.0**	**2 331.1**	**11.7**	**14.1**	**10.0**	**12.5**	**12.9**
1100 Of individuals	584.7	1 224.5	1 224.5	1 774.7	1 926.1	9.8	11.9	8.2	10.2	10.6
1200 Corporate	117.0	229.3	267.0	398.3	405.0	2.0	2.2	1.8	2.3	2.2
1300 Unallocable between 1100 and 1200	0.0	0.0	0.0	0.0	0.0	0.0	0.0	0.0	0.0	0.0
2000 Social security contributions	**397.0**	**683.1**	**917.8**	**1 078.0**	**1 124.0**	**6.6**	**6.6**	**6.1**	**6.2**	**6.2**
2100 Employees	173.9	305.6	406.4	479.1	502.4	2.9	3.0	2.7	2.7	2.8
2200 Employers	204.1	343.2	462.1	540.0	560.4	3.4	3.3	3.1	3.1	3.1
2300 Self-employed or non-employed	19.0	34.4	49.3	59.0	61.3	0.3	0.3	0.3	0.3	0.3
2400 Unallocable between 2100, 2200 and 2300	0.0	0.0	0.0	0.0	0.0	0.0	0.0	0.0	0.0	0.0
3000 Taxes on payroll and workforce	**0.0**	**0.0**	**0.0**	**0.0**	**0.0**	**0.0**	**0.0**	**0.0**	**0.0**	**0.0**
4000 Taxes on property	**180.3**	**295.2**	**462.1**	**485.3**	**490.0**	**3.0**	**2.9**	**3.1**	**2.8**	**2.7**
4100 Recurrent taxes on immovable property	161.5	254.7	435.0	453.6	456.6	2.7	2.5	2.9	2.6	2.5
4200 Recurrent taxes on net wealth	0.0	0.0	0.0	0.0	0.0	0.0	0.0	0.0	0.0	0.0
4300 Estate, inheritance and gift taxes	15.8	35.6	19.5	24.1	25.6	0.3	0.3	0.1	0.1	0.1
4400 Taxes on financial and capital transactions	0.0	0.0	0.0	0.0	0.0	0.0	0.0	0.0	0.0	0.0
4500 Non-recurrent taxes	0.0	0.0	0.0	0.0	0.0	0.0	0.0	0.0	0.0	0.0
4600 Other recurrent taxes on property	3.0	4.8	7.5	7.7	7.8	0.1	0.0	0.1	0.0	0.0
5000 Taxes on goods and services	**273.5**	**468.4**	**644.4**	**782.1**	**807.3**	**4.6**	**4.6**	**4.3**	**4.5**	**4.5**
5100 Taxes on production, sale, transfer, etc	235.2	404.1	542.1	657.7	681.5	3.9	3.9	3.6	3.8	3.8
5110 General taxes	125.6	221.4	294.4	352.8	367.2	2.1	2.2	2.0	2.0	2.0
5111 Value added taxes	0.0	0.0	0.0	0.0	0.0	0.0	0.0	0.0	0.0	0.0
5120 Taxes on specific goods and services	109.6	182.7	247.6	304.9	314.3	1.8	1.8	1.7	1.7	1.7
5121 Excises	65.0	108.6	145.3	154.5	154.7	1.1	1.1	1.0	0.9	0.9
5200 Taxes on use of goods and perform activities	38.2	64.3	102.3	124.4	125.8	0.6	0.6	0.7	0.7	0.7
5300 Unallocable between 5100 and 5200	0.0	0.0	0.0	0.0	0.0	0.0	0.0	0.0	0.0	0.0
6000 Other taxes	**0.0**	**0.0**	**0.0**	**0.0**	**0.0**	**0.0**	**0.0**	**0.0**	**0.0**	**0.0**
Non-wastable tax credits										
Non-wastable tax credits against 1000	6.2	36.5	171.9	144.6	157.2	0.1	0.4	1.1	0.8	0.9
Transfer component	4.4	26.9	101.8	99.8	113.9	0.1	0.3	0.7	0.6	0.6
Tax expenditure component	1.8	9.6	70.1	44.8	43.4	0.0	0.1	0.5	0.3	0.2

Note: More detailed country data and country notes are available in online chapter 5: http://dx.doi.org/10.1787/9789264283183-en. Full time series can be accessed at http://oe.cd/full-time-series.

Source: Federal estimates are derived from the US Budget, the Final Monthly Treasury Statement and the Annual Report of the US Treasury Department. The State and Local estimates are derived from Government Finances, published by the Bureau of the Census.

StatLink http://dx.doi.org/10.1787/888933613482

Table 4.70. **United States, tax revenue and % of GDP by level of government and main taxes**

	Billion USD					% of GDP				
	1990	2000	2010	2014	2015	1990	2000	2010	2014	2015
Federal or Central government										
Total tax revenue	**632.2**	**1 316.6**	**1 288.6**	**1 916.9**	**2 059.0**	**10.6**	**12.8**	**8.6**	**11.0**	**11.4**
1000 Taxes on income, profits and capital gains	569.7	1 201.3	1 176.7	1 763.5	1 899.4	9.5	11.7	7.9	10.1	10.5
2000 Social security contributions	0.0	0.0	0.0	0.0	0.0	0.0	0.0	0.0	0.0	0.0
3000 Taxes on payroll and workforce	0.0	0.0	0.0	0.0	0.0	0.0	0.0	0.0	0.0	0.0
4000 Taxes on property	11.6	28.1	15.1	18.8	20.2	0.2	0.3	0.1	0.1	0.1
5000 Taxes on goods and services	50.9	87.3	96.8	134.6	139.4	0.9	0.8	0.6	0.8	0.8
6000 Other taxes	0.0	0.0	0.0	0.0	0.0	0.0	0.0	0.0	0.0	0.0
State/Regional										
Total tax revenue	**309.7**	**547.6**	**724.1**	**888.3**	**923.7**	**5.2**	**5.3**	**4.8**	**5.1**	**5.1**
1000 Taxes on income, profits and capital gains	120.2	231.0	282.0	370.1	390.9	2.0	2.2	1.9	2.1	2.2
2000 Social security contributions	0.0	0.0	0.0	0.0	0.0	0.0	0.0	0.0	0.0	0.0
3000 Taxes on payroll and workforce	0.0	0.0	0.0	0.0	0.0	0.0	0.0	0.0	0.0	0.0
4000 Taxes on property	10.1	17.6	18.1	18.4	18.9	0.2	0.2	0.1	0.1	0.1
5000 Taxes on goods and services	179.4	299.0	424.0	499.7	513.9	3.0	2.9	2.8	2.9	2.8
6000 Other taxes	0.0	0.0	0.0	0.0	0.0	0.0	0.0	0.0	0.0	0.0
Local government										
Total tax revenue	**213.6**	**353.2**	**585.3**	**635.2**	**645.7**	**3.6**	**3.4**	**3.9**	**3.6**	**3.6**
1000 Taxes on income, profits and capital gains	11.9	21.6	32.8	39.3	40.8	0.2	0.2	0.2	0.2	0.2
2000 Social security contributions	0.0	0.0	0.0	0.0	0.0	0.0	0.0	0.0	0.0	0.0
3000 Taxes on payroll and workforce	0.0	0.0	0.0	0.0	0.0	0.0	0.0	0.0	0.0	0.0
4000 Taxes on property	158.6	249.4	428.9	448.1	450.8	2.7	2.4	2.9	2.6	2.5
5000 Taxes on goods and services	43.1	82.1	123.6	147.8	154.0	0.7	0.8	0.8	0.8	0.9
6000 Other taxes	0.0	0.0	0.0	0.0	0.0	0.0	0.0	0.0	0.0	0.0
Social Security Funds										
Total tax revenue	**397.0**	**683.1**	**917.8**	**1 078.0**	**1 124.0**	**6.6**	**6.6**	**6.1**	**6.2**	**6.2**
1000 Taxes on income, profits and capital gains	0.0	0.0	0.0	0.0	0.0	0.0	0.0	0.0	0.0	0.0
2000 Social security contributions	397.0	683.1	917.8	1 078.0	1 124.0	6.6	6.6	6.1	6.2	6.2
3000 Taxes on payroll and workforce	0.0	0.0	0.0	0.0	0.0	0.0	0.0	0.0	0.0	0.0
4000 Taxes on property	0.0	0.0	0.0	0.0	0.0	0.0	0.0	0.0	0.0	0.0
5000 Taxes on goods and services	0.0	0.0	0.0	0.0	0.0	0.0	0.0	0.0	0.0	0.0
6000 Other taxes	0.0	0.0	0.0	0.0	0.0	0.0	0.0	0.0	0.0	0.0

Note: More detailed country data and country notes are available in online chapter 6: http://dx.doi.org/10.1787/9789264283183-en. Full time series can be accessed at http://oe.cd/full-time-series.

Source: Federal estimates are derived from the US Budget, the Final Monthly Treasury Statement and the Annual Report of the US Treasury Department. The State and Local estimates are derived from Government Finances, published by the Bureau of the Census.

StatLink http://dx.doi.org/10.1787/888933613501

4.2. Memorandum tables

Table 4.71 shows different sources for financing social benefits, beyond compulsory social security contributions reported in section 4.1. In addition, this table shows also data on other taxes, on voluntary contributions to government and on compulsory contributions to private sector.

Table 4.72 shows social security contributions and payroll taxes paid by government. During the revision of the Interpretative Guide in 1984, the question arose of how to treat taxes paid by government. The two most prominent examples of such taxes are social security contributions and payroll taxes paid by government in respect of its employees. After a long discussion it was decided that the data shown in this publication should continue to include taxes paid by government (see §5 of the Interpretative Guide in Annex A).

Whilst it was recognised that for certain purposes (e.g. to show the cash flow to the government sector from the private sector) it would be appropriate to eliminate taxes paid by one sector of government to another or tax payments between different units of the same sector of government, the view was taken that to record tax flows in the context of the economy as a whole required that taxes paid by government should be included in the data. This treatment ensures that the different resource flows of an economy, including the calculation of the output of government, are measured consistently in after-tax units. Nevertheless, it was decided that data on identifiable taxes paid by government should be separately identified in a memorandum item and this is the purpose of the country tables which follow.

The data that are reproduced in the following tables refer to actual compulsory payments made by general government in respect of their employees. Fictive, voluntary and imputed contributions are excluded from these data. The definitions of social security contributions, payroll taxes and general government are those set out in §35 to §41, §42 and §3 to §4 of the Interpretative Guide. Information on the other taxes paid by government (namely property taxes and consumption taxes) is not available in most countries, although it is believed that in all countries taxes based upon payroll are the most important taxes paid by government. In many cases, the data are estimates and are not always constructed on a basis consistent with that used in the main tables.

Table 4.71. **Financing of social security benefits**

National currency

	Currency	Total					2015				
		1990	2000	2010	2014	2015	Social security contributions	Other taxes	Voluntary contributions to government	Compulsory contributions to private sector	**Total**
Australia	Million AUD	0.0	0.0	0.0	0.0	0.0	..	..	..	..	**0.0**
Austria	Million EUR	17.9	30.7	41.8	48.6	50.2	49.9	0.0	0.3	0.0	**50.2**
Belgium	Million EUR	24.1	40.1	67.3	76.0	71.0	58.6	12.3	0.1	0.0	**71.0**
Canada	Million CAD	29.7	53.1	76.8	93.4	96.2	96.2	0.0	0.0	0.0	**96.2**
Chile	Million CLP	487.7	2 598.4	6 902.7	10 305.3	11 170.1	2 252.5	0.0	0.0	8 917.6	**11 170.1**
Czech Republic	Million CZK	..	345.5	582.8	632.3	666.9	659.7	0.0	0.4	6.7	**666.9**
Denmark	Million DKK	9.5	26.5	22.9	19.2	19.1	1.4	0.0	14.7	3.0	**19.1**
Estonia	Million EUR	..	0.7	1.9	2.5	2.7	2.3	0.0	0.0	0.4	**2.7**
Finland	Million EUR	11.1	16.9	23.5	26.9	27.6	26.6	0.0	0.3	0.6	**27.6**
France	Million EUR	194.1	312.9	461.2	534.0	540.1	369.9	170.2	0.0	0.0	**540.1**
Germany	Million EUR	184.9	328.9	369.8	425.9	443.4	424.6	0.0	8.2	10.6	**443.4**
Greece	Million EUR	3.5	14.3	24.7	18.6	18.8	18.8	0.0	0.0	0.0	**18.8**
Hungary	Million HUF	..	1 759.3	3 539.6	4 245.4	4 538.8	4 293.7	243.9	1.2	0.0	**4 538.8**
Iceland	Million ISK	37.6	95.3	236.5	295.8	317.5	79.7	98.0	0.0	139.8	**317.5**
Ireland	Million EUR	1.7	3.9	8.4	9.6	10.2	10.2	0.0	0.0	0.0	**10.2**
Israel	Million ILS	..	27.6	54.4	88.6	94.8	59.6	0.0	0.0	35.2	**94.8**
Italy	Million EUR	87.3	144.1	209.7	210.4	215.1	214.4	0.0	0.7	0.0	**215.1**
Japan	Billion JPY	34.6	48.0	54.5	62.3	64.5	64.5	0.0	0.0	0.0	**64.5**
Korea	Billion KRW	3.8	22.8	69.1	98.2	104.7	104.7	0.0	0.0	0.0	**104.7**
Latvia	Million EUR	..	0.7	1.6	2.1	2.1	2.0	0.1	0.0	0.0	**2.1**
Luxembourg	Million EUR	1.0	2.2	4.4	5.4	5.6	5.6	0.0	0.0	0.0	**5.6**
Mexico	Million MXN	21.0	205.6	423.6	568.7	616.1	409.2	0.0	0.0	206.8	**616.1**
Netherlands	Million EUR	45.0	101.6	..	..	..	96.4	0.0	0.0	..	**..**
New Zealand	Million NZD	0.0	0.0	0.0	0.0	0.0	..	..	..	..	**0.0**
Norway	Million NOK	79.7	132.2	243.0	312.9	326.0	326.0	0.0	0.0	0.0	**326.0**
Poland	Million PLN	..	96.4	156.0	209.9	224.8	224.8	0.0	0.0	0.0	**224.8**
Portugal	Million EUR	4.1	10.6	16.2	16.6	17.2	16.2	1.0	0.0	0.0	**17.2**
Slovak Republic	Million EUR	..	4.4	8.9	10.6	11.3	10.9	0.0	0.0	0.4	**11.3**
Slovenia	Million EUR	..	2.6	5.4	5.4	5.6	5.6	0.0	0.0	0.0	**5.6**
Spain	Million EUR	36.7	76.0	129.7	122.2	124.5	124.5	0.0	0.0	0.0	**124.5**
Sweden	Million SEK	205.9	321.3	412.3	419.9	437.4	404.9	0.0	32.6	0.0	**437.4**
Switzerland	Million CHF	41.8	62.1	90.4	102.8	104.7	43.9	7.8	0.0	53.0	**104.7**
Turkey	Million TRY	0.0	7.5	71.7	143.4	170.3	170.3	0.0	0.0	0.0	**170.3**
United Kingdom	Million GBP	45.7	73.9	122.3	134.1	139.5	114.1	0.0	20.0	5.5	**139.5**
United States	Million USD	408.7	705.7	979.6	1 150.5	1 199.1	1 124.0	0.0	75.0	0.0	**1 199.1**

StatLink http://dx.doi.org/10.1787/888933613520

Table 4.72. Social security contributions and payroll taxes paid by government

Million national currency

	Currency	Total					2015				
		1990	2000	2010	2014	2015	Federal or Central government	State/Regional	Local government	Social security Funds	**Total**
Australia[1]	Million AUD	0.1	0.3	0.6	0.7	0.8	0.0	0.0	0.0	0.0	**0.8**
Austria	Million EUR	1.3	2.9	5.6	6.3	6.6	2.4	1.9	1.9	0.3	**6.6**
Belgium	Million EUR	1.8	3.1	5.3	6.6	7.4	0.7	2.3	4.0	0.4	**7.4**
Canada	Million CAD	..	6.4	10.2	11.9	12.1	1.5	6.5	4.1	0.0	**12.1**
Chile	Million CLP	..	54.6	190.0	248.5	269.3	205.1	..	63.6	0.6	**269.3**
Czech Republic	Million CZK	..	34.2	55.8	58.5	80.5	37.6	..	42.0	1.0	**80.5**
Denmark	Million DKK	0.0	0.0	0.0	0.0	0.0	..	..	..	..	**0.0**
Estonia	Million EUR	..	0.2	0.5	0.6	0.7	0.4	..	0.2	0.0	**0.7**
Finland	Million EUR	1.9	3.8	5.6	6.3	6.2	1.2	..	4.9	0.1	**6.2**
France	Million EUR	23.4	36.3	53.7	59.2	60.1	14.8	..	22.4	22.9	**60.1**
Germany	Million EUR	13.6	21.7	20.3	22.5	23.3	1.5	6.6	12.3	2.9	**23.3**
Greece	Million EUR	0.1	1.7	3.6	2.7	2.7	2.4	..	0.0	0.3	**2.7**
Hungary	Million HUF	..	367.0	544.9	637.7	697.4	543.2	..	151.2	3.1	**697.4**
Iceland	Million ISK	..	..	..	..	..	..	..	..	..	**..**
Ireland	Million EUR	0.1	0.4	1.2	1.3	1.4	0.5	..	0.9	0.0	**1.4**
Israel	Million ILS	..	4.1	6.7	9.3	9.3	7.4	..	1.9	0.0	**9.3**
Italy	Million EUR	..	36.7	50.6	49.5	49.2	0.0	..	0.0	49.2	**49.2**
Japan	Billion JPY	2.0	2.9	3.0	3.4	3.5	0.9	..	2.6	0.0	**3.5**
Korea	Billion KRW	..	..	..	..	..	..	..	..	..	**..**
Latvia	Million EUR	..	0.0	0.2	0.2	0.3	..	..	..	..	**0.3**
Luxembourg	Million EUR	0.3	0.3	0.5	0.6	0.6	0.6	..	0.0	0.0	**0.6**
Mexico	Million MXN	3.0	44.9	103.4	135.4	145.3	145.3	0.0	0.0	0.0	**145.3**
Netherlands	Million EUR	0.3	2.0	0.0	0.0	0.0	..	..	..	..	**0.0**
New Zealand	Million NZD	0.0	0.0	0.0	0.0	0.0	..	..	..	..	**0.0**
Norway	Million NOK	17.9	36.7	77.6	106.2	112.4	52.9	..	59.5	0.0	**112.4**
Poland	Million PLN	..	9.0	18.4	23.6	24.3	9.6	..	14.2	0.6	**24.3**
Portugal	Million EUR	0.0	0.2	0.0	0.0	0.0	..	..	..	..	**0.0**
Slovak Republic	Million EUR	..	0.6	1.3	1.6	1.7	1.0	..	0.6	0.0	**1.7**
Slovenia	Million EUR	..	0.3	0.6	0.6	0.6	0.4	..	0.2	0.0	**0.6**
Spain	Million EUR	4.0	9.6	18.5	17.9	18.7	2.2	11.4	4.6	0.5	**18.7**
Sweden	Million SEK	69.3	101.6	136.7	155.4	163.9	37.9	..	125.9	0.0	**163.9**
Switzerland	Million CHF	1.8	2.2	3.0	3.3	3.3	0.5	1.8	1.0	0.0	**3.3**
Turkey	Million TRY	0.0	3.6	39.4	80.0	95.1	95.1	..	0.0	0.0	**95.1**
United Kingdom	Million GBP	4.1	6.0	11.7	12.2	12.5	7.7	..	4.8	0.0	**12.5**
United States	Million USD	28.9	44.1	71.6	73.7	75.2	26.7	48.4	0.0	0.0	**75.2**

1. For Australia, the total differs from the sum of the four levels of government. The difference is due to a multi-jurisdictional (University) sector specific to this country. This sector contains units where jurisdiction is shared between two or more governments, or where classification of a unit to a jurisdiction is otherwise unclear. The main type of units currently falling into this category is public universities.

StatLink http://dx.doi.org/10.1787/888933613539

Chapter 5

Detailed country tables, 1965-2015

This chapter provides statistical tables with a detailed breakdown of tax revenues by country for the years between 1965 and 2015. Two memorandum tables show how countries finance their social benefits, and report taxes and social security contributions paid by general government.

This chapter is available online at http://dx.doi.org/10.1787/9789264283183-en.

Chapter 6

Tax revenues by subsectors of general government

This chapter attributes tax revenues to general government by the following sub-sectors: central, state, local and social security funds. It contains a set of comparative statistical tables for the years 1975-2015 and a second series of tables with a detailed breakdown of tax revenues by country for the years between 1975 and 2015.

This chapter is available online at http://dx.doi.org/10.1787/9789264283183-en.

ANNEX A

The OECD classification of taxes and interpretative guide

Table of contents

A.1 The OECD Classification of taxes

1. 1000 Taxes on income, profits and capital gains
   - 1100 Taxes on income, profits and capital gains of individuals
     - 1110 On income and profits
     - 1120 On capital gains
   - 1200 Corporate taxes on income, profits and capital gains
     - 1210 On income and profits
     - 1220 On capital gains
   - 1300 Unallocable as between 1100 and 1200
2. 2000 Social security contributions
   - 2100 Employees
     - 2110 On a payroll basis
     - 2120 On an income tax basis
   - 2200 Employers
     - 2210 On a payroll basis
     - 2220 On an income tax basis
   - 2300 Self-employed or non-employed
     - 2310 On a payroll basis
     - 2320 On an income tax basis
   - 2400 Unallocable as between 2100, 2200 and 2300
     - 2410 On a payroll basis
     - 2420 On an income tax basis
3. 3000 Taxes on payroll and workforce
4. 4000 Taxes on property
   - 4100 Recurrent taxes on immovable property
     - 4110 Households
     - 4120 Other
   - 4200 Recurrent taxes on net wealth
     - 4210 Individual
     - 4220 Corporate
   - 4300 Estate, inheritance and gift taxes
     - 4310 Estate and inheritance taxes
     - 4320 Gift taxes
   - 4400 Taxes on financial and capital transactions

4500 Other non-recurrent taxes on property

4510 On net wealth

4520 Other non-recurrent taxes

4600 Other recurrent taxes on property

5. 5000 Taxes on goods and services

5100 Taxes on production, sale, transfer, leasing and delivery of goods and rendering of services

5110 General taxes

5111 Value added taxes

5112 Sales taxes

5113 Other general taxes on goods and services

5120 Taxes on specific goods and services

5121 Excises

5122 Profits of fiscal monopolies

5123 Customs and import duties

5124 Taxes on exports

5125 Taxes on investment goods

5126 Taxes on specific services

5127 Other taxes on international trade and transactions

5128 Other taxes on specific goods and services

5130 Unallocable as between 5110 and 5120

5200 Taxes on use of goods, or on permission to use goods or perform activities

5210 Recurrent taxes

5211 Paid by households in respect of motor vehicles

5212 Paid by others in respect of motor vehicles

5213 Other recurrent taxes

5220 Non-recurrent taxes

5300 Unallocable as between 5100 and 5200

6. 6000 Other taxes

6100 Paid solely by business

6200 Paid by other than business or unidentifiable

A.2 Coverage

General criteria

1. In the OECD classification the term "taxes" is confined to compulsory unrequited payments to general government. Taxes are unrequited in the sense that benefits provided by government to taxpayers are not normally in proportion to their payments.

2. The term "tax" does not include fines, penalties and compulsory loans paid to government. Borderline cases between tax and non-tax revenues in relation to certain fees and charges are discussed in §9-12.

3. General government consists of the central administration, agencies whose operations are under its effective control, state and local governments and their administrations, certain social security schemes and autonomous governmental entities, excluding public enterprises. This definition of government follows that of the 2008 *System of National Accounts* (SNA).[1] In that publication, the general government sector and its sub-sectors are defined in chapter 4, section F, pages 80-84.

4. Compulsory payments to supra-national bodies and their agencies are no longer included as taxes as from 1998, with some exceptions. However, custom duties collected by EU member states on behalf of the European Union are still identified as memorandum items and included in overall tax revenue amounts in the country tables (Chapter 4) of the country in which they are collected. (See §94). In countries where the church forms part of general government church taxes are included, provided they meet the criteria set out in §1 above. As the data refer to receipts of general government, levies paid to non-government bodies, welfare agencies or social insurance schemes outside general government, trade unions or trade associations, even where such levies are compulsory, are excluded. Compulsory payments to general government earmarked for such bodies are, however, included, provided that the government is not simply acting in an agency capacity.[2] Profits from fiscal monopolies are distinguished from those of other public enterprises and are treated as taxes because they reflect the exercise of the taxing power of the state by the use of monopoly powers (see §61-63), as are profits received by the government from the purchase and sale of foreign exchange at different rates (see §69).

5. Taxes paid by governments (e.g. social security contributions and payroll taxes paid by governments in their capacity as an employer, consumption taxes on their purchases or taxes on their property) are not excluded from the data provided. However, where it is possible to identify the amounts of revenue involved,[3] they are shown in Chapter 4.3 of this Report.

6. The relationship between this classification and that of the System of National Accounts (SNA) is set out in Sections A.9 and A.11 below. Because of the differences between the two classifications, the data shown in national accounts are sometimes calculated or classified differently from the practice set out in this guide. These and other differences are mentioned where appropriate (e.g. in §25 below) but it is not possible to refer to all of them. There may also be some differences between this classification and that employed domestically by certain national administrations (e.g. see §10 below), so that OECD and national statistics data may not always be consistent: any such differences, however, are likely to be very slight in terms of amounts of revenues involved.

Social security contributions

7. Compulsory social security contributions, as defined in §34 below, paid to general government, are treated here as tax revenues. Being compulsory payments to general government they clearly resemble taxes. They may, however, differ from other taxes in that the receipt of social security benefits depends, in most countries, upon appropriate contributions having been made, although the size of the benefits is not necessarily related to the amount of the contributions. Better comparability between countries is obtained by treating social security contributions as taxes, but they are listed under a separate heading so that they can be distinguished in any analysis.

8. Social security contributions which are either voluntary or not payable to general government (see §1) are not treated as taxes, though in some countries, as indicated in the country footnotes, there are difficulties in eliminating voluntary contributions and certain compulsory payments to the private sector. Imputed social security contributions are also not treated as taxes.

Fees, user charges and licence fees

9. Apart from vehicle licence fees, which are universally regarded as taxes, it is not easy to distinguish between those fees and user charges which are to be treated as taxes and those which are not, since, whilst a fee or charge is levied in connection with a specific service or activity, the strength of the link between the fee and the service provided may vary considerably, as may the relation between the amount of the fee and the cost of providing the service. Where the recipient of a service pays a fee clearly related to the cost of providing the service, the levy may be regarded as requited and under the definition of §1 would not be considered as a tax. In the following cases, however, a levy could be considered as "unrequited":

a) where the charge greatly exceeds the cost of providing the service;

b) where the payer of the levy is not the receiver of the benefit (e.g. where government is not providing a specific service in return for the levy which it receives even though a licence may be issued to the payer (e.g. where the government grants a hunting, fishing or shooting licence which is not accompanied by the right to use a specific area of government land);

c) where benefits are received only by those paying the levy but the benefits received by each individual are not necessarily in proportion to his payments (e.g. a milk marketing levy paid by dairy farmers and used to promote the consumption of milk).

10. In marginal cases, however, the application of the criteria set out in §1 can be particularly difficult. The solution adopted – given the desirability of international uniformity and the relatively small amounts of revenue usually involved – is to follow the predominant practice among tax administrations rather than to allow each country to adopt its own view as to whether such levies are regarded as taxes or as non-tax revenue.[4]

11. A list of the main fees and charges in question and their normal[5] treatment in this publication is as follows:

Non-tax revenues:	court fees; driving licence fees; harbour fees; passport fees; radio and television licence fees where public authorities provide the service.
Taxes within heading 5200:	permission to perform such activities as distributing films; hunting, fishing and shooting; providing entertainment or gambling facilities; selling alcohol or tobacco; permission to own dogs or to use or own motor vehicles or guns; severance taxes.

12. In practice it may not always be possible to isolate tax receipts from non-tax revenue receipts when they are recorded together. If it is estimated that the bulk of the receipts derive from non-tax revenues, the whole amount involved is treated as a non-tax revenue; otherwise, such government receipts are included and classified according to the rules provided in §27 below.

Royalties

13. Royalty payments for the right to extract oil and gas or to exploit other mineral resources are normally regarded as non-tax revenues since they are property income from government-owned land or resources.

Fines and penalties

14. In principle, fines and penalties charged on overdue taxes or penalties imposed for the attempted evasion of taxes should not be recorded as tax revenues. However it may not be possible to separate payments of fines or other penalties from the revenues from the taxes to which they relate. In this case the fines and penalties relating to a particular tax are recorded together with the revenues from that tax and fines and penalties paid with revenue from unidentifiable taxes are classified as other taxes in Category 6000. Fines not relating to tax offences (e.g. for parking offences), or not identifiable as relating to tax offences, are also not treated as tax revenues.

A.3 Basis of reporting

Accrual reporting

15. The data reported in this publication for recent years are predominantly recorded on an accrual basis, i.e. recorded at the time that the tax liability was created. Further information is provided in the footnotes to the country table in Chapter 4 of the Report.

16. However, data for earlier years are still predominantly recorded on a cash basis, i.e. at the time at which the payment was received by government. Thus, for example, taxes withheld by employers in one year but paid to the government in the following year and taxes due in one year but actually paid in the following year are both included in the receipts of the second year. Corrective transactions, such as refunds, repayments and drawbacks, are deducted from gross revenues of the period in which they are made.

17. Data on tax revenues are recorded without offsets for the administrative expenses connected with tax collection. Similarly, where the proceeds of tax are used to subsidise particular members of the community, the subsidy is not deducted from the yield of the tax, though the tax may be shown net of subsidies in the national records of some countries.

18. As regards fiscal monopolies (heading 5122), only the amount actually transferred to the government is included in government revenues. However, if any expenditures of fiscal monopolies are considered to be government expenditures (e.g. social expenditures undertaken by fiscal monopolies at the direction of the government) they are added back for the purpose of arriving at tax revenue figures (see §61 below).

The distinction between tax and expenditure provisions[6]

19. Because this publication is concerned only with the revenue side of government operations, no account being taken of the expenditure side, a distinction has to be made between tax and expenditure provisions. Normally there is no difficulty in making this distinction as expenditures are made outside the tax system and the tax accounts and under legislation separate from the tax legislation. In borderline cases, cash flow is used to distinguish between tax provisions and expenditure provisions. Insofar as a provision affects the flow of tax payments from the taxpayer to the government, it is regarded as a tax provision and is taken into account in the data shown in this publication. A provision

which does not affect this flow is seen as an expenditure provision and is disregarded in the data recorded in this publication.

20. Tax allowances, exemptions and deductions against the tax base clearly affect the amount of tax paid to the government and are therefore considered as tax provisions. At the other extreme, those subsidies which cannot be offset against tax liability and which are clearly not connected with the assessment process, do not reduce tax revenues as recorded in this publication. Tax credits are amounts deductible from tax payable (as distinct from deductions from the tax base). Two types of tax credits are distinguished, those (referred to here as wastable tax credits) which are limited to the amount of the tax liability and therefore cannot give rise to a payment by the authorities to the taxpayer, and those (referred to as non-wastable tax credits) which are not so limited, so that the excess of the credit over the tax liability can be paid to the taxpayer.[7] A wastable tax credit, like a tax allowance, clearly affects the amount of tax paid to the government, and is therefore considered as a tax provision. The practice followed for non-wastable tax credits[8] is to distinguish between the "tax expenditure component",[9] which is that portion of the credit that is used to reduce or eliminate a taxpayer's liability, and the "transfer component", which is the portion that exceeds the taxpayer's liability and is paid to that taxpayer. Reported tax revenues should be reduced by the amount of the tax expenditure component but not by the amount of the transfer component. In addition, the amounts of the tax expenditure and transfer components should be reported as memorandum items in the country tables. Countries that are unable to distinguish between the tax expenditure and transfer components should indicate whether or not the tax revenues have been reduced by the total of these components, and provide any available estimates of the amounts of the two components. Further information is given in Chapter 2 of the Report, which illustrates the effect of alternative treatments of non-wastable tax credits on tax to GDP.

Calendar and fiscal years

21. National authorities whose fiscal years do not correspond to the calendar year show data, where possible, on a calendar year basis to permit maximum comparability with the data of other countries. There remain a few countries where data refer to fiscal years. For these the GDP data used in the comparative tables also correspond to the fiscal years.

A.4 General classification criteria

The main classification criteria

22. The classification of receipts among the main headings (1000, 2000, 3000, 4000, 5000 and 6000) is generally governed by the base on which the tax is levied: 1000 income, profits and capital gains; 2000 and 3000 earnings, payroll or number of employees; 4000 property; 5000 goods and services; 6000 multiple bases, other bases or unidentifiable bases. Where a tax is calculated on more than one base, the receipts are, where possible, split among the various headings (see §27 and §77). The headings 4000 and 5000 cover not only taxes where the tax base is the property, goods or services themselves but also certain related taxes. Thus, taxes on the transfer of property are included in 4400[10] and taxes on the use of goods or on permission to perform activities in 5200. In headings 4000 and 5000 a distinction is made in certain sub-headings between recurrent and non-recurrent taxes: recurrent taxes are defined as those levied at regular intervals (usually annually) and non-recurrent taxes are levied once and for all (see also §42 to §45, §48, §49 and §75 for particular applications of this distinction).

23. Earmarking of a tax for specific purposes does not affect the classification of tax receipts. However, as explained in §34 on the classification of social security contributions, the conferment of an entitlement to social benefits is crucial to the definition of the 2000 main heading.

24. The way that a tax is levied or collected (e.g. by use of stamps) does not affect classification.

Classification of taxpayers

25. In certain sub-headings distinctions are made between different categories of taxpayers. These distinctions vary from tax to tax:

a) Between individuals and corporations in relation to income and net wealth taxes

The basic distinction is that corporation income taxes, as distinct from individual income taxes, are levied on the corporation as an entity, not on the individuals who own it, and without regard to the personal circumstances of these individuals. The same distinction applies to net wealth taxes on corporations and those on individuals. Taxes paid on the profits of partnerships and the income of institutions, such as life insurance or pension funds, are classified according to the same rule. They are classified as corporate taxes (1200) if they are charged on the partnership or institution as an entity without regard to the personal circumstances of the owners. Otherwise, they are treated as individual taxes (1100). Usually, there is different legislation for the corporation taxes and for the individual taxes.[11] The distinction made here between individuals and corporations does not follow the sector classification between households, enterprises, and so on of the System of National Accounts for income and outlay accounts. The SNA classification requires certain unincorporated businesses[12] to be excluded from the household sector and included with non-financial enterprises and financial institutions. The tax on the profits of these businesses, however, cannot always be separated from the tax on the other income of their owners, or can be separated only on an arbitrary basis. No attempt at this separation is made here and the whole of the individual income tax is shown together without regard to the nature of the income chargeable.

b) Between households and others in relation to taxes on immovable property

Here the distinction is that adopted by the SNA for the production and consumption expenditure accounts. The distinction is between households as consumers (i.e. excluding non-incorporated business) on the one hand and producers on the other hand. However, taxes on dwellings occupied by households, whether paid by owner-occupiers, tenants or landlords, are classified under households. This follows the common distinction made between taxes on domestic property versus taxes on business property. Some countries are not, however, in a position to make this distinction.

c) Between households and others in relation to motor vehicle licences

Here the distinction is between households as consumers on the one hand and producers on the other, as in the production and consumption expenditure accounts of the SNA.

d) Between business and others in relation to the residual taxes (6000)

The distinction is the same as in c) above between producers on the one hand and households as consumers on the other hand. Taxes which are included under the heading 6000 because they involve more than one tax base or because the tax base does not fall within any of the previous categories but which are identifiable as levyable only on producers and not on households are included under "business". The rest of the taxes which are included under the heading 6000 are shown as "other" or non-identified.

Surcharges

26. Receipts from surcharges in respect of particular taxes are usually classified with the receipts from the relevant tax whether or not the surcharge is temporary. If, however, the surcharge has a characteristic which would render it classifiable in a different heading of the OECD list, receipts from the surcharge are classified under that heading separately from the relevant tax.

Unidentifiable tax receipts and residual sub-headings

27. A number of cases arise where taxes cannot be identified as belonging entirely to a heading or sub-heading of the OECD classification and the following practices are applied in such cases:

a) The heading is known, but it is not known how receipts should be allocated between sub-headings: receipts are classified in the appropriate residual sub-heading (1300, 2400, 4520, 4600, 5130, 5300 or 6200).

b) It is known that the bulk of receipts from a group of taxes (usually local taxes) is derived from taxes within a particular heading or sub-heading, but some of the taxes in the group whose amount cannot be precisely ascertained may be classifiable in other headings or sub-headings: receipts are shown in the heading or sub-heading under which most of the receipts fall.

c) Neither the heading nor sub-heading of a tax (usually local) can be identified: the tax is classified in 6200 unless it is known that it is a tax on business in which case it is classified in 6100.

A.5 Commentaries on items of the list

1000 – *Taxes on income, profits and capital gains*

28. This heading covers taxes levied on the net income or profits (i.e. gross income minus allowable tax reliefs) of individuals and enterprises. Also covered are taxes levied on the capital gains of individuals and enterprises, and gains from gambling.

29. Included in the heading are:

a) taxes levied predominantly on income or profits, though partially on other bases. Taxes on various bases which are not predominantly income or profits are classified according to the principles laid down in §27 and §77;

b) taxes on property, which are levied on a presumed or estimated income as part of an income tax (see also §42(a), (c) and (d));

c) compulsory payments to social security fund contributions that are levied on income but do not confer an entitlement to social benefits. When such contributions do confer an entitlement to social benefits, they are included in heading 2000 (see §34);

d) receipts from integrated scheduler income tax systems are classified as a whole in this heading, even though certain of the scheduler taxes may be based upon gross income and may not take into account the personal circumstances of the taxpayer.

30. The main subdivision of this heading is between levies on individuals (1100) and those on corporate enterprises (1200). Under each subdivision a distinction is made between taxes on income and profits (1110 and 1210), and taxes on capital gains (1120 and 1220). If certain receipts cannot be identified as appropriate to either 1100 or 1200, or if in practice this distinction cannot be made (e.g. because there are no reliable data on the recipients of payments from which withholding taxes are deducted) they are classified in 1300 as not-allocable.

Treatment of credits under imputation systems

31. Under imputation systems of corporate income tax, a company's shareholders are wholly or partly relieved of their liability to income tax on dividends paid by the company out of income or profits liable to corporate income tax. In countries with such systems,[13] part of the tax on the company's profits is available to provide relief against the shareholders' own tax liability. The relief to the shareholder takes the form of a tax credit, the amount of which may be less than, equal to, or more than the shareholder's overall tax liability. If the tax credit exceeds this tax liability the excess may be payable to the shareholder. As this type of tax credit is an integral part of the imputation system of corporate income tax, any payment to the shareholders is treated as a repayment of tax and not as expenditure (compare the treatment of other tax credits described in §20).

32. As the tax credit under imputation systems (even when exceeding tax liability) is to be regarded as a tax provision, the question arises whether it should be deducted from individual income tax receipts (1110) or corporate income tax receipts (1210). In this Report, the full amount of corporate income tax paid is shown under 1210 and no imputed tax is included under 1110. Thus, the full amount of the credit reduces the amount of 1110 whether the credit results in a reduction of personal income tax liability or whether an actual refund is made because the credit exceeds the income tax liability. (Where, however, such tax credits are deducted from corporation tax in respect of dividends paid to corporations the amounts are deducted from the receipts of 1210).

1120 and 1220 – Taxes on capital gains

33. These sub-headings comprise taxes imposed on capital gains, 1120 covering those levied on the gains of individuals and 1220 those levied on the gains of corporate enterprises, where receipts from such taxes can be separately identified. In many countries this is not the case and the receipts from such taxes are then classified with those from the income tax. Heading 1120 also includes taxes on gains from gambling.

2000 – Social security contributions

34. Classified here are all compulsory payments that confer an entitlement to receive a (contingent) future social benefit. Such payments are usually earmarked to finance social benefits and are often paid to institutions of general government that provide such benefits. However, such earmarking is not part of the definition of social security contributions and is not required for a tax to be classified here. However, conferment of an entitlement is required for a tax to be classified under this heading. So, levies on income or payroll that are earmarked for social security funds but do not confer an entitlement to benefit are excluded from this heading and shown under personal income taxes (1100) or taxes on payroll and workforce (3000). Taxes on other bases, such as goods and services, which are earmarked for social security benefits are not shown here but are classified

according to their respective bases because they generally confer no entitlement to social security benefits.

35. Contributions for the following types of social security benefits would, *inter alia*, be included: unemployment insurance benefits and supplements, accident, injury and sickness benefits, old-age, disability and survivors' pensions, family allowances, reimbursements for medical and hospital expenses or provision of hospital or medical services. Contributions may be levied on both employees and employers.

36. Contributions may be based on earnings or payroll ("on a payroll basis") or on net income after deductions and exemptions for personal circumstances ("on an income tax basis"), and the revenues from the two bases should be separately identified if possible. However, where contributions to a general social security scheme are on a payroll basis, but the contributions of particular groups (such as the self-employed) cannot be assessed on this basis and net income is used as a proxy for gross earnings, the receipts may still be classified as being on a payroll basis. In principle, this heading excludes voluntary contributions paid to social security schemes. When separately identifiable these are shown in the memorandum item on the financing of social security benefits. In practice, however, they cannot always be separately identified from compulsory contributions, in which case they are included in this heading.

37. Contributions to social insurance schemes which are not institutions of general government and to other types of insurance schemes, provident funds, pension funds, friendly societies or other saving schemes are not considered as social security contributions. Provident funds are arrangements under which the contributions of each employee and of the corresponding employer on his/her behalf are kept in a separate account earning interest and withdrawable under specific circumstances. Pension funds are separately organised schemes negotiated between employees and employers and carry provisions for different contributions and benefits, sometimes more directly tied to salary levels and length of service than under social security schemes. When contributions to these schemes are compulsory or quasi-compulsory (e.g. by virtue of agreement with professional and union organisations) they are shown in the memorandum item (refer to Chapter 4.2 of the Report).

38. Contributions by government employees and by governments in respect of their employees, to social security schemes classified within general government are included in this heading. Contributions to separate schemes for government employees, which can be regarded as replacing general social security schemes, are also regarded as taxes.[14] Where, however, a separate scheme is not seen as replacing a general scheme and has been negotiated between the government, in its role as an employer, and its employees, it is not regarded as social security and contributions to it are not regarded as taxes, even though the scheme may have been established by legislation.

39. This heading excludes 'imputed' contributions, which correspond to social benefits paid directly by employers to their employees or former employees or to their representatives (e.g. when employers are legally obliged to pay sickness benefits for a certain period).

40. Contributions are divided into those of employees (2100), employers (2200), and self-employed or non-employed (2300), and then further sub-divided according to the basis on which they are levied. Employees are defined for this purpose as all persons engaged in activities of business units, government bodies, private non-profit institutions, or other

paid employment, except the proprietors and their unpaid family members in the case of unincorporated businesses. Members of the armed forces are included, irrespective of the duration and type of their service, if they contribute to social security schemes. The contributions of employers are defined as their payments on account of their employees to social security schemes. Where employees or employers are required to continue the payment of social security contributions when the employee becomes unemployed these contributions, data permitting, are shown in 2100 and 2200 respectively. Accordingly, the sub-heading 2300 is confined to contributions paid by the self-employed and by those outside of the labour force (e.g. disabled or retired individuals).

3000 – *Taxes on payroll and workforce*

41. This heading covers taxes paid by employers, employees or the self-employed either as a proportion of payroll or as a fixed amount per person, and which do not confer entitlement to social benefits. Examples of taxes classified here are the United Kingdom national insurance surcharge (introduced in 1977), the Swedish payroll tax (1969-1979), and the Austrian Contribution to the Family Burden Equalisation Fund and Community Tax.

4000 – *Taxes on property*

42. This heading covers recurrent and non-recurrent taxes on the use, ownership or transfer of property. These include taxes on immovable property or net wealth, taxes on the change of ownership of property through inheritance or gift and taxes on financial and capital transactions. The following kinds of tax are excluded from this heading:

a) taxes on capital gains resulting from the sale of a property (1120 or 1220);

b) taxes on the use of goods or on permission to use goods or perform activities (5200); see §72;

c) taxes on immovable property levied on the basis of a presumed net income which take into account the personal circumstances of the taxpayer. They are classified as income taxes along with taxes on income and capital gains derived from property (1100);

d) taxes on the use of property for residence, where the tax is payable by either proprietor or tenant and the amount payable is a function of the user's personal circumstances (pay, dependants, and so on). They are classified as taxes on income (1100);

e) taxes on building in excess of permitted maximum density, taxes on the enlargement, construction or alteration of certain buildings beyond a permitted value and taxes on building construction. They are classified as taxes on permission to perform activities (5200);

f) taxes on the use of one's own property for special trading purposes like selling alcohol, tobacco, meat or for exploitation of land resources (e.g. United States severance taxes). They are classified as taxes on permission to perform activities (5200).

4100 – *Recurrent taxes on immovable property*

43. This sub-heading covers taxes levied regularly in respect of the use or ownership of immovable property.

- these taxes are levied on land and buildings;
- they can be in the form of a percentage of an assessed property value based on a national rental income, sales price, or capitalised yield; or in terms of other characteristics of real

property, (for example size or location) from which a presumed rent or capital value can be derived.

- such taxes can be levied on proprietors, tenants, or both. They can also be paid by one level of government to another level of government in respect of property under the jurisdiction of the latter.
- debts are not taken into account in the assessment of these taxes, and they differ from taxes on net wealth in this respect.

44. Taxes on immovable property are further sub-divided into those paid by households (4110) and those paid by other entities (4120), according to the criteria set out in §25(*b*) above.

4200 – Recurrent taxes on net wealth

45. This sub-heading covers taxes levied regularly (in most cases annually) on net wealth, i.e. taxes on a wide range of movable and immovable property, net of debt. It is sub-divided into taxes paid by individuals (4210) and taxes paid by corporate enterprises (4220) according to the criteria set out in §25(*a*) above. If separate figures exist for receipts paid by institutions, the tax payments involved are added to those paid by corporations.

4300 – Estate, inheritance and gift taxes

46. This sub-heading is divided into taxes on estates and inheritances (4310) and taxes on gifts (4320).[15] Estate taxes are charged on the amount of the total estate whereas inheritance taxes are charged on the shares of the individual recipients; in addition the latter may take into account the relationship of the individual recipients to the deceased.

4400 – Taxes on financial and capital transactions

47. This sub-heading comprises, *inter alia*, taxes on the issue, transfer, purchase and sale of securities, taxes on cheques, and taxes levied on specific legal transactions such as validation of contracts and the sale of immovable property. The heading does not include:

a) taxes on the use of goods or property or permission to perform certain activities (5200);

b) fees paid to cover court charges, charges for birth, marriage or death certificates, which are normally regarded as non-tax revenues (see §9);

c) taxes on capital gains (1000);

d) recurrent taxes on immovable property (4100);

e) recurrent taxes on net wealth (4200);

f) once-and-for-all levies on property or wealth (4500).

4500 – Other non-recurrent taxes on property[16]

48. This sub-heading covers once-and-for-all, as distinct from recurrent, levies on property. It is divided into taxes on net wealth (4510) and other non-recurrent taxes on property (4520). Heading 4510 would include taxes levied to meet emergency expenditures, or for redistribution purposes. Heading 4520 would cover taxes levied to take account of increases in land value due to permission given to develop or provision of additional local facilities by general government, any taxes on the revaluation of capital and once-and-for-all taxes on particular items of property.

4600 – Other recurrent taxes on property

49. These rarely exist in OECD member countries, but the heading would include taxes on goods such as cattle, jewellery, windows, and other external signs of wealth.

5000 – Taxes on goods and services

50. All taxes and duties levied on the production, extraction, sale, transfer, leasing or delivery of goods, and the rendering of services (5100), or in respect of the use of goods or permission to use goods or to perform activities (5200) are included here. The heading thus covers:

a) multi-stage cumulative taxes;

b) general sales taxes – whether levied at manufacture/production, wholesale or retail level;

c) value-added taxes;

d) excises;

e) taxes levied on the import and export of goods;

f) taxes levied in respect of the use of goods and taxes on permission to use goods, or perform certain activities;

g) taxes on the extraction, processing or production of minerals and other products.

51. Borderline cases between this heading and heading 4000 (taxes on property) and 6100 (other taxes on business) are referred to in §42, §47 and §74. Residual sub-headings (5300) and (5130) cover tax receipts which cannot be allocated between 5100 and 5200 and between 5110 and 5120, respectively; see §27.

5100 – Taxes on the production, sale, transfer, leasing and delivery of goods and rendering of services

52. This sub-heading consists of all taxes, levied on transactions in goods and services on the basis of their intrinsic characteristics (e.g. value, weight of tobacco, strength of alcohol, and so on) as distinct from taxes imposed on the use of goods, or permission to use goods or perform activities, which fall under 5200.

5110 – General taxes on goods and services

53. This sub-heading includes all taxes, other than import and export duties (5123 and 5124), levied on the production, leasing, transfer, delivery or sales of a wide range of goods and/or the rendering of a wide range of services, irrespective of whether they are domestically produced or imported and irrespective of the stage of production or distribution at which they are levied. It thus covers value-added taxes, sales taxes and multi-stage cumulative taxes. Receipts from border adjustments in respect of such taxes when goods are imported are added to gross receipts for this category, and repayments of such taxes when goods are exported are deducted. These taxes are subdivided into 5111 value-added taxes, 5112 sales taxes, 5113 other general taxes on goods and services.

54. Borderline cases arise between this heading and taxes on specific goods (5120) when taxes are levied on a large number of goods, for example, the United Kingdom purchase tax (repealed in 1973) and the Japanese commodity tax (repealed in 1988). In conformity with national views, the former United Kingdom purchase tax is classified as a general tax (5112) and the former Japanese commodity tax as excises (5121).

5111 – *Value-added taxes*

55. All general consumption taxes charged on value-added are classified in this sub-heading, irrespective of the method of deduction and the stages at which the taxes are levied. In practice, all OECD countries with value-added taxes normally allow immediate deduction of taxes on purchases by all but the final consumer and impose tax at all stages. In some countries the heading may include certain taxes, such as those on financial and insurance activities, either because receipts from them cannot be identified separately from those from the value-added tax, or because they are regarded as an integral part of the value-added tax, even though similar taxes in other countries might be classified elsewhere (e.g. 5126 as taxes on services or 4400 as taxes on financial and capital transactions).

5112 – *Sales taxes*

56. All general taxes levied at one stage only, whether at manufacturing or production, wholesale or retail stage are classified here.

5113 – *Other general taxes on goods and services*

57. This sub-heading covers multi-stage cumulative taxes (also known as "cascade taxes") where tax is levied each time a transaction takes place without deduction for tax paid on inputs, and also those general consumption taxes where elements of value-added, sales or cascade taxes are combined.

5120 – *Taxes on specific goods and services*

58. Excises, profits generated and transferred from fiscal monopolies, and customs and imports duties as well as taxes on exports, foreign exchange transactions, investment goods and betting stakes and special taxes on services, which do not form part of a general tax of 5110, are included in this category.

5121 – *Excises*

59. Excises are taxes levied on particular products, or on a limited range of products, which are not classifiable under 5110 (general taxes), 5123 (import duties) and 5124 (export duties). They may be imposed at any stage of production or distribution and are usually assessed by reference to the weight or strength or quantity of the product, but sometimes by reference to value. Thus, special taxes on, for example, sugar, beetroot, matches, chocolates, and taxes at varying rates on a certain range of goods, as well as those levied in most countries on tobacco goods, alcoholic drinks and hydrocarbon oils and other energy sources, are included in this sub-heading.

60. Excises are distinguished from:

a) 5110 (general taxes). This is discussed in §53-54;

b) 5123 (import duties). If a tax collected principally on imported goods also applies, or would apply, under the law by which the tax is imposed to comparable home-produced goods, the receipts there from would be classified as excises (5121). This principle applies even if there is no comparable home production or no possibility of it (see also §64);

c) 5126 (taxes on services). The problem here arises in respect of taxes on electricity, gas and energy. All of these are regarded as taxes on goods and are included under 5121.

5122 – *Profits of fiscal monopolies*

61. This sub-heading covers that part of the profits of fiscal monopolies which is transferred to general government or which is used to finance any expenditures considered to be government expenditures (see §18). Amounts are shown when they are transferred to general government or used to make expenditures considered to be government expenditures.

62. Fiscal monopolies reflect the exercise of the taxing power of government by the use of monopoly powers. Fiscal monopolies are non-financial public enterprises exercising a monopoly in most cases over the production or distribution of tobacco, alcoholic beverages, salt, matches, playing cards and petroleum or agricultural products (i.e. on the kind of products which are likely to be, alternatively or additionally, subject to the excises of 5121), to raise the government revenues which in other countries are gathered through taxes on dealings in such commodities by private business units. The government monopoly may be at the production stage or, as in the case of government-owned and controlled liquor stores, at the distribution stage.

63. Fiscal monopolies are distinguished from public utilities such as rail transport, electricity, post offices, and other communications, which may enjoy a monopoly or quasi-monopoly position but where the primary purpose is normally to provide basic services rather than to raise revenue for government. Transfers from such other public enterprises to the government are considered as non-tax revenues. The traditional concept of fiscal monopoly is not generally extended to include state lotteries, the profits of which are usually accordingly regarded as non-tax revenues. However, they can be included as tax revenues if the prime reason for their operation is to raise revenues to finance government expenditure. Fiscal monopoly profits are distinguished from export and import monopoly profits (5127) transferred from marketing boards or other enterprises dealing with international trade.

5123 – *Customs and other import duties*

64. Taxes, stamp duties and surcharges restricted by law to imported products are included here. Also included are levies on imported agricultural products which are imposed in member countries of the European Union and amounts paid by certain of these countries under the Monetary Compensation Accounts (MCA) system.[16] Starting from 1998, customs duties collected by European Union member states on behalf of the European Union are no longer reported under this heading in the country tables (in Chapter 4 of the Report). Excluded here are taxes collected on imports as part of a general tax on goods and services, or an excise applicable to both imported and domestically produced goods.

5124 – *Taxes on exports*

65. In the 1970s, export duties were levied in Australia, Canada and Portugal as a regular measure and they have been used in Finland for counter-cyclical purposes. Some member countries of the European Union pay, as part of the MCA system, a levy on exports (see note 16 to §64). Where these amounts are identifiable, they are shown in this heading. This heading does not include repayments of general consumption taxes or excises or customs duties on exported goods, which should be deducted from the gross receipts under 5110, 5121 or 5123, as appropriate.

5125 – *Taxes on investment goods*

66. This sub-heading covers taxes on investment goods, such as machinery. These taxes may be imposed for a number of years or temporarily for counter-cyclical purposes. Taxes on industrial inputs which are also levied on consumers [e.g. the Swedish energy tax which is classified under (5121)] are not included here.

5126 – *Taxes on specific services*

67. All taxes assessed on the payment for specific services, such as taxes on insurance premiums, banking services, gambling and betting stakes (e.g. from horse races, football pools, lottery tickets), transport, entertainment, restaurant and advertising charges, fall into this category. Taxes levied on the gross income of companies providing the service (e.g. gross insurance premiums or gambling stakes received by the company) are also classified under this heading. Tax revenues from bank levies and payments to deposit insurance and financial stability schemes are provisionally included here for the 2012 edition. The detailed classification is set out in paragraph 104.

68. Excluded from this sub-heading are:

a) taxes on services forming part of a general tax on goods and services (5110);

b) taxes on electricity, gas and energy (5121 as excises);

c) taxes on individual gains from gambling (1120 as taxes on capital gains of individuals and non-corporate enterprises) and lump-sum taxes on the transfer of private lotteries or on the permission to set up lotteries (5200);[17]

d) taxes on cheques and on the issue, transfer or redemption of securities (4400 as taxes on financial and capital transactions).

5127 – *Other taxes on international trade and transactions*

69. This sub-heading covers revenue received by the government from the purchase and sale of foreign exchange at different rates. When the government exercises monopoly powers to extract a margin between the purchase and sales price of foreign exchange, other than to cover administrative costs, the revenue derived constitutes a compulsory levy exacted in indeterminate proportions from both purchaser and seller of foreign exchange. It is the common equivalent of an import duty and export duty levied in a single exchange rate system or of a tax on the sale or purchase of foreign exchange. Like the profits of fiscal monopolies and import or export monopolies transferred to government, it represents the exercise of monopoly powers for tax purposes and is included in tax revenues.

70. The sub-heading covers also the profits of export or import monopolies, which do not however exist in OECD countries, taxes on purchase or sale of foreign exchange, and any other taxes levied specifically on international trade or transactions.

5128 – *Other taxes on specific goods and services*

71. This item includes taxes on the extraction of minerals, fossil fuels and other exhaustible resources from deposits owned privately or by another government together with any other unidentifiable receipts from taxes on specific goods and services. Taxes on the extraction of exhaustible resources are usually a fixed amount per unit of quality or weight, but can be a percentage of value. The taxes are recorded when the resources are

extracted. Payments from the extraction of exhaustible resources from deposits owned by the government unit receiving the payment are classified as rent.

5200 – *Taxes on use of goods or on permission to use goods or perform activities*

72. This sub-heading covers taxes which are levied in respect of the use of goods as distinct from taxes on the goods themselves. Unlike the latter taxes – reported under 5100 –, they are not assessed on the value of the goods but usually as fixed amounts. Taxes on permission to use goods or to perform activities are also included here, as are pollution taxes not based upon the value of particular goods. It is sometimes difficult to distinguish between compulsory user charges and licence fees which are regarded as taxes and those which are excluded as non-tax revenues. The criteria which are employed are noted in §9-10.

73. Although the sub-heading refers to the "use" of goods, registration of ownership rather than use may be what generates liability to tax, so that the taxes of this heading may apply to the ownership of animals or goods rather than their use (e.g. race horses, dogs and motor vehicles) and may apply even to unusable goods (e.g. unusable motor vehicles or guns).

74. Borderline cases arise with:

a) taxes on the permission to perform business activities which are levied on a combined income, payroll or turnover base and, accordingly, are classified following the rules in §77;

b) taxes on the ownership or use of property of headings 4100, 4200 and 4600. The heading 4100 is confined to taxes on the ownership or tenancy of immovable property and – unlike the taxes of 5200 – they are related to the value of the property. The net wealth taxes and taxes on chattels of 4200 and 4600 respectively are confined to the ownership rather than the use of assets, apply to groups of assets rather than particular goods and again are related to the value of the assets,

5210 – *Recurrent taxes on use of goods and on permission to use goods or perform activities*

75. The principal characteristic of taxes classified here is that they are levied at regular intervals and that they are usually fixed amounts. The most important item in terms of revenue receipts is vehicle licence taxes. This sub-heading also covers taxes on permission to hunt, shoot, fish or to sell certain products and taxes on the ownership of dogs and on the performance of certain services, provided that they meet the criteria set out in §9-10. The sub-divisions of 5210 are user taxes on motor vehicles paid by households (5211) and those paid by others (5212).[18] Sub-heading 5213 covers dog licences and user charges for permission to perform activities such as selling meat or liquor when the levies are on a recurring basis. It also covers recurrent general licences for hunting, shooting and fishing where the right to carry out these activities is not granted as part of a normal commercial transaction (e.g. the granting of the licence is not accompanied by the right to use a specific area which is owned by government).

5220 – *Non-recurrent taxes on use of goods and on permission to use goods or perform activities*

76. This section covers non-recurrent taxes levied on the use of goods or on permission to use goods or perform activities and taxes levied each time goods are used. It includes

taxes levied on the emission or discharge into the environment of noxious gases, liquids or other harmful substances.

- Payments for tradable emission permits issued by governments under cap and trade schemes should be recorded here at the time the emissions occur. No revenue should be recorded for permits that governments issue free of charge. The accrual basis of recording means that there can be a timing difference between the cash being received by government for the permits and the time the emission occurs. In the national accounts, this timing gives rise to a financial liability for government during the period.
- Payments made for the collection and disposal of waste or noxious substances by public authorities should be excluded as they constitute a sale of services to enterprises.

77. Other taxes falling under heading 5200 that are not levied recurrently are also included here. Thus, once-and-for-all payments for permission to sell liquor or tobacco or to set up betting shops are included provided they meet the criteria set out in §9-10.

6000 – Other taxes

78. Taxes levied on a base, or bases, other than those described under headings 1000, 3000, 4000 and 5000, or on bases of which none could be regarded as being predominantly the same as that of any one of these headings, are covered here. As regards taxes levied on a multiple base, if it is possible to estimate receipts related to each base (e.g. the Austrian and German "Gewerbesteuer") this is done and the separate amounts included under the appropriate headings. If the separate amounts cannot be estimated, but it is known that most of the receipts are derived from one base, the whole of the receipts are classified according to that base. If neither of these procedures can be followed, they are classified here. The sub-headings may also include receipts from taxes which governments are unable to identify or isolate (see §27). Included here also are fines and penalties paid for infringement of regulations relating to taxes but not identifiable as relating to a particular category of taxes (see §14). A subdivision is made between taxes levied wholly or predominantly on business (6100) and those levied on others (6200).

A.6 Conciliation with National Accounts

79. This section of the tables provides a re-conciliation between the OECD calculation of total tax revenues and the total of all taxes and social contributions paid to general government as recorded in the country's National Accounts. Where the country is a member of the European Union (EU), the comparison is between the OECD calculation of total tax revenues and the sum of tax revenues and social contributions recorded in the combination of the general government and the institutions of the EU sectors of the National Accounts.

A.7 Memorandum item on the financing of social security benefits

80. In view of the varying relationship between taxation and social security contributions and the cases referred to in §34 to §40, a memorandum item collects together all payments earmarked for social security-type benefits, other than voluntary payments to the private sector. Data are presented as follows (refer Chapter 4.2 of the Report):

a) Taxes of 2000 series.

b) Taxes earmarked for social security benefits.

c) Voluntary contributions to the government.

d) Compulsory contributions to the private sector.

Guidance on the breakdown of (a) to (d) above is provided in §34 to §40.

A.8 Memorandum item on identifiable taxes paid by government

81. Identifiable taxes actually paid by government are presented in a memorandum item classified by the main headings of the OECD classification of taxes. In the vast majority of countries, only social security contributions and payroll taxes paid by government can be identified. These are, however, usually the most important taxes paid by governments (refer to Chapter 4.3 of the Report).

A.9 Relation of OECD classification of taxes to national accounting systems

82. A system of national accounts (SNA) seeks to provide a coherent framework for recording and presenting the main flows relating respectively to production, consumption, accumulation and external transactions of a given economic area, usually a country or a major region within a country. Government revenues are an important part of the transactions recorded in SNA. The final version of the 2008 SNA was jointly published by five international organisations: the United Nations, the International Monetary Fund, the European Union, the Organisation for Economic Co-operation and Development, and the World Bank in August 2009. The *System* is a comprehensive, consistent and flexible set of macroeconomic accounts. It is designed for use in countries with market economies, whatever their stage of economic development, and also in countries in transition to market economies. The important parts of the SNA's conceptual framework and its definitions of the various sectors of the economy have been reflected in the OECD's classification of taxes.

83. There are, however, some differences between the OECD classification of taxes and SNA concepts that are listed below. They arise because the aim of the former is to provide the maximum disaggregation of statistical data on what are generally regarded as taxes by tax administrations.

a) OECD includes compulsory social security contributions paid to general government in total tax revenues. Imputed and voluntary contributions plus those paid to private funds are not treated as taxes (§7 and §8 above);

b) there are different points of view on whether or not some levies and fees are classified as taxes (§9 and §10 above);

c) OECD excludes imputed taxes or subsidies resulting from the operation of official multiple exchange rates or from the central bank paying a rate of interest on required reserves that is different from other market rates;

d) there are differences in the treatment of non-wastable tax credits

84. As noted in §1 and §2, headings 1000 to 6000 of the OECD list of taxes cover all unrequited payments to general government, other than compulsory loans and fines. Such unrequited payments including fines, but excluding compulsory loans can be obtained from adding together the following figures in the 2008 SNA

- value-added type taxes (D.211);
- taxes and duties on imports, excluding VAT (D.212);
- export taxes (D.213);
- taxes on products, excluding VAT, import and export taxes (D.214);

- other taxes on production (D.29);
- taxes on income (D.51);
- other current taxes (D.59);
- social contributions (D.61), excluding voluntary contributions;
- capital taxes (D.91).

A.10 The OECD classification of taxes and the International Monetary Fund (GFS) system

85. The coverage and valuation of tax revenues in the GFS system and the 2008 SNA are very similar. Therefore, the differences between the OECD classification and that of the 2008 SNA (see §83 above) also apply to the GFS. In addition the International Monetary Fund subdivides the OECD 5000 heading into section IV (Domestic Taxes on Goods and Services) and section V (Taxes on International Trade and Transactions). This reflects the fact that while the latter usually yield insignificant amounts of revenue in OECD countries, this is not the case in many non-OECD countries.

A.11 Comparison of the OECD classification of taxes with other international classifications

86. The table below describes an item by item comparison of the OECD classification of taxes and the classifications used in the following:

a) System of National Accounts (2008 SNA);

b) European System of Accounts (2010 ESA);

c) IMF *Government Finance Statistics Manual* (GFSM2014).

87. These comparisons represent those that would be expected to apply in the majority of cases. However in practice some flexibility should be used in their application. This is because in particular cases, countries can adopt varying approaches to the classification of revenues in National Accounts.

A.12 Attribution of tax revenues by sub-sectors of general government

88. The OECD classification requires a breakdown of tax revenues by sub-sectors of government. The definition of each sub-sector and the criteria to be used to attribute tax revenues between these sub-sectors are set out below. They follow the guidance of the 2008 SNA and GFSM 2014.

Sub-sectors of general government to be identified

a) Central government

89. The central government sub-sector includes all governmental departments, offices, establishments and other bodies which are agencies or instruments of the central authority whose competence extends over the whole territory, with the exception of the administration of social security funds. Central government therefore has the authority to impose taxes on all resident and non-resident units engaged in economic activities within the country.

OECD Classification	2008 SNA	2010 ESA	GFSM2014
1000 Taxes on income, profits and capital gains			
1100 Individuals			
1110 Income and profits	D51-8.61a	D51A	1111
1120 Capital gains	D51-8.61c, d	D51C, D	1111
1200 Corporations			
1210 Income and profits	D51-8.61b	D51B	1112
1220 Capital gains	D51-8.61c	D51C	1112
1300 Unallocable as between 1100 and 1200			1113
2000 Social security contributions			
2100 Employees	D613-8.85	D613	1211
2200 Employers	D611-8.83	D611	1212
2300 Self-employed, non-employed	D613-8.85	D613	1213
2400 Unallocable as between 2100, 2200 and 2300			1214
3000 Taxes on payroll and workforce	D29-7.97a	D29C	112
4000 Taxes on property			
4100 Recurrent taxes on immovable property			
4110 Households	D59-8.63a	D59A	1131
4120 Other	D29-7.97b	D29A	1131
4200 Recurrent net wealth taxes			
4210 Individual	D59-8.63b	D59A	1132
4220 Corporations	D59-8.63b	D59A	1132
4300 Estate, inheritance and gift taxes			
4310 Estate and inheritance taxes	D91-10.207b	D91A	1133
4320 Gift taxes	D91-10.207b	D91A	1133
4400 Taxes on financial and capital transactions	D59-7.96d; D29-7.97e	D214B, C	114114; 1161
4500 Other non-recurrent taxes on property	D91-10.207a	D91B	1135
4600 Other recurrent taxes on property	D59-8.63c	D59A	1136
5000 Taxes on goods and services			
5100 Taxes on production, sale and transfer of goods and services			
5110 General taxes on goods and services			
5111 Value-added taxes	D211-7.89	D211; D29G	11411
5112 Sales taxes	D2122-7.94a; D214-7.96a	D21224; D214I	11412
5113 Other general taxes on goods and services	D214-7.96a	D214I	11413
5120 Taxes on specific goods and services			
5121 Excises	D2122-7.94b; D214-7.96b	D21223; D214A, B, D	1142
5122 Profits of fiscal monopolies	D214-7.96e	D214J	1143
5123 Customs and other import duties	D2121-7.93	D2121; D21221, 2	1151
5124 On exports	D213-7.95a	D214K	1152-4
5125 On investment goods			
5126 On specific services	D2122-7.94c; D214-7.96c	D21225; D214E, F, G, H; D29F	1144; 1156
5127 Other taxes on international trade and transactions	D2122-7.94d D29-7.95b D29-7.97g D59-8.64d	D21226; D29D; D59E	1153; 1155-6
5128 Other taxes on specific goods and services			1146
5130 Unallocable between 5110 and 5120			
5200 Taxes on use of goods and on permission to use goods or perform activities			
5210 Recurrent taxes on use of goods and on permission to use goods or perform activities			
5211 Motor vehicle taxes households	D59-8.64c	D59D	11451
5212 Motor vehicles taxes others	D29-7.97d	D214D; D29B	11451
5213 Other recurrent taxes on use of goods and on permission to use goods or perform activities	D29-7.97c, d, f D59-8.64c	D29B, E, F; D59D	11452
5220 Non-recurrent taxes on permission to use goods or perform activities			11452
5300 Unallocable as between 5100 and 5200			
6000 Other taxes			
6100 Payable solely by business			1161
6200 Payable by other than business, or unidentifiable	D59-8.64a, b	D59B, C	1162

b) State, provincial or regional government

90. This sub-sector consists of intermediate units of government exercising a competence at a level below that of central government. It includes all such units operating independently of central government in a part of a country's territory encompassing a number of smaller localities, with the exception of the administration of social security funds. In unitary countries, regional governments may be considered to have a separate existence where they have substantial autonomy to raise a significant proportion of their revenues from sources within their control and their officers are independent of external administrative control in the actual operation of the unit's activities.

91. At present, federal countries comprise the majority of cases where revenues attributed to intermediate units of government are identified separately. Spain is the only unitary country in this position. In the remaining unitary countries, regional revenues are included with those of local governments.

c) Local government

92. This sub-sector includes all other units of government exercising an independent competence in part of the territory of a country, with the exception of the administration of social security funds. It encompasses various urban and/or rural jurisdictions (e.g. local authorities, municipalities, cities, boroughs, districts).

d) Social security funds

93. Social security funds form a separate sub-sector of general government. The social security sub-sector is defined in the 2008 SNA by the following extracts from paragraphs 4.124 to 4.126 and 4.147:

"Social security schemes are social insurance schemes covering the community as a whole or large section of the community that are imposed and controlled by government units. The schemes cover a wide variety of programmes, providing benefits in cash or in kind for old age, invalidity or death, survivors, sickness and maternity, work injury, unemployment, family allowance, health care, etc. There is not necessarily a direct link between the amount of the contribution paid by an individual and the benefits he or she may receive." (Paragraph 4.124).

"When social security schemes are separately organised from the other activities of government units and hold their assets and liabilities separately from the latter and engage in financial transactions on their own account they qualify as institutional units that are described as social security funds." (Paragraph 4.125).

"The amounts raised, and paid out, in social security contributions and benefits may be deliberately varied in order to achieve objectives of government policy that have no direct connection with the concept of social security as a scheme to provide social benefits to members of the community. They may be raised or lowered in order to influence the level of aggregate demand in the economy, for example. Nevertheless, so long as they remain separately constituted funds, they must be treated as separate institutional units in the SNA. (Paragraph 4.126).

"The social security funds sub-sector (of general government) consists of the social security funds operating at all levels of government. Such funds are social insurance schemes covering the community as a whole or large section of the community that are imposed by government units." (Paragraph 4.147).

94. This definition of social security funds is followed in the OECD classification with the two following exceptions which are excluded:

- Schemes imposed by government and operated by bodies outside the general government sector, as defined in §3 of this manual; and
- Schemes to which all contributions are voluntary.

Supra-national Authorities

95. This sub-sector covers the revenue-raising operations of supra-national authorities within a country. In practice, the only relevant supra-national authority in the OECD area is that of the institutions of the European Union (EU). As from 1998, supra-national authorities are no longer included in the *Revenue Statistics*, to achieve consistency with the SNA definition of general government which excludes them. For example, income taxes and social security contributions collected by European Institutions and paid by European civil servants who are resident of EU member countries should not be included. However the specific levies paid by the member states of the EU continue to be included in total tax revenues and they are shown under this heading.

Criteria to be used for the attribution of tax revenues

96. When a government collects taxes and pays them over in whole or in part to other governments, it is necessary to determine whether the revenues should be considered to be those of the collecting government which it distributes to others as grants, or those of the beneficiary governments which the collecting government receives and passes on only as their agent. The criteria to be used in the attribution of revenues are set out in §97 to §100 which replicate paragraphs 3.70 to 3.73 from the 2008 SNA.

97. In general, a tax is attributed to the government unit that:

a) exercises the authority to impose the tax (either as a principal or through the delegated authority of the principal),

b) has final discretion to set and vary the rate of the tax

98. Where an amount is collected by one government for and on behalf of another government, and the latter government has the authority to impose the tax, and set and vary its rate, then the former is acting as an agent for the latter and the tax is reassigned. Any amount retained by the collecting government as a collection charge should be treated as a payment for a service. Any other amount retained by the collecting government, such as under a tax-sharing arrangement, should be treated as a current grant. If the collecting government was delegated the authority to set and vary the rate, then the amount collected should be treated as tax revenue of this government.

99. Where different governments jointly and equally set the rate of a tax and jointly and equally decide on the distribution of the proceeds, with no individual government having ultimate overriding authority, then the tax revenues are attributed to each government according to its respective share of the proceeds. If an arrangement allows one government unit to exercise ultimate overriding authority, then all of the tax revenue is attributed to that unit.

100. There may also be the circumstance where a tax is imposed under the constitutional or other authority of one government, but other governments individually set the tax rate in their jurisdictions. The proceeds of the tax generated in each respective government's jurisdiction are attributed as tax revenues of that government.

Levies paid by member states of the European Union

101. The levies paid by the member states of the EU take the form specific levies which include:

a) custom duties and levies on agricultural goods (5123);

b) gross monetary compensation accounts (5123 if relating to imports and 5124 if relating to exports); and

c) Steel, coal, sugar and milk levies (5128).

102. The custom duties collected by member states on behalf of the EU are recorded

- on a gross of collection fee basis;
- using figures adjusted so that duties are shown on a "final destination" as opposed to a "country of first entry" basis where such adjustments can be made. These adjustments concern in particular duties collected at important (sea) ports. Although the EU duties are collected by the authorities of the country of first entry, when possible these duties should be excluded from the revenue of the collecting country and be included in the revenue of the country of final destination.

103. This is the specific EU levy that most clearly conforms to the attribution criterion described in §95 above. Consequently as from 1998, these amounts are footnoted as a memorandum item to the EU member state country tables (in Chapter 4) and no longer shown under heading 5123. However the figures are included in the total tax revenue figures on the top line for all the relevant years shown in the tables.

A.13 Provisional classification of revenues from bank levies and payments to deposit insurance and financial stability schemes

104. The OECD have adopted the following interim approach to reporting revenue from bank levies plus deposit insurance and stability fees for the 2012 and subsequent editions of *OECD Revenue Statistics*. It is recommended that the amounts should be recorded under category 5126.

- Compulsory payments of stability fees, bank levies and deposit insurance should generally be treated as tax revenues where the payments are made to General Government and allocated to the governments' consolidated or general funds so that the Government is free to make immediate use of the money for the purposes that it chooses. This principle would apply regardless of whether the Government is promising to make payments to guarantee the banks' customer deposits in some future contingency.
- If the compulsory payments are made to general government and placed in funds that are earmarked to be entirely channelled back to the sector of the economy that comprises the companies that are subject to the payment, they would still generally be treated as tax revenues on the grounds that the funds would be available for the government and would reduce its budget deficit, the fee is unrequited for an individual entity and the amounts raised could be unrelated to any eventual pay out to depositors or expenditure on wider support for the financial sector.
- Payments to made to the smaller long-standing schemes for insuring 'retail' deposits, where the payment levels are consistent with the costs of insurance should be classified as fee for service.
- Any payments which involve governments realising the assets of a failed institution or receiving a priority claim on its assets in liquidation in order to fund payments of

compensation to customers for their lost deposits would be treated as a fee for a service as opposed to tax revenues.

- Compulsory payments that are made to funds operated outside the government sector and non-state institutions backed by the deposit takers and all payments to voluntary schemes should not be treated as tax revenues.

Notes

1. All references to SNA are to the 2008 edition.
2. See section A.12 of this guide for a discussion of the concept of agency capacity.
3. It is usually possible to identify amounts of social security contributions and payroll taxes, but not other taxes paid by government.
4. If, however, a levy which is considered as non-tax revenue by most countries is regarded as a tax – or raises substantial revenue – in one or more countries, the amounts collected are footnoted at the end of the relevant country tables, even though the amounts are not included in total tax revenues.
5. Names, however, can frequently be misleading. For example, though a passport fee would normally be considered a non-tax revenue, if a supplementary levy on passports (as is the case in Portugal) were imposed in order to raise substantial amounts of revenue relative to the cost of providing the passport, the levy would be regarded as a tax under 5200.
6. A more detailed explanation of this distinction can be found in the special feature, "Current issues in reporting tax revenues", in the 2001 edition of the *Revenue Statistics.*
7. Sometimes the terms "non-refundable" and "refundable" are used, but it may be considered illogical to talk of 'refundable' when nothing has been paid.
8. A different treatment, however, is accorded to non-wastable tax credits under imputation systems of corporate income tax (§31-33).
9. This is not strictly a true tax expenditure in the formal sense. Such tax expenditures require identification of a benchmark tax system for each country or, preferably, a common international benchmark. In practice it has not been possible to reach agreement on a common international benchmark.
10. Unless based on the profit made on a sale, in which case they would be classified as capital gains taxes under 1120 or 1220.
11. In some countries the same legislation applies to both individual and corporate enterprises for particular taxes on income. However, the receipts from such taxes are usually allocable between individuals and enterprises and can therefore be shown in the appropriate sub-heading.
12. For example, "...sufficiently self-contained and independent that they behave in the same way as corporations....... (including) keeping a complete set of accounts" (2008 SNA, section 4.44).
13. In Canada – a country also referred to as having an imputation system – the (wastable) tax credit for the shareholder is in respect of domestic corporation tax deemed to have been paid whether or not a corporation tax liability has arisen. As there is no integral connection between the corporation tax liability and the credit given against income tax under such systems, these credits for dividends are treated, along with other tax credits, on the lines described in §20.
14. This may also apply where a scheme for government employees existed prior to the introduction of a general social security scheme.
15. In the 2008 SNA these are regarded as capital transfers and not as taxes (see section A.8).
16. This is the system by which the European Union adjusts for differences between the exchange rates used to determine prices under the Common Market Agricultural Policy and actual exchange rates. Payments under the system may relate to imports or exports and where these amounts are separately identifiable they are shown under the appropriate heading (5123 or 5124). In this Report, these amounts are shown gross (i.e. without deducting any subsidies paid out under the MCA system).
17. Transfers of profits of State lotteries are regarded as non-tax revenues (see also §63).
18. See §25(c) as regards this distinction.

ANNEX B

Date of data submission

	Date of data submission
Australia	31 July 2017
Austria	8 June 2017
Belgium	22 June 2017
Canada	10 July 2017
Chile	1 August 2017
Czech Republic	11 July 2017
Denmark	2 June 2017
Estonia	18 June 2017
Finland	13 July 2017
France	30 May 2017
Germany	12 June 2017
Greece	29 June 2017
Hungary	4 July 2017
Iceland	8 June 2017
Ireland	19 July 2017
Israel	25 July 2017
Italy	6 June 2017
Japan	1 August 2017
Korea	15 June 2017
Latvia	10 August 2017
Luxembourg	19 June 2017
Mexico	19 July 2017
Netherlands	13 July 2017
New Zealand	2 June 2017
Norway	20 June 2017
Poland	31 August 2017
Portugal	21 June 2017
Slovak Republic	2 June 2017
Slovenia	17 July 2017
Spain	1 August 2017
Sweden	7 June 2017
Switzerland	8 May 2017
Turkey	9 June 2017
United Kingdom	10 July 2017
United States	5 July 2017

ORGANISATION FOR ECONOMIC CO-OPERATION AND DEVELOPMENT

The OECD is a unique forum where governments work together to address the economic, social and environmental challenges of globalisation. The OECD is also at the forefront of efforts to understand and to help governments respond to new developments and concerns, such as corporate governance, the information economy and the challenges of an ageing population. The Organisation provides a setting where governments can compare policy experiences, seek answers to common problems, identify good practice and work to co-ordinate domestic and international policies.

The OECD member countries are: Australia, Austria, Belgium, Canada, Chile, the Czech Republic, Denmark, Estonia, Finland, France, Germany, Greece, Hungary, Iceland, Ireland, Israel, Italy, Japan, Korea, Latvia, Luxembourg, Mexico, the Netherlands, New Zealand, Norway, Poland, Portugal, the Slovak Republic, Slovenia, Spain, Sweden, Switzerland, Turkey, the United Kingdom and the United States. The European Union takes part in the work of the OECD.

OECD Publishing disseminates widely the results of the Organisation's statistics gathering and research on economic, social and environmental issues, as well as the conventions, guidelines and standards agreed by its members.

OECD PUBLISHING, 2, rue André-Pascal, 75775 PARIS CEDEX 16
(23 2017 31 1 P) ISBN 978-92-64-28317-6 – 2014

www.ingramcontent.com/pod-product-compliance
Ingram Content Group UK Ltd.
Pitfield, Milton Keynes, MK11 3LW, UK
UKHW051502290926
15471UKWH00008B/1366

9 789264 283176